# Alcoholism and the Family
## A Guide to Treatment and Prevention
## Second Edition

**Ann Lawson, PhD**
Professor
U.S. International University
San Diego, California

**Gary Lawson, PhD**
Professor
U.S. International University
San Diego, California

pro·ed
An International Publisher
8700 Shoal Creek Boulevard
Austin, Texas 78757-6897
800/897-3202   Fax 800/397-7633
www.proedinc.com

© 1998 by PRO-ED, Inc.
8700 Shoal Creek Boulevard
Austin, Texas 78757-6897
800/897-3202   Fax 800/397-7633
www.proedinc.com

**Library of Congress Cataloging-in-Publication Data**

Lawson, Ann W.
    Alcoholism and the family : a guide to treatment and prevention / Ann W. Lawson, Gary
    Lawson.—2nd ed.
       p. cm.
    Originally published: Gaithersburg, Md. : Aspen, 1998.
    Includes bibliographical references and index.
    ISBN 0-944480-03-9
       1. Alcoholics—Family relationships. 2. Alcoholism—Treatment. 3.
    Alcoholism—Prevention. I. Lawson, Gary. II. Title.

    HV5132.L39   2004
    362.292'3—dc21

                                                                                    2003046561

(Previously published by Aspen Publishers
as ISBN 0-8342-1058-4)

Printed in the United States of America

1  2  3  4  5  6  7  8  9  10     08  07  06  05  04

*To all who have been affected by alcoholism*

# TABLE OF CONTENTS

# PREFACE

Alcoholism continues to be a major problem in our society. Alcohol ranks second only to tobacco as a legal drug that kills more Americans than any other, with more than 150,000 deaths each year directly related to alcohol use. This far exceeds the number of deaths from all of the illegal drugs combined. Volumes of statistics document the physical, emotional, and cultural effects of alcohol abuse. In terms of suicide, divorce, crime, economic loss, and mental and physical health problems, alcoholism affects our entire society.

Yet one group probably feels the effects of alcoholism more than any other—the family. However, despite the efforts of many practitioners and researchers in the addictions and the family therapy fields, the alcoholic family continues to be undertreated.

In general, writings about family treatment of alcoholism have underscored the importance of the family as a dynamic system that is the primary source of alcoholism and related problems. In the early 1980s there was a flurry of publications about how alcoholism affects all of the members of the family, spurring the Adult Children of Alcoholics movement and the codependency dispute. Although this did allow for treatment of family members other than the alcoholics themselves, treatment providers have mostly missed the concept of the alcoholic family system. Mental health practitioners and alcohol counselors continue to focus rehabilitation efforts on the alcoholic member of the family while simply instructing other family members on how best to work with this person. Generally, the problem drinker goes off for treatment and the rest of the family is, at best, a secondary consideration. We propose a different perspective. Instead of treating just one member, we view the entire alcoholic family as the client. Each individual within the family structure should be an integral part of treatment, not just the drinking member. Usually, the development of alcoholism does not happen in a vacuum; it is an outgrowth of an ailing family system. Even if an alcoholic has no current family, it must be remembered that he or she was once a member of a family and is a product of that system. It may be argued that some families do not cause alcoholism but that alcoholism causes these families' problems. However, this is an academic point. By the time an alcoholic seeks treatment, the family is most likely in disarray and in need of treatment.

There are three central reasons for viewing the family system as the client. First, it is less productive, or even harmful, to rehabilitate an alcoholic in isolation and then return him or her to the same destructive family system that created or maintained the problem in the first place. Second, family members may be under as much stress and in as much need of help as the alcoholic. All family members should be encouraged to receive help. Third, only when the family in toto participates in the rehabilitation process can its members understand the family dynamics and adopt new behaviors.

Our treatment approach attempts to trace alcoholism back to its origins and identifies how the problem is passed from generation to generation. The book describes many ways people perpetuate alcoholism, both consciously and unconsciously, and how it can be identified and treated. Specific procedures are included for prevention and for the diagnosis and treatment of alcoholic families.

This book is primarily designed to aid alcoholism counselors who wish to work with families, as well as family counselors who encounter problems associated with alcohol abuse. Each chapter can be consulted independently for specific information. However, sections are designed to build on one another so that background information can be applied to specific methods. The material selected for this book represents a broad spectrum of contemporary thought and intervention approaches; our intent is not only to explain this material but demonstrate its application in real-life situations.

Part I is a review of alcoholism treatment and etiological theories provided for readers unfamiliar with them. Parts II, III, and IV, covering etiology, treatment, and prevention, are based on the family systems model and offer a different and exciting way to view alcoholism and to treat and prevent it. The reader who is knowledgable in traditional alcoholism treatment may wish to begin with any of these parts, depending on his or her need.

In this second edition we have added new material to every chapter. The latest research and theory concerning etiology, treatment, and prevention is presented in each section. Readers familiar with the first edition will find new family therapy theories, diagnostic instruments, etiological research, and treatment models, a new section on Adult Children of Alcoholics, a new discussion of codependency, and current treatment outcome studies and prevention ideas.

Although we collaborated on each chapter, primary responsibility for various sections was assumed individually. Dr. Gary Lawson was the major contributor in the area of prevention and Part I, and also made major contributions to the chapters on etiology (chapters 1, 2, 4, 5, 13, and 14). Dr. Ann Lawson was the major contributor in the treatment section, and also made major contributions to the etiology section (chapters 3, 6, 7, 8, 9, 10, 11, and 12).

*Note:* Although the title of this book is *Alcoholism and the Family*, it is rare that therapists encounter a pure alcoholic today. Thus, the terms *alcoholic/addict, substance abuser, chemically dependent,* and *alcoholic* have been used interchangeably to denote people whose alcohol and other drug abuse is problematic for them and their families.

# ACKNOWLEDGMENTS

We would like to give a special thank you to Robert F. Partridge, Jr., for his valuable contribution to the graphics and charts in this second edition. He redesigned and improved all of the original figures and charts.

# Part I

# Background of the Problem

The first section of this book is designed to provide the reader with a review of current issues and theories in the field of alcoholism and alcoholism treatment. The first chapter will examine the theories of etiology or the causes of alcoholism. The second chapter will discuss the important elements of the treatment of alcoholism and what the alcohol counselor needs to know to be effective. Those readers just beginning to work in the alcoholism treatment field will find these two chapters particularly useful. These two chapters combined should provide background information and a solid basis for the remaining chapters in the book.

# CHAPTER 1

# Explanations of the Cause of Alcoholism

The purpose of this chapter is to provide the reader with an overview of existing thought on the etiology or cause of alcoholism. Although there has been a great deal of new research on the topic since this book was first published in 1983, little has changed regarding the basic theories of alcoholism or addiction in general. For economic, political, and other reasons new treatment approaches have been developed during the past 15 years and some old approaches are not as popular as they were in the past. These will be discussed in the next chapter. However, these changes in approaches to treatment are based on the standard theories of etiology, which still fall into three major categories: (1) physiological theories of alcoholism, (2) psychological theories of alcoholism, and (3) sociological theories of alcoholism. Of course, combinations of aspects of two or even three of these areas yield new theories, and the acceptance of these combinations may be what has changed the most in the area of etiology of alcoholism and addiction over the past 10 to 15 years.

Thus, today's treatment provider is less likely to get stuck with one treatment paradigm and the therapeutic approach derived from that paradigm. Shaffer and Robbins (1995) point out the utility of considering different theories of addiction and suggest that theories be time limited and should change as essential new information is assimilated. This constant reframing of etiology allows the person designing or guiding the treatment to apply the most effective method or approach at any given time. This view of etiology is most important for the family therapist who must consider the systemic dynamics involved in alcoholism or addiction.

Consider the ramifications of a family therapist who truly believes alcoholism is only excessive behavior, or a moral weakness, or a symptom of character pathology or a metabolic deficiency, or a primary disease. Each of these views suggests a different course of treatment. Family therapists need to be open to all models of etiology and flexible enough to adjust their view as new information is gathered. In other words, family therapists must be flexible in their approach to therapy or treatment planning.

## IS ALCOHOLISM A DISEASE? (DOES IT MATTER?)

During the 1980s and even early 1990s, when practitioners in the field were asked to define alcoholism, they often responded categorically that alcoholism was a disease. And yet, when asked to elaborate, many were hard pressed to explain what this phrase really means. This was primarily due to the manner in which this concept was developed and is used. Most advocates of the disease concept base their position on various interpretations of the well-known book *The Disease Concept of Alcoholism* by Jellinek (1960).

Jellinek based his ideas on questionnaire studies done in 1946 and 1952, along with a synthesis of existing thought on alcoholism (Jellinek, 1946, 1952). His findings can be reduced to two essential concepts: (1) there are several different types (species) of alcoholism, and (2) some types of alcoholics (Delta and Gamma) progress irreversibly through a series of ever-worsening stages, unless there is therapeutic intervention. Regarding the first concept, Jellinek used the Greek alphabet for labeling purposes and described five distinct types of alcoholism: Alpha, Beta, Gamma, Delta, and Epsilon.

*Alpha alcoholism* represents purely psychological dependence on the abusive effects of alcohol. However, the Alpha alcoholic is nonetheless an abusive drinker and is often very resistant to treatment. Because Alpha drinkers are not physically addicted to alcohol, they do not experience withdrawal symptoms if they temporarily stop drinking, nor do they progress through stages.

The *Beta alcoholic*, on the other hand, has physical complications (e.g., gastritis or cirrhosis) related to alcohol consumption. There is no indication of physical or psychological dependence or progression with Beta alcoholics, but heavy drinking often continues despite medical complications.

*Gamma alcoholism* involves physical addiction with withdrawal symptoms (shakes and nausea when drinking is stopped), a definite progression from psychological to physical dependence, and loss of control—uncontrollable drinking against the alcoholic's own wishes. The Gamma alcoholic experiences a physical craving for alcohol and undergoes marked behavioral and personality changes. The damage to the alcoholic's health and financial and social standing is more prominent than in other types of alcoholism.

*Delta alcoholism* is similar to the Gamma variety, but in this case the drinker can control his or her intake in a given situation. However, it is known that Gamma drinkers may abstain ("go on the wagon") from time to time, but Delta alcoholics cannot go a single day without drinking. Delta alcoholism is more prominent in Europe, and Gamma alcoholism is much more common in the United States.

Finally, *Epsilon alcoholism* refers to the periodic drinker who may drink infrequently but does so in abusive binges. Although Jellinek only described five different kinds of alcoholism, he felt that many more exist but have yet to be defined. The key to understanding this aspect of Jellinek's work is that alcoholism is a global concept encompassing many varieties of problem drinking. To simply label someone an alcoholic is to overlook differences that may exist between that person and other drinkers.

Jellinek's second major concept was that many alcoholics go through a series of ever-worsening stages or phases. At the first stage, the *prealcoholic symptomatic phase*, the drinker begins to consume alcohol for relief. As the prealcoholic increases his or her consumption to combat stress, other forms of tension reduction are discarded, and soon alcohol becomes the major response to any stress. Drinking becomes an almost daily habit, and an increase in tolerance is often noted.

The next phase is called *prodromal* and is characterized by five definite symptoms: (1) blackouts or periods of memory loss while drinking, (2) surreptitious drinking, which involves sneaking drinks, (3) gulping drinks, (4) preoccupation with drinking, and (5) guilt associated with inappropriate behavior while intoxicated. At this phase, a denial or alibi system is formulated.

The next stage, called the *crucial phase*, involves loss of control and signals physical addiction. Loss of control can be described as a chain reaction—one drink leads to the next. Individuals drink to unconsciousness or until they are forced to quit, even though they know the consequences will be negative. This phase may best be understood as the loss phase—loss of job, friends, health, etc.

The final phase is called *chronic* and is the last phase before death. Alcoholics who progress to the chronic phase have a total obsession with alcohol consumption and have often lost their families, friends, and jobs. In many cases they have been treated for alcoholism. Major symptoms of the chronic phase are a loss of tolerance for alcohol, morning and day drinking, loss of memory, and ethical or moral deterioration.

It was thought for some time that alcoholics needed to reach the chronic stage ("hit rock bottom") before treatment could be effective because only then would the alcoholic be motivated to quit. Currently most practitioners agree that intervention should take place as soon as possible, at a time when the problem drinker still has the major support systems (job, family, health, friends) intact.

Even though the disease concept of alcoholism has enjoyed wide acceptance by counselors, physicians, and recovering alcoholics, especially those associated with Alcoholics Anonymous, things have begun to change. Today many textbooks on alcoholism and substance abuse hardly mention the disease model, if at all (Howard, Harrison, Carver, & Lightfoot, 1993; Washton, 1995; Walters, 1996). The disease concept was an attractive position for three reasons: (1) it is easy to grasp conceptually, (2) it has, to some extent, removed the negative stigma associated with alcoholism, and (3) it calls for total abstinence from alcohol as the only plausible treatment goal, which is also simple, straightforward, and, therefore, attractive.

The problem with the disease concept, as interpreted from Jellinek's work, is that it has been widely misunderstood and misused. Jellinek himself explained that of all the various types of alcoholism, only the Gamma and Delta varieties could be considered diseases. He based this conclusion on the progressive physical and behavioral changes that these alcoholics undergo. However, he felt the other kinds of alcoholism could not really be thought of as diseases.

What does this mean? First of all, not all problem drinkers are alike, and they may require different types of treatment. Based on the goals of the individual client, treatment may range anywhere from training in responsible drinking to complete abstinence. Specific treatment approaches will be addressed in detail in the following chapter.

The disease concept has come under increasing attack from a variety of critics. Their arguments were summed up by Levin (1995) and include:

- Progression is not inevitable nor invariant, as reported in the disease model.
- Medicalization of alcohol addiction is essentially a political decision made primarily for economic reasons.
- Loss of control is refuted by the scientific evidence.
- Teaching alcoholics that they have an uncontrollable disease becomes a self-fulfilling prophecy.
- The disease concept is antitherapeutic and responsibility is denied and undermined by those holding the disease concept.

Still many, including Levin, regard the disease concept as helpful and useful. He agreed with Vaillant (1983) when he said, after exhaustively reviewing the evidence, that alcoholism is best compared with a chronic metabolic disease such as diabetes, which can be significantly controlled by proper self-care. It appears both sides have valid points in certain situations. The key for the family therapist on this issue appears to be flexibility.

## PHYSIOLOGICAL THEORIES OF ALCOHOLISM

Research has shown a clear genetic component of alcoholism and there are correlates between drinking behavior with abnormal biological or genetic factors. Because alcoholism is such a multifaceted disorder, many of these studies are flawed. It has always been difficult to separate environmental influences from genetic influences. New research methods and statistical procedures are making it more likely that some useful information will be forthcoming. Crabbe and Goldman (1992) stated that alcoholism does not appear to be the result of a single gene but rather an interaction of multiple genes (i.e., polygenic) and important environmental factors.

## Is Alcoholism Inherited?

The theory that alcoholism is genetic has generated a great deal of discussion and research. A very large amount of money has been spent on this research. However, this effort has not provided much in the way of a definitive answer to the nature of alcoholism. It is interesting to speculate about what would really change if a gene for alcoholism were discovered. Would those with the gene be banned from buying and drinking alcohol? Would they have a red *A* stamped on their birth certificate or driver's license? Would they attempt to engineer a new gene that allowed them to drink without becoming alcoholic? This research effort has been described by those more interested in the environmental and family aspects of the etiology of alcoholism as rats jumping onto a sinking ship. Perhaps this research money could be spent in a more efficient way—perhaps not. Only time will tell.

Indeed, research on genetics and alcoholism has actually raised more questions than it has answered. For example, it is known that despite the country of origin, alcoholism consistently runs in families. Without known exception, every family study of alcoholism has shown much higher rates of alcoholism among the relatives of alcoholics than in the general population (Goodwin, 1971). Indeed, a study by Winokur and Clayton (1968) showed a very high prevalence of alcoholism among the full siblings of alcoholics. A full 46 percent of the brothers and 5 percent of the sisters of male alcoholics sampled were also alcoholics. Siblings of female alcoholics had even higher rates of alcoholism: 50 percent of the male siblings and 8 percent of the female siblings were alcoholics. However, this research doesn't answer the question: Are these factors due to inheritance of a propensity for alcoholism or can they be explained through learned attitudes and behaviors that are passed from adults to their offspring?

A second area of genetic inquiry involves comparing the alcohol consumption of identical (monozygotic) and fraternal (dizygotic) twins. Researchers assume that because both identical and fraternal twins are typically raised in the same family environment (same parents, home, and so on), they will differ mostly to genetic makeup. Parenthetically, identical twins share 100 percent of their genes, but fraternal twins share only 50 percent and are no more genetically similar than any other sibling combination. Therefore, it is theorized that genetic disorders will more often be concordant between identical twins than fraternal twins. Two large-scale studies relating to this subject are cited that represent typical findings in the research literature. The first (Kaij, 1960) was conducted in Sweden and compared

174 male twin pairs of which one member was registered as an alcoholic. In short, Kaij found that the concordance (agreement) rate was higher in monozygotic twins than dizygotic twins. Monozygotic twins showed a rate of 54 percent, but dizygotic twins had a rate of only 28 percent. The implication is that heredity accounts for the difference in alcoholism rates. On the other hand, a similar study conducted in Finland by Partanen, Brunn, and Markhanen (1966) compared 902 male twins but found no difference in alcoholism rates between monozygotic and dizygotic twins. Unfortunately, such contradictory research does little to clarify the question of inheritance as a factor in alcoholism.

Research in genetics and alcohol use is also being conducted with laboratory animals. In a study by Rogers and McClearn (1962), strains of mice were identified that seem to voluntarily consume alcohol at varying rates (i.e., high versus low volumes). A combination of these strains produced offspring that consumed "moderate" amounts, suggesting a genetic predisposition for alcohol preference in these animals.

In another area of genetic research, genetic marker studies have explored associations between inherited characteristics (color blindness, blood type, etc.) and alcoholism. In general, this research tends to be contradictory. For example, Cruz-Coke and Varela (1966) found that color blindness, cirrhosis, and alcoholism were associated, and they proposed that alcoholism was transmitted by a sex-linked recessive gene. However, similar research was conducted by Fialkow, Thuline, and Fenster (1966), who concluded that color blindness was more likely due to the toxic and/or nutritional effects of heavy drinking than to a sex-linked gene.

Although this review of genetic research represents only a tiny sample of the many studies that have been conducted, the unsolved problems are representative. First, as mentioned earlier, the cause-and-effect relationship is difficult to establish. Second, the age-old nature versus nurture controversy is still largely unanswered. Do families inherit alcoholism or learn it? Third, findings with laboratory animals cannot always be generalized to human beings. Finally, conclusions can be hard to draw from the contradictory research studies in this area. Even though genetic research has contributed valuable information, it still has not led to an understanding of the causes of alcoholism.

**Is Alcoholism Caused by Abnormal Biophysiological Conditions?**

Some researchers have postulated that alcoholism may be due to biophysiological causes. Some of the major biophysiological conditions that have been investigated include: (1) the production of morphine-like substances in the brain (tetrahydropapaveroline), (2) abnormalities in sugar metabolism, (3) food allergies, and (4) endocrine abnormalities. These will be reviewed briefly.

According to the first hypothesis, acetylaldehyde (the first major breakdown product of alcohol) combines under certain unknown conditions with other body chemicals to form a morphine-like addictive substance. This theory could explain the addictive effect alcohol has on some individuals but not others. However, there currently is not enough evidence to prove this reaction actually happens (Editorial, 1972).

The second theory, abnormalities in sugar metabolism, has also been in vogue of late (Lundquist, 1971). It has been noted that many alcoholics suffer from hypoglycemia and other abnormalities related to sugar or carbohydrate metabolism. But nowhere is the cause-and-effect quandary more evident. Because these problems are discovered in alcoholics with long drinking histories, it seems just as likely that sugar metabolism problems could be the result of abusive drinking and not the cause.

Another hypothesis, alcoholism as a food allergy or craving, has been forwarded by Williams (1981) and others. This theory holds that some people crave or have an appetite for alcohol (it is also felt that this appetite may be inherited). Several alcoholism treatment programs feature specialized diets that include high-protein food as well as vitamins and minerals to offset this craving. Again, cause and effect are difficult to determine. Does an appetite for alcohol cause heavy drinking or result from it, as in addiction?

Finally, the concept of an endocrine dysfunction, researched by Senior (1967) and elsewhere, has emerged as a possible contributing factor to alcoholism. In this framework, some individuals lack the enzyme (NAD) that aids in the metabolism of alcohol. When alcohol is insufficiently broken down, an abundance of acetylaldehyde remains in the system and creates symptoms akin to alcohol withdrawal (nausea, shakes, etc.). Therefore, the person repeats his or her drinking to alleviate these symptoms, and a vicious cycle is created. In evaluating this theory, two problems arise. First, the cause-and-effect relationship is unclear; second, this process does not seem to occur in a large percentage of heavy drinkers.

As is the case with genetic research and alcoholism, studies of biophysical abnormalities contribute to the knowledge base without explaining the nature of alcoholism. To resolve the cause-and-effect problem, research must be conducted with people before they become problem drinkers. In this way, those who exhibit biophysical abnormalities, along with a suitable control group, could be followed throughout their lives, and rates of alcoholism could be compared.

After reviewing three of the major adoption studies that have been published, Searles (1991) concluded that:

> Research examining a possible genetic basis for alcoholism suggests that environmental factors play a relatively minor etiologic role. Methodological limitations of the three major adoption studies that converge on

this finding . . . may not be as compelling on close inspection of the design and results of the studies. A major problem is that the investigations did not use standard and uniform criteria for diagnosis, which resulted in considerable variation among studies as to obtained prevalence rates of alcoholism. (p. 8)

He suggested using a more complex model incorporating both genetic and environmental effects, particularly one that takes into account different types of environmental influences. Several years earlier Lester (1989) examined the research from 1943 to 1970 on the heritability of alcoholism and concluded that factual support for the belief is "at best weak—and that the consensus in the main reflects a victory for ideology over rigorous scientific methodology and solid data." As mentioned later in chapter 4, the family therapist can use a family history of alcoholism as a risk factor to provide more in the way of prevention for those at risk and to understand the family dynamics of those in therapy.

## PSYCHOLOGICAL THEORIES OF ALCOHOLISM

### Personality and Alcohol Use

Psychological theories of alcoholism involve the association of psychological factors and individuals' drinking behaviors. These include but are not limited to personality factors, certain behavior variables, temperament, self-concept, field dependence, ego weakness, and specific cognitive styles. Once again, however, this research area is plagued with some of the same methodological problems discussed earlier as well as others. In this case, it is difficult to determine if psychological factors are the cause of alcoholism or are the result of years of heavy drinking. Another problem inherent in these studies is the imprecise nature of psychological measurement. To begin this review, theories of personality and alcohol use will be discussed.

There are several problems with the concept of an alcoholic personality. First is the lack of empirical psychological findings in alcoholic populations. Second, almost all studies have been done only on males (Levin, 1995). Another problem referred to by Levin is that many patients are involved in research during or shortly after periods of intoxication or alcohol addiction and follow-up studies after significant periods of abstinence and sobriety have rarely been done.

The terms *addictive personality* and *alcoholic personality* are often used in the field of alcoholism rehabilitation and are meant to describe an individual who is impulsive, aggressive, overly emotional, agitated, and easily frustrated. There is, in fact, some evidence to support these theories. Studies seem to show the Sixteen Personality Factor Questionnaire (16PF) and the Minnesota Multiphasic Personality Inventory (MMPI) (Kammeier, Hoffmann, & Loper,1973) can be used to discriminate personality differences between alcoholics and nonalcoholics. With the MMPI, alcoholics tended to have consistently more depressive profiles, and on the 16PF they score higher for aggressiveness and impulsiveness than nonalcoholics (Walton, 1968). And yet, given the limitations of these studies, as cited earlier, it is really not possible to define an alcoholic personality per se. Furthermore, other research indicates that there is no definite alcoholic personality and that the range of personality types of alcoholics is not different from that found in the general population (Gorad, 1971). There are those, however, who propose an addictive personality model of drug and alcohol vulnerability (Nathan, 1988) according to which the individual is seen as engaging in a self-defeating pattern of activity as a consequence of various character flaws or personality traits.

One theory related to personality that seems to hold up over various research studies is that antisocial behavior during childhood can be predictive of alcohol problems as an adult. Also, shyness, aggressive behavior, and hyperactivity have been reported to relate to alcohol problems. However, a family therapist is more likely to see antisocial behavior during childhood as a symptom of inadequate parenting, neglect, or abuse—a systemic viewpoint. This has also been a topic of research. The 1989 Institute of Medicine publication *Prevention and Treatment of Alcohol Problems* listed over 20 studies that have looked at these variables; the conclusion is that the studies have made an important contribution to the understanding of the etiology of alcohol problems. Again, the important limitations of prospective research of this nature are emphasized.

Kaufman (1994) concluded that the vast majority of substance abusers (including alcoholics) have at least one personality disorder—usually antisocial personality, borderline personality, or dependent personality. If this is in fact the case the family therapist treating alcoholism and other addictions would be wise to include some form of personality assessment in the treatment process.

Using MMPI, 16PF, or another measure of a psychological nature can offer the family therapist clinically relevant information about underlying etiologies of a person's alcohol problems; this may help in planning an appropriate treatment program. But before administering evaluative instruments, a detailed clinical interview with a family history is recommended. During this interview all of the psychological variables important to a treatment plan should be examined.

Another important psychological variable is cognitive style. In other words, how individuals thinks about the world they live in has a great deal to do with their choices and decisions regarding the use or abuse of alcohol as well as other drugs. Some valuable findings suggest that alcoholics think differently than nonalcoholics. One area where alcoholics have differed is in the way they organize their perceptive field. Using measurements such as the Rod and Frame Test and the Embedded Figure Test, researchers have shown that alcoholics are more likely to be field dependent rather than field independent. What that means is that the alcoholic is more likely to rely on his or her environment and external cues rather than on introceptive or internal cues in orienting to the world.

Walters (1996) presented an interesting theory relating to the cognitive styles of substance abusers. He believed that they develop a lifestyle based on their life conditions, the choices they make, and, most importantly, the cognitions or thoughts they have about the choices they make. He suggested that the first step in a program of change is to arrest the lifestyle. This is done by changing the cognitive style. This approach will be discussed in more detail in chapter 2.

Levin (1995) reported another psychological variable that seems to surface with regularity in the research literature—impoverished self-concept. Active alcoholics and those entering treatment seem to have these problems with self-concept. The question that has yet to be answered is: Did alcoholics have these poor self-concepts before they began drinking alcoholically or did they get them as a result of their drinking? Was it a cause of their drinking? Regardless of the answer to that question, it can be assumed as a result of the existing research that part of a good treatment plan should involve raising self-esteem.

Levin (1995) also listed evidence that ego weakness manifested by impulsivity, the inability to delay gratification, low affect tolerance, a propensity toward panic-level anxiety, prolonged depression, a confused sense of identity, a lack of clear boundaries, and poor reality testing most likely play a role in the etiology of alcoholism. Again, perhaps it is more important to consider how these factors will be addressed in treatment.

## Transactional Theory

Steiner's transactional analysis (TA) approach (1979) should interest people working with alcoholic families. Steiner maintained that alcoholism is not a disease at all but a series of distorted communications within families that he labels "games." The theory is that if an alcoholic were stranded alone on an island, he or she would stop drinking voluntarily even if plenty of alcohol were available because the "alcoholic game" could not be played. This contradicts the disease concept, which maintains that addiction leads to alcoholic behavior. TA theory holds that alcoholic behavior (games) leads to addiction and that addiction can often be cured.

Two major concepts in TA theory are games and scripts. *Games*, as previously cited, are defined as a sequence of interactions with one or more people in which the actor has an ulterior motive and some expectation of profit. A *script* is a person's life plan that was assumed during childhood and represents basic decisions the individual has made about him- or herself and others (e.g., "I'm no good and neither is anyone else.").

Steiner outlined three games that he feels alcoholics play. The first of these he labeled "drunk and proud of it," or D & P. D & P is a three-handed game between the alcoholic and another person who vacillates between two roles, Patsy and Persecutor. The D & P player is basically interested in getting persecuting parents so angry and frustrated that they show their impotence and foolishness. This relationship starts with a domineering parent or parents and is transferred later in life to spouse, friends, counselors, etc. It is an attempt by the alcoholic to get even with the domineering people in their lives. A typical scenario is when the D & P alcoholic gets drunk, acts out, and then pleads for forgiveness or promises not to do it again. The person (usually a spouse) with whom the game is being played is then forced into one of two roles: (1) he or she can forgive the D & P player and become the Patsy (it always will happen again), or (2) he or she can become the Persecutor and angrily denounce the behavior. And on and on it goes, with the same game being repeated in many families for years.

The second alcoholic game is colloquially called "Lush." In this game there are four players: the alcoholic (Lush), the Persecutor, the Patsy, and the Rescuer. Lush involves an alcoholic who has been cut off from emotional and (usually) sexual support and who drinks abusively as a response. It is a game because the nondrinking members of the family maintain an appearance of self-righteousness and virtuousness. The family denies any responsibility for the problem and treats the drinker as a scapegoat. The Lush, deprived of warmth or rewards ("strokes") at home, often tries to meet these needs through extramarital affairs and drinking buddies. On the other hand, the underlying guilt feelings of the family (usually the spouse) surface periodically, and this person changes from Persecutor to Rescuer. The game is maintained because the love-starved alcoholic settles for the costly strokes obtained when being rescued. However, as long as the alcoholic continues to drink, family members can camouflage their own emotional shortcomings as well as their part of the game. It is important to note that counselors are often a part of the lush game, first playing Patsy and then Persecutor when the alcoholic returns to drinking (in order to be rescued again).

Game three is called "Wino." In this game alcoholics obtain strokes by becoming physically ill and forcing others to literally save their lives and take care of them. Interestingly, the Wino player uses the disease model concept as an excuse to maintain abusive drinking: "I have a disease, therefore I cannot control my drinking, and therefore I cannot really be held responsible for my behavior." To the Wino, the fact that he or she must be at death's door to get aid from those in positions of strength and power implies that others are really not okay. The Wino operates from the conviction that he or she is okay but the rest of the world is not.

In order to reverse these games and cure the alcoholic, Steiner believed that all those involved in the alcoholic's life must stop playing the game. In this framework the family structure can be seen as the client, as opposed to the alcoholic in isolation. Games take on many additional forms in addition to those outlined here. Although the TA conceptualization of alcoholism is primarily theoretical, it has contributed creatively to the alcoholism field in terms of the analysis and description of interpersonal dynamics within the alcoholic family. Similarly, the view of the alcoholic as "curable" and not diseased has offered a controversial and thought-provoking perception.

## Psychodynamic Theory and Alcoholism

Psychodynamic theory explains alcoholism as a manifestation of unconscious processes that originated during early stages of the individual's development. These processes are malignant in that they serve as ineffective and destructive attempts to counter early unresolved conflicts. For example, Blume (1966), after a review of psychodynamic literature, concluded that "oral stage fixation" was a problem for most alcoholics. The result of being fixated (stuck) in the oral stage supposedly accounts for the infantile behavior exhibited by many alcoholics (i.e., narcissism, demanding behavior, passivity, and dependence). The fixation is a result of early deprivation by parents during childhood. Because this dependency and other needs cannot be met by others (until oral fixation is resolved), they lead to anxiety and compensatory needs for control, power, and achievement. For this person, alcohol serves to tranquilize the anxiety as well as create a sense of strength and invulnerability, also known as "false courage."

However, after sobering up from a drinking episode, the alcoholic is flooded with his or her feelings of insecurity, inadequacy, and guilt. Therein lies the motivation to drink again, and a degenerative cycle is established. Because alcoholics can artificially exercise control over their emotional states by drinking, it feeds their grandiose self-images. This need for self-importance is labeled "reactive grandiosity" and is seen as a key dynamic in alcoholics.

The psychodynamic school, like the TA orientation, concedes that alcoholism eventually becomes a physical addiction but holds that it is primarily a symptom and not a disease. Psychoanalysts part company with TA advocates when it comes to treatment, however, seeing alcoholism recovery as a much longer process. The exact treatment strategy of the psychodynamic approach will be outlined in the next chapter.

## Reinforcement Theories

Reduced to its fundamental elements, operant conditioning simply states that if a behavior is followed by a reward (reinforced), the likelihood that this behavior will occur again is increased. This principle transfers logically to drinking behavior. Consider, for example, the many rewards that follow drinking: relief from tension, euphoria, a sense of well-being, increased gregariousness, etc. Alcohol does have a definite effect, often initially positive, on those who use it.

Most young people sample their first drink of alcohol under parental supervision and consequently enjoy the positive results of drinking (mild euphoria) as opposed to negative results (intoxication and nausea) as an initial experience. This positive first experience is therefore reinforced, which increases the likelihood of subsequent drinking. As additional drinking episodes are similarly rewarded, the bond is further strengthened, and the individual learns that alcohol consumption is good. According to behaviorists, the longer and more often a behavior is reinforced, the harder the behavior is to stop. This is true even if the behavior is not always reinforced, which may explain why many people continue to drink even though the consequences eventually become aversive.

Another reinforcement system, classical conditioning, involves the occurrence of an object or phenomenon in nature (stimulus) that is reinforcing (such as food or affection) at the same time as a neutral stimulus (such as a bell). If these two stimuli occur together often enough, the previously neutral stimulus will become reinforcing on its own. For example, animals have been taught to salivate at the sound of a bell. The application to alcoholism may be unclear at first, but in our culture many associations between alcohol and/or events are already reinforcing. Adult status, parties, companionship, masculinity, and youthfulness are only a few of the perceived benefits of alcohol use. Such associations are not only a part of our acculturation process but also are promoted by liquor distributors, who tell us through advertising that liquor is linked with good looks, youth, and wealth.

These two processes help to explain why Americans drink so much. We learn from our first drink that alcohol is pleasant, and we associate liquor with a wide variety of enjoyable events.

The use of reinforcement concepts in alcoholism rehabilitation is elaborated in depth in the following chapter.

Although psychological factors are clearly involved in alcoholism, the following three problems affect our understanding of: (1) the lack of accuracy in measuring psychological factors, (2) the difficulty of establishing a cause-and-effect relationship, and (3) the lack of agreement on operational definitions of psychological factors (e.g., depression, anxiety).

## SOCIOLOGICAL THEORIES OF ALCOHOLISM

### The Socialization Process and Alcohol

After a longitudinal study that included two relatively large research samples followed from childhood into their forties. Vaillant (1983) concluded that culture was a far more powerful determinant than any other factor in the development of alcoholism.

While there are regional and other sociocultural variations in drinking patterns, the consumption of alcoholic beverages by most adults in American society is normative social behavior (Barnes, 1977). Thus, drinking behavior by youths seems to be an integral part of the passage into adulthood and is introduced and fostered by the family. Jessor, Graves, Hanson, and Jessor (1968) elaborated on this process:

> The role of the family as socializer can be seen as primary and pervasive. The family is, after all, the most proximal social system to which patterned exposure occurs; it generally guarantees a continuance exposure extending back in time to the earliest consciousness of social meanings; and it is the single milieu that encompasses at preadolescence, the widest range of experience and involvement for the child. Analysis of socialization as it occurs within the family should reveal a significant amount of information about the influence exerted by the culture on the developing child.

It can be assumed that the influence of the family on drinking behavior is great. In the discussion of genetics and alcoholism, the point was made that alcoholism runs in families. However, not only does problem drinking tend to be passed on from generation to generation, but moderate drinking and abstinence are similarly perpetrated along family lines.

The research of Cahalan, Cisin, and Crossley (1969) indicates that, for males in their study, frequent drinking by the father (three times a week or more) was highly correlated with later heavy drinking on the part of the son. Of the males who reported their fathers were frequent drinkers, 35 percent were heavy drinkers themselves, as opposed to 12 percent of the men who reported that their fathers never drank or drank less than once a year. Corresponding differences based on the mother's drinking were even more pronounced. In this case, 44 percent of men who were heavy drinkers had mothers who drank frequently, as compared with only 15 percent of heavy drinkers who had mothers that never drank or drank less than once a year.

The same tendency was true of parents' attitudes toward drinking. Although 28 percent of the men who reported that their fathers approved of drinking were heavy drinkers themselves, only 12 percent of the men whose fathers disapproved were heavy drinkers. When the respondents' mothers approved of drinking, 33 percent of the men drank heavily, but only 15 percent drank heavily when their mothers disapproved. Women's drinking behaviors are similarly influenced by parental attitudes.

Many additional sociological theories have both general and culture-specific applications. In terms of general concepts, three cultural principles are thought to affect the drinking problems of a society. The first is the degree to which a culture induces inner tensions in its members. For example, the Irish peasantry of the 19th century suffered from oppression and poverty at the hands of the English. Few personal liberties existed, and life was limited to austerity and hard work. Writings from the period indicate intemperance was a way of life for many, and the words *Irishman* and *drunkard* became synonymous (Bales, 1980). Incidentally, statistics in the United States for hospital admissions for alcoholism currently indicate the Irish to have rates two to three times higher than any other ethnic group.

A second general principle holds that the attitudes a culture has toward drinking markedly influences the level of consumption and the nature of the consequences. In general, those cultures that have few sanctions against drunkenness have higher rates of alcoholism than those who denounce intoxication. In the first case, American Indians represent a culture that suffers from rampant alcoholism. This group has traditionally tolerated drunken behavior and has often excused violence due to intoxication. It is felt by many tribes that the intoxicated individual is possessed during these times and is not responsible for his or her actions (Hammer, 1965). In the second case, the Jewish culture offers an example of people who use alcohol but denounce intoxication. In virtually every cross-ethnic study of alcoholism rates in the United States, Jews are at the bottom, just as the Irish are on the top. Although more than one explanation has been forwarded for this phenomenon, the low rate of alcoholism among Jews is thought to be related to the ritualistic manner in which alcohol is consumed. Jews learn to use alcohol in a rational manner from the time they are children, using it primarily for ceremonies and in a family context where intoxication is discouraged.

The third cultural influence on drinking is the degree to which a society provides suitable substitutes for alcohol use. Unfortunately, other kinds of drug abuse may be substituted. For example, many Muslim cultures regularly use hashish, and the Japanese culture has a high incidence of opium use. Other societal alternatives may include an emphasis on vigorous recreation, higher standards of living, or a just and democratic system of government. However, the amount and kinds of alternatives a society could offer as suitable alternatives to drinking are mostly speculative and unproven.

Other influences on drinking behavior can be cited, such as religious affiliation, socioeconomic status, and ethnic identity. Our view is that these categories may not in themselves influence drinking but constitute an amalgamation of values that is primarily responsible for the shaping of attitudes and subsequent drinking behavior.

The exact role that socialization and inheritance play, separately or together, in the shaping of an alcoholic is as yet unknown. Is alcoholism learned or inherited?

A reasonable and likely possibility is that both processes may be at work, to a larger or lesser degree, depending on circumstances. Defining the conditions under which each is most influential is a continuing challenge in this field.

## SUMMARY

There are many theories on the etiology of alcoholism; only a few are presented here. For a more thorough coverage see chapters 6, 7, and 8 of the 1996 Levin reference listed at the end of this chapter. We observe, after reviewing theories of alcoholism's etiology, that the various hypotheses fail to show a definite, single cause. The most reasonable conclusion to draw is that all these theoretical factors can contribute to the problem under individual circumstances. This book focuses on family influences. We draw from the existing theories of alcoholism and have used our considerable clinical experience to devise a unique perspective on the alcoholic family that constitutes a new approach to intervention, prevention, and treatment strategies. This approach is described in detail throughout the subsequent chapters.

## REFERENCES

Bales, F. (1980). Cultural differences in roles of alcoholism. In D. Ward (Ed.), *Alcoholism: Introduction to theory and treatment*. Dubuque, IA: Kendall-Hunt,

Barnes, G.M. (1977). The development of adolescent drinking behavior: An evaluative review of the impact of the socialization process within the family. *Adolescence, 12* (48), 571–591.

Blume, E.M. (1966). Psychoanalytic views of alcoholism: A review. *Quarterly Journal of Studies on Alcohol, 27*, 259–299.

Cahalan, D., Cisin, H., & Crossley, H. (1969). *American drinking practices*. New Brunswick, NJ: Journal of Studies on Alcohol, Inc.

Crabbe, J.C., & Goldman, D. (1992). Alcoholism: A complex genetic disease. *Genetics, 16* (4), 297–303.

Cruz-Coke, R., & Varela, A. (1966). Inheritance of alcoholism. *Lancet, 2*, 1282.

Editorial. (1972). Alcohol addiction: A biochemical approach. *Lancet, 2*, 24–25.

Fialkow, P.J., Thuline, M.C., & Fenster, R.F. (1966). Lack of association between cirrhosis of the liver and the common types of colorblindness. *New England Journal of Medicine, 275*, 584.

Goodwin, D.D. (1971). Is alcoholism hereditary? *Archives of General Psychiatry, 25*, 518–545.

Gorad, S.L. (1971). A communications approach to alcoholism. *Quarterly Journal of Studies of Alcohol, 32*, 651–668.

Hammer, J.H. (1965). Acculturation stress and the functions of alcohol among forest Potawatomi. *Quarterly Journal of Studies of Alcohol, 26*, 19–25.

Howard, B.M., Harrison, S., Carver, V., & Lightfoot, L. (Eds.). (1993). *Alcohol and drug problems: A practical guide for counsellors.* Toronto, Canada: Addiction Research Foundation.

Institute of Medicine. (1989). *Prevention and treatment of alcohol problems.* Washington, DC: National Academy Press.

Jellinek, E.M. (1946). Phases in the drinking history of alcoholics. *Quarterly Journal of Studies of Alcohol, 7*, 1–88.

Jellinek, E.M. (1952). Current notes: Phases of alcohol addiction. *Quarterly Journal of Studies of Alcohol, 7*, 673–684.

Jellinek, E.M. (1960). *The disease concept of alcoholism.* New Haven, CT: United Printing Service, Inc.

Jessor, R., Graves, T., Hanson, R., & Jessor, S. (1968) *Personality and deviant behavior: A study of a tri-ethnic community.* New York: Holt, Rinehart & Winston, Inc.

Kaij, L. (1960) *Studies on the etiology and sequels of abuse of alcohol.* Mimeographed. Lund, Sweden: University of Lund.

Kaij, L. (1970). Biases in a Swedish social register of alcoholics. *Social Psychiatry, 5*, 216–218.

Kammeier, M.L., Hoffmann, H., & Loper, R.S. (1973). Personality characteristics of alcoholics as college freshmen at the time of treatment. *Quarterly Journal of Studies of Alcohol, 34*, 390–399.

Kaufman, E. (1994). *Psychotherapy of addicted persons.* New York: Gilford Press.

Lester, D. (1989). The heritability of alcoholism: Science and social policy. *Drugs and Society, 3* (3/4), 29–68.

Levin, J.D. (1995). *Introduction to alcoholism counseling: A bio-psycho-social approach* (2nd ed.). Washington, DC: Taylor & Francis.

Lundquist, F. (1971). Influence of ethanol on carbohydrate metabolism. *Quarterly Journal of Studies of Alcohol, 32*, 1–12.

Nathan, P.E. (1988). The addictive personality is the behavior of the addict. *Journal of Consulting and Clinical Psychology, 56*, 183–188.

Partanen, J., Brunn, K., & Markhanen, T. (1966). *Inheritance of drinking behavior.* Mimeographed. New Brunswick, NJ: Rutgers University Center of Alcohol Studies.

Rogers, D.A., & McClearn, G.E. (1962). Alcohol preferences in mice. In Bliss (Ed.), *Roots of behavior.* New York: Harper & Row.

Searles, J.S. (1991). The genetics of alcoholism: Impact on family and sociological models of addiction. *Family Dynamics of Addiction Quarterly, 1*(1), 8–21.

Senior, J.R. (1967). Ethanol and liver disease. *Postgraduate Medicine, 41*, 65.

Shaffer, H.J., & Robbins, M. (1995). Psychotherapy for addictive behavior: A stage-change approach to meaning making. In A.M. Washton (Ed.), *Psychotherapy and substance abuse: A practitioner's handbook*, (pp. 103–123). New York: Gilford Press.

Steiner, G.M. (1979). *Healing alcoholism.* New York: Grove Press.

Vaillant, G.E. (1983). *The natural history of alcoholism: Causes, patterns and paths to recovery*. Cambridge, MA: Harvard University Press.

Walters, G.D. (1996). *Substance abuse and the new road to recovery: A practitioner's guide*. Washington, DC: Taylor & Francis.

Walton, J.H. (1968). Personality as a determinant of the form of alcoholism. *British Journal of Psychiatry, 114*, 761–766.

Washton, A.M. (Ed.). (1995). *Psychotherapy and substance abuse: A practitioner's handbook*. New York: Gilford Press.

Williams, R.J. (1981). *The prevention of alcoholism through nutrition*. New York: Bantam.

Winokur, G., & Clayton, P.J. (1968). Comparison of male and female alcoholics. *Quarterly Journal of Studies of Alcohol, 29*, 885–891.

Zimbler, S., Wallace, J., & Blum, S. (Eds.). (1978). *Practical approaches to alcoholism psychotherapy*. New York: Plenum Press.

# CHAPTER 2

# Skills and Knowledge Alcoholism Therapists Need and Treatment Approaches to Alcoholism

This book was written for both the alcoholism counselor who wants to do family therapy and the family therapist who wants to learn to treat alcoholism. In the first edition this chapter provided an overview of several major treatment approaches mainly for the family therapist unfamiliar with alcoholism treatment. In the 15 years since that edition was published there have been major changes in the way alcoholism is treated. Some traditional treatment approaches are still used today just as they were 15 years ago. However, due to the major changes in our health care system, including HMOs and managed care, the traditional 30-day inpatient treatment program has become a last resort rather than a front-line treatment approach, and other treatment approaches such as solution-focused brief therapy (Berg, 1994), motivational interviewing (Miller & Rollnick,1991), rational-emotive behavior therapy (REBT) (Ellis, Mcinerney, DiGuiseppe, & Yeager, 1988), and alternative self-help methods such as rational recovery (RR) (Trimpey, 1992) have become popular. The fact that insurance companies are now reluctant to pay for expensive inpatient treatment programs, given the lack of evidence that they work better than much cheaper outpatient programs, has changed the field of alcoholism treatment.

## SKILLS AND KNOWLEDGE FOR COUNSELORS

Another change that has had a major impact is that more and more professionals are beginning to offer alcoholism treatment as part of their practice. When this book was first published the majority of those working in the field of alcoholism treatment were paraprofessionals; most of whom were recovering alcoholics. Professionals such as psychiatrists, psychologists, social workers, and family therapists were adjunct to treatment programs if they were involved at all. Now there are active professional groups in most all major mental health professions that give exams and certifications to those in their discipline who want to work in the treatment of addictions. This chapter lists some of the knowledge skills those who treat alcoholism might need and it provides an overview of alcoholism treatment. It also suggests additional readings that will give the family therapist the background needed to work in this field. Although there has yet to be research to support this fully, based on our clinical experience and for reasons explained later in this book, we believe that in most instances family therapy is the most appropriate and useful treatment for alcoholism. However, there are times when adjunct treatments are called for. The more family therapists know about these treatment approaches, the better they will be able to serve their clients and make appropriate referrals when necessary.

What knowledge and skills do family therapists need to treat alcoholism—that is, beyond the knowledge and skills they have as a family therapist? What knowledge and skills are necessary for one to be a good alcohol counselor? There have been major attempts by different organizations to answer these questions. It is not the purpose of this book to cover these in detail; however, a brief presentation will allow the reader to take action to bring his or her skills and knowledge to an appropriate level.

Lawson, Lawson, and Rivers (1996) listed the basic chemical dependency counselor skills as developed by the Curriculum Review Committee of the federally funded Addiction Training Center Programs (now called Addiction Technology Transfer Centers). These centers are funded by the National Center for Substance Abuse Treatment. The centers have attempted to describe the knowledge, skills, and attitudes essential to the competent practice of chemical dependency counseling (Curriculum Review Committee, 1995). In general, these include clinical evaluation skills such as screening and assessment; treatment planning; referral skills; case management including implementing the treatment plan, consulting, and continuing assessment and treatment planning; individual counseling skills; documentation; supervision; and client and community education.

Psychologists have, through the American Psychological Association Practice Directorate, compiled the results of a survey of psychologists regarding knowledge domains needed for psychologists working in the field of addictions. These included clinical pharmacology and clinical epidemiology of psychoactive substances; etiology of psychoactive substance use disorders (PSUDs); initiation, progression, and maintenance of PSUDs; course/natural history of PSUDs; prevention, early intervention, and harm reduction; screening and assessment of psychoactive substance use; diagnosis and comorbidity; treatment models and approaches; treatment planning and implementing and managing treatment and course of recovery; issues in specific populations; research knowledge; legal and ethical issues; and, finally, policy and economics of substance use disorders.

The reality is that there is no end to the amount of useful information available to those working in the treatment of alcoholism. It is an area one could study for a lifetime and not exhaust. Those who choose to treat alcoholics using family therapy should be on a lifelong learning quest in both the family therapy and addictions fields. The suggested readings at the end of this chapter offer a start toward this goal. The remainder of the chapter provides an overview of the current status of treatment for alcoholism.

## ASSESSMENT FOR TREATMENT

An initial evaluation or screening to help determine a treatment approach may or may not be done by the family therapist. This will depend on where the referral came from or the setting in which the family therapist works. Such questions as the client's motivation and resources to pay for treatment and physical condition (e.g., is detoxification necessary?) will determine choices for treatment. Family therapy may be the primary treatment or it may be adjunct to some other form of treatment such as Alcoholics Anonymous. For the family therapist who works primarily in a family therapy setting, assessment might be a different process than for an alcohol therapist who does family therapy in an alcohol treatment setting. When a patient comes to an alcohol treatment facility it is not difficult to determine that alcohol is at least part of the problem. When a family comes for family counseling, alcohol may be part of a presenting problem or it may be a hidden problem. These issues will be discussed in the chapter on diagnosis. The focus of this chapter is to provide the family therapist with background on what treatment approaches are available and an idea of what other kind of treatment the alcoholic is, has, or will be receiving.

## AN OVERVIEW OF TREATMENT APPROACHES

In general, therapeutic approaches to alcoholism very closely follow the various theories of alcoholism etiology that were addressed in chapter 1. In this chapter we will review several widely recognized traditional models of alcoholism treatment as well as some of the newer approaches.

### Alcoholics Anonymous Model

Alcoholics Anonymous (AA) is the most widespread and widely utilized treatment approach in the field of alcoholism. AA was founded in 1935 by two alcoholics called, in what became a tradition of anonymity, Bill W. and Dr.

Bob S. Their idea was to develop a fellowship composed of problem drinkers who would lend each other assistance in conquering their obsession with alcohol. From this beginning, AA has spawned a truly remarkable following that spans geographic, cultural, and socioeconomic lines. Nearly every community in the United States, large or small, has AA meetings on a regular basis. This scope is especially remarkable because AA is composed totally of anonymous volunteers, receives no outside funding, and has no central administration or organized leadership. Over the years AA has evolved both a set of bylaws, called "traditions," and a relatively uniform procedure of rehabilitation known as the "12 steps." In general, AA philosophy holds the following beliefs: (1) alcoholism is an incurable, progressive disease that will result in death without therapeutic intervention, (2) the only remedy for alcoholism is complete abstinence from drinking, (3) once an alcoholic, always an alcoholic—no cure is possible, only remission, and (4) no one can cure his or her own alcoholism without help.

These beliefs form the core of the structure and function of AA. All anyone need do to become a member is have a sincere desire to stop drinking. However, initiation into an AA group usually takes place through "sponsorship," where an experienced member acts as an advocate. Sponsorship may include introducing the new member to the AA group, picking him or her up for the meeting, and in general providing support and advice. Sponsorship is an integral part of AA recovery, and members believe that being a sponsor is important to their own recovery. In order to get a sponsor, a person can simply call a local AA member and request one. Sponsorship is part of the 12th (and last) step.

Upon becoming a member, each person learns the philosophy of AA and is given encouragement and support to give up drinking. Other members share their own drinking experiences and describe how they overcame associated problems. This mutual sharing is one of the most effective aspects of AA because it provides practical solutions and alleviates guilt by demonstrating that others have also behaved irrationally while drinking. AA also alleviates guilt by assuring members that their drinking behavior and all the negative consequences associated with it are a manifestation of a disease. However, AA does hold people responsible for their behavior; in other words, it is largely up to them to seek help and maintain their sobriety. In addition to these advantages, AA is helpful in the following ways:

- AA offers a regular support group composed of individuals who are striving for the same goal—abstinence from alcohol.
- AA meetings are available daily in most communities and can help alcoholics structure much of their time.
- Friends and acquaintances are often AA members. This is important because often alcoholics simply do not know many nondrinkers.

- AA often acts as an important adjunct to professionals who provide psychotherapy to alcoholic clients.
- AA has no fee and does not discriminate on racial, sexual, or socioeconomic grounds.
- AA has comprehensive goals, including emotional, behavioral, and spiritual change; the aim is to teach the person a new lifestyle with new values.

Although AA is an effective treatment method for many problem drinkers, it has some limiting factors that the professional counselor should take into account. First, AA is religiously oriented, which may be repugnant to some clients who resist the idea of spiritual surrender. Second, AA has a uniform view of alcoholism, and everyone is indoctrinated into the same basic credo. Research has demonstrated that there are many kinds of problem drinkers, and a complete lifestyle change may be overly rigorous for some who could benefit from lesser modifications in their drinking patterns. And third, AA calls for surrender to God and others as an important first step. This may be confusing for mental health clients who are being helped toward independence and personal responsibility. Counselors should discuss and clarify these issues with clients before referring them to AA.

Finally, it should be pointed out that AA is not a scientific theory but a set of beliefs and procedures that has evolved through years of trial and error. Evaluation research is somewhat difficult to conduct because many AA groups take on unique characteristics and are hard to compare with each other. The anonymous nature of the organization adds to this problem. There is surprisingly little scientific evidence to indicate the effectiveness (success rate) of AA. Some research has looked at the characteristics of individuals who are most likely to maintain affiliation with AA (Boscarino, 1980; Glaser & Ogborne, 1982). Emrick (1987) has concluded that favorable outcomes in AA are not limited to particular types of persons. There have also been correctional studies to support a relationship between AA attendance and abstinence (Alford, 1980; Polich, Armor, & Braiker, 1980; Hoffman Harrison, & Belille,1983).

## Al-Anon

Al-Anon largely incorporates AA principles but focuses on the alcoholic's spouse or significant others. Although Al-Anon often works with family members while the alcoholic is in treatment, in many cases it provides support independent of the alcoholic's actions. Basically, Al-Anon helps those close to an alcoholic face their own problems and see their role in contributing to the family's dysfunction. Participants are encouraged to learn to take care of their own needs and stop their world from revolving around the alcoholic's pathology. They are told the alcoholic will not stop drinking until he or she is ready and that many attempts at control (withholding money, hiding liquor, etc.) are counterproductive.

It should be remembered that all family members are negatively influenced by alcoholism and that all contribute to the problems. In our view, it is equally important for those in an alcoholic family to receive help as it is for the alcoholic.

### Additional Self-Help Groups

Alcoholics Anonymous was the prototype for self-help groups. However, many new groups have developed over the past decade to meet the needs of individuals who find AA unappealing for some reason. Rational recovery (RR) is based on the principles of rational-emotive behavior therapy (REBT). It was developed by a dissatisfied member of AA named Jack Trimpey. Like other cognitive approaches, RR teaches that alcoholism is a result of irrational beliefs, and it tries to replace them with rational ones. AA has the "Big Book" (Alcoholics Anonymous, 1976); RR has the *The Small Book* (Trimpey, 1992). Other spin-off groups are Women for Sobriety (Kirkpatrick, 1977), SOS, or the Secular Organization for Sobriety, and the SMART program (Self-Management and Recovery Training). Both SMART and RR utilize principles and techniques drawn from REBT. Newer self-help groups are available in different parts of the country. It is important for the family therapist to know the self-help scene in their geographic area as well as all treatment programs that are available.

## NATURAL RECOVERY

It should be noted that there are those who reject all forms of treatment, including self-help groups, yet they get better. It has been estimated that as many as 90 percent of problem drinkers never enter treatment and many suspend problematic use without it (Hingson, Scotch, Day, & Culbert, 1980). Important factors in the success of these "natural recoverers" include breaking off relationships with drug users, leaving a drug-using environment, and using social networks of friends and family that help provide support for their newly emerging status as drug- or alcohol-free (Grandfield & Cloud, 1996). It has been hypothesized that the self-labeling process that goes on in most self-help groups may be deleterious to the termination of addictive behaviors for some people. Several individuals who recovered on their own stated in interviews that they believed that a permanent identity as an addict would impede their continued social development, as reported by Grandfield and Cloud (1996). These authors also found that a major opposition to the 12-step approach seemed to be a reluctance to admit powerlessness over addiction, as these people saw themselves as strong and powerful. Other important factors for this group of people interviewed included education and other credentials, job skills, meaningful family attachments, and support mechanisms. None of the individuals in this group was from a disadvantaged background. Also, they still had family and other support ties and they had not yet burned their social bridges. So the family appears to be an important resource for those who get sober without treatment.

## Transactional Analysis Model

The transactional analysis (TA) treatment model is in marked philosophical contrast to the Alcoholics Anonymous model. In some ways it shares more in theory with models such as REBT (Ellis et al., 1980) and is cognitive in nature. TA, as described in chapter 1, holds that alcoholism is a game or series of destructive interpersonal dynamics rather than a disease. TA consequently believes that alcoholism can be cured, as opposed to being controlled, and that (theoretically) the alcoholic can return to non-problem drinking.

In his book *Healing Alcoholism*, Steiner (1979) described his TA approach. First, Steiner believed that alcoholics must sincerely want to seek help for their drinking because many alcoholics initially enter therapy not to be rehabilitated but to involve the counselor in a game. Unless therapists are effective in identifying clients genuinely requesting help, they may become unwilling participants in the alcoholic game. This assessment involves careful and direct questioning of the person requesting help and "contracting" or committing the client to a specific course of action.

When screening potential alcoholic clients, therapists must examine their motives for seeking help. For example, if potential clients are evasive about having a drinking problem or are being coerced into therapy by family, friends, or the courts, Steiner believed they should be told to delay counseling until they believe a problem exists and they want help. Steiner also avoided diagnoses ("you are an alcoholic") or collaboration with others who want the person to stop drinking. A direct request for help from the person is required. Once a request for help is made, a contract for treatment is specified by the therapist; this contract must be agreed to by the client without qualifications. More specifically, successful treatment requires alcoholic clients to:

- maintain complete sobriety for a minimum of a year
- attend group therapy sessions regularly every week for two hours during the one-year period

- involve themselves in specific homework including diet and other lifestyle changes addressed to their specific problems
- attend monthly body work sessions (as an example)

The establishment of a mutual informed consent relationship (contract) involves three transactions:

1. the request for treatment from the client
2. the offer of treatment by the therapist
3. an acceptance of treatment by the client

Also underlying the TA conception of treating alcoholics is the avoidance of counselor responses called "rescues." Steiner (1979) cited 10 rules to avoid rescues:

1. When three or more suggestions to an alcoholic have been rejected, you are Rescuing. Instead, offer one or two and wait to see whether they are acceptable. If they are not, stop making suggestions. Don't play "Why don't you . . . Yes, but . . ."
2. It's okay to investigate possible therapists for an alcoholic, but never make an appointment for him or her. Any therapist who is willing to make an appointment with an alcoholic through a third person is probably a potential Rescuer and eventual Persecutor.
3. Do not remove liquor, pour liquor down the drain, or look for hidden stashes of liquor in an alcoholic's house unless you're asked to do so by the alcoholic. Conversely, do not ever buy, serve, mix for, or offer alcohol to an alcoholic.
4. Do not engage in lengthy conversations about alcoholism or a person's alcoholic problem while the person is drunk or drinking; that will be a waste of time and energy and will be completely forgotten by him/her in most cases.
5. Never lend money to a drinking alcoholic. Do not allow a drunk alcoholic to come to your house, or, worse, to drink in your house. Instead, in as loving and nurturing a way as possible, ask to see him/her again when he/she is sober.
6. Do not get involved in errands, repair jobs, cleanups, long drives, pickups, or deliveries for an alcoholic who is not actively participating in fighting his/her alcoholism.
7. When you are relating to an alcoholic, do not commit the common error of seeing only the good and justifying the bad. "He's so wonderful when he's not drunk" is a common mistake people make with respect to alcoholics. The alcoholic is a whole person, and his personality includes both his good

part and his bad part. They cannot be separated from each other. Either take the whole person or none at all. If the ledger comes out consistently in the red, it is foolish to look only on the credit side.

8. Do not remain silent on the subject of another's alcoholism. Don't hesitate to express yourself freely on the subject: what you don't like, what you won't stand for, what you think about it, what you want, or how it makes you feel. But don't do it with the expectation of creating a change—do it just to be on record. Often your outspoken attitude will be taken seriously and appreciated, though it may not bring about immediate changes.

9. Be aware of doing anything that you don't want to do for the alcoholic. It is bad enough if you commit any of the above mistakes willingly. But when you add to them the complications of doing them when you would prefer not to, you are compounding your error and fostering an eventual Persecution.

10. Never believe that an alcoholic is hopeless. Keep your willingness to help ready, offer it often, and make it available whenever you detect a genuine interest and effort on the alcoholic's part. When that happens, don't overreact, but help cautiously and without Rescuing, doing only what you want to do and no more than your share. (pp. 156, 157)

After the alcoholic client has requested help, has been offered help by the counselor, and has agreed to its terms, the course of therapy involves the frank and thorough examination of the person's games and their payoffs. This is usually done in both individual and group therapy sessions. Not only do clients explore current behaviors but they are also helped to identify the root causes of their games, which can often be traced back to early childhood experiences. In childhood, basic decisions about life are made ("I have to be perfect to be okay") and life scripts are formed. TA also holds that people mirror qualities learned from their parents (e.g., being critical or accepting), and these early learnings are explored in light of current behaviors and attitudes.

Once these factors have been integrated by the client, new and healthier ways of getting needs met are explored. Because games involve other people, it is advantageous if other participants (usually the family) are involved in treatment. This is important because others in the alcoholic's life may resist the changes he or she may make because they are also game players and consequently receive their own payoffs. It should be underscored that games are played unconsciously by all involved.

In addition, TA therapists make the point that their approach is not to outwit alcoholics or put them down. In fact, TA emphasizes a true valuing of the individual as well as support and empathy. Essentially, the therapist must avoid becoming a game member because that serves only to prolong and reinforce the alcoholic's self-destructive behaviors. The therapist should be direct and confrontational but in a truly nurturing way.

Like AA, transactional analysis has little research to support its clinical success. In fact, TA is not often referred to in the literature after the mid-1980s. However, as a model it may be useful in understanding human communications, and it has played a role in some of the more current approaches to treatment.

### Psychodynamic Model

Psychodynamic theorists describe several principles for the treatment of alcoholism. First, they believe that all drinking must be terminated if rehabilitation is to be effective. Without detoxification and initial sobriety, it is felt that treatment will be unsuccessful and a power struggle will develop between the client and the therapist. Second, it is important to understand the transference that will be established by the client. *Transference* refers to the attachment of unresolved older feelings in a newer relationship. In this case, the alcoholic client will attach the paradoxical feelings of extreme dependency along with hostility, manipulation, and testing behaviors to the therapist. This leads to the third principle, countertransference, which the therapist may attach to the client. An understanding of this process is very important because it is easy for a therapist to take the client's resistance personally and become disgusted and discouraged. Instead, the therapist should see clients' behaviors objectively, as a symptom of their pathological condition. It is also underscored that therapists should not see themselves as omnipotent, and they should realize that no one can stop an alcoholic determined to drink.

The fourth principle is that the alcoholic's defenses should not be smashed by heavy confrontation during initial therapy but should be redirected in a supportive manner. Under this model, insight is not the initial goal of therapy—sobriety is the first goal. For example, Wallace (1978) believed denial can be used to benefit the alcoholic during initial treatment. He pointed out that rather than make clients face up to all their irrationalities of the past, clients need to preserve some self-worth and save face. Denial can be an effective coping mechanism in fending off overwhelming anxiety. Coming to grips with the past, Wallace believed, should come later in the treatment process.

The fifth principle is that therapeutic leverage, or therapist potency, can only come from a clear understanding of the client's developmental past. Not that therapists will bring these issues out, but they need to know what defenses should be left in place (for the present) in order to maximize treatment. The sixth and final principle is the concept of stages. According to psychodynamic theory, three stages are necessary for total recovery. Stage one is the client's recognition that "I can't drink." This is an initial stage where a good deal of external control is necessary: detoxification, hospitalization, Antabuse, Alcoholics Anonymous, and family support. In this stage, the alcoholic needs protection against his or her own impulses to drink. The second phase is "I won't drink," or the internalization of controls. At this stage the conflict about drinking is mostly unconscious. Many AA members and other recovering alcoholics are at this stage and can function adequately. The third stage is "I don't have to drink" and represents conflict resolution. It is at this point, psychodynamic theorists believe, that insight should be sought, but only after sobriety and stabilization have occurred. They also point out that few alcoholics successfully complete the third stage because their lives are manageable for the most part at the second, and the impetus for further change may be diminished. The completion of all three stages is felt to be a relatively long-term process but needed before the alcoholic can truly be rid of conflict.

## Behavioral Models of Treatment

The principles of operant and classical conditioning were outlined in chapter 1. How these principles are manifested in specific treatment models is now described.

### *Aversive Conditioning Techniques*

Nowhere can the classical conditioning model be more clearly demonstrated than in aversive conditioning paradigms. Essentially, a noxious substance is administered to a client at the same time that liquor is consumed. If this procedure is repeated enough times, the liquor itself becomes a noxious stimulus and further alcohol consumption becomes impossible. The first example of aversive conditioning to be cited involves the use of nausea-inducing chemicals.

The two chemicals most widely used in aversive conditioning are apomorphine and emetine. This procedure was explored as early as 1941 by Voegthlin, Lemere, Broz, and O'Hollaren, who reported success rates as high as 60 percent after one year. The procedure involves the administration of emetine shortly before the sipping of the alcoholic's favorite beverage. This is followed by prolonged vomiting of 45 minutes or more. This sequence is repeated two or three times in a row, every other day, for three or four days. In addition, individual and family counseling often accompany the treatment.

A second form of aversive conditioning is electric shock. The treatment format is very similar to the chemical aversion model, but here the client is given painful (but not harmful) shocks via electrodes on the arms as he or she sips a preferred beverage. Often a shock is terminated when the drink is spit out. A variation of this approach is aimed at controlled drinking. The first stage of this process is to teach clients to accurately estimate their blood alcohol levels (BALs) through feedback exercises in which they estimate their BALs. Once different BALs can be discriminated, clients drink to a predetermined level, above which a shock is administered. The goal is to create an aversive experience only after an elevated BAL occurs. Research by Nathon and Bridell (1977), however, indicates this technique is only moderately successful and the effects short-lived.

### Operant Conditioning

An example of operant conditioning (contingency management) is individualized behavior therapy (IBT), initially developed at Patton State Hospital in 1970. This research represented the first major attempt in the United States to treat alcoholic clients in which the treatment outcome was non–problem drinking. It was the contention of researchers that diagnosed Gamma alcoholics could learn new drinking responses that were felt (by the client) to be nonabusive. Alcoholics were taught to avoid abusive drinking behaviors such as ordering a straight drink, gulping (versus sipping) drinks, ordering a drink within 20 minutes of a previous drink, and ordering more than three drinks in a 90-minute period. Other components of this treatment regime included videotape replays where drinking antecedents (e.g., anxiety due to social pressure) were analyzed and modified. This technique represents aversive avoidance. Behavior connected to abusive drinking resulted in electric shocks, but new positive behavior was not punished. This is an operant conditioning model in that reinforcement (in this case, lack of shock) is contingent upon the client's behavior.

Work done in Baltimore City Hospitals (Bigelow, Liebson, & Griffiths, 1974) showed that chronic alcoholics moderated their drinking in order to live in an enriched environment (i.e., phone privileges, visitors, regular diet) and to avoid a more austere environment in which these privileges were unavailable. Briefly, researchers concluded that alcoholics could and would voluntarily control their drinking in order to improve their lives in a structured setting. How they would fare in society is another matter.

### Assertiveness Training and Systematic Desensitization

Other forms of behavioral techniques can be used without elaborate equipment and in an outpatient setting. Two of these are assertiveness training and systematic desensitization. Assertiveness training is thought to be appropriate for many alcoholics because the expression of anger, resentment, and other forms of confrontation often occurs only during intoxication and is usually destructive. Assertiveness training is aimed at helping an individual better manage interpersonal relationships. Typically, alcoholic clients will describe situations to their therapists in which they were unassertive (accepted a drink when they really did not want one). This scenario is role-played and analyzed, and then new, more assertive responses are rehearsed.

This is followed by a homework session in which the client tries out the new behavior in real life. The next step is to analyze what took place. For example, how did the other person react, and how did the client feel? Following this, other new responses are discussed and practiced, especially focusing on areas of conflict in the client's life. Eventually, the client should be able to generalize new responses (which are more rewarding) in a variety of previously stress-producing situations. This procedure is invaluable for many alcoholic clients who tend to avoid confrontation, feel guilty or ashamed, and then drink as a coping response. Alcoholic clients often avoid confronting marital, work, or social interaction problems, and this avoidance is usually followed by a drinking spree and an explosion of feelings.

Systematic desensitization (Wolpe, 1973) is similar in that stress-producing life situations (which often cue drinking) are the focus of treatment. The general idea behind systematic desensitization is to teach clients to relax while imagining stressful circumstances. The first step in training is deep muscle relaxation, which is accomplished through the contraction and relaxation of muscles. Next, the client and therapist construct a hierarchy of stressfulness, from the least stressful to the most stressful event. Following this, the patient is instructed to imagine being in a low-stress situation while fully relaxed. Progression up the scale takes place until the client can imagine the most stressful situation in a relaxed state. Eventually, the client actually enters these situations with reduced anxiety. Because many alcoholics experience anxiety and stress and drink to cope with these states, systematic desensitization, like assertiveness training, is seen as appropriate treatment to offset the immediate impulse to drink in reaction to stress.

## Cognitive Approaches

Cognitive approaches are based on the three postulates that cognitive activity (1) affects behavior, (2) can be monitored, and (3) can be modified to effect changes in behavior (Dobson & Block, 1988). Given that drinking alcohol is in fact a behavior this seems to be a viable approach. Cognitive behavior therapy usually includes imagery training, self-regulation, cognitive reframing, and cognitive restructuring (Walters, 1994).

### Rational-Emotive Therapy

Originated by Albert Ellis in 1955, rational-emotive therapy (RET) has become one of the most popular schools of psychotherapy. It has been adapted for use with alcohol problems (Ellis et al., 1988) and like AA has been the basis of many other approaches to the treatment of alcoholism. It differs from other major schools of psychotherapy in the amount of importance it places on the role of cognition or the thinking process in human problems. The basic tenet of RET is that although negative life events are accompanied by negative emotional states, these events *do not directly cause emotional reactions.* Ellis developed the ABC theory:

$A$ = *a*ctivating event
$B$ = *b*eliefs, attitudes, thoughts, self-statements
$C$ = emotional and behavioral *c*onsequences

Ellis believed that most problems are based on the belief that $A$ causes $C$. However, if it were true that $A$ causes $C$ then $A$ would always cause $C$ and it does not. $A$, or the activating event, does not cause $C$, or the emotional and behavioral consequences, but $C$ is a result of $B$, or beliefs, attitudes, thoughts, and self-statements. In fact, beliefs or cognitions are the primary determinants of emotions. Ellis believed that low frustration tolerance (LFT) and the cognitive thoughts that sustain it keep an individual from being able to maintain abstinence. Some of these beliefs include:

- I cannot stand avoiding a drink.
- I cannot function without a drink.
- I am not strong enough to resist alcohol.
- Life is too hard so I am entitled to have a drink.
- I must not abstain when it's so enjoyable to imbibe.

These irrational beliefs lead to the emotional disturbance of LFT, or discomfort anxiety, which leads to drinking. Alcoholics learn to overcome this problem by changing this addictive thinking. Obviously the theory is more complex than presented here. For a more detailed discussion of RET, see the references suggested at the end of the chapter.

### Lifestyle Theory

In two recent publications, Glenn Walters (1994 & 1996) presented a model he developed during his experience working with criminal addicts in the Bureau of Prisons substance abuse treatment program. This model is based on a theory that is an alternative to traditional perspectives on substance abuse, including the disease model, and it deemphasizes—but does not ignore—psychological and social conditions that promote substance abuse. It examines the lifestyle that forms from continued involvement in drug or alcohol abuse. Habitual drug use is seen as a response to existential fear, the expression of which is a complex function of the conditions, choices, and cognitions that define a person's life space.

This theory, as well as REBT, discussed previously, are useful and well-thought-out theories. However, both seem to underestimate the role of the family in the development of cognitive and emotional factors involved in alcoholism and substance abuse. Where do we get most of our ideas about how the world operates and our place in the world? Our view of alcohol and drugs and their usefulness, our view of ourselves in relation to the world, come primarily from our early family experiences. If we were treated well we treat others well. If we were treated poorly we treat others poorly. If our parents behaved in a rational way we see the world as a rational place. If our parents were irrational we see the world as a threatening and irrational place. A great deal of useful information can be gained from studying cognitive approaches to the treatment of substance abuse and alcoholism. However, they should remain in a family perspective.

## Biological Approaches

### Pharmacotherapies

The use of medication to treat alcohol problems has been divided into three major strategies (Institute of Medicine, 1989): (1) antidipsotropic medications, (2) effect-altering medications, and (3) psychotropic medications. The first antidipsotropics (meaning anti-alcoholism drugs) include agents that cause an adverse reaction if the person consumes alcohol. These reactions vary in severity but in some cases can be deadly. The primary drug used for this purpose is disulfiram (Antabuse). In its review of treatment effectiveness the Institute of Medicine reported mixed results and several studies that failed to show benefits from disulfiram. Effect-altering drugs reduce the reinforcing properties of ethanol without producing negative side effects. Drugs such as Naltrexone (RiVia) block the high of alcohol and have been widely reported to decrease craving. Psychotropic drugs are usually used to treat alcoholics with a dual diagnosis—a mental illness in addition to alcoholism. Antidepressants, antipsychotics, and lithium, an antimania drug, have all been used in alcoholism treatment. Certain psychotropics such as anti-anxiety drugs are used during detoxification.

### Nutritional Approaches

Most detoxification centers and residential treatment facilities include proper nutrition as an integral part of their treatment regimen. It is generally felt that alcoholic clients neglect proper diet and often suffer the effects of malnutrition. But malnutrition has also been forwarded as more than a side effect of alcoholism; Williams (1981) and others considered nutrition a contributing factor in its development. According to this theory, people vary greatly in their inherent tolerance and appetite for liquor. Williams felt many are therefore born with a predisposition to alcohol abuse and are at high risk to become alcoholics from birth. He made two essential points in this regard: (1) alcoholism may be prevented through proper nutrition, and (2) it may also be treated in this manner.

For prevention, Williams described seven principles to follow.

1. Know one's unique physiological needs.
2. Eat high-quality foods.
3. Avoid low-quality foods (e.g., sugars and starches).
4. Exercise.
5. Cultivate inner peace through moderation and emotional health.
6. Use nutritional supplements (vitamins and minerals).
7. Use glutamine, an amino acid, as a food supplement.

For alcoholism treatment, Williams underlines the importance of glutamine. This naturally occurring substance is thought to protect bacterial cells that are important in the metabolism of food. Research with laboratory animals has shown rats to lower their voluntary consumption of alcohol by 40 percent through the use of glutamine. With humans, Williams relied on case histories rather than experimental research but insisted that some alcoholics' craving for alcohol can be significantly reduced by adding glutamine to their diets. More on the subject can be found in Williams's book *The Prevention of Alcoholism through Nutrition*.

## Sociological Approaches

Social environment can have an impact on individuals' use or abuse of drugs or alcohol. The messages they receive from those around them are important. Besides their family, other institutions they are involved in can give messages that help determine their behavior related to drug or alcohol use. Work settings, schools, churches, and social settings all affect how a person uses alcohol or drugs. These institutions can also have an impact on treatment if they are so utilized.

### Employee Assistance Programs

The Employee Assistance Program (EAP) is not a model of alcoholism treatment but a model for intervention and referral of alcohol abusers at a worksite. These programs have proliferated in recent years as businesses have discovered their financial and humanitarian value. Essentially, an employee whose work has slipped consistently is no longer simply fired. He or she is instead approached by a trained supervisor who offers the worker an option—accept confidential help or face possible job action. Often this comes as an ultimatum: Get help or lose the job.

In the majority of cases, the problems are alcohol-related—absenteeism, tardiness, or a decline in performance. The company benefits because a trained employee can be rehabilitated and return to work. Employees obviously benefit because they are forced to accept help (which they otherwise might refuse), and they often keep their jobs. All supervisors are trained and are told not to attempt to diagnose but to base the referral strictly on work performance. The entire procedure is confidential and does not go into the employee's personnel file. Often insurance carriers for the company have a special clause that pays for hospitalization for alcoholism and other problems that interfere with the employee's ability to perform. EAPs also serve the insurance agency because it is less costly to rehabilitate a worker than to pay for years of disability. Also, the rate of accidents and injuries is reduced because impaired workers are not allowed to remain on duty.

Typically, the initial referral is made by the EAP coordinator, who assesses the nature of the employee's problem and makes a referral to an appropriate rehabilitation agency. Progress is monitored. When the treatment agency, the EAP coordinator, and the employee feel the time is right, he or she returns to the worksite. Upon the employee's return to work, the immediate supervisor monitors work performance. EAP programs in such companies as Kemper Insurance, Eastman Kodak, Consolidated Edison, Du Pont, and many, many others have reported both savings and a high rate of success—up to 80 percent (Rouse). These results may be due to the high level of motivation created when an individual's job is on the line and the relatively high level of functioning of the population served.

### Alcoholism Services

The most available alcoholism service, as mentioned earlier, is Alcoholics Anonymous. Nearly every community has AA groups that meet on a regular basis. AA also functions as an adjunct to many public and private alcoholism treatment centers. Meetings are usually held once a week; however, many communities hold meetings often enough that an individual can attend one nearly every day if so desired. Larger communities have a wide variety of AA groups consisting of individuals with homogeneous socioeconomic backgrounds. In some areas there are AA groups specifically for physicians and priests. It is therefore often possible and desirable to refer a client to a meeting where he or she will find people with similar backgrounds. Information about AA can be obtained from a variety of sources, including local mental health centers, physicians, clergymen, the peronals section of many newspapers, or General Services Office, Grand Central Station, New York, NY 10017.

Other alcoholism services include public and private rehabilitation facilities as well as counselors, psychologists, psychiatrists, and other practitioners who specialize in alcoholism rehabilitation. Public alcoholism centers are often (but not always) incorporated within a community mental health center and consist of inpatient (hospital) or halfway house residential care (one to three months long), outpatient counseling, and social setting detoxification (one to five days long). These programs can be found through local, state, and federal government departments of health and mental health. Private alcoholism rehabilitation programs offer basically the same range of services as the public ones but are more often freestanding, which means they are not a part of a larger mental health system. Also, most private programs are affiliated with hospitals administratively and are often housed in those hospitals. Most public and private alcoholism programs, as well as AA, provide outreach services and will therefore make home visits if necessary.

## SUMMARY

Although not covered in this review, many additional forms of alcoholism treatment do exist. For example, Glasser's reality therapy techniques, gestalt methods, Kern's *Addiction Alternatives*, the community reinforcement approach (Hunt & Azirin, 1973), and others have been used in the treatment of alcoholic clients. What we have done, however, is present those models that have addressed themselves directly to the treatment of alcoholism and are most widely used.

Evaluation of these models is difficult because treatment outcome data are either not available (e.g., AA) or are not generally agreed upon by various theoretical orientations. Even programs that do publish outcome results, such as aversive conditioning programs, are subject to question because it can be argued that private programs serve higher-functioning clients than does AA, for example. Private facilities require payment, and the clientele usually are (or were recently) employed and/or have health insurance; therefore, lower socioeconomic groups are screened out.

We recommend an eclectic approach; the treatment should fit the needs of the client and should be individualized.

Many similarities exist among the models presented. For example, all call for initial abstinence. In this vein, it can be argued that the specific model of treatment may not be as important as the competence of the practitioner and the motivation and readiness of the client. Our conclusions are that no one model is universally true or appropriate and that all the models presented can be effective, depending on the unique needs of the client. It is also important to point out that no presentation of family therapy approaches was made. Traditionally accepted approaches, by and large, have not visualized alcoholism treatment in a family context. Rather, the identified-patient medical model has predominated.

This book was written to offer an alternative and, we feel, a superior concept of alcoholism treatment. Obviously, family therapy is not the only true effective approach. Many models of treatment can be adapted to focus on the family system (as opposed to the individual) as the client. The family is usually affected by the alcoholism of a family member and therapy for the family can help everyone.

---

## REFERENCES

Alcoholics Anonymous World Service. (1976). *Alcoholics anonymous* (3rd ed.). New York: Author.

Alford, G. (1980). Alcoholics Anonymous: An empirical study. *Addictive Behavior, 5*, 359–370.

Berg, I.K. (1994). *Family-based services: A solution-focused approach.* New York: W.W. Norton.

Bigelow, G., Liebson, I.A., & Griffiths, R.R. (1974). Alcoholic drinking suppression by a behavioral time out period. *Behavior Research and Therapy, 12*, 107–115.

Boscarino, J. (1980). Factors related to "stable" and "unstable" affiliation with Alcoholics Anonymous. *International Journal of Addiction, 15,* 839–848.

Curriculum Review Committee, Addiction Training Center Program (Sept. 1995). *Addiction counselor competencies.* Albany, NY: State University of New York.

Dobson, K.S., & Block, L. (1988). Historical and physiological bases of the cognitive behavioral therapies. In K.S. Dobson (Ed.), *Handbook of cognitive-behavioral therapies* (pp. 3–38). New York: Gilford Press.

Ellis, A., Mcinerney, J., DiGiuseppe, R., & Yeager, R. (1988). *Rational-emotive therapy with alcoholics and substance abusers.* New York: Pergamon Press.

Emrick, C.D. (1987). Alcoholics Anonymous: Affiliation processes and effectiveness as treatment. *Alcoholism Clinical Experience and Research, 011*, 416–423.

Glaser, F.B., & Ogborne, A.C. (1981). Does A.A. really work? *British Journal of Addiction, 77,* 123–129.

Grandfield, R., & Cloud, W. (1996). The elephant that no one sees: Natural recovery among middle-class addicts. *Journal of Drug Issues, 26*(1), 45–61.

Hingson, R., Scotch, N., Day, N., & Culbert A. (1980). Recognizing and seeking help for drinking problems. *Journal of Studies on Alcohol, 41*, 1102–1117.

Hoffman, N.B., Harrison, P., & Belille, C. (1983). Alcoholics Anonymous after treatment: Attendance and abstinence. *International Journal of Addiction, 18,* 111–318.

Hunt, G.M., & Azirin, N.H. (1973). A community- reinforcement approach to alcoholism. *Behaviour Research and Therapy, 11*, 91–104.

Institute of Medicine. (1989). *Prevention and treatment of alcohol problems.* Washington, DC: National Academy Press.

Kirkpatrick, J. (1977). *Turnabout: Help for a new life.* New York: Doubleday.

Lawson, G., Lawson, A., & Rivers, C. (1996). *Essentials of chemical dependency counseling.* Gaithersburg, MD: Aspen Publishers.

Miller, W.R., & Rollnick, S. (1991). *Motivational interviewing: Preparing people to change addictive behavior.* New York: Gilford Press.

Nathon, P.E., & Bridell, D.W. (1977). *Behavioral treatment and assessment of alcoholism.* In B. Kissin & H. Begleiter (Eds.), *The biology of alcoholism* (Vol. 5). New York: Plenum Press.

Polich, J.M., Armor, D.J., & Braiker, H.B. (1980). Patterns of alcoholism over four years. *Journal on Studies of Alcohol, 41,* 397–416.

Rouse, K.A. *What to do about the employee with a drinking problem.* Kemper Insurance Companies, public relations, Tongrove, IL.

Steiner, C.M. (1979). *Healing alcoholism.* New York: Grove Press.

Trimpey, J. (1992). *The small book.* New York: Delacorte.

Voegthlin, W.L., Lemere, F., Broz, W.R., & O'Hollaren, P. (1941). Conditioned reflex therapy of chronic alcoholism IV: A preliminary report on the value of reinforcement. *Quarterly Journal of Studies on Alcohol, 2,* 505–511.

Wallace, J. (1978). Working with the preferred defense structure of the recovering alcoholic. In A. Zimberg, J. Wallace, & S. Blume (Eds.), *Practical approaches to alcoholism psychotherapy.* New York: Plenum Press.

Walters, G.D. (1994). *Escaping the journey to nowhere: The psychology of alcohol and other drug abuse.* Washington, DC: Taylor & Francis.

Walters, G.D. (1996). *Substance abuse and the new road to recovery: A practitioner's guide.* Washington, DC: Taylor & Francis.

Williams, R.J. (1981). *The prevention of alcoholism through nutrition.* New York: Bantam.

Wolpe, J. (Ed.). (1973). *The practice of behavior therapy* (Vol. 2). New York: Pergamon Press.

## RECOMMENDED READINGS

Alcoholics Anonymous World Service. (1976). *Alcoholics anonymous* (3rd ed.). New York: Author.

   The basis for the AA program. A book that has sold millions of copies and is a must-read for those working in the alcoholism field.

Ellis, A., Mcinerney, J., DiGiuseppe, R., & Yeager, R. (1988). *Rational-emotive therapy with alcoholics and substance abusers.* New York: Pergamon Press.

   A primer on RET and an alternative to the disease model.

Lawson, G., Lawson, A., & Rivers, C. (1996). *Essentials of chemical dependency counseling.* Gaithersburg, MD: Aspen Publishers.

   A basic text on alcoholism counseling. A best-selling text that is readable and full of useful information about topics from ethics to basic counseling skills.

Lenin, J.D. (1995) *Introduction to alcoholism counseling: A bio-psycho-social approach* (2nd ed.). Washington, DC: Taylor & Francis.
An interesting and enlightening book with lots of social and biological information related to alcoholism.

Trimpey, J. (1992). *The small book.* New York: Delacorte.
*The* book about rational recovery.

Walters, G.D. (1994). *Escaping the journey to nowhere: The psychology of alcohol and other drug abuse.* Washington, DC: Taylor & Francis.
This book has a more detailed description of the lifestyle model. If you only buy one of Dr. Walters's books, buy this one.

Walters, G.D. (1996). *Substance abuse and the new road to recovery: A practitioner's guide.* Washington, DC: Taylor & Francis.
This book has a large appendix with 30 sample forms used in the lifestyle treatment model. It is useful for those developing treatment programs but is light on family issues.

Washton, A.M. (Ed.). (1995). *Psychotherapy and substance abuse: A practitioner's handbook.* New York: Gilford Press.

# PART II

# Etiology

The previous chapters discussed traditional and contemporary theories of the etiology and treatment of alcoholism. Therapists choose treatment methods based on their views of the cause of alcoholism. In many of the theories, the assumption was that drinking problems originated with the drinker, and the treatment was therefore directed toward the individual. However, excessive drinking behavior may lead to disruption of a social system or it may be a *result* of a dysfunctional social system such as a family. The drinking behavior may even have a function in the family system that acts and reacts to perpetuate the behavior. It is less important for family therapists to understand the cause or etiology of alcoholism than how it is being maintained. Family therapists are acutely aware of the environmental, biological, and interpersonal factors that may lead a family member to abuse alcohol. This family viewpoint focuses on interpersonal relationships and transactions rather than on personal pathology. The therapist works interactionally with the entire family. Rather than involving family members simply to enhance the treatment of the identified patient, the focus is shifted to the family itself as the patient. Thus, the goal of treatment is an improvement in family functioning and not just sobriety for the alcoholic member. With this approach the therapist works for a healthy family system that has no need for a symptomatic member—a family that communicates freely, both emotionally and cognitively, with each other on every subject and whose members have their needs met in the family.

A large portion of this book is dedicated to understanding the role the family members of an alcoholic play in the onset, progression, treatment, and prevention of alcoholism and problem drinking. The etiology part addresses the interlocking relationships of family members as they relate to the drinking behavior of the alcoholic and examines the role these relationships play in perpetuating this destructive cycle. The roots of alcoholism must be understood not only to aid in choosing the proper treatment method but also to help prevent alcohol abuse in families, especially those with long-standing histories of alcoholism.

It is important to have some understanding of the complex patterns in families that lead to a family member developing alcoholism. This understanding improves the chances of stopping not only the active alcoholism but also the intergenerational transmission of alcoholism in the family. One certainty about the etiology of alcoholism is that it runs in some families generation after generation and does not exist in others. A pioneer in the addiction and family field, M. Duncan Stanton, studied genograms (family trees) that cover four to seven generations, looking for "the first alcoholic." He studied the patterns of drinking conveyed from one generation to another and noted that drinking began as a result of loss or grief. The generation just preceding the first alcoholic suffered a great loss from which it was unable to recover. Stanton uses this process with the families he treats to give them a new perspective. It depathologizes past family members and casts them in a new light of being pained. This frees up the family to make a choice whether to keep, revise, or replace these intergenerational patterns (Daw, 1995).

---

**REFERENCE**

Daw, J.L. (1995, December). Alcohol problems across generations. *Family Therapy News*. Washington, DC: AAMFT.

# CHAPTER 3

# Viewing the Family as a Client

The first part of this chapter discusses the roots of family therapy, the nuclear family, and the family of origin, and examines these interlocking relationships in terms of their value for treatment. The second section covers the overlapping yet distinct theories of the etiology of family dysfunction as proposed by the structural and strategic models of family therapy, Bowen therapy, communication/experiential therapy, and behavioral family therapy.

## ROOTS OF FAMILY THERAPY

Family therapists took from the anthropological approach of functionalism the notion that deviant behavior may serve a protective function for a social group and applied this to symptoms of family members (Nichols & Schwartz, 1995). Functionalists believe that families need to adapt to their environment. Symptoms (i.e., alcoholism) in family members mean that the family is not adapting to the environment and is unable to meet its needs.

Ludwig von Bertalanffy, a biologist, developed a model of *general systems theory* that relates to any system, whether physical (a machine), biological (a dog), psychological (a personality), or sociological (a labor union or set of laws). A system can be made up of smaller systems or be a part of a larger system (Davidson, 1983). These systems also have properties or rules, such as "a system is more than the sum of its parts." In other words, when the parts of a system come together, they create something like a watch telling time when all of its parts are assembled. Therapists therefore should not concentrate just on the people in a family but should also observe the interaction and process of these family parts.

Bertanlanffy also espoused the idea that living systems, people, are not machines and have special properties. *Equifinality* is the principle that organisms

45

have the ability to reach final goals from different initial conditions and in different ways, and have the ability to protect and restore their wholeness (Davidson, 1983). He also promoted a belief in the importance of values and ecological protection of the environment.

*Cybernetics,* another major influence on family therapy, was developed by a mathematician studying machines, Norbert Weiner. The core of the theory is the *feedback loop,* which is the process of a system getting information for self-correction to maintain a balance or progress toward a goal (Nichols & Schwartz, 1995). These can be *positive feedback loops*, which amplify deviation from a course or state, or negative feedback loops, which reduce deviation. An example of how this works is the effect of rising temperature outside of a house; this creates a *negative feedback loop* that activates the thermostat and starts the air conditioner to bring the temperature back to the original state.

Gregory Bateson, an anthropologist, brought cybernetics to family therapy with the notion of *circular causality*: psychopathology is not caused by events in the past but it is part of ongoing circular feedback loops (Nichols & Schwartz, 1995). These ideas are applied to families by studying their rules that govern behavior; negative feedback loops, or the process used to enforce the rules; the sequence of events around the problem, or how the family reacts to a problem, and in what order; and what happens if the negative feedback loop does not solve the problem or if positive feedback loops do not push for new solutions.

This is evident in alcoholic families when the family has a set pattern of reaction to the intoxication of the alcoholic member. Rules are established to attempt to solve the problem: "Don't make noise. It will disturb your father." The nonalcoholic spouse takes on most of the responsibility for running the family. All family members learn not to talk about the alcoholic behavior. Secrets are kept and role behaviors develop in an attempt to fix the problem. All of this leads to maintenance of the status quo in an attempt to keep the family together, but the sequences of family behavior become part of the problem. Instead of the drinking behavior being the deviation from the stable state, it becomes part of the status quo of the family. Family members learn how to adapt to it, thus keeping it stuck. This usually results when negative feedback loops about the drinking behavior (nagging and complaining) fail to correct the deviation. An example of a negative feedback loop that does not work is the classic communication pattern, "I drink because you nag." This usually leads to increased or at least a continued pattern of drinking.

Murray Bowen, a psychiatrist, was strongly influenced by biological sciences because he wanted to draw his concepts from a science that concerned living organisms. His concept of *differentiation of self,* which is the core of this theory, was taken from the process by which cells differentiate from each other or are fused together. He saw this process in families with schizophrenic children who appeared highly emotionally reactive to each other and formed what Bowen called an *undifferentiated family ego mass,* like an undifferentiated cell (Nichols & Schwartz, 1995). Bowen was also influenced by the theory of evolution in adopting his premise of the *multigenerational transmission process,* whereby low levels of differentiation are passed down through the generations, creating symptoms in family members. This concept is relevant to chemical dependency that has become part of the multigenerational process in families. Bowen described the transmission of alcoholism across generations in the only paper he wrote about a specific symptom or problem (Bowen, 1974).

## THE NUCLEAR FAMILY AND THE FAMILY OF ORIGIN

The nuclear family consists of those individuals with whom the alcoholic is presently living. The husband and wife of this family originated in separate families of origin. These families of origin are the parents and in-laws of the marital partners and the future grandparents of their children. In discussing the family it is impossible to explain the nuclear family without intertwining it with families of origin in a circular fashion. The nuclear family, in turn, becomes a family of origin for all of the next generation.

The nuclear family begins with the decision of a man and a woman, both from separate social systems with unique values, beliefs, and interactional dynamics, to marry and form a third system, bringing with them parts from their original systems (families of origin). The attraction these two people feel for each other is invariably linked to the marital relationships of their parents or the role they played in the family. The woman, for example, may be looking for someone strong like her father because she is weak like her mother, or she may be looking for someone she can dominate and who will allow her to maintain her compulsively intense relationship with her mother. The man, on the other hand, may feel weak but defensively appears strong to impress his mate. Because his father was the family authority, the man may wish to recreate this role for himself.

Bowen (1978) believed people with equal levels of differentiation from their parents are attracted to each other. He said, "It is common for young people to get into marriage blaming their parents for past unhappiness, and expecting to find perfect harmony in the marriage" (p. 263). However, people who are overly dependent on their parents and have a low capacity for independent problem solving are often unable to form new attachments in marital relationships.

Framo (1976) wrote that "the relationship problems that adults have with their spouses and children are reconstructions and elaborations of earlier conflicts from the family of origin" (p. 194). He stated that people perceive their spouses based on their own needs and make demands that are irrational but are needed to fill the voids they experienced in their own families. Mate selections, according to Framo, are "made with exquisite accuracy, and unconscious deals are made—e.g.,

I will be your conscience if you will act out my impulses" (p. 194). Thus, a wife with a large superego will control her antisocial husband within limits, while he acts out her rebellious needs that she is unable to fulfill. The two personalities become dependent on each other and increasingly intertwined, making it difficult for either to leave regardless of the dysfunction of the relationship.

Marital partners enmeshed in these relationships (based on their inability to function as an individual) can manifest dysfunctions leading to superficial relationships, emotional upheaval, and possible drinking behavior (if this drinking model was present in their family of origin). Often these marital partners reach out to each other for identity and fuse into a single entity in the marriage. To achieve some separateness the marital partners must set up emotional distance. One spouse may take the dominant position in the relationship with the remaining spouse adapting to the other and further losing identity. "If this pattern is continued long enough, the adaptive one is vulnerable to some kind of chronic dysfunction, which can be physical illness, emotional illness, or a social dysfunction such as drinking, the use of drugs or irresponsible behavior" (Bowen, 1978, p. 263).

Fogarty (1976) described marital relationships as having an emotional pursuer and an emotional distancer. Usually the pursuer is the wife and the distancer is the husband, but these roles can be reversed. As the wife works toward emotional closeness, the husband distances. A diagram of this process is shown in Figure 3–1.

In healthy systems these roles are interchangeable, with both parties pursuing at times and achieving intimacy. Often the pursuer in one area will be the distancer in another area. If mutual distancing remains over a prolonged period of time, a fixed distance occurs that may place the husband in a peripheral position in the family. This result may be functional for the husband's identity but dysfunctional for the marriage. Often in these cases the wife can become overinvolved with one or several children, passing on the inability to differentiate from the parents. Alcoholism as a coping mechanism can be transmitted from generation to generation. Emotional distancing is frequently seen between every member of an alcoholic family. The discussion in the chapters to follow deals with overprotective and overinvolved parents as predisposers of alcoholism.

## Case Histories

A case example of marital difficulty resulting from emotional distancing in the wife's family of origin was seen at a child guidance clinic. Judy, age 33, and Marvin, age 47, were referred to the center for parenting information and help with their son Chris, age 4. A large portion of the therapy hours was concerned with Judy's complaints about her husband's behaviors, in addition to withdrawal of love and deterioration of their sexual relationship since the birth of their son.

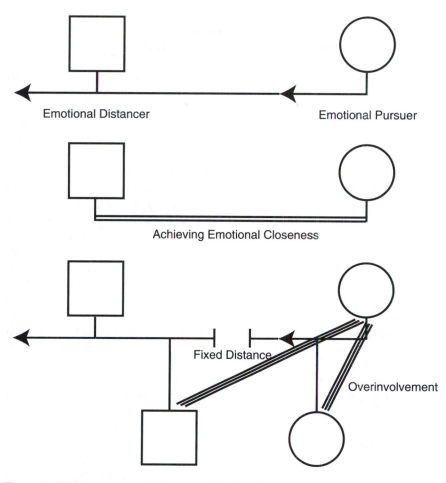

**Figure 3–1** Distance, Pursuit, Closeness, Overinvolvement.

The therapists at this point began to focus on the marital relationship. Judy explained that this was the second marriage for both her and her husband. Her husband had three children by a previous marriage and did not wish to have any in this marriage. Judy had been told that it would be very difficult for her to have children, and she was unable to have children during her first marriage. The assumed marital agreement was marriage for love and companionship—not to raise a family. When Judy became pregnant, she was extremely happy but feared Marvin would feel she had deceived him. After Chris's birth, Judy became very suspicious of Marvin. His work took him on the road five days a week while Judy stayed home and became overinvolved with Chris. She also accused Marvin of not caring for Chris and stated she was working very hard to have a loving family that would be different from the unfeeling family she grew up in.

During a history-taking session the therapist discovered that Judy had never felt loved by her alcoholic father and was jealous of his relationship with her sister. She tearfully admitted, "If he would just put his arms around me once and tell me everything was all right, maybe I could finally believe he cares."

Judy continued to criticize Marvin in the family sessions for minor issues that Marvin would attempt to change. Repeatedly, Marvin assured Judy that he had neither felt trapped nor tricked by Chris's birth and that he really loved her and their son. Judy was unable to believe him and complained about the infrequency of sexual activity. Upon investigation, Marvin explained that Judy's critical remarks during sex had angered him and he had been avoiding her (setting up the distance). This pattern of criticism was a repetition of the conflict between Judy's mother and father that distanced her father from the family.

As improvements began to occur in the relationship due to the therapy, Judy continued to find fault and state that she did not believe Marvin loved her. Although Judy protested that she was pursuing intimacy, all of her actions were distancing the relationship. Finally, she demanded to have another baby, knowing that Marvin was opposed to the idea. This demand gave Marvin a further excuse to avoid sexual activity and also provided Judy with further proof of Marvin's lack of love. At this point in the therapy, Marvin became weary of working toward intimacy and refused to attend further sessions.

During Judy's remaining individual sessions, she began to understand that she was unable to feel love from her child or her husband because she had never felt it from her father. Because Judy did not feel worthy of love, she created situations in her marriage to prove to herself that her husband was so angry at her for having a child that he was seeing other women and withholding love from her.

Because Marvin felt frustrated when Judy thwarted all his attempts to show love, he increased his drinking, stayed away from home long periods of time, and eventually left the marriage. Judy moved home with her parents. In this marriage, Judy became the emotional distancer, hoping to gain emotional closeness that she had never felt as a child.

The marital relationship may be functional or dysfunctional depending on the hopes, fears, and needs of the individuals and their motivations to marry. To a great degree these needs are influenced by the roles the individuals played in their families of origin and the degree of differentiation from these family members. If, as a child, a wife took on caretaking duties in her family to gain self-worth and protect an alcoholic parent, she may seek a husband who needs similar protection, thus maintaining her self-worth as a caretaker.

Because children have a great need for acceptance and verification, they record and copy their parents' behaviors. Parents often hear themselves repeated. While playing house, Susie yells at Johnnie for coming home late and then turns to her dolls to lecture them on the disarray of their toys. Parents want their children to be like them and carry on their family traditions and positive traits. However, children mirror bad habits as well and may cause negative responses from their parents. Some children learn that negative attention is acceptable if the positive kind is infrequent. If Mommy does not show love, the child may be able to elicit anger, which is better than indifference. Children cannot verify themselves with indifference.

Unfortunately, negative attention sets up inner conflict that cannot be resolved. The more children repeat negative behavior to gain acceptance, the more rejection they receive. Siblings may divide this attention. The oldest child may be the family darling who does no wrong, leaving no room for the second child to outshine this perfectionist. However, there is much negative attention left for a rebellious troublemaker. "Every rebellious child is raging inside over his parent's failure to show him love he desperately needs and wants. What he is angry about is that he does not feel loved despite the loving words he may hear" (Hoffman, 1979, p. 26). These children have a faulty belief that they can only belong in this family by hurting others as they feel hurt. This revenge cycle teaches passive-aggressive ways of dealing with the anger over loss of love.

Jenny is an example of a passive-aggressive child. At age 4, she accidentally dropped and broke her mother's favorite crystal vase that had been a wedding present from her mother's parents. At age 10 Jenny went to a friend's softball game after school and missed dinner with her grandparents, who had driven all day to visit her. Jenny's parents were humiliated and hurt when they could not explain where Jenny was. When Jenny was 14, she ran away from home the day before the family was to attend her grandparents' 50th wedding anniversary. None of these incidents involved direct confrontation with Jenny's parents, but she wanted them to feel the hurt she felt as a result of past negative experiences. She forgot rules, disobeyed at times that would affect her parents the most, and caused further disapproval of her parents' parenting skills from the grandparents. These were not isolated incidents in Jenny's family—they were representative of a pattern that developed when Jenny felt she could not belong to this family without hurting others.

Revenge cycles are present in many families for periods of time. In the alcoholic family, these patterns can become chronic. Alcoholic parents may model these behaviors and may be unable to give their children the love and approval they ask for by their behavior.

The emotional vacuum just described is further compounded if the parents are unable to love one another and one spouse sees negative mirroring of the other spouse in a child. If the family rule is that spouses do not fight, these children are vulnerable for attack on the negative mirrored behavior. In this situation, the spouse erroneously combats misplaced marital issues with the children. This pattern often appears in divorced or separated families when one parent is not living with the family and the custodial parent has not settled the marital issues with the other spouse. The pattern is certain to reduce the self-image of the child in a downward spiral. The children mirror the parents, and the parents further reject them. Self-destructive patterns like these can continue on to adulthood. Hoffman (1979) believed self-destructive problems of adulthood (such as alcoholism) can be traced to the rebellion of a child who is still holding on to anger with mother and father. These individuals may know they are endangering their lives with drinking but are daring their parents to stop them. Hoffman continued to say:

> This conflict between the intellect and the emotions is the reason most attempts to permanently solve addiction are ineffective. No amount of information or encouragement is powerful enough to counter the force of our angry rebellious child underneath the veneer of our intellect. In the most extreme cases even the fear of untimely death is not a strong enough deterrent. (p. 27)

This inability to love and show love becomes a multigenerational problem. If father and mother did not really love each other, then their children will have difficulty maintaining loving relationships. This is a real problem for many. Hoffman wrote, "We pursue the love our parents did not know how to give and become unloving in spite of our quest for love" (p. 22). Bowen (1971) said that children are unable to raise their level of differentiation above their parents' level, and Hoffman believed children are unable and do not dare to rise above the emotional giving of their parents.

In healthy families destructive patterns often correct themselves, but in alcoholic families the avoidance of intimacy becomes chronic and predictable.

The children of alcoholics often seek mates who remind them of the parents who withheld love. The daughter of an alcoholic who marries an alcoholic is saying to her father, "I've not turned my back on you. I've married someone who acts like you. Now, will you love me?" To her mother she says, "I'm a martyr like you. We are alike; please love me." In the case history of Judy and Marvin, Judy copied her parents' emotional distance in her own marriage, even though she said she wanted a marriage different from her mother's. The conflict occurred when she rebelled against the unfeeling patterns of her parents, which caused guilt. Eventually, Judy used this rebellion to recreate emotional distance and continue to beg for parental love.

Many needs for acceptance go unspoken during courtship, and as the initial defenses used by each partner fade with time, disillusionment sets in. The fantasized white knight becomes a human being who squeezes the toothpaste tube in the middle and fails to replace the cap. This disillusionment can lead to detachment and can end either in divorce or in a changed perspective that allows growth in the relationship. Feelings of disillusionment may lead to the decision to have a child who will presumably rejuvenate the marriage and change the couple into a family. Unfortunately, parenthood usually divides the couple more by adding a heavy responsibility to an already strained relationship. If the parents' self-esteem is low, they may look to the child to fill this void and prove the family's worth to the community. Many hopes ride with these first children, and at their birth the family becomes a social and psychological unit that is more than just the sum of its parts.

## KEY CONCEPTS IN VIEWING THE FAMILY AS THE CLIENT

The following are definitions of commonly used family therapy terms. It is important for therapists to understand this terminology, which may be new to them, before moving on to the theoretical models and techniques of family therapy.

### Homeostasis

Jackson (1957) coined the term *family homeostasis* to define a balancing behavior in families. "This balance or equilibrium shifts in response to changes which occur within the family (illness, aging, death, unemployment) and influential forces from without (economic, political, social)" (Meeks & Kelly, 1970, p. 400). Ewing and Fox (1968) adopted theoretical concepts from Jackson's theory of homeostasis in families. They viewed the alcoholic marriage as a "homeostatic mechanism" that is "established . . . to resist change over long periods of time. The behavior of each spouse is rigidly controlled by the other. As a result, an effort by one person to alter typical role behavior threatens the family equilibrium and provokes renewed efforts by the spouse to maintain status quo" (p. 87). Alcohol is often a key part in the balance of the alcoholic family.

Jackson believed that a lack of need satisfaction on the part of the family members leads to an imbalance in family functioning and produces tension. Jackson (1968) found that healthy family systems seek alternative ways of gaining need satisfaction, but that dysfunctional families, because of their lack of adequate problem-solving techniques, project this tension onto a family member who becomes the symptom bearer for the family. Ironically, both of these methods reduce family tension and restore homeostasis (see Figure 3–4). Jackson referred to this process as the *homeostatic mechanism*. He said this mechanism is found at times in all families, but when it is in constant motion, it produces disturbed individual members to whom he referred as "scapegoats." If alcohol is a central force in this balance and it is removed without helping the family to find new alternatives, the system may break up (divorce), or a new symptom bearer may emerge to maintain tension reduction.

Wegscheider (1981) drew a parallel between the homeostasis of the alcoholic family and an art form, the mobile, in this excerpt:

> A family system resembles a mobile. A mobile is an art form made up of rods and strings upon which are hung various parts. The beauty of the mobile is in the balance and its flexibility. The mobile has a way of responding to changing circumstances such as wind. It changes position but always maintains connections with each part. If one flicks one of the suspended parts, energy, the whole system moves to gradually bring itself to equilibrium. The same thing is true of a family. In a family where there is stress, the whole organism shifts to bring balance, stability, survival. (Wegscheider, 1981, pp. 36–37)[1]

Wegscheider explained that in the chemically dependent family each person is affected by the chemical abuse of one member and said that "in an attempt to maintain balance, members compulsively repress their feelings and develop survival behaviors and walls of defense to protect them from pain" (p. 37).

Family balance is often achieved in the alcoholic family with drinking as a central point. When this drinking is removed through treatment, the family is thrown into turmoil as if it were a mobile in a windstorm. Mother is not needed as the overly responsible martyr when Dad returns to take over running the household. Brother has no reason to stay away from home and must reevaluate his relationship with Dad. The family suddenly notices little sister's hyperactive mannerisms. The emotional distance of the marriage may still exist, and the precipitating environment that began the drinking may still exist. Without family intervention, drinking behavior may recur, the family may separate; or a new family member may become symptomatic.

## Family Roles

The basic principles of homeostasis include predictable roles for family members to act out and a set of rules, both overt and covert, for interaction of these roles. These family roles are diagrammed in Figure 3–2. Family roles include husband, wife, father, mother, daughter, son, grandmother, grandfather, aunt, uncle, cousin, stepfather, stepmother, stepbrother, stepsister, and many more. Each of these roles comes with a set of expectations that depend on the cultural

---

[1]Reprinted with permission.

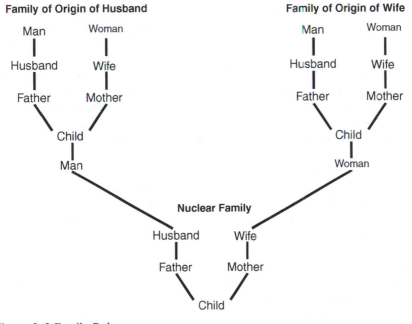

**Figure 3–2** Family Roles.

---

and ethnic backgrounds of the families and the current societal parameters of appropriate behavior.

Other roles played by family members are more subtle and derive from a person's birth order and requirements of the family. Many firstborns, for instance, are high achievers. They are born into a family of adults who have high expectations for the first child. A son may be groomed to take over the family business or follow in his father's footsteps. Oldest daughters are often encouraged to be responsible and help parent younger siblings. They become little adults who make the family proud and give stability to the system. However, if active alcoholism is present when they are born, they may become a problem child to take the focus off of the marital problems around the drinking.

Subsequent children come along and dethrone the firstborn, and competition is setup. This can be healthy or unhealthy competition. If the oldest is good in school, the second may excel in sports or music. If the family needs a focus for its problems, the secondborn can fill a need for a scapegoat and be the family's worst child. Youngest children are born into a system that has already established rules and patterns of operation. They are often left out of family matters because they are too young and usually have many bosses. They may tend to act out to get attention from this established family. If the youngest is the third child, the second becomes a middle child. Middle children can be concerned with finding their places and making certain they are treated fairly. These birth position roles can shift with the demands of the family. Middle children can become like the oldest when the oldest leaves home. Families with large gaps between children's ages can have two oldest children.

Marital and parental roles of the parents of the family are often derived from their families of origin. People who marry have their own ideas, values, and notions of appropriate sex roles. They are unique individuals who, given the conglomerate of their life experiences, act and react in a predictable way. Their job is to blend into a single marital unit the values, beliefs, and behaviors they embraced in their own families. In today's American society, many of these marriages attempt to share leadership responsibilities in an equitable manner. This produces a new set of rules different from those of their ancestors, whose families may have been ruled by an autocratic father with mother as second in command and the children in a pecking order under both parents. The women's movement and economic stresses have produced the two-income family and restructured the traditional family diagram.

This new dual leadership approach creates a situation not found in most social systems. What corporation could function with two chairpersons? During the 1980 presidential elections there was a flurry of excitement at the Republican National Convention when Ronald Reagan hinted at choosing Gerald Ford as his running mate. The negotiations reportedly fell through when the two men could not agree on the mechanics of a copresidency. Although the concept is difficult to envision—two men running a country with equal power—it is this theory many marital relationships struggle to enact. Continued spoken and unspoken negotiations are required to keep the relationship functional. Money, religion, in-laws, friends, sex, child rearing, and recreation are key issues in these negotiations.

With the addition of a child to this unit, the husband and wife take on a third role. The man must add the new role of father to his other roles as an individual with personal needs and as a husband working out a marital relationship. The woman also juggles three roles, and further negotiations take place on child rearing and discipline philosophies. Who will punish? How will we discipline? What is the role of the father? Should the mother work?

## Family Rules

Decisions are made or not made according to the rules, boundaries, and alliances of family members. Families have rules about the expression of feelings such as love, hurt, or anger. These rules include who can express feelings, how they are expressed, and how they are received. In an alcoholic family the unspoken rule may be that anger can only be expressed during intoxication or that affection and intimacy can occur only when one or both spouses are drinking.

Barnard (1981) believed other areas where rules are formulated for family functioning are: (1) what, when, and how family members may comment on what they see, feel, and think; (2) who can speak to whom and about what; (3) how a member can be different; (4) how sexuality can be expressed; (5) what it means to be male or female; and (6) how a person can acquire self-worth and how much is appropriate to possess. These rules are the basis for dyadic and triadic relationships and interactions in the family subsystems that are formed by generation, gender, mutual interest, or duties.

Rules that govern alcoholic/addict families typically concern the best way to deal with the intoxicated or high person, secret keeping, and family preservation. Black (1981) listed three rules that children of alcoholics often live by: Don't talk. Don't trust. Don't feel. Talking, especially about the substance abuse, might cause even more problems. Trusting usually leads to disappointment when parents do not come through with their promises. Feeling is too painful, and expression of feelings is not allowed because it might cause more trouble.

## Family Subsystems

A subsystem is simply a part of a system that has a job that affects the larger system. Family subsystems can include the couple, the parents, the children, the grandparents, the daughters, the sons, and so on. Each subsystem contributes to the entire system's maintenance. A family has a number of coexisting subsystems that can be formed by a generation (mother and father), by gender (mother and daughter), by interest (intellectual pursuits), or by function (parents) (Goldenberg & Goldenberg, 1996).

The first subsystem in the family is the marital subsystem; membership is closed and duties are performed by the husband and wife. The second subsystem, the parental subsystem, usually emerges with the birth of the first child. These duties are usually carried out by the husband and wife, but in an alcoholic family, the alcoholic parent may abdicate his or her role and a grandparent or sibling may fill the parental gap. This may blur the generational boundaries or parentify the child. The child who takes on early parenting responsibilities is at risk for losing his or her childhood when strapped with the adult responsibilities of raising siblings.

The third main category is the sibling subsystem. There may be one or many subsystems depending on the number of children and their gender, age differences, and common interests. In healthy families the subsystems are fluid and members can move between them as the overall system changes and balances. Children can act like adults when they learn to do chores or babysit for their younger siblings for short times. Parents can act like children and play and be silly for short times. Flexibility is important in defining subsystems; however, these shifts to other subsystems need to be temporary.

In an alcoholic family subsystems may become rigid and uncertain of their tasks. Parenting may be ignored, children may take on adult roles, and children may be allowed into the marital subsystem if incestuous relationships occur between a parent and one or several children. Children get stuck in the parental subsystem; addicts and alcoholics become rigidly childlike and irresponsible.

## Boundaries

The term boundaries has been misused in the popular literature and in the chemical dependency field. Boundaries are not rules for behavior of children, nor are they processes of limit setting. Boundaries exist between each member of the family, between subsystems, and between the family and society. These are the rules of interaction and the methods of functioning. Minuchin (1974) defined three types of boundaries: (1) enmeshed, (2) clear, and (3) disengaged. In reality most boundaries fall somewhere on a continuum from the very rigid to the very diffuse, with the clearly defined boundaries falling in the center.

Clear boundaries are found in most healthy relationships that are based on mutual respect. Clear boundaries allow separateness for each member yet maintain closeness among them. Freedom and flexibility in these relationships promote clear and direct communication patterns.

Enmeshed or diffuse boundaries leave no room for flexibility and no room for differences. Sameness and unity are stressed in these relationships and there is little space for individuality. Living in an enmeshed family is like living in a house with no doors. In other words, "What's yours is mine." Emotions are also shared and a child in this type of family might cry because her mother is sad. The fused marital relationship is an example of the loss of self-identity that occurs when the individual personality of each partner is sacrificed for the sake of the marriage. Although this enmeshment can reduce independence of the family members, it is only harmful to them if they experience it as a problem. Ethnic and cultural factors have an effect on the amount of connectedness a family should have and can tolerate. Many families with a cultural heritage of close relationships with extended families can tolerate a great degree of diffusion in boundaries without causing problems for the family members.

Disengaged or rigid boundaries are often seen in alcoholic families and are identified as isolation of the members or isolation of the family from society. The rules in these families are: (1) do not talk about the alcoholism, (2) do not confront drinking behavior, and (3) protect and shelter the alcoholic so that things don't become worse. These rules perpetuate the drinking and the drinking maintains the need for isolation. Often, marital relationships in these families have arrived at a fixed distance. Similarly, siblings in this situation lack a sense of belonging, and very little love is transmitted to build self-worth. These children may use alcohol to numb the pain of rejection, or they may act out inappropriately to try to get the recognition they want. Misbehavior may escalate to attract others' attention.

This pattern of rigid boundaries can be found in families who have children in their 20s who have not left home. They often have chronic drug problems that keep them from gaining steady employment and, thus, moving out. Research indicates that these young adults and adolescents with drug problems have never felt connected to their families and are hanging on to try to get those needs met (Friedman, A.S., Tomko, & Utada, 1991; Olson & Killorin, 1987). Olson and Killorin (1987) compared chemically dependent families and nondependent families using the *circumplex model* of measuring family cohesion (see chapter 6). Forty-four percent of the chemically dependent adolescents perceived their families as disengaged compared with 8 percent of the nondependent adolescents. Fifty-two percent of these same adolescents rated their families as chaotic compared with 20 percent of nondependent adolescents. On the outside looking in, these families might look enmeshed and stuck together. It would be tempting for a therapist to tell the parents to kick these kids out, and although this is the end goal, it can be disastrous if the children don't first feel connected to their families at times when they are not taking money or getting bailed out of trouble.

### Case History

A case example of an alcoholic family shows how both of these maladaptive boundaries can be present in the same family.

Susan, age 34, and John, age 40, were practicing alcoholics and drug abusers before their marriage. They married because they felt sorry for each other, and they became fused in "we-ness" to fight the world. Both spouses lost self-identity, and in order to achieve an individual identity, they pulled back to a fixed distance in their relationship. They set up a covert marital rule that Susan would be the dominant spouse and breadwinner, while John would be adaptive, lose self-identity, and be unable to hold a job. Both of these positions reflect the role that each played in his or her family of origin. Susan was the oldest child in her family and felt she had to be perfect to win her mother's love. When she failed to meet her mother's expectations, she felt very guilty and began to drink. John was an adopted only child who was raised in an overprotective and overdemanding family. He was forced into college against his wishes and paid his parents back with repeated failures, job losses, and drug abuse. His rage at his parents was unresolved and colored his role in the nuclear family.

The disengaged marital relationship did not allow for direct confrontation, and issues between spouses were ignored. When the first child, Denise, was born, the father made a strong alignment with her. Denise was repeatedly compared with her father by members of the family, and when the second daughter was born, she was rejected by the father and aligned with the mother. Wars could now be fought between the enmeshed father-daughter subgroup and the mother-daughter sub-group without having direct marital confrontation. The undercurrent was, "If I confront my spouse directly, things will get worse."

A further dynamic of this family centered around Susan's belief that she would not be an alcoholic if she did not drink before four o'clock in the afternoon. When Denise arrived home from school at three o'clock, using the same figures of speech and mannerisms as her father, she reminded Susan of her issues with John, and Susan would beat Denise. Then, feeling guilty, Susan would begin to drink at four o'clock. Denise blamed herself for these attacks, although she never understood them. Susan inflated her guilt and increased her drinking. Denise suffered from her enmeshed relationship with her father and failed to gain her own identity in the family.

Eventually, both parents sought alcoholism treatment and maintained sobriety. However, the marital roles and the emotional distance between the spouses and between Denise and her mother remained. The family balance became unachievable, and the spouses divorced. Family therapy was initiated with this family when Denise became progressively withdrawn.

Denise is now learning to relate to her mother for the first time in family therapy sessions that involve Susan (the custodial parent) and her daughters. Denise is making friends for the first time and has been able to complete her school work, thereby recovering from years of underachievement. Because Denise had been often told that she had no sense, like her father, she had hidden her intelligence to gain acceptance from him. Denise is at high risk to marry an alcoholic if she fails to fully gain the approval she has longed for from her parents. She will be saying, "See, I married someone like you. Now will you accept me?"

### Family Values

As family roles, rules, and boundaries begin to develop, so do the values of the nuclear family. These values again are a blend of those values transmitted from the spouses' families of origin. They may be shared by the couple or be more strongly supported by one spouse or the other. Possible values in families are athletics, musical ability, money, work, education, power, control, winning, social status, conservatism, and radicalism, to name a few. Conflict can occur when the mother embraces music and education as her strong values and wants her son to become a musical virtuoso, while the father longs for an athlete who is competitive and values winning. In some cases, children make adaptations and combine values to please both parents, but when the values are in direct opposition, the child must choose one or none of the conflicting values. This is a no-win situation for the child because one of the parents will withhold approval. The children in the family have the option of accepting or rejecting any or all of the family values and are not bound by pure imitation of their parents. However, it is often true that the parent who sees his or her values mirrored in the child will come forth with more approval. Depending on the boundaries and rules of the family, children who choose different values may be allowed this differentiation, or they may defy a family rule that says family members must not be different.

Other conflicts arise when a female child is born in a family that values boys and needs an heir for the family business or when a male child is born to a family that needs a girl for balance or to satisfy a parent's psychological need.

As the family develops, it takes on an overall atmosphere, depending on the amount of conflict involved in balancing of roles, family values, and interaction rules. The interactions produce an atmosphere that is friendly, competitive, or cooperative, or an environment that is hostile, autocratic, or permissive.

While it is important for therapists to understand the values of families and of the family members, it is also important for them to understand their own values. In the early years of family therapy the effort to understand each family member's perspective, treat each fairly, and not blame any one person for the family's problems, ignored societal realities of power, and gender differences in families. Recent criticisms of pure systems thinking have caused family therapists to be more aware of the values and belief systems that they bring with them to the therapy session. Therapists do not check them at the door. For instance, in working with a marital couple, the gender of the therapist is a fact that is easy for the couple to see and may make the same gender person in the couple feel more understood. Therapists who try to hide their belief that women are not treated equally in society are not actually being fair to the woman by assuming everyone is equal in the therapy.

## Alliances, Coalitions, Triangles, and Relationships with the Family of Origin

The discussions of homeostasis, family roles, family rules, family subsystems, boundaries, family values, and birth order pertained chiefly to the nuclear family, although references were made to the families of origin. This section will deal more directly with relationships between the nuclear family and the families of origin.

Alliances are connections between two people in a family about an issue or a position. Mom and Dad, for instance, can be in alliance about their children's bedtimes. Two sisters can form an alliance to defend themselves against their brothers. Families, however, most often work in triangles that can operate in many ways: two against one, two form one, one pulled between two others, one bridging a gap between two others, etc. It is very difficult for two family members to talk for very long without "triangulating" a third member into the discussion. For instance, if two sisters are debating an issue, it is common to hear, "But Mom said. . . ."

Coalitions form in a family when two people are allied against a third. When a wife is afraid to confront her husband directly because he hits her, she many entice her son to fight her battles with her husband for her. A daughter who feels her father treats her mother badly may pick fights with him to even the score. Many coalitions are problematic because they cross generational boundaries and shift people into inappropriate subsystems.

In healthy families, the strongest alliances form in a horizontal pattern within generations (Figure 3–3). That is, grandparents have an alliance between themselves; parents have a marital and parental alliance; and the children have special relationships among themselves. These alliances can become vertical in nature if, for instance, there is a cross-generational alliance between one spouse and his or her parent that takes the place of marital closeness. In the discussion on boundaries, a cross-generational alliance was described between one spouse and a child when a fixed distance occurred in the marriage. "Whenever generational boundaries are consistently violated and members of one generation supply what should be received in another generation, pathology can be expected" (Haley, 1976, p. 39).

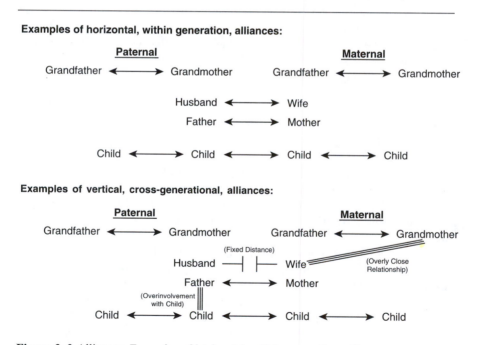

**Figure 3–3** Alliances. Examples of horizontal, within generation, alliances

Cross-generational alliances and coalitions are far more prevalent among alcoholic families (30 of 39 families) than in recovered families (21 of 44 families) or control families (14 of 42 families) (Preli & Protinsky, 1988). The same study found that alcoholic families also had disturbed hierarchies. The alcoholic families more frequently lacked clear hierarchical structures (23 of 39 families) than recovered (6 of 44 families) or nonalcoholic families (1 of 42 families) (Preli & Protinsky, 1988). The most frequent disturbance of hierarchy in the alcoholic families was that of mothers and children at the same level, either superior or inferior to the males. The researchers point out that 41 percent of the alcoholic families reported no hierarchical reversals and were able to avoid this structural problem in the face of severe stress.

Cross-generational alliances disturb the balance of the nuclear family by changing role definitions and pulling members of the family of origin into the dynamics and workings of the nuclear family. Marital issues cannot be resolved if they are discussed only between the wife and her mother. If the maternal grandmother was overprotective of her daughter and is reluctant to allow her to break away and become an independent person, this attachment may continue through their adult lives. If the daughter married and had children because the expectations of society were stronger than the overprotective tie with her mother, she may be very angry with her husband for taking her away from her mother and angry with her children for keeping her in a difficult position.

This anger often is not shown directly but is manifested in the same overprotective parenting style with which the mother was raised. The mother's underlying wish to be rid of her husband and children must be repressed and covered with overconcern. Her anxiety and overprotection often produce symptoms in one of the children and may cause an overinvolvement between the parent and child, thus passing on a cross-generational alliance and maladaptive behavior. Overprotection has been identified as one of the parenting styles that increase the risk of children becoming alcoholic and drug addicted. These parenting styles are discussed at length in the next chapter.

As the nuclear family develops as a social system, the spouses define themselves in terms of their relationships with their families of origin. Framo (1976) identified four categories of relationships with families of origin.

The first category is the overinvolved relationship, which may resemble the enmeshed subsystems in the nuclear family. These families may live close together—maybe even down the street. The people in these families often talk daily on the telephone. In families that are forced to move apart, this daily phone contact may continue long distance. These families usually have very little social life outside their own confines and are closed off from the rest of society. The (other) spouse in these relationships may resent the spouse's overinvolvement or may welcome the relationship with a parent substitute. Difficulty occurs in these situations if grandparents give advice on home management, parenting, marital relationships, and areas that are typically roles of the marital and parental subsystems. Self-identity and self-worth as a spouse and parent are sabotaged with messages from the family of origin to the effect that "you are inadequate, and you need our help." What the family of origin may really mean is "we need you to need help so we can busy ourselves with your problems and not look at our own marital difficulties."

The second type of relationship is superficial. It involves infrequent, nonpersonal contact, usually revolving around ceremonies or family rituals. Framo described people in these relationships as seeing themselves as having resolved their difficulties with their families in a mature way. They have used space, distance, and time to reduce conflict.

The third pattern occurs when people completely cut themselves off from their families. They proclaim that the absence of contact is the only way to maintain their own sanity and virtually deny the existence of other family members, treating them as if they were already dead. Framo believed that these people have the greatest chance of repeating the irrational patterns of their parents.

The last category is a positive one in which a person establishes an identity within the family of origin before leaving. This differentiation occurs when families have clear boundaries and parents can solve their own problems without projecting them onto their children or involving their children in the resolution process. These children consequently have no need either to stay in the family or to escape its clutches. There is neither overattachment nor angry rebellion. These families do have a sense of belonging, but it is balanced with a respect for independence. The parents in this type of family of origin love their children enough to let them leave. The adult children relate more in an adult-to-adult manner with their parents than remaining to react to and interact with their parents as if they were still young children.

"In general, the more a nuclear family is emotionally cut off from parental families, the higher the incidence of problems and symptoms in the nuclear family" (Bowen, 1978, p. 264). Children from families with alcoholism and drug addiction may leave their families in many ways but they usually feel that although they never really belonged to the family they can never really leave. How children are launched from their families colors the rest of their history and has an effect on all subsequent relationships. Families have a life cycle development just as individuals do. This process of the child moving from the family of origin and creating another family of his or her own has the potential to replicate the dynamics of the original family, passing on symptoms generation after generation. A launching that is not a launching or is a cutoff has the highest potential of this.

Carter and McGoldrick (1980) described the family life cycle state thus:

> In outlining the stages of the family life cycle, we have departed from the traditional sociological depiction of the family life cycle as commencing

at courtship or marriage and ending with the death of one spouse. Rather than considering the family to be the operative emotional unit from the cradle to the grave, we see a new family life cycle beginning at the stage of the "unattached young adult," whose adequate or inadequate completion of the primary task of coming to terms with his or her family of origin will most profoundly influence whom, when and how he or she marries and all succeeding stages of the new family life cycle. Adequate completion of this task would require that the young adult separate from the family of origin without cutting off or fleeing reactively to a substitute emotional refuge. (p. 13)

## Symptoms

The family roles, rules, boundaries, values, atmosphere, birth order issues, and alliances all combine to constitute the family homeostasis. Meeks and Kelly (1970) state:

> Any attempt to shift the family equilibrium either from within (i.e., change in a member) or from without (i.e., input from a therapist) may evoke resistance from the family system which seeks to maintain the status quo (equilibrium). No matter how sick it may appear to the outside observer, the established equilibrium represents that family's attempt to minimize the threats of disruption and pain. (p. 400)

In the alcoholic family, a balance is maintained with the presence of alcohol, and the family may resist all attempts to remove this part of the balance, although they may also ask for the drinking to cease. They believe that change may be worse than the pain they are already suffering. Steinglass (1976) said, "[T]he presence or absence of alcohol becomes the single most important variable determining the interactional behavior not only between the identified drinker and other members of the family but among non-drinking members of the family as well" (p. 106).

When families present themselves to a therapist, it is usually due to a symptom in one member resulting from a disturbance in family homeostasis or is a result of the suggestion of someone outside the family. Bowen (1971) defined three areas within the nuclear family in which symptoms are expressed: (1) marital conflict, (2) dysfunction in a spouse, and (3) projection to one or more children. Bowen labeled this third area the *family projection process*, which he believed exists to some extent in all families. In this process, families project their problems onto their children, who become the symptom bearers for the family. The symptom bearer often unconsciously volunteers for this position and may be instrumental in bringing a family into therapy where alcohol abuse or dysfunctional family patterns can be corrected, thus relieving the symptoms in the child. These children have a stake in saving their families and themselves in the symptom bearer role. "Children, and adults as well, will forego their own nature in order to save a parent from going crazy or in order to become the kind of person a parent (or parent representative) can love" (Framo, 1976, p. 207). Children may mirror the behavior of the parent to gain acceptance, but instead they receive rejection. The child's symptoms may be labeled as inappropriate, causing conflict and anxiety in the child.

Family therapy has evolved around the notion of the identified patient or the symptom bearer as the person who expresses a particular dysfunction for the whole family. Therefore, the context of the alcoholic person is reframed as the alcoholic family, with the alcoholic as the identified patient. Steinglass (1976) pointed out that, uniquely, symptoms occur in the parental subsystem in the alcoholic family. This is in contrast to the majority of dysfunctional families, in which children are the symptom bearers. The adult alcoholic/addict, however, may have developed the seeds of his or her addiction as an adolescent in response to disruption in the family of origin and has just brought it into his or her current family as part of an intergenerational family process. This does not mean that the children are not symptomatic. Children of alcoholics/addicts suffer from a variety of problems.

The alcoholic family may also be unique in the process of triangulation, in which the tension between two people is displaced onto an issue or a substance (e.g., alcohol or drugs) instead of being projected onto the child. Unfortunately, the removal of the substance may result in a worsening of tension or another displacement. Post-treatment divorces are common.

Because of the intergenerational nature of addiction, however, there is usually more than one person in a family with substance abuse problems. It is not unusual for a family to have a drug-abusing son, an alcoholic father, an obese, compulsive overeater mother, two or three addicted grandparents, and a daughter with anorexia. Chemical dependency is a unique symptom in that it can take on a life of its own. Changing the family system may not stop the addictive behavior. Often the addiction needs to be treated in conjunction with changing the family patterns that maintain the addiction. It can be just as counterproductive to treat the family and ignore the addictive behavior as can treating the addiction and ignoring the family dynamics and problems of other family members.

The term *symptom* has been borrowed by the family therapy field from the psychoanalytic or individual model of abnormal behavior and mental illness. Therefore, there is often confusion about whether family therapists see alcoholic drinking as merely a symptom of a dysfunctional family that will disappear if the family structure is realigned or if they see it as the focus of treatment. The function of the "symptom" of alcoholism is far more complicated and embedded in family systems than most symptoms. It needs to be the central focus of treatment.

Framo (1982) used an object relations theory perspective to explain, very eloquently, what is meant by symptoms in a family context, what produces symptoms, how symptoms are chosen, and how they are maintained or reduced. In terms of etiology, he believed that symptoms may be created in several ways in families. Children may develop symptoms from parents' irrational role assignments and projective transference distortions. These children come to represent valued or feared expectations of parents that are based on parental introjects. "In every family of multiple siblings there is 'the spoiled one,' 'the concience of the family,' and 'the wild one'; the assigned roles are infinite" (Framo, 1982, p. 28). Framo also stated that symptoms can evolve from blurring generational boundaries and changes in the family relationship system such as death of a parent or child, hospitalization or imprisonment of a parent, marital separation or divorce, accidents, physical handicaps, and economic reverses, which produce catastrophic strain and disruption in a family (Framo, 1982).

From a relationship point of view, Framo (1982) believed that a symptom in one member of an intimate relationship may be necessary for the maintenance or even survival of the relationship. For instance, a marriage may consist of one partner being functioning or "independent" and the other being "dependent" or helpless. Framo used quotation marks around "independent" and "dependent" to indicate that these roles are subject to shift. There are also marital relationships that appear stable. For instance, in a couple where an executive is married to an alcoholic whom he has to take care of, the nurtured one ensures the relationship will continue while hiding the dependency of her husband. If she changes through therapy, there can be a rapid role reversal.

It is important for a therapist working with chemical dependency to understand the meaning and purpose that the symptom of alcoholism or other drug abuse plays in the family. It is possible to successfully treat the alcoholic only to find the spouse or another family member becoming symptomatic to maintain the family balance. The goals of the family therapist are to treat the symptom and to make second-order change in the system in order to reduce the need for the symptom.

## AN OVERVIEW OF FAMILY THERAPY THEORY IN TERMS OF ETIOLOGY

This section reviews five schools of family therapy theory. Although there are many other schools of thought and new ideas that have developed since the first generation of theories, these are the approaches most often used to treat substance abuse: structural family therapy, strategic family therapy, intergenerational family therapy, experiential family therapy, and behavioral family therapy. Each is examined in terms of its origin and the therapists involved in it, basic etiological concepts, and relevance to the alcoholic family.

Family therapists have created their own models of doing family therapy; these approaches are called *schools*. The models were influenced by the therapists' personalities, cultural backgrounds, previous training in psychology, psychiatry, or social work, social trends, and the zeitgeist in which they lived.

## Structural Family Therapy

The founder of structural family therapy was Salvador Minuchin, a psychiatrist from Argentina. His theory grew out of his work with male juvenile delinquents at the Wyltwyck School, where he worked with poor, multiproblem families. These families required techniques that were concrete and action-oriented. Minuchin would have these families enact their problems in the therapy sessions so he could see firsthand what was happening in the family and so determine its organization and structure. Structural family therapists are interested in the structure (rules, roles, and sequences of behaviors), subsystems, and boundaries of families. Minuchin was also concerned with environmental factors and found the family to be the interpreter of societal values, rules, and behaviors. Children, he felt, learn either functional or dysfunctional behaviors in the family through observing and interpreting the family structure.

The family structure is defined as transactions that are unique to a family: levels of authority, power structure, and mutual expectations. The structure is created with the marriage and the agreement of the spouses to satisfy each other's needs. The evolution of spousal functions creates the core of the nuclear family. The structure changes when the first child is born and parental functions are negotiated. On this child rides the potential for family growth or destruction. If the family cannot clearly differentiate the spousal and parental functions, dysfunction in the family may occur. This theory is similar to Bowen's concepts of the family projection process and cross-generational alliances.

Within the family structure, Minuchin defined subsystems as one or more family members who share something in common: generation, gender, interests, or family duties. He defined boundaries as the rules of the subsystems that are either rigid, diffuse, or clear. Dysfunction occurs when rigid boundaries create isolation and discourage family communication, or when diffuse boundaries do not clearly define areas of authority or responsibility. These diffuse boundaries can discourage individual responsibility and promote random and confused problem solving.

The fourth concept in Minuchin's structural model categorizes the family's methods of experiencing stress:

1. Stress can be caused in one family member by someone outside of the family, such as the father's boss. This stress is transmitted to the wife, who in turn is angry with the children, who kick the dog.

2. Stress can be caused in the entire family by an outside force, such as economic change or a move to a new location, that affects everyone.
3. Stress can be caused by life crisis transitions, such as the birth of a child, a child attending school for the first time, adolescence, adolescents leaving home (particularly the last child), or midlife crises, such as the mother's return to the workforce (which may occur simultaneously with the adolescence of the children).
4. Stress can result from the presence of a chronically ill person in the family, including an alcoholic or addict.

Minuchin felt that dysfunction in the family occurs when there are unclear levels of authority and power, expectations are misunderstood, there is confusion as to the functions of subgroups, or rigid or diffuse boundaries exist.

Alcoholic families have many different patterns of structure, but some are more common than others. They more frequently see themselves as disengaged and lacking cohesion. The power structure and hierarchy are often reversed, with the children acting like parents and the parents not taking a responsible position. There is frequently a cross-generational alliance between a nonalcoholic spouse and a child who becomes the parent's emotional support. This comes with a great cost to the child, who sacrifices his or her childhood to become parentified. Such children are often given information about the alcoholic's infidelity or other marital dysfunction that is the business of the marital subsystem only. These children have difficulty leaving home.

The goal of structural family therapy is to alter the family structure so that the family can problem solve. The therapist alters boundaries and realigns subsystems to change the behavior and experiences of each of the family members (Nichols & Schwartz, 1995). A common goal is to help parents function as a united parental unit without division or conflict. Parents, also, need to be in charge of the children and not act as their buddies or peers.

There are three main overlapping processes in structural family therapy (Minuchin, 1974). First, the therapist joins the family as a director of the therapy process. Minuchin referred to this as joining the family like a wise uncle. The second process is mapping the underlying structure of the family. Minuchin devised a system of symbols to graphically map out the family structure, boundaries, and interactions. The third process is the intervention to change the family structure. Structural techniques are further discussed in chapter 7.

*double bind theory*

## Strategic Family Therapy: An Outgrowth of the Communication Model

Strategic family therapy grew out of the communications model that was developed by the Mental Research Institute (MRI) in Palo Alto, California.

Gregory Bateson began working with interpersonal communications in schizo-phrenic families and applying cybernetics to family therapy. Bateson was joined in this project by Jay Haley, John Weakland, Don Jackson, and, later, Virginia Satir. They developed a belief that communication between members was the most important factor of family life (Bateson, Jackson, Haley, & Weakland, 1956). These theorists believed that blocked forms of communication in the individual were symptoms of overall dysfunctional communication in the family. They proposed that dysfunctional communication patterns produced family ten-sion that was projected onto one or more family members (Figure 3–4).

The MRI group developed the theory of the double bind and later related it to clinical work (Jackson, 1960). The double bind is a communication pattern involving a victim or scapegoat and a message sender. The sender gives two messages at the same time. Often one is verbal and the other nonverbal. In order

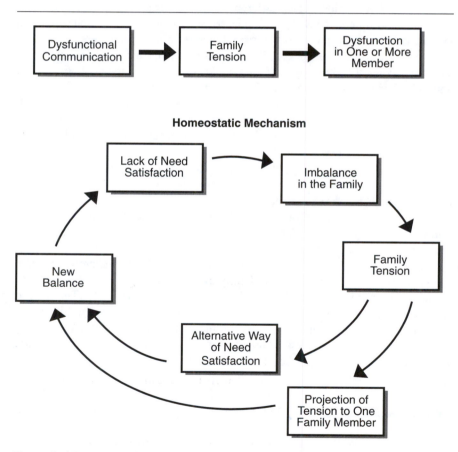

**Figure 3–4** Patterns Explained by the Communication Model.

for these messages to be defined as a double bind, they must be conflicting and be repeatedly sent over a long period of time. One message must convey a negative connotation or punishment (which may seem life threatening) and the other must be more abstract and contradictory. The victims are trapped in this pattern by their need for love and approval.

Children can feel frustrated and angry with their parents when they receive these double-bind messages. A case history involves Bobby, who was unable to express his anger to his mother when he felt frustration. The mother would say in therapy sessions that she wanted Bobby to show his anger and not bottle it up. She had done this in her family, and it had caused her pain. At home, however, when Bobby got angry, the mother would send him to his room until he could calm down and show his anger nicely. Bobby was confused and could not figure out how to please his mother. As much as he tried, he found it impossible to express anger nicely. When Bobby confronted her with this dilemma, she cited several occasions when this was not the case. His mother had denied Bobby's feelings and further frustrated him by not allowing him to show the anger she demanded he express.

If double-bind patterns of communication continue over prolonged periods, the victims have three ways of responding (Figure 3–5):

1. They can continue to repeat the behaviors that elicit the double-bind responses to try to find their meaning, which will lead to frustration and possible escape to drugs and alcohol.
2. They may try to go in both directions but find no meaning in either. Often they develop a belief that communication is worthless and that the world is a meaningless place. This process may lead to withdrawal from the environment and possible drug and alcohol abuse.
3. They can completely withdraw from the relationship and turn to alcohol and drugs or retreat with psychotic behaviors, as in schizophrenic families. "Double binds are present in all families, but more so in families of substance abusers than in 'normal' or 'neurotic' ones" (Kaufman, 1979, p. 269).

The communication model of family therapy relies heavily on identifying faulty communication patterns in a system that produces tension, disturbing homeostasis and producing symptomatic problems for an identified patient. Dysfunctional behavior, including alcohol abuse, can result from a lack of appropriate problem-solving techniques, a chronic double-bind communication pattern, unclear and cross-generational alliances, a lack of interpersonal skills, and an inability to accept differences and fixed role behaviors in the family. It should also be stressed that these behaviors are transmitted across generational boundaries.

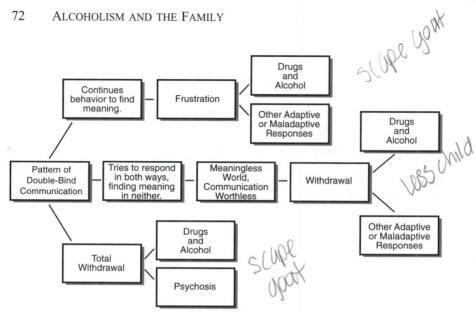

Figure 3–5 Reactions to the Double Bind.

One of the communication model therapists, Haley, developed a philosophy involving personal alliances in the family (1976). In the healthy family, he noticed mutually satisfying and need-fulfilling relationships. In the dysfunctional family, he found confused communication patterns and shifting alliances. Haley hypothesized that confused, out-of-order communication patterns can lead to misinterpretations, assumptions, guessing, and misunderstanding among family members. If children cannot interpret what their parents' needs and wishes are, they certainly cannot fulfill them. Haley also found that cross-generational alliances produced confused communication and misunderstanding in the power hierarchy of the family. He believed that change in family communication patterns and alliances would change the overall functioning of the family and reduce symptoms in the symptom bearer.

Haley was highly influenced by the work of Milton Erickson and Salvador Minuchin as well as Gregory Bateson. The combination of these influences—communication theory, cybernetics, Ericksonian hypnosis, and structural theory—became Haley's strategic approach. Strategic therapists are more concerned with changing a family's behavior than in changing their understanding; consequently, they are very interested in technique (Nichols & Schwartz, 1995). The goal of therapy is to resolve the presenting problem. These therapists are not interested in insight or understanding. The strategic therapist takes on most of the responsibility for change in the family and devises novel strategies for bringing about change. Strategic therapists have been criticized for being manipulative and deceiving the family, but they have responded with treatment outcome data indicating the power of their techniques in producing change.

Strategic therapists borrow concepts from cybernetics and are interested in positive feedback loops, family rules, creating second-order change (changing the family structure), and reframing behavior to expose the function of the symptom. This means the adaptive function that the problem serves in the family—why it is so hard to give up. (See the Adaptive Consequences section of chapter 6 for further discussion.) This is another way of trying to understand why people do things that are apparently opposite to the goal they are trying to achieve.

Strategic therapists use paradoxical techniques to bypass a family's or a family member's resistance to change. A simple paradox is prescribing the symptom. If, for instance, a daughter is doing poorly in school, the therapist might suggest that she continue to fail at her school work. If she continues to fail, she has followed the therapist's directive. (If she begins to succeed, the intervention has worked.) If there is strong resistance to change, sometimes going with the resistance will produce more change than confronting it directly. If the therapist believes that the daughter is failing because it gets her mother involved with her around homework and studies and takes her mother's focus away from a "failing" marriage or her alcoholic husband, the therapist may say, "You really need to continue to fail at school, because your mother feels needed when you do," or the therapist might compliment the daughter for being so sensitive to her mother's need and being willing to sacrifice her school work for her mother.

Haley also believed that the symptoms presented by the symptom bearer are metaphors for what is really wrong with the family or the marriage, and without changing the family structure the symptom will return or change to another one. Another type of paradoxical message is the restraint of change. Because families are used to their homeostatic balance, even if it is unhealthy, change may be very frightening for them. The therapist can acknowledge this ambivalence to change by instructing the family to go slow with change, because it can be dangerous. There is an art to devising paradoxical interventions, and they should not be used if a straightforward directive will be followed or if the therapist has not had sufficient training and supervision in these techniques. The process of Haley's strategic family therapy is covered in chapter 7.

## Intergenerational Family Therapy

Although structural and strategic approaches to family therapy are useful in working with chemically dependent families, the process of addiction in families is most clearly understood from an intergenerational perspective. The only definite statement the chemical dependency field can make is that chemical dependency and other addictions run in families, generation after generation, and more in some families than in others. Whether this is caused by nature (genetics) or nurture (environment) is really not as important as how to intervene in a problem with a tremendous history in a family.

Intergenerational family therapists share an interest in family dynamics across generations and come from a background in psychodynamic theory. Their interest in history is fueled by the belief that people's pasts influence their current behavior and relationships. Three pioneers in the school developed their theories at approximately the same time and were influenced by each other: Murray Bowen, Ivan Boszormenyi-Nagy, and James Framo. Bowen was also influenced by biological science, as mentioned earlier. He developed a theoretical model called Bowen therapy that features six interlocking concepts: (1) differentiation of self, (2) triangles, (3) nuclear family emotional process, (4) family projection process, (5) multigenerational transmission process, and (6) sibling position. He added two concepts in the 1970s: (1) emotional cutoff, and (2) societal emotional process.

Nagy and Framo worked together at the Eastern Pennsylvania Psychiatric Institute developing a process for working with schizophrenic families. Nagy developed a contextual family therapy, which was based on loyalty, trust, and ethics in family relationships. He emphasized the loyalty commitments people have to their families of origin, which is particularly useful in understanding what appears as undeserved loyalty in substance-abusing families.

Framo was influenced by Bowen, but he drew the foundations for his theory from object-relations theory. Framo brought adult children together with their parents and siblings for intensive family-of-origin therapy sessions (Framo, 1991). The goals of these sessions were to heal old wounds, correct family mythology, and help the adult children relate on an adult-to-adult level with their parents instead of regressing to a child in their presence. This is similar to Bowen's concept of differentiation from the family of origin; however, Bowen coached clients to return to their families and practice a nonreactive presence in response to their family or origin, whereas Framo brought them all together in the therapy session.

Because Bowen directly addressed the intergenerational transmission of alcoholism, this section covers his theory more thoroughly. This model can be used with individuals in treatment and is particularly effective with adults who were raised in alcoholic/addict families. Bowen (1974) saw the transmission process that occurs in alcoholic families as involved with levels of differentiation of self in the family. This is a function of the relationship the child has with his or her parents and the way the child's unresolved emotional attachment to his or her parents is handled in young adulthood. This model of family theory and therapy, which emerged during the birth of the family movement, defines symptoms in one member as a function of the family system of more than one generation (Bowen, 1974).

This theory can be used to understand the etiology of alcoholism in the family (Bowen, 1974). Bowen developed it during his work with schizophrenic families. He began seeing distinctions in affective states and cognitive processes that led to his *scale of differentiation*. This early work defined the family as a system operated by the same principles as other systems, such as societies, corporations, and institutions. Thus, the family is a system in that a change in one family member is followed automatically by a change in another. Bowen was willing to work with the most motivated individual (i.e., the nonalcoholic spouse) in the family to bring about change. He believed that a person's current behavior was caused by a transference process that inappropriately applied past history and behaviors to present situations. Bowen's initial focus was on the mother-daughter relationship, which fostered his theory of the family projection process. When he began to add grandparents to his sessions, he developed his theories on multi-generational transmission.

Bowen observed families that exhibited a feeling of oneness or lack of individual identity among the members. He found varying degrees of this oneness in families that seemed overly dependent on one another and labeled it "stuck togetherness." This stuck togetherness was the families' defense against crises or tensions; under threat, family members pulled together to restore balance. A delicate balance was created, with changes in one member affecting all others. If self-destructive behaviors, such as substance abuse, helped to maintain the balance, the families tolerated them.

In this system, the smallest unit (consisting of three people) was the triangle, as Bowen felt that dyads (two people) that could not handle stress would bring a third person into play to stabilize the unit. In alcoholic families the third member of the triangle can be the alcohol itself. In states of calm, the triangle has two comfortable sides and one in conflict. Over a period of time, these roles become fixed. When conflict occurs between the two comfortable members, they project conflict onto the third, who develops symptoms in a family projection process. A familiar example is the mother, father, and child triangle. When conflict occurs in the marriage, tension rises in the mother and is projected onto the child, who accepts it to maintain the family oneness. In this case, the father may be the adaptive spouse, giving up his identity for the sake of the marriage and supporting the other spouse's needs as well as her projection to the child. This father may also withdraw from the conflict by working long hours, drinking with his buddies in the local tavern, or finding endless chores out in the garage. Several other patterns of response to stress or conflict may occur among the three members.

The child selected for the projection is often the one closest to the mother. It may be the oldest boy or girl (depending on the gender valued by the family), the only child, a child born during a crisis, or one born with a defect. When this child leaves the family, another takes its place. When all the children are gone, the marital problems may come to the fore or the projection passed on to those outside the family.

The adolescent who leaves this family creates a pseudoindependence based on anxiety that will be transmitted to his or her own marital relationship in a multigenerational transmission process. Thus the patterns of the family of origin are repeated in the nuclear family.

Families with a high degree of "stuck togetherness" produce children who become distancers in an attempt to gain self-identity. They may become rebellious adolescents or withdraw destructively, gain physical distance by moving away from home, or emotionally distance themselves, which also creates physical distance. These children never differentiate themselves from their parents and are consequently unable to become problem solvers in crisis situations. Some of these children may become substance abusers who say, "I can't take pressure or I can't cope; I'm an alcoholic."

Bowen devised a scale for determining self-differentiation in family members (Figure 3–6). The scale ranges from 0 to 100. The range from 0 to 25 contains those who are dominated by their emotions. These people live from day to day, unable to make decisions or form opinions. Essentially, they lack a self; their only feeling of self-worth comes from others. The two rules of behavior for these people are: (1) "Does it make me feel good?" and (2) "Will others approve of me?"

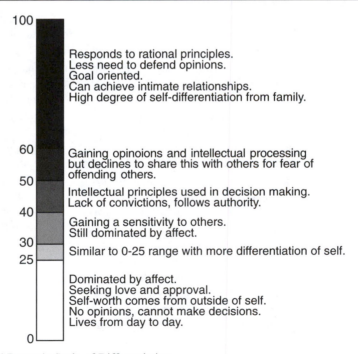

**Figure 3–6** Bowen's Scale of Differentiation.

Moving up the scale, differentiation is added to the profile of people who begin to use intellectual processes in decision making and who gain personal opinions. The upper half of the scale reflects goal orientation and includes those who can respond with rational principles and have less need to be defensive. They have achieved a self with a high degree of differentiation from their families. These people are able to achieve intimate relationships and are problem solvers.

Self-differentiation "is the degree to which the person has a 'solid self' or solidly held principles by which he lives his life. This is in contrast to a 'pseudoself' made up of inconsistent life principles that can be corrupted by coercion for the gain of the moment. The 'differentiation of self' is roughly equivalent to the concept of emotional maturity" (Bowen, 1978, p. 263). The rating is based on the amount of a person's differentiation from his or her parents, the type of relationship that exists with the parents, and the quality of emotional separation from the parents in young adulthood.

Bowen stated that people with similar scores tend to be attracted to one another, and they pass on similar degrees of differentiation to their children. The child with the lowest degree of differentiation is at highest risk for the family projection process and later problems. It is common for people to flee their families, blaming their parents for their problems and seeking happiness in their marriages. These two pseudoselves fuse and create impairments in one of the spouses. The most common way couples handle this marital fusion is by one spouse becoming dominant and the other being adaptive to the other. The adaptive one becomes a "no-self." "If this pattern is continued long enough, the adaptive one is vulnerable to some kind of chronic dysfunction, which can be physical illness, emotional illness, or a social dysfunction such as drinking, the use of drugs, or irresponsible behavior" (Bowen, 1978, p. 263). Families can use marital conflict or projection of their immaturity onto the children as ways to adapt. These patterns were programmed into the spouses by their families of origin.

Bowen believed there is a continuum of behaviors that lead to alcoholism. At one end is the person who denies the emotional attachment to his or her family of origin and maintains a superindependent posture. The actual level of emotional attachment, however, is intense. As this person becomes increasingly emotionally isolated he or she finds relief in alcohol. At the other end of the continuum is the person who is so attached to his or her parents that he or she is never able to manage a productive life. These people become de-selfed in the emotional fusion with the family of origin. They deny the intense need for the parents and begin drinking heavily early in life. Bowen states that most people with drinking problems fall somewhere in between these two extremes. "A high percentage of adult alcoholism is in people who are married, and who have the same kind of emotional attachment in marriage that they had in their parental families" (Bowen, 1978, p. 265).

Framo (1982) described a similar process of symptom development. He stated, "Symptoms are concomitants of the universal conflict between individuation, autonomous strivings, and loyalty to the family relationship system" (Framo, 1982, p. 127).

Treatment involves helping the patient differentiate from the family of origin and reducing emotional reactivity to this system. The goal is to help the patient to create his or her own nuclear family with a minimum of the multigenerational transmission process. This lengthy process usually transpires between the therapist and the family member wishing to differentiate from the family of origin. The therapist coaches the patient in this work. "Differentiation is the lifelong process of striving to keep one's being in balance through the reciprocal external and internal processes of self-definition and self-regulation" (Friedman, E.H., 1991).

The following case example of a family demonstrates several of the principles of systems theory. The family was seen at a child guidance clinic when the daughter, the identified patient, refused to attend school even when she was physically carried there. She would run out of the building and return home. Although the school tried its traditional methods of working with a school phobia, it had no success and, therefore, made a referral for family therapy. During the evaluation sessions, which included a family history, the therapist learned that the mother and the maternal grandmother had been excessively close. They had talked for hours every day—even long distance during the time the family had been transferred halfway across the United States. On further questioning, it was learned that this mother-daughter alliance had gone on for many generations in the past in the mother's family.

Sally, 8 years old, was the youngest of three children. Her sister was 14 and her brother 10. When the mother was pregnant with Sally, her mother (the maternal grandmother) and her sister were killed in a car wreck. The mother formed a strong attachment to Sally, probably as a replacement for the alliance with her mother (Sally's grandmother). This was seen as a passing on of a family intergenerational pattern and possibly as a repression of anger toward her children and husband for taking her away from her mother. She may have wished they would all disappear so she could return to the safety of her family of origin. However, this unconscious wish caused anxiety for the mother, and as a result she felt her children needed constant protection. This protection became a more rigid pattern when a neighborhood girl was struck and killed by a car while riding her bicycle. This vividly showed that bad things really can happen to family members.

As the family talked about their daily behavior, patterns of overprotection emerged. The mother would not let the children ride with their father to a town 50 miles away because she feared they would all be killed. Whenever one of the children was out of the house, the mother would worry and often shared this worry with Sally. She would ask Sally to run and make sure father was all right or check on the other children. Mother also disclosed that she had agoraphobia and often would have to run out of stores and rush home because of a panic attack.

Although the marital couple insisted they were happy, they agreed that they never went out without the children and that the mother did most of the parenting because the father was usually busy in the garage or drinking at the local bar. The mother stated that during the previous summer she had begun to worry about what would happen when her children grew up and left home. She felt she and her husband no longer "knew each other." In response to this worry they planned a three-day trip for the two of them to rejuvenate their marriage. Following her mother's habit of excessive worrying when a family member was out of the house, Sally cried throughout the three days and refused to participate in activities that her aunt had planned for her while her parents were away.

In later family sessions, Sally talked about her mother's constant threats to leave home. Several times the mother had gotten in the car after screaming that she was going to drive off a bridge, not returning for several hours. Another time she packed a suitcase and looked in the want ads for apartments to rent. Her mother's behavior terrified Sally, and she feared that if she let her mother out of her sight she might not return. The mother felt this was ridiculous and said she had never meant to leave. She just wanted the children to see how their behavior upset her and she was using these threats to communicate her unhappiness to her husband. Sally continued to strengthen the mother-daughter alliance by picking up her mother's phobic behaviors. Sally would not go into her room alone, would not go down into the basement, and began to refuse to leave the house for any reason.

This is an example of the family projection process in which the marital couple had reached fixed distance. The mother was the dominant spouse and the father adapted to her power and satisfied her need to control while giving up his own need fulfillment. He was withdrawn from parental duties and spent most of his time at a bar. The mother's tension about the loss of a marital partner had been projected onto Sally, who produced symptoms that reinforced the mother-daughter alliance. For Sally, these symptoms were an attempt to keep the family together.

The mother was very uncomfortable when the focus of therapy was not on Sally, and between sessions she took Sally to psychiatrists in an attempt to reinforce the notion of a sick child as well as to get approval for the family projection process. The therapist made a contract with the family, who agreed to stop seeing other therapists for four weeks. Sessions were started with the marital couple only.

Sally came to the first marital session and was left in the lobby. When she decided she was no longer the focus of therapy and her parents were getting the help she felt they needed, she returned to school. By the third marital session, Sally was in school full time and had returned to her other activities outside the home.

The father's drinking behavior was reduced significantly when he was given an equal share of the parenting responsibilities, and the marital couple began planning social engagements without the children.

In summary, Bowen believed that dysfunctional behavior in the nuclear family should be looked at in terms of the lack of differentiation of family members, repression of individuality, and the inability of spouses to differentiate from their parents' past behaviors.

## Experiential Family Therapy

"Experiential family therapists focus on the subjective needs of the individual in the family and work to facilitate a family process that will address the individuality of each member" (Hanna & Brown, 1995, p. 13). They incorporate elements of intergenerational theory but put more emphasis on emotional expressions and growth. They also resemble the structural and strategic therapists in their focus on the present interactions in the therapy session. Experiential family therapy draws from individual humanistic therapy, Gestalt therapy, and encounter groups that emphasize here-and-now experiences. The arts and psychodrama also influenced techniques of family sculpting and family drawing.

The two most influential therapists in this school were Virginia Satir and Carl Whitaker. Satir began seeing families in her private practice in Chicago and later joined Bateson, Haley, Jackson, and Weakland in Palo Alto, California, at the Mental Research Institute, where she added her perspectives to the communication model (Satir, 1967). These theorists believed that blocked forms of communication in the individual were symptoms of overall dysfunctional communication in the family. They proposed that dysfunctional communication patterns produced family tension that was projected onto one or more family members (see Figure 3–4.).

Satir saw communications as a key factor in functional and dysfunctional relationships, and believed that homeostasis was more valuable to a family than an individual member's well-being. Satir also stated that parents bring their faulty patterns of communication to the marriage from their families of origin and that children learn these patterns in a multigenerational process. Her version of the communication model, however, grew to be a more holistic health model dedicated to self-esteem building, personal growth, and spirituality. Satir was a dynamic, nurturing therapist who genuinely cared for her fellow human beings. She was a master at creating peak experiences in therapy with her gift of a healing touch, generating family dramas in the therapy sessions. Her technique of family sculpting was adapted by the chemical dependency field to help families experience their connections, boundaries, and hierarchies.

Satir (1967) continued to develop the communication model with her theories of conjoint family therapy. She referred to the symptom bearer as the identified patient (IP), and to the symptoms as pain. She stated that individual pain is a symptom of pain that is present in the larger system of the family and the society the family lives in. This pain is seen as having a purpose in the interworkings of the family process.

In terms of etiology, Satir believed that dysfunctional people have not learned how to effectively interact with others. They either lack a model of appropriate communications in their family or they have been sheltered and spared responsibility for interpersonal relationships. Alcohol treatment centers often focus on teaching interpersonal skills when it becomes clear that their patients have not developed such skills as beginning conversations, giving compliments, joining a group of peers, finding a job, or expressing feelings. Goldstein was similarly successful in teaching these social skills to alcoholics using behavior modification techniques described in his book, *Structured Learning Therapy* (1976).

Satir further found that dysfunction occurs due to people's inaccurate perception of interactions and their unwillingness to accept differences in others as well as themselves. Walsh (1981) stated:

> Parents who depreciate a child because of the development of different characteristics or behaviors, are creating the basis for self-doubt and insecurity. As he grows, any display of differentness on the part of others can be perceived as threatening to [an] already weak self-concept. He may feel, "If this person is right, and I believe differently, I am wrong and less of a person." This attitude can lead to a rigid approach to the world or a rejection of others through withdrawal. (p. 13)

Satir developed four basic role types that family members typically adopt when dealing with crises, such as substance abuse, in the family:

1. The *placater* is a person who reduces tension by smoothing things over. The person may be a martyr, a role often played by the alcoholic's spouse. This role parallels Bowen's adaptive spouse who allows the partner to become dominant and risks losing self-identity. The placater avoids confrontation of abusive drinking behavior and denies personal emotions.
2. The *blamer* role is often played by people with low self-esteem, who attack to keep the focus off themselves. The alcoholic plays this role by blaming others and insisting that his or her drinking behavior was caused by the spouse's nagging or the children's misbehavior. The spouse can also shift to this role when conflict is high.
3. The *irrelevant* role is played by people in the family who avoid conflict by changing the subject, responding inappropriately, distracting others, or having temper tantrums.

4. The *superresponsible* role is characterized by ultrareasonable communication. These people act calm, cool, and collected, but internally they feel
vulnerable.

Satir used these roles to create family sculptures so that family members could
experience from a symbolic and dramatic perspective the roles they play and how
this is all part of a family dance in response to stress or problems in the family.
Family sculptures in the therapy room are created by placing the family members
physically in positions that are representative of the roles they play in the family.
These positions portray the closeness/distance of the relationships and the power
hierarchy of the family, so the family members can recognize and experience
these dynamics (see the section on family sculpting in chapter 6). She believed
that these roles covered real feelings that people were afraid to share because of
their low self-esteem. In her work, Satir clarified communications, helped families find solutions, supported each family member's self-esteem, and taught
families how to touch and be affectionate.

Carl Whitaker, another experiential family therapist, was raised on an isolated
dairy farm in New York. He attributed his shyness and his ability to connect with
schizophrenic patients to this experience of isolation. He was originally trained as
a doctor of obstetrics and gynecology, but during World War II was pressed into
working as a psychiatrist and became fascinated by psychotic patients. Because he
had no formal training in psychiatry, he was unencumbered by traditional ideas.
Whitaker went on to establish a training program at Emory University. He later
left Emory with several of his colleagues to establish the Atlantic Psychiatric
Clinic, where his version of experiential family therapy, symbolic-experiential
family therapy, was further developed.

Whitaker's theory evolved from his work with schizophrenic families and
collaboration with other family therapists. The goal of his therapy was individual
growth as well as strengthening the family as a whole. He believed that personal
growth requires family integration and that family integration depends on personal growth of its members (Nichols & Schwartz, 1995). Toward this goal of
growth, Whitaker created an experience in therapy for its own sake. He further
believed that a therapist should approach a therapy session with the expectation
that he or she would also experience growth from these existential encounters.

Whitaker often referred to his therapy as "therapy of the absurd," and he relied
on his intuition and flashes of thoughts created by the encounter with families. He
talked of falling asleep in sessions and dreaming about the family. Upon waking,
he would tell the family what he dreamed in a symbolic way. He was known to
blurt out statements about the undercurrent of process in the family such as,
"Someone is having murderous thoughts!" "Whitaker advocates 'craziness,' non-
rational, creative experiencing and functioning, as a proper goal of therapy. If they

let themselves become a little crazy, he believes, families will reap the rewards of zest, emotionality, and spontaneity" (Nichols & Schwartz, 1995, p. 299).

In contrast to Bowen, Whitaker liked to raise the anxiety of the family and create emotional exchanges. He believed that sometimes family members had to get angry with each other to clear the air and allow for closeness and loving feelings.

Although these experiential therapists are difficult to emulate because their personalities were part of their therapies, their beliefs, goals, and processes can be adapted by others. Focusing on feelings, self-esteem, and the experiences of the therapy process can be useful in working with substance-abusing families, who usually have low levels of self-esteem and a strong taboo against expressing feelings. They often need to learn to be spontaneous, loving, and growing individuals and families. Couples who have been struggling with addiction for long periods are full of anger, resentment, disappointment, and fear. Experiential therapy can be useful to help couples get beyond the stockpiles of negative emotions that keep them from growing in their recovery process.

**Behavioral Family Therapy**

Behavioral family therapy emerged in the mid-1970s largely through the efforts of Gerald Patterson at the Oregon Research Institute in Eugene, Oregon (Patterson, 1971). He was able to take the major step of transferring the assessment and intervention for families from the clinic environment to the home (Falloon, 1991). He trained families to use social learning strategies themselves.

Richard Stuart (1969) developed an approach to promoting positive family milieu in troubled families through contingency contracting of an exchange of pleasing behaviors between family members. He believed the best strategy to shift the homeostatic balance was for each family member to provide unconditional positive rewards to other family members, particularly those with whom he or she was experiencing conflict (Falloon, 1991).

This theory is based on the principles of behaviorism and behavior modification, many of which were developed by Skinner and then applied to the family unit. Patterson stated that all behaviors of family members, whether functional or dysfunctional, are learned through correct or faulty training of individual family members by other family members. Children are taught how to behave by their parents, siblings, and other relatives, and, conversely, children teach parents and others about themselves with their reactions to the parents' teaching. Problems occur in the family when individuals cannot discriminate between teaching positive and negative behaviors and when parents unknowingly teach negative behaviors. This theory is similar to Hoffman's idea of negative love that children receive through mirroring parents' negative habits while in search of love and approval.

Patterson, like other family theorists, believed in looking to the families of origin to understand the patterns of behavior in the nuclear family. He believed that an individual's present behaviors are determined by the reactions they received from their families in the past. These behaviors become predictable and repetitive and are seen as fixed patterns, similar to the Satir role patterns, that can be observed and changed by the family. These learned behaviors can be unlearned by changing the response pattern to the undesired behaviors, while new replacement behaviors can be conditioned to substitute for dysfunctional behaviors.

The main principle propounded by Patterson is that reinforcement increases the probability that desired behaviors will be repeated and nonreinforcement decreases the probability or causes extinction of the behavior. There are four types of reinforcers:

1. *Positive reinforcement* is a reward for appropriate behavior. These rewards can be material, such as paychecks, candy, or desired gifts; social, such as kisses, hugs, or verbal praise; or intrinsic, such as self-worth and positive internal feelings. The first two are external reinforcers and require a second person. The third is internal and is a solitary process. An important consideration is for the second person to know what type of reinforcement will motivate the individual. Therapists use these reinforcers in a hierarchical method beginning with material reinforcers but moving to social and then to intrinsic reinforcers as soon as possible.

   The recovering alcoholic who obtains money from a job, receives love and approval from the family, and begins to gain intrinsic self-worth from sobriety is responding to positive reinforcers. However, if drinking behavior is rewarded by a reduction of personal tension and escape from responsibility, reduced guilt, a diminished demand from the spouse and children, and a reduction of family tension, the drinking behavior is being reinforced.

2. *Negative reinforcement* occurs when some unwanted experience is removed. For example, if a child cries and refuses to comply with a request, parents negatively reinforce crying if they withdraw the request. If responsibility and pressure are withdrawn because the family reduces demands when the alcoholic drinks, the behavior is negatively reinforced.

3. *Punishment* is any aversive stimulus in the person's environment, such as hitting or yelling. Therapists avoid punishment because of a carryover to positive behaviors and the chance that children will imitate punishing behaviors. Children learn that if a person is not pleased with someone's behavior he or she can hit that person, and if individuals are not pleased with their own behavior they can be self-destructive.

This theory may be useful in understanding why people continue to drink when they are aware of the self-destructive nature of alcohol. Research has also shown that parents who were physically abused themselves are at higher risk to abuse their children.

4. *Nonreinforcement* is the removal of a positive reinforcer such as praise and attention or the removal of the person from the reinforcing environment. The removal of a child from a group interaction to an isolated timeout chair is a nonreinforcer.

Although behavioral family therapists assume that each member of a family is doing his or her best to cope, given the restraints of life, there are some common deficits that seem to produce children with difficulties. Falloon (1991) identified three of these patterns:

1. *Families that have difficulty in recognizing deviant behavior.* Age-appropriate behavior can be seen as deviant, while true deviant behavior is ignored. These are found in families that are dealing with depression and anxiety, high stress, or those with a lack of understanding of appropriate development.
2. *Families with a lack of clearly defined family rules.* This is common in families with adolescents and families where drug and alcohol abuse occur. There is a lack of clear structure of how the household is to be managed.
3. *Families with dysfunction in emotional communication.* These families have a low rate of expression of positive feelings and a high rate of expression of negative feelings. These negative communications may be direct or indirect through nonverbal gestures or posturing. This pattern has been found when alcoholic families are compared with nonalcoholic families. Alcoholic families have a much lower level of open and direct expression of feelings but exhibit a high level of open expression of anger, aggression, and generally conflictual interactions (Filstead, McElfresh, & Anderson, 1981).

An important outgrowth of behavioral family therapy is behavioral marital therapy (BMT). The focus is shifted from behavior of children to the marital couple. The goal is to induce couples to collaborate to produce an environment supportive of a desirable relationship (Holtzworth-Munroe & Jacobson, 1991).

BMT was the focus of several studies that used this approach in the treatment of alcoholism. A promising approach is the use of BMT with couples in alcoholism treatment. BMT combines a focus on the drinking with work on more general marital relationship issues. This method instigates positive couple and family activities and teaches communication and conflict resolution skills (McCrady et al., 1986; O'Farrell & Choquette, 1991; O'Farrell & Cutter, 1982; O'Farrell, Cutter, & Floyd, 1985).

In summary, behavioral family therapy and behavioral marital therapy look at the dysfunctional behavior as learned behavior that is taught by others, especially family members. This behavior can be unlearned and replaced with functional behavior by using operant conditioning and reinforcement techniques.

## REFERENCES

Barnard, C.P. (1981). *Families, alcoholism and therapy*. Springfield, IL: Charles C. Thomas.

Bateson, G., Jackson, D., Haley, J., & Weakland, J. (1956). Toward a theory of schizophrenia. *Behavioral Science, 1*, 251–264.

Black, C. (1981). *It will never happen to me*. Denver, CO: M.A.C. Publishers.

Bowen, M. (1971). Family therapy and family group therapy. In H. Kaplan & B. Sadock (Eds.), *Comprehensive group psychotherapy*. Baltimore: Williams & Wilkins.

Bowen, M. (1974). Alcoholism as viewed through family systems theory and family psychotherapy. *Annals of the New York Academy of Science, 233*, 115–122.

Bowen, M. (1978). *Family therapy in clinical practice*. New York: Jason Aronson.

Carter, E., & McGoldrick, M. (1980). *The family life cycle: A framework for family therapy*. New York: Gardner Press.

Davidson, M. (1983). *Uncommon sense: The life and thought of Ludwin von Bertalanffy*. Los Angeles: J.P. Tarcher.

Ewing, I.A., & Fox, R.E. (1968). Family therapy of alcoholism. In S. Messerman (Ed.), *Current psychiatric therapies*. New York: Grune & Stratton.

Falloon, I.R.H. (1991). Behavioral family therapy. In A. Gurman & D. Kniskern (Eds.), *Handbook of family therapy: Vol. 2*. (pp. 65–95). New York: Brunner/Mazel.

Filstead, W.J., McElfresh, O., & Anderson, C. (1981). Comparing the family environments of alcoholics and normal families. *Journal of Alcohol and Drug Education, 26*, 24–31.

Fogarty, T. (1976). Marital crisis. In P. Guerin (Ed.), *Family therapy: Theory and practice*. New York: Gardner Press.

Framo, J.L. (1976). Family of origin as a therapeutic resource for adults in marital and family therapy: You can and should go home again. *Family Process, 15*, 193–209.

Framo, J.L. (1982). Symptoms from a family transactional viewpoint. In C. Sager and H.S. Kaplan (Eds.), *Progress in group and family therapy*. New York: Brummer/Mazel.

Framo, J.L. (1991). *Family of origin therapy: An intergenerational approach*. New York: Brunner/Mazel.

Friedman, A.S., Tomko, L.A., & Utada, A. (1991). Client and family characteristics that predict better family therapy outcome for adolescent drug abusers. *Family Dynamics of Addiction Quarterly, 1*(1), 77–93.

Friedman, E.H. (1991). Bowen theory and therapy. In A. Gurman & D. Kniskern (Eds.), *Handbook of family therapy: Vol. 2*. (pp. 134–170). New York: Brunner/Mazel.

Goldenberg, I., & Goldenberg, H. (1996). *Family therapy: An overview* (4th ed.). Pacific Grove, CA: Brooks/Cole.

Goldstein, A.P. (1976). *Structured learning therapy*. New York: Academic Press.

Haley, J. (1976). *Problem solving therapy*. New York: Harper & Row.

Hanna, S.M., & Brown, J.A. (1995). *Family therapy: Key elements across models*. Pacific Grove, CA: Brooks/Cole.

Hoffman, B. (1979). *No one is to blame: Getting a loving divorce from your parents*. Palo Alto, CA: Science and Behavior Books.

Holtzworth-Munroe, A., & Jacobson, N.S. (1991). Behavioral marital therapy. In A. Gurman & D. Kniskern (Eds.), *Handbook of family therapy: Vol. 2*. (pp. 96–133). New York: Brunner/Mazel.

Jackson, D.D. (1957). The question of family homeostasis. *Psychiatric Quarterly Supplement, 31*, 79–90.

Jackson, D.D. (Ed.). (1960). *The etiology of schizophrenia*. New York: Basic Books.

Jackson, D.D. (1968). *Communication, family and marriage*. Palo Alto, CA: Science and Behavior Books.

Kaufman, E. (1979). The application of the basic principles of family therapy to the treatment of drug and alcohol abusers. In E. Kaufman & P. Kaufman (Eds.), *Family therapy of drug and alcohol abuse*. New York: Gardner Press.

McCrady, B.S., Noel, N.E., Abrams, D.B., Stout, R.I., Nelson, H.F., & Hay, W.M. (1986). Comparative effectiveness of three types of spouse involvement in outpatient behavioral alcoholism treatment. *Journal of Studies on Alcohol, 47*(67), 459–466.

Meeks, D., & Kelly, C. (1970). Family therapy with the families of recovering alcoholics. *Quarterly Journal of Studies on Alcoholism, 31*(2), 399–413.

Minuchin, S. (1974). *Families and family therapy*. Cambridge, MA: Harvard University Press.

Nichols, M.P., & Schwartz, R.C. (1995). *Family therapy: Concepts and methods*. Boston: Allyn & Bacon.

O'Farrell, T.J., & Choquette, K. (1991). Marital violence in the year before and after spouse-involved alcoholism treatment. *Family Dynamics of Addiction Quarterly, 1*(1), 32–40.

O'Farrell, T.J., & Cutter, H.S.G. (1982, February). Effect of adding a behavioral or an interactional couples group to individual outpatient alcoholism counseling. In T.J. O'Farrell (Chair), *Spouse involved treatment for alcohol abuse*. Symposium conducted at the Sixteenth Annual Convention of the Association for the Advancement of Behavior Therapy, Los Angeles, CA.

O'Farrell, T.J., Cutter, H.S.G., & Floyd, F.J. (1985). Evaluating behavioral marital therapy for male alcoholics: Effects on marital adjustment and communication from before to after therapy. *Behavior Therapy, 16*, 147–167.

Olson, D.H., & Killorin, E.A. (1987). Chemically dependent families and the circumplex model. Unpublished research report, University of Minnesota, St. Paul, MN.

Patterson, G. (1971). *Families*. Champaign, IL: Research Press.

Preli, R., & Protinsky, H. (1988). Aspects of family structures in alcoholic, recovered, and nonalcoholic families. *Journal of Marital and Family Therapy, 14*(3), 311–314.

Satir, V. (1967). *Conjoint family therapy*. Palo Alto, CA: Science and Behavior Books.

Steinglass, P. (1976). Experimenting with family treatment approaches to alcoholism, 1950–1975: A review. *Family Process, 15,* 97–123.

Stuart, R. (1969). Operant-interpersonal treatment for marital discord. *Journal of Consulting and Clinical Psychology, 33,* 675–682.

Walsh, W.M. (1980). *A primer in family therapy.* Springfield, IL: Charles C. Thomas.

Wegscheider, S. (1981). From the family trap to family freedom. *Alcoholism, (Jan./Feb.),* 36–39.

# CHAPTER 4

# Physiological, Sociological, and Psychological Influences on the Family

This chapter presents the three primary theoretical models of the etiology of alcoholism—physiological, sociological, and psychological—and describes the relationship of these models to the family. In each of these areas, the major research is covered and a framework provided for a central theory of etiology that includes the critical influences of the family. This chapter should give the reader a clear understanding of the role the family plays in the development of alcoholism.

At the end of each major section, several questions are presented that the reader can use to determine whether an individual is at high, low, or medium risk for alcoholism. By asking these questions and completing the chart in Figure 4–1, it is possible to determine the alcoholism risk factor for an individual.

Although the physiological and sociological models of etiology have a solid basis in empirical research, alcoholism treatment personnel have little control over genetic and cultural factors. However, a knowledge of these areas is important both for the treatment specialist and the prevention worker to provide them with a complete picture of the patient and his/her disorder.

## PHYSIOLOGICAL THEORIES OF ETIOLOGY AND THE FAMILY

This section examines the physiological/genetic factors of alcoholism etiology and their relationship to the family, particularly the family of origin. Is alcoholism hereditary? If so, what factors are inherited? What makes a person physically at high risk for alcoholism? Some of the major studies in this area were presented in the overview in chapter 1. They will be reviewed briefly here with a focus on the role the family plays in the development of a high or low risk for alcoholism.

Although there has been a decade of research since the first edition of this book, it is surprising how few studies have added significant information to the etiology

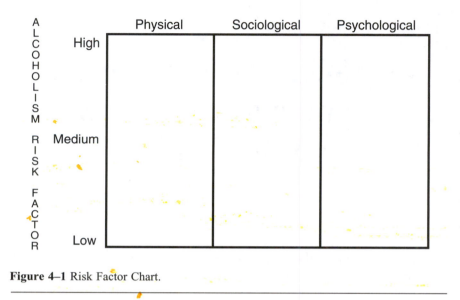

**Figure 4–1** Risk Factor Chart.

of alcoholism in the physiological arena. After a review of some of the contemporary studies in this area, Searles (1991) concluded that because most of these studies had design problems such as lack of uniform criteria for a diagnosis of alcoholism, results may not be as compelling as they first were thought to be.

## Family Studies

It is apparent that children of alcoholics have more problems with alcohol than children from families with nonalcoholic parents. Without exception, every family study of alcoholism, no matter what the country of origin, shows higher rates of alcoholism among the relatives of alcoholics than in the population in general (Goodwin, 1971). Cotton's review of the literature (1979) found that all 39 of the studies reviewed revealed that the rates of alcoholism were substantially higher in relatives of alcoholics than in relatives of nonalcoholics, even when nonalcoholics were psychiatric patients.

## Twin Studies

Others in the field approach the problem of genetics by studying pairs of twins. These studies compare the degree of similarity, or concordance, in alcohol consumption between identical twins (monozygotic or one-egg twins) and fraternal twins (dizygotic or two-egg twins). Monozygotic (MZ) twins have 100 percent genetic likeness, but dizygotic (DZ) twins have only about 50 percent genetic likeness and are no more similar than any brother and sister. This idea assumes that MZ and DZ twins differ mainly in genetic makeup and that the environment is the same for both sorts of twins.

Two major studies have been reported using this technique. The first was by Kaij (1960) of Sweden, who identified 174 male pairs of twins in which at least one twin was registered at a temperance board because of a legal conviction for drunkenness or other alcohol abuse. He interviewed 90 percent of the subjects and established zygosity by a blood test. The concordance rate for alcohol abuse in the MZ group was 54 percent as compared with 28 percent for the DZ group; the difference was statistically significant. He also noted that the more severe the drinking problem in the first identified twin, the higher the concordance rate. In an interesting follow-up, he discovered that the social and brain function deterioration aspects of alcohol abuse correlated more closely with zygosity than did the amount and frequency of alcohol intake.

In a somewhat different approach, the Finnish group of Partanen, Bruun, and Markkanen (1966) studied 133 MZ pairs and 471 DZ pairs, 28 to 37 years of age. This nonalcoholic population did show more concordance with regard to frequency and amount of drinking among MZ twins than among DZ twins. However, there was no report of heritability for the presence of "addictive" symptoms or drinking consequences (i.e., arrest for drunkenness).

It appears that in both of these studies inherited traits passed on by families (parents) played a contributing role in drinking behavior. However, the studies have been faulted because of the greater physical resemblance between MZ twins than DZ twins. This is thought to be a pertinent factor because identical twins are often treated more similarly (i.e., similar clothing) than fraternal twins, and therefore their life experiences are more alike.

## Adoption Studies

Another family method used to separate nature from nurture is the adoption study. Some see this method as the most productive way to approach the problem. Goodwin, Schlosinger, Hermansen, Guze, and Winaker (1973) went to Denmark to take advantage of a pool of 15,000 known adoptees, most of whom were separated from their biological nuclear families at birth or during early childhood and were raised by nonrelatives. It would be very difficult to attempt such a study in the United States because of the lack of access to adoption records.

The experimental group in Denmark consisted of 55 male adoptees who had at least one biological parent who had been hospitalized primarily for alcoholism. Each had been separated from the parents in the first six weeks of life, had no subsequent contact with his biological parents, and was adopted by nonrelatives.

A control group used for comparison consisted of 78 adopted males who met the same criteria except that they had no biological alcoholic parents. The groups were matched for adult age and approximate age at adoption. The mean age in both groups at the time they were interviewed was 30, with a range of 25 to 45. All adoptees were interviewed by a Danish psychiatrist who did not know to which group they belonged. The information obtained included demographic factors, information on adoptive parents, psychopathology in adoptees, drinking practices and problems, and a variety of life experiences. Of the 55 subjects with alcoholic parents, 10 were classified as alcoholic, a rate nearly four times that of the controls. Almost without exception, this group had more drinking problems than the controls. Differences were significant in five types of problems, including hallucinations, inability to control drinking, morning drinking, amnesia, and tremor. Goodwin's conclusions were that severe forms of alcohol abuse may have a genetic predisposition, but that heavy drinking itself, even when problems resulted from the drinking, reflected predominantly nongenetic factors.

A follow-up study by Goodwin (1974) also suggested a relationship between the severity of alcoholism and increased tendencies toward alcohol problems in offspring. Goodwin (1988) concluded that rather than a *genetic* inheritability for alcoholism a *biological* vulnerability is inherited. He speculated that what makes for vulnerability may be low levels of serotonin, a neurotransmitter, and he cited evidence that alcoholic rats have low levels of serotonin in certain parts of their brains and that serotonin reuptake blockers such as Prozac decrease appetite for alcohol in those rats.

More recently, Swan, Carmelli, and Cardon (1996), using an elaborate statistical model, compared a cohort of 173 MZ twins and 183 DZ twins on their use of alcohol, tobacco, and coffee. They concluded that significant heritabilities were obtained for smoking (56 percent), alcohol consumption (50 percent), and coffee consumption (36 percent), after controlling for common and subject-specific environmental effects. They also concluded that a common factor underlies the joint use of alcohol, tobacco, and coffee. They did encourage caution when generalizing the results of the study for several reasons. First, the findings were based entirely on self-report. Second, unassessed variables that underlie the joint use of these substances, including environmental stress and depression, could be confounding factors in the results of the study.

## Half-Sibling Studies

In another variant of family genetic research, Schuckit, Goodwin, and Winakur (1972) studied 60 male and 9 female subjects who were diagnosed as primary alcoholics and who also had half-siblings. A number of detailed analyses were done on these subjects. Using this approach, the incidence of alcoholism was measured in children who had biological alcoholic parents but were raised in foster homes with no alcoholic parent figures. Conversely, the alcoholism outcome was determined for children without biological alcoholic parents who were raised in homes with an alcoholic parent. In this study, of the 32 alcoholic half-siblings and the 32 nonalcoholic half-siblings, 62 percent of the former and only 19 percent of the latter had at least one alcoholic biological parent, clearly indicating a strong genetic relationship. The rates of alcoholic and nonalcoholic half-siblings who lived with an alcoholic parent figure were almost identical, suggesting a stronger relationship with hereditary than with environmental factors. Drew, Moon, and Buchanan (1974) graphically reported the situation.

Does this research prove conclusively that alcoholism is inherited? No, there are some definite problems with the studies just cited. Even though alcoholism may run in families, this tendency does not constitute proof of inheritance. Many things run in families, such as language, eating habits, and occupations, but these are sociocultural in nature and are not due to heredity. Although many studies link alcoholism to heredity, none have demonstrated heredity to be more than a contributing factor in the etiology of alcoholism.

An authority in the area of alcoholism and heredity, Goodwin (1981) felt this type of research is plagued with difficulties. For example, the sources of information may be faulty, or conflicting stories may be reported to researchers. Problems with definitions (particularly in the field of alcoholism) are also significant, as are many other inherent methodological problems. As Goodwin points out, problems must be acknowledged and improvements made. However, the apparent consistency of results across studies is encouraging, and the volume of work done in this area should not be ignored. Indeed, studies of families are not the only evidence of genetic factors in alcoholism. Several other methods have been developed to examine this issue.

## Animal Studies

Although some feel that alcoholism is a human condition and animal research is irrelevant, this type of research continues to provide useful information about the hereditary determinants of alcoholism. For example, it has been shown that different strains of mice and rats seek out and ingest different amounts of alcohol. And, if members of nondrinking strains and heavy-drinking strains mate, they produce moderate-drinking offspring with intermediate alcohol intake. This suggests that voluntary alcohol consumption was "regulated by numerous genes" (Goodwin, 1971). The primary reason that research is conducted with animals is that experimental manipulations can be carried out on animals that would be detrimental or unwise for people, such as the mating procedure in the experiment mentioned above. It is clear that these experiments have produced strains of animals that have different responsiveness to alcohol. It is entirely possible that such hereditary factors exist in humans and that they are passed on from family to family.

## Other Physiological Studies of Alcoholism Etiology

Several theories are relevant to this section, including biochemical, nutritional, and endocrine system theories of alcoholism and neurobiochemical factors.

Cloninger and his associates studied a large sample of alcoholics and concluded that there are two basic types of alcoholics, each related to a set of familial factors (Cloninger, Bohman, & Sigvardsson, 1981), and a personality cluster that has a neurochemical basis (Cloninger, 1987). Cloninger suggested in his study there were two basic types of alcoholics. Type I is the most common and occurs in both men and women. It consists of either mild or severe alcoholism and is characterized by an inability to control drinking. Type II alcoholics are predominantly men and usually have drinking-related problems at a very early age. They also are very likely to be aggressive and to engage in antisocial behavior, such as fighting and driving under the influence. These individuals rarely abstain from alcohol for any period and show no guilt or fear of alcohol dependence. The fathers of Type II alcoholics are likely to be alcoholic and to have a history of criminality. Although there is a genetic component to both types of alcoholism , the degree of genetic predisposition varies considerably. Cloninger concluded that Type I alcoholics have a genetic predisposition but that environmental factors account for the severity and likelihood of their becoming alcoholic. On the other hand, Type II alcoholics are under a greater genetic control and have a much greater chance of becoming alcoholic.

Schuckit (1985) examined body sway in young men with a family history of alcoholism compared with men without a family history of alcoholism after drinking moderate amounts of alcohol. Men with a family history showed much less body sway after drinking, though the two groups were even in body sway in predrinking trials. Schuckit concluded that men from alcoholic families might have a genetic factor that caused them to be less affected by alcohol, thus increasing their risk for becoming alcoholic. However, it could have been that living with an alcoholic made them learn to control outward signs of intoxication because they didn't want to be like the alcoholics in their family. It is possible to learn to improve psychomotor skills while under the influence of alcohol. This has been shown in both animal and human studies.

Some researchers have focused on the biochemistry of the brain. Certain chemicals produced in the brain are involved in the transmission of neuroimpulses, particularly those related to emotional expression, and these chemicals may affect alcohol intake. According to one of these hypotheses, alcohol may produce a morphine-like substance in the brains of certain individuals that is responsible for alcohol addiction (Davis & Walsh, 1970). Schuckit and Gold (1988) examined the difference between high-risk college students (those who came from alcoholic families) and low-risk students (from families free of alcoholism) on levels of biological markers, including platelet MAO levels, before and after drinking and found no significant difference.

In the nutritional area, Williams (1959) postulated that alcoholism may be caused by a metabolic pattern that is inherited and results in nutritional deficiencies. For example, a glutamine deficiency results in a craving for another nutrient, alcohol. In certain cases, glutamine has been given to alcoholics, and they have subsequently been reported to lose their taste for liquor.

Another major physiological theory, the endocrine theory, postulates that alcoholism is caused by a dysfunction of the endocrine system. Experimental clinical evidence, however, does not provide a great deal of support for this theory. The available information suggests that heavy drinking may be the cause rather than the result of endocrine dysfunctions.

The above discussion presents only a sample of the evidence that physiological and genetic factors contribute to alcoholism. The reader who is interested in a detailed review should consult Goodwin (1988), McClearn (1970), and Lindsey, Loehlin, Monosevitz, and Thiessen (1971).

Although heredity has never been demonstrated to explain alcoholism in total, it is clearly one of the many contributing factors. If people can inherit brown eyes from their parents, they may also inherit the way alcohol is metabolized by their body. The genetic endowment a person receives may only set down a predisposition to alcoholism, the final outcome depending on a combination of physiological, sociological, and psychological factors. However, some people clearly are at a higher physical risk for alcoholism than others, and this trait may be passed on from family to family. A genetic involvement does not mean the condition is hopeless. Genetically influenced diabetes can be modified by injections of insulin; genetically influenced myopia can be modified by lenses; and future alcoholism can be modified by intervention and prevention techniques.

Like so many pathologies, the earlier the predictions of future alcohol problems can be made, the better the chance of effective prevention.

Who is at high risk and who is at low risk physically for alcoholism? By asking the following three questions, an approximate risk factor for the physiological area can be determined:

1. Do you have a parent or grandparent who was or is alcoholic?
2. If you have started drinking, are you or were you able to drink larger amounts of alcohol than most of your friends with fewer physical consequences (i.e., hangover)?
3. Did you drink large amounts of alcohol from the first time you started drinking?

The rationale for the first question is obvious. If the client has a parent or grandparent who is alcoholic, he or she has a better than average chance of being physically at high risk. However, there are a few problems with this first question. For example, if none of the relatives drink, there is no way to know if they would have alcohol problems if they did. The other possibility is that there are conflicting views on the grandparent's or parent's status. To the teetotaler, the person who has two drinks every day might be considered a problem drinker. However, to an alcoholic, a person who drinks a fifth of liquor a day might seem quite normal. Despite these problems, the first question will be easy for most people to answer. If alcoholic aunts or uncles exist, the client is at least at medium physical risk.

The second question is for those who have started to drink, and it is an excellent indicator of a high physical risk factor. The rationale for this question comes from our personal experience with alcoholics. Of the hundreds of alcoholics we interviewed in the past 25 years, a significant number fit the description detailed in question two. Some people believe that alcoholics are in an endless search for good feelings, without the negative consequences that were present when they first began drinking. However, for most alcoholics, early drinking experiences were mainly pleasant.

The third question has the same rationale as the second. Many alcoholics claim they became alcoholic with their first drink. A person who answers yes to question three should be considered at high physical risk for alcoholism.

The risk factors in each of the three theoretical models can change. However, the physical risk factors are less likely to change than either the sociological or psychological factors. Physical risk does increase slightly with age because the body's ability to metabolize alcohol deteriorates as a person ages. For example, people over age 65 would need much less alcohol to gain the same effect they received at age 25. Similarly, a physical injury or disease can change the physical risk factor. A person with a liver ailment might become at higher physical risk for alcoholism. Abusing the body with alcohol or drugs can raise the physical risk factor. People who drink heavily for many years may increase their risk.

Who is at low risk? People who answer no to all three questions, people who almost always get sick when they drink too much (unless they are in the advanced stages of alcoholism), and people who never drink alcohol all have a low risk for alcoholism.

## SOCIOCULTURAL THEORIES OF ETIOLOGY AND THE FAMILY

In the previous section, biological or physiological characteristics that make a person a high risk for alcoholism were presented. This section examines the sociological or sociocultural factors that influence alcoholism. Generally, a person's physical capacity to handle alcohol is inherited from parents or grandparents. Social attitudes toward alcohol use result from family orientation. The family has multiple ways of influencing drinking behavior. As with physiological risk factors, parents again are the major contributors to the development of high risk factors for their children in the sociocultural area.

Social factors determine not only whether people will drink but also how people will view themselves after drinking. In a review of a 33-year prospective study of alcoholism, Vaillant and Milofsky (1982) found data suggesting that ethnicity (South European) and the number of alcoholic relatives accounted for most of the variance in adult alcoholism. Other social factors, such as age, sex, religion, socioeconomic class, and family background, have been studied to help explain the diversity in alcoholism rates among different groups of people. Tarter and Schneider (1976) identified 14 variables that affect an individual's decision to start, continue, or stop drinking:

1. childhood exposure to alcohol and drinking models
2. the quantity of alcohol that is considered appropriate or excessive
3. drinking customs
4. type of alcoholic beverage used
5. levels of inhibition considered safe
6. symbolic meaning of alcohol
7. attitude toward public intoxication
8. the social group associated with drinking
9. activities associated with drinking
10. the amount of pressure exerted on the individual to drink and continue drinking
11. use of alcohol in social or private context
12. the individual's mobility in changing drinking reference groups
13. the permanence of
14. and the social rewards or punishments for drinking

The importance of these social variables is largely discounted by the majority of people in the field of alcoholism rehabilitation. This is due in part to the incompatibility of these theories with the predominantly accepted disease model of alcoholism.

One author who has rejected the disease model, primarily due to conclusions based on his research, is Cahalan (1970). In a national survey published in 1970, he concluded that social environment, to a large extent, determines whether an individual will or will not drink. Social/psychological variables also determine the level of drinking maintained. Variables cited by Cahalan include:

- an attitude favorable to drinking
- the amount and type of environmental support for heavy drinking

- the individual's impulsiveness and his or her desire for conformity or nonconformity
- the degree of the individual's alienation and maladjustment
- the individual's expectations for success
- the looseness of social control

To become a problem drinker, Cahalan said, a person must permit heavy drinking under at least some circumstances. The social variables of age, sex, ethnicity, and social position influence the probability of drinking as a dominant response.

Loss of control occurs when the reinforcing effects of alcohol become stronger than the negative effects of the physiological and psychological conditions that follow the termination of drinking. This loss of drinking control is commonly assumed to be caused by alcohol's effect on the brain. The area of the brain that controls inhibition is said to be temporarily inoperative. On the other hand, MacAndrew and Edgerton (1969) came to a different conclusion. By surveying evidence from many diverse societies provided by anthropologists, historians, missionaries, explorers, and other observers, they showed that in many parts of the world drinking is followed by either no change in behavior or a wide variety of changes. The drunken "misconduct" that does take place occurs within socially defined limits.

On this basis, drunken behavior cannot be explained simply as a result of alcohol's effect on the brain. Instead, changes in behavior can be explained on the basis of social definitions of drunkenness as a state of reduced responsibility or of "time out." MacAndrew and Edgerton (1969) argued that excuses are of great importance in all social systems and that drunkenness is one such excuse.

Our personal experiences corroborate somewhat the findings of MacAndrew. We spent five of the past 25 years in England, Holland, Germany, Greece, and Spain and traveled extensively throughout the rest of Europe. The drinking habits of at least eight separate cultures (all different from one another and all very different from the United States) were observed at first hand. European people, in general, seem to have a healthier attitude about drinking than people in the United States. Although drinking seemed to be more thoroughly integrated into social custom and routine, drunkenness was far less acceptable and less evident in these cultures.

Anthropological studies of alcohol use are fascinating. In a study of two distinct groups of Mayan Indians, the Chichicastenango of Guatemala and the Chamula of Mexico, Bunzel (1940) reported that although both of these tribes were hard-drinking and the drinking was sanctioned by the culture, the Chichicastenango experienced guilt and hangovers after each binge while the Chamula did not. It is very important for the family therapist to understand the cultural aspects of drinking for each family.

Myerson (1940) used the term *social ambivalence* in reference to American cultural attitudes toward drinking. He believes that this ambivalence limits the development of the more stable attitudes toward drinking shown in certain other cultures. He further stated that this ambivalence restricts the meaning of drinking to hedonism and insulates drinking practices from social control. Drinking becomes an extreme and uncontrolled form of behavior for many people.

Some observations based on personal experience verify this view. During the five years we spent in Europe, most people observed drunk in public places were American tourists or American military personnel. Stolnick (1958) found alcoholic complications in students from abstinent backgrounds. He stated, "Total abstinence, teaching which imposes and implants a repugnance to drinking and inebriety, tends to identify the act of drinking with personal and social disorganization. This inadvertently suggests inebriety as a pattern of drinking and encourages the behavior it most deplores."

Stolnick suggested that people who become alienated from their abstinence background may use excessive drinking to express their frustration with early familial, religious, and community teachings. Problem drinking is a symbol of revolt against early family values that became overly rigid during adulthood. Again, our personal experience confirms this idea, as a significant number of the more than 1000 people personally seen in treatment during the past 25 years came from homes where at least one parent had a strong religious and moralistic bias against alcohol. However, there is some evidence that a strong religious sanction against alcohol keeps a significant number of people from using alcohol to begin with (Belcastro, 1992).

Some people believe that if drinking were more thoroughly integrated into American social custom and routine, these competing attitudes (abstinence and hedonism) would be neutralized along with alcoholism. To substantiate this position, they refer to the low alcoholism rate among Jews (Lolli, Serianni, Golden, & Luzzatto -Fegiz, 1958) and Italians (Pittman & Snyder, 1962), and the high rate among Irish and Scandinavian groups (Pittman & Snyder, 1962). They point to the high integration of drinking into the Jewish subculture and the negative status drunkenness has for Jews. They also indicate that drinking plays a significant part in Jewish family ritual. By contrast, the Irish male's drinking is disassociated from the church and is also not part of the family's social routine. For Jews, drinking is integrated into the subculture, but for the Irish, it is the subject of ambivalence (Pittman, 1968).

*Hedonism* and *utilitarianism* are terms first used by Bales (1946) to describe what he saw as the major functions that drinking may serve other than religious and ceremonial purposes. Bales proposed that a society that produces acute inner tensions (such as the suppression of aggression, guilt, and sexual tension) and that condones the use of alcohol to relieve those tensions is susceptible to high rates of alcoholism. Bales also listed the collective attitudes toward alcohol that influence drinking practices as follows: (1) abstinence, (2) ritual use connected with religious rites, (3) convivial drinking in a social setting, and (4) utilitarian—the use of drinking for personal, self-interested reasons. These reasons for drinking were thought by Bales to cause most drinking problems for a society.

Bales also cited the degree to which the culture offers alternatives for the release of tension as a significant variable in drinking practices. If there are few alternative means for tension release, more drunkenness will occur.

Because tension is a societal factor in alcoholism, Cloward (1959) focused on the difference between the socially desirable aspirations instilled in an individual and the opportunity that society affords the person to achieve such aspirations. He felt that if the means to meet these goals are not available, the person is likely to retreat into alcoholism. Many other sociocultural theories exist. Merton (1957) postulated that anomie, or normlessness, is brought about by a discrepancy between goals shared by persons in the same society and the means available for achieving them. Deviant behavior (such as alcoholism) results from the strain between perceived goals and the means available to meet them. Similarly, Horman (1979) identified alienation and the depression, nonspecific anxiety, and rebellion that stem from it as key causes of the increase in adolescent drinking in this country. Bacon (1974) believed that alcoholism occurs in any society that combines a lack of indulgence of children with demanding attitudes toward achievement and negative attitudes toward dependent behavior in adults. The low rate of alcoholism among Italians seems to support this theory, but Bacon ignores the much higher rate of alcoholism among the French, despite the similarity of cultures.

In terms of the family, O'Connor (1975) identified eight characteristics that correlate with a low incidence of alcoholism:

1. Children are exposed early to alcohol in family or religious situations.
2. The parents present an example of moderate drinking.
3. The beverages most commonly used contain large amounts of nonalcoholic components.
4. The beverages are viewed mainly as a food and are usually served with meals.
5. No moral importance is attached to drinking.
6. Drinking is not viewed as proof of adulthood or virility.
7. Abstinence, but not excessive drinking or intoxication, is considered socially acceptable.

8. There is virtually complete agreement among group members on standards of drinking behavior.

There are additional sociocultural theories that are not covered here due to practical limitations, although many questions are yet to be answered in this area. For example, why do Native Americans have such a high rate of alcoholism? Is it because they have been drinking a relatively short period of time compared with other groups (300 years compared with, for example, 3000 years for Jews)? Is it because they are caught between two cultures? Or is it a combination of these factors and more? More research will be conducted in this area. The purpose, for now, has been to establish that the sociocultural area is an important factor in the etiology of alcoholism. For interesting and informative readings on the cultural factors in alcoholism see *Journal of Studies on Alcohol*, January 1981, Supplement No. 9. The sociological view, along with the physiological and psychological views, is necessary for a comprehensive theory of alcoholism etiology. It is important for the reader to keep in mind the important role the family plays in each of these areas.

For the sociological area there are five questions that can help establish a client's risk factor. In this format, each question is worth one point. A score of zero is low risk, a score of one or two is medium, and a score of three to five is high risk. The questions are:

1. Do/Did one or both of your parents have strong religious or moral views against drinking alcohol?

    yes + 1 no +0

2. Are either of your parents alcoholic?

    yes + 1 no + 0

3. Do you come from an ethnic background that has a reputation for a high rate of alcoholism?

    yes + 1 no +0

4. Would most people in society consider your friends to be heavy drinkers?

    yes + 1 no + 0

5. Does your social status match your concept of where you feel you should be in society?

    yes + 0 no + 1

Just as in the section on physiological factors, a high risk score does not mean a person is or will become an alcoholic. Many people have high risk scores in this area but never experience drinking problems; they are discussed in chapter 5. For now, this score is to be used with the other two risk scores shown on the chart in Figure 4–1.

The rationale for the questions comes from various researchers and from personal experience. The first question is derived from a combination of the research of Stolnick (1958), mentioned earlier in the chapter, and our personal experiences. Question two was used in the last section and is used again for different reasons. In the last section, the reasons were biological and genetic, but this time they are sociological. A person growing up in an alcoholic home experiences alcoholism as a model for adjustment. By using the question twice in determining risk factors, both nature and nurture, environment and heredity, are accounted for. The psychological ramifications are discussed in the next section.

The third question is open to some interpretation. Some groups are generally accepted as having high rates of alcoholism (for example, Native Americans and Irish Catholics). However, in other groups the distinction is not clear. Many Southern Baptists, for example, do not drink at all, and they are not only low risk but no risk. However, those Southern Baptists who do drink have a higher rate of alcoholism than the population in general. If you cannot determine an answer to this question, ask as many people as you can who you do not know and who are not from your client's ethnic group and go with the consensus.

Question four is also open to interpretation. If a client drinks a case and a half of beer a day and his friends only drink a case, he might not consider them heavy drinkers. However, if a client drinks a case and a half a day, put the book down and refer him to the nearest treatment center—and take his friends along. Seriously, opinions vary as to what constitutes heavy drinking. For example, people from both coasts drink somewhat more than those in other parts of the country. When asking this question, the regional norm should be taken into consideration. Three drinks a day might seem normal in New York or San Francisco, but that amount may be considered excessive in Iowa or Oklahoma.

If the client has reached the point in his drinking where he no longer has friends and only drinks alone, forget about the questions and give him checkmarks in the high risk category.

The fifth and final question might be the most difficult to answer objectively. Some people of very low social status in this country may feel as if that's where they belong. On the other hand, some high-status people do not feel comfortable and would prefer to be in a lower position. These dynamics are difficult to understand, and cognitive dissonance and association theories complicate the matter (for a discussion of these see a recent social psychology text). In order to determine a risk factor if the question is too difficult for the client to answer, the question "Are you happy with your life?" can be substituted (yes +0, no +1). However, many alcoholics may answer "yes, I'm happy" during sobriety and "no, I'm not happy" when drunk or vice versa.

Sociological theories of the etiology of alcoholism are not foolproof. Even the low rates of alcoholism for Jews have become suspect (Blume, 1978). However, they do fill in some pieces of the puzzle, and the next section on psychological theories of etiology will fill in the puzzle even more. Finally, chapter 5 will address some important questions about the treatment and prevention of alcoholism.

## PSYCHOLOGICAL THEORIES OF ETIOLOGY AND THE FAMILY

The previous two sections discussed the sociological and physiological theories of the etiology of alcoholism. Although these areas are important, the most important area, in terms of treatment and prevention, appears to be the psychological area. Some say it is the personality of the individual that has more to do with the way he or she deals with the environment than any other factor. This section examines the psychological causes of alcoholism and shows a relationship between the family and psychological risk for alcoholism. The original research in the psychological aspect of alcoholism attempted to answer the question "What causes people to become dependent on alcohol?" This question proved much too broad, and an alternate question took its place: "How do alcoholics differ from the population in general?"

Much of the literature on personality types combined all substance abuse and in some cases compulsive behaviors as well (Esterly & Neely, 1997). There does not seem to be a specific personality typology of the "addictive personality." However, some characteristics help to understand addictive behavior. For alcoholics, characteristics such as dependency, denial, depression, superficial sociability, emotional instability, suspiciousness, low tolerance for frustration, impulsivity, self-devaluation, and chronic anxiety occur with high frequency. Kaufman (1994) believed that there are "addictive personalities" that have common personality traits, symptoms, and psychodynamic factors that occur in clusters. These individuals can and often do become addicted to almost anything, from drugs, including alcohol, to food, jogging, and even high-risk behaviors like gambling and skydiving.

Gross and Adler (1970) reported that 266 male alcoholics tested on the 16PF personality inventory showed traits that differentiated them from the general population, with significant differences on 12 of the 16 personality traits assessed. Jones (1968) identified adult problem drinkers as being uncontrolled, impulsive, and rebellious.

The problem with these studies is that they leave several important questions unanswered. For example, does excessive drinking cause these personality traits, or do the personality traits cause the drinking? Furthermore, a considerable number of problem drinkers do not possess these traits, and many people who do have them are not problem drinkers. In another study, Robins (1966) found that, as adults, alcoholics closely resemble sociopaths, even though nonalcoholic sociopaths may have many of the same personality characteristics. Robins also found evidence that the childhoods of alcoholics resembled the childhoods of sociopaths. The difference between the two groups may lie in the sociological and physiological areas of risk. The sociopath becomes the person who shows up as high risk in the psychological area but low risk in the other two areas. Again, for a complete picture of the individual, all three of the risk areas must be considered.

Alcoholism is apparently caused not by a single factor but by many complicated interrelated factors. Seven factors have been identified that differentiate those who abuse alcohol from those who do not. The characteristics show the difference between the low-risk person and the high-risk person in the psychological area of the etiology of alcoholism, and they all involve the family. Not limited to alcoholism, these factors also predict success in a variety of other areas.

As presented by Glenn (1981) at a prevention seminar, the characteristics of high-risk people are:

1. Low identification with viable role models, which refers to a person's self-concept and reference group (family). Persons who are vulnerable in this area see themselves as different from people whose attitudes, values, and behaviors allow them to function and "survive" in their total environment. For instance, a child might not relate to his or her family and may reject their values.

2. Low identification with and responsibility for "family" process. In this instance, people do not identify strongly with things greater than themselves (e.g., relationships with other people, groups, humankind, or God). They also do not see how this behavior affects others. This process refers to shared investments in outcomes, shared responsibility for achieving outcomes, and accountability to others.

3. High faith in "miracle" solutions to problems. This area involves the skills and attitudes necessary to work through problems and includes the belief that problems can be solved through application of personal resources. When these skills are poorly developed, people believe that problems have been escaped when they cannot feel them (involving the use of drugs and alcohol, for example). These individuals do not believe that there is any way to affect the present or future—things just happen. (The role parents play in fostering this attitude is discussed later in this section.)

4. Inadequate intrapersonal skills. This area includes the skills of self-discipline, self-control, and self-assessment. Weakness in these areas shows up as

inability to cope with personal stresses and tensions, dishonesty with self, denial of self, and the inability to defer gratification.

5. Inadequate interpersonal skills. These skills involve communication, cooperation, negotiation, empathy, listening, and sharing. Poor performance in this area shows up as dishonesty with others, a lack of empathetic awareness, resistance to feedback, unwillingness to share feelings, or the inability to give or receive love or help.

6. Inadequate systemic skills. This area involves the ability to respond to the limits inherent in a situation (responsibility) and the ability to constructively adapt behavior to a situation in order to get needs met (adaptability). Irresponsibility, refusal to accept consequences of behavior, and scapegoating are all expressed when there is a weakness in this area.

7. Inadequate judgment skills. This area includes the ability to recognize, understand, and apply appropriate meanings to relationships. Weaknesses in judgment are expressed as crises in sexual, natural, consumer, and drug and alcohol environments and as repetitive self-destructive behavior.

The person who is successful in life and is unlikely to abuse alcohol or drugs has well-developed skills in these areas.

Successful individuals tend to identify with viable role models and take responsibility within the family. They have problem-solving abilities and strong intrapersonal and interpersonal skills. They are skilled at working within "the system" and have good judgment. The remainder of this section looks at the role of the family in thwarting the development of these traits in the individual.

The parents play the most important part in a child's early development. In our experience, there are four major problem parent types. Each alcoholic almost always has one or both parents in one or more of the categories. We presented this theory to perhaps 1000 alcoholics who were students or workshop participants. Only one person indicated that her parents did not fit this scheme. The theory has had virtually unanimous support. However, many people who are not alcoholic also have parents who fit into one or more of these categories. In these cases, the other two risk categories become useful.

The four parent types are: (1) alcoholic, (2) teetotaler, (3) overdemanding, and (4) overprotective.

## The Alcoholic Parent

Alcoholic parents foster alcoholism in their offspring in many ways. Probably the single most important factor is modeling. Children learn acceptable behavior by watching those around them. If a parent deals with problems through alcohol, the child learns that drinking is an option.

Even if the child is initially repulsed by parental drinking behavior, abusive drinking is a possibility for him or her. A child may say to himself, "I will never drink like Daddy," only to find himself later in life doing just that. Some people feel that sons become alcoholic to say to their parents, "See, I love you; I'm just like you." Many daughters of alcoholics marry alcoholics. They essentially are saying, "See Daddy, I love you. I married someone just like you" (Hoffman, 1979). Both of these reactions come from feelings of being unloved and neglected as children and, perhaps, from guilt about a parent's drinking. A child often feels responsible for a parent's drinking or for a poor relationship between parents. The child may reason that "if only I had been good or if only I had kept my room clean, Daddy would not have hit Mommy." Unfortunately, treatment for the alcoholic often heightens the guilt experienced by children. The child may hate Daddy because of his drinking behavior. When the child hears that Daddy didn't mean it and that Daddy has a disease, the child may feel guilty for hating a "sick" person who "couldn't help it." Unless the family is treated concurrently with the alcoholic, the children may not be better off than they were before the parent's treatment. They may worry constantly about what will happen when Daddy gets sick again, or they may continue to feel guilty about hating a sick person.

In addition, the alcoholic parent is in no position to promote general mental health and development in his or her children. It is understandable that alcoholics, in their uncomfortable, guilt-ridden, and anesthetized state, are unable to establish a loving and meaningful relationship with their children. The alcoholic is usually self-centered and self-occupied. Children similarly cannot turn to the spouse of the alcoholic for attention, because he or she is often too overcome with anger, frustration, and futility to be of any comfort.

Many other factors account for the psychological trauma that leads children of alcoholics to become alcoholics themselves. The disruption of important family rituals (e.g., holidays, dinnertime, weekends, vacations) due to drinking has serious implications. In families where rituals were maintained despite alcoholism, recurrence of alcoholism in children was low compared with high alcoholism rates in children from families that did not maintain rituals (Wolin, Bennett, Noonan, & Teitelbaum, 1977).

Whatever the reason, children of alcoholics often are weak in major areas of psychological functioning, and they often have very poor self-images. These problems will not necessarily be resolved just because a parent has entered treatment. The entire family also needs treatment.

## The Teetotaler Parent

The next parent type that shows up often among the parents of alcoholics is the teetotaler. The term *teetotaler* in this context is not implied to mean merely a person who has chosen not to drink—it refers to a person who chooses not to drink and condemns those who make a different choice. For some reason, usually moral or religious, the teetotaler feels that all drinking is immoral and indecent. The contrast to a teetotaler is a person who merely chooses not to drink but does not condemn the drinking of others. The last section presented the teetotaler parent in the sociological perspective; here, the teetotaler parent is addressed in terms of the psychological outcome of the children.

The psychological effects on a child who grows up in a home in which one or both parents are teetotalers or one parent is a teetotaler and the other parent is alcoholic are rarely positive.

One of the problems with parents who have a rigid stance against alcohol is that they also tend to have a rigid, moralistic approach to life. Problems are presented to children with right and wrong, black and white answers. The children grow up with the words *shouldn't* and *should* ringing in their ears. They learn that parents, teachers, ministers, and others in positions of authority have all the right answers and that there is a right and a wrong position on every issue. They become intolerant of any but their own viewpoints. When they are presented with life problems that do not have right and wrong answers, their rigid stance only causes difficulties. Living in a world of gray with only a black and white rule book can be a trying experience (e.g., Rush Limbaugh). This approach to life is similarly detrimental for people associated with this person.

In short, the teetotaler parent gives the child a set of rules and expectations that is inconsistent with basic human needs and impossible to live by. In turn, the child has the perfect opportunity to graphically show contempt for these rules by abusing alcohol, usually during adolescence or early adulthood. Basically, the individual says to his or her parents, "How dare you give me rules that are impossible to live by. I reject your rules, and I reject you as my parent. To make sure you understand this, I will abuse alcohol to the point that you cannot ignore it. I will become alcoholic." To complicate matters, this person usually has a low self-image due to guilt about not being able to live up to the parents' expectations. This last example crosses into the "overdemanding parent" type. However, it is not unusual for one parent type to show the tendencies of another. The overdemanding parent, for example, comes in several forms.

**The Overdemanding Parent**

The most common type of overdemanding parents makes it quite clear to the child what it is they expect, but these expectations are generally unrealistic. It is not uncommon for a child to excel in one area (e.g., math, sports, spelling, or social skills), but very few excel in all areas. Many do not excel in any area. Often, when the parents ask a great deal from their children, they are living vicariously through them. These parents may be heard to say something like "By damn, I never had a chance to go to college, so you're going to go." Parents who choose career fields for their children often fit into this category. "You're going to be a doctor!" It's only natural for parents to want the best for their children, and no parent wants his or her child to make the same mistakes he or she did. Such overdemanding parents often do not cause serious psychological problems unless their expectations are extreme.

The overdemanding parent likely to have a son or daughter with a problem models a high degree of success. These parents inadvertently place high expectations on their offspring even if their only wish for their children is that they be happy. The parents' own achievement level makes it impossible for their children to develop a positive self-image when comparing themselves with parents who are extremely successful. Often, these parents achieve success at the expense of the family. Children find it hard to feel good about themselves when parents seem to care more about their career than about them. This is often a tragic situation because the parents may truly believe they are working extra hard so the family can benefit financially and otherwise.

*Siblings and Spouses*

This phenomenon is not limited to children and parents. Brothers and sisters may compare themselves with one another; often, there is a brother-to-brother or sister-to-sister competition. But family rivalry does not stop there. Mom can compare herself with Dad or Dad with Mom—the dynamics and the results are the same. When people compare themselves with someone they see as "better," they perceive themselves as less than they want to be or should be, and their self-image suffers as a consequence. Alcoholism and drug abuse are not always the solution for these people; sometimes they inadvertently choose to commit suicide or become mentally ill. The large number of sons and daughters of movie stars who have these problems graphically shows these dynamics at work. Similarly, an example of brother-to-brother rivalry is shown in the relationships of President Clinton and his brother Roger and of Jimmy and Billy Carter. Examples of husband-and-wife conflict involving alcoholism or substance abuse can be seen in the relationship of Betty and Gerald Ford and Joan and Edward Kennedy and Michael and Kitty Dukakis.

Of course, many other factors are also involved. Human behavior is complex; very few behaviors are simple to justify or explain. There may be hundreds of reasons why people become alcoholic, but the ones mentioned here seem to be very important, based on research and personal experience. The one person, mentioned earlier in the section, whose parents did not fit into any of these categories described her parents this way: "My parents were not alcoholic; they drank moderately. They were not teetotalers, and they were not overly protective or overly demanding. In fact," she said, "they were perfect parents." Someone in the class pointed out that it must have been hard to live up to "perfect parents," and she got the point.

## Overly Protective Parents

The final parent type is overly protective. The dynamics here are complex, but the outcome is simple. The child never gets a chance to develop a sense of self-worth and a positive self-image. After a childhood and adolescence of being taken care of it is very difficult to handle life's problems because there has been no chance to practice.

Three of the possible dynamics here include, first, the parent or parents who are overinvested in their children. Too much of their own self-worth and ego needs are met through the children. Second, the parent or parents may be suffering from a reaction formation. They may have some doubts about if they even really like their children. This thought is so unacceptable that they react by showing their children, as well as the rest of the world, how much they care through their overprotective behavior. Third, and perhaps most common, is a parent who had a particularly bad childhood, such as growing up with an abusive alcoholic parent, and tries to protect his own children from anything bad, even the natural developmental hurdles involved in growing up. Again, children in these families have little chance to grow up and develop coping skills or the sense of self-worth that comes from being self-sufficient.

The common element among all of these parent types is that their children do not develop a positive sense of self-worth. In many cases, children are not exposed to a sufficient number of life's problems to prove to themselves that they can succeed or can fail without falling apart. They fail to learn to adjust to their environment when necessary and very often have low interpersonal communication skills. This is not an indictment of parents. Parents do not cause alcoholism, although they do have a hand in its development. But blaming parents for alcoholism is an exercise in futility. If someone must bear the blame it should be the cultural system that fails to teach parents how to parent effectively.

Six questions determine high, medium, and low risk for alcoholism in the psychological area. A positive answer to any item could indicate a high psychological risk for alcoholism. But, as in the last section, number values have been assigned to answers. To be high risk on this scale requires a score of five to six. Medium risk is three to four, and low risk is one to two. The questions are:

1. Did you have a parent who was alcoholic or chemically dependent?
   yes + 1 no +0
2. Were one or both of your parents teetotalers as described in this section?
   yes + 1 no + 0
3. In your opinion, were your parents overly protective of you?
   yes + 1 no +0
4. Were your parents, in your opinion, overdemanding of you, in words or deeds?
   yes + 1 no + 0
5. Do you have something to do in life that makes you feel worthwhile (e.g., a job, a hobby)?
   yes + 0 no +1
6. Do you have someone who loves you and someone you love?
   yes + 0 no +1

Although the first two questions were used in the last section on sociological reasons for alcoholism, they are also used here because of their psychological ramifications. Questions three and four address overly protective and demanding parent types. It is possible to score one point for each type. For example, the person who had an overprotective mother and an overdemanding father would score a point for each. The final two questions come from the writings of William Glasser, founder of the Reality Therapy Institute, who believes that successful people must have someone who loves them and someone they love, as well as something they feel is worthwhile to do.

In an abbreviated version of this process, simply ask "How do you rate yourself compared with others?" The risk factor is inverse to self-image. Figure 4–2 presents a way to picture this.

Now that the importance of each of the three risk areas is established, it is time to determine what all this means in terms of the treatment and prevention of alcoholism. What good does it do to know that alcoholism is caused by factors falling into either physiological, sociological, or psychological areas? These and other questions are answered in chapter 5.

---

**REFERENCES**

Bacon, M.K. (1974). The dependency-conflict hypothesis and the frequency of drunkenness. *Quarterly Journal of Studies on Alcohol, 35,* 863–876.

Bales, R. (1946). Cultural differences in rates of alcoholism. *Quarterly Journal of Studies on Alcohol, 6,* 480–499.

Belcastro, P.A. (1992). Pedagogical patronizing of the pharmacodynamic promises of illicit drugs. *Journal of Drug Education, 22*(1), 9–13.

Blume, S. (1978). Jews shown not to be immune to alcoholism. *NIAAA Information and Feature Service,* HEW, September 20.

Bunzel, A. (1940). The role of alcoholism in two Central American cultures. *Psychiatry, 3,* 361–387.

Cahalan, D. (1970). *Problem drinkers: A national survey.* San Francisco: Jossey-Bass.

Cloninger, C.R. (1987). Neurogenetic mechanisims in alcoholism. *Science, 236,* 410–416.

Cloninger, C.R., Bohman, M., & Sigvardsson, S. (1981). Inheritance of alcohol abuse: Cross-fostering analysis of alcoholic men. *Archives of General Psychiatry, 38,* 861–868.

Cloward, R. (1959). Illegitimate means, anomie and deviate behavior. *American Sociological Review, 24,* 164–176.

Cotton, N.S. (1979). The familial incidence of alcoholism: A review. *Journal of Studies on Alcohol, 46*(1), 17–34.

Davis, V.E., & Walsh, M.J. (1970). Alcohol, amines, and alkaloids: A possible biochemical basis for alcohol addiction. *Science, 167,* 1005–1007.

Drew, L.R.H., Moon, J.R., & Buchanan, F.H. (1981). *Alcoholism: A handbook.* Melbourne, Australia: Heinemann Health Books.

Esterly, R.W., & Neely, W.T. (1997). *Chemical dependency and compulsive behaviors.* Mahwah, NJ: Lawrence Erlbaum Associates.

Glenn, S. (1981, February). *Directions for the 80's.* Paper presented at the Nebraska Prevention Center, Omaha.

Goodwin, D.W. (1971). Is alcoholism hereditary? *Archives of General Psychiatry, 25,* 518–545.

Goodwin, D. W. (1974). Drinking problems in adopted and nonadopted sons of alcoholics. *Report submitted to the National Institute on Alcohol Abuse and Alcoholism,* January 15.

Goodwin, D.W. (1981). Family studies on alcoholism. *Journal of Studies on Alcohol, 42*(1).

Goodwin, D.W. (1988). *Is alcoholism hereditary?* New York: Ballantine Books.

Goodwin, D.W., Schlosinger, F., Hermansen, L., Guze, S.B., & Winaker, G. (1973). Alcoholism problems in adoptees reared apart from alcoholic biological parents. *Archives of General Psychiatry, 28,* 238–243.

Gross, W.F., & Adler, L.O. (1970). Aspects of alcoholics' self-concepts as measured by the Tennessee self-concept scale. *Psychological Reports, 27,* 431–434.

Hoffman, B. (1979). *No one is to blame.* Palo Alto, CA: Dutton.

Horman, R.E. (1979). The impact of sociological systems on teenage alcohol abuse in youth alcohol and social policy. In H.T. Blane & M.E. Chafetz (Eds.), *Youth, alcohol and social policy.* New York: Plenum Press.

Jones, M.C. (1968). Personality correlates and antecedents of drinking patterns in adult males. *Journal of Consulting and Clinical Psychology, 32*, 2–12.

Kaij, L. (1960). *Studies on the etiology and sequels of abuse of alcohol.* Lund, Sweden: Department of Psychiatry, University of Lund.

Kaufman, E. (1994). *Psychotherapy with addicted persons.* New York: Gilford Press.

Lindsey, G., Loehlin, I., Monosevitz, M., & Thiessen, P. (1971). *Annual Review of Psychology, 22*, 39.

Lolli, G.S., Serianni, E., Golden, G., & Luzzatto-Fegiz, P. (1958). *Alcohol in Italian culture.* Glencoe, IL: Free Press.

MacAndrew, C., & Edgerton, R.B. (1969). *Drunken comportment: A social explanation.* Chicago: Aldins.

McClearn, G.E. (1970). *Annual Review of Genetics, 4*, 437.

Merton, R.K. (1957). *Social theory and social structure.* New York: Free Press.

Myerson, A. (1940). Alcohol: A study of social ambivalence. *Quarterly Journal of Studies on Alcohol, 1*.

O'Connor, J. (1975). Social and cultural factors influencing drinking. *Irish Journal of Medical Science, June*, 65–71.

Partanen, J., Bruun, K., & Markkanen, T. (1966). *Inheritance of drinking behavior.* New Brunswick, NJ: Rutgers Center for Alcohol Studies.

Pittman, D.J. (1968). Drinking and alcoholism in American society. In R.J. Catanzaro (Ed.), *Alcoholism: The total treatment approach.* Springfield, IL: Charles C. Thomas.

Pittman, D.G., & Snyder, C.R. (Eds.). (1962). *Society, culture and drinking patterns.* New York: Wiley.

Robins, L.N. (1966). *Deviant children grown up: A sociological and psychiatric study of sociopathic personality.* Baltimore: Williams & Wilkins.

Schuckit, M.A. (1985). Ethanol-induced changes in body sway in men at high alcoholism risk. *Archives of General Psychiatry, 42*, 375–379.

Schuckit, M.A., & Gold, F.O. (1988). A simultanous evaluation of multiple markers of ethanol and placebo challenges in sons of alcoholics and controls. *Archives of General Psychiatry, 45*, 211–216.

Schuckit, M.A., Goodwin, D.W., & Winakur, G. (1972). *Life history research in psychopathology.* Minneapolis, MN: University of Minnesota Press.

Searles, J.S. (1991). The genetics of alcoholism: Impact on family and sociological models of addiction. *Family Dynamics of Addiction Quarterly, 1*(1), 8–21.

Stolnick, J.H. (1958). Religious affiliation and drinking behavior. *Quarterly Journal of Studies on Alcohol, 19*, 452–470.

Swan, G., Carmelli, D., & Cardon. (1996). The consumption of tobacco, alcohol, and coffee in caucasian male twins: A multivariate genetic analysis. *Journal of Substance Abuse, 8*(1), 19–31.

Tarter, R.E., & Schneider, D.V. (1976). Models and theories of alcoholism. In R.E. Tarter & A.A. Sugleman (Eds.), *Alcoholism: Interdisciplinary approaches to an enduring problem.* Reading, MA: Addison-Wesley.

Vaillant, G.E., and Milofsky, E.S. (1982). The etiology of alcoholism: A prospective viewpoint. *American Psychologist, 37*(5), 494–503.

Williams, R.J. (1959). Biochemical individuality and cellular nutrition: Prime factors in alcoholism. *Quarterly Journal of Studies on Alcohol, 20*, 452–463.

Wolin, S., Bennett, L., Noonan, D., & Teitelbaum, M. (Study conducted from 1974 to 1977). *Families at risk: The intergenerational recurrence of alcoholism.* National Institute of Alcohol Abuse and Alcoholism Grant #2 R01 AA 01 454.

# CHAPTER 5

# The Relevance of Etiology for Treatment and Prevention

Designing a treatment or prevention program for alcoholism without a thorough understanding of its etiology is like taking a trip without a map. You may or may not arrive at your destination, and if you do arrive, you may not be sure whether you took the shortest route or even how you got there. The fields of mental health and medicine often recognize an illness or a disease before its cause is discovered or a treatment is developed. Very rarely is an effective treatment developed before the cause is known. In medicine, the cause of an illness is often limited to a single factor, such as a germ, a virus, a genetic predisposition, perhaps a vitamin deficiency or an environmental hazard. In mental health, illnesses are often multicausal. Depression, for example, can have many causes, including environmental or cultural factors (some cultures have a much higher rate of depression than others), a biological predisposition (depression runs in families), and psychological makeup of the individuals. Conditions with several causal factors are often perplexing to treatment personnel. Treatment approaches are developed by different branches of the same profession. Cancer, for example, may be treated with chemotherapy, radiation therapy, or surgery. Physicians and patients unsure of the outcome of these treatments may use them in combination. This multimodality treatment is often used for conditions whose causes are unclear.

Another way to approach treatment is by trial and error. When an effort relieves major symptoms it becomes accepted by everyone as "the way" to treat that disorder. Many psychotropic drugs were discovered in this manner. A drug's side effect for one disorder may become a treatment effect in another disorder. For example, a common antidepressant has the side effect of urinary retention, so physicians began to give it to children who wet the bed. On scientific investigation, however, some of these hit-or-miss approaches prove to be counterproductive in the long run. For example, for many years milk or dairy products were taken by people with ulcers in an attempt to reduce acid in the stomach, thus reducing the pain of the ulcer. Later, findings indicated that long after the antacid effect of milk wears off, the calcium left in the stomach causes an increase in acidity levels and makes the use of milk counterproductive. However, because milk seems to reduce pain, many people continue to use it for ulcers. More recently, a virus rather than acid levels has been suspected of causing ulcers, which sheds a whole new light on what an appropriate treatment should be.

Although the actual causes of alcoholism are unknown, most experts agree that there are many causes, not just one or two. Research and observation lead to the conclusion that three main factors must be considered regarding the etiology of alcoholism—physiological, sociological, and psychological factors. Knowledge about the causes of alcoholism must be used to bridge the gaps between research, treatment, and prevention.

The primary line of thinking in the past was that alcoholism is a disease. Although the cause is unknown and the disease is incurable, it can be arrested if the alcoholic stops drinking. According to this concept, the most effective way for the alcoholic to give up drinking is through the fellowship of Alcoholics Anonymous (AA). The utility of the disease concept of alcoholism has often been either questioned or supported in the literature (Levin, 1995; Walters, 1992; Peele and Brodsky, 1991; Fingarette, 1990; Vogler & Bartz, 1982). We choose not to take sides and to accept whatever way patients and their family choose to frame alcoholism.

The disease model of alcoholism poses interesting problems. For example, the only people who can be accepted for treatment and who can successfully complete it are those willing to give up alcohol completely for the rest of their lives. What if Masters and Johnson ran a sex clinic and required, as a criterion for admission, that clients abstain from sex altogether? The implication would be that sex itself is the problem, and if people abstain from sex they will have no difficulties with it. Many people believe that alcohol itself is the problem and that, if the client or patient gives up drinking, the problem will be resolved. Unfortunately, in most cases, this is not true. In fact, it is possible for an individual to have lifelong alcohol-related problems even if that person doesn't drink. Many children of alcoholics suffer their entire lives because of their parents' alcoholism. People can have alcohol problems without drinking, just as they can have sexual problems without having sex.

When alcohol consumption is seen as the major concern in treatment, the issue of denial becomes a problem. Denial is considered a primary symptom of alcoholism, and a good part of many treatment programs is spent in breaking down the alcoholic's denial. The irony here is that almost anyone can be considered an alcoholic when asked if drinking causes a problem. If people say "yes," they are alcoholic, and if they say "no," they are denying alcoholism. With this philosophy, it is not difficult to keep inpatient alcoholism treatment beds full.

However, because of this approach to diagnosis and treatment many inpatient treatment programs have been shut down under the scrutiny of managed care. Also, many early cases of problem drinking are unidentified. People who could return to nonproblem drinking, as suggested by Miller and Munoz (1982), are never given a chance to reach this goal. If they do reach it, the alcoholism rehabilitation community may simply discount the successful effort by considering the person a nonalcoholic or predict that problem drinking will, in time, return, which it may or may not.

Of course, in some cases, denial is a serious issue for the alcoholic in treatment. However, the denial that exists among those who work in the field of alcoholism is a far more serious problem. Practitioners deny that they know enough about the causes of alcoholism to plan successful treatment programs for problem drinkers who refuse to take a vow of lifetime abstinence. They deny that a person who drinks half the amount that they did before they came to treatment is better off than before. They deny that most often it is the behavior of the alcoholic that causes the problem and that there is not always a direct relationship between drinking and problematic behavior. They deny that there are many types of alcoholism and that some people may respond to treatment approaches other than AA. Similarly, they deny that alcoholism may not truly be a disease but a complicated condition caused by physiological, sociological, and psychological factors. Finally, alcoholism treatment personnel may deny the role that the family plays in the etiology of alcoholism, that the family members should be treated, not just educated, and that alcoholism can be *prevented* by recognizing its etiology.

Treating all alcoholics and all alcoholism the same is like prescribing castor oil for all stomachaches. Although some stomach problems will respond and improve, many will not. Some believe that as many as 10 million people have responded to AA and have improved (1994 Congressional hearings on alcoholism), but there are many millions of alcoholics and problem drinkers in the United States and not all are responding to AA, or total abstinence. We estimate that only about one out of 10 alcoholics or problem drinkers is being helped through AA.

If the standard procedure for a stomachache was exploratory surgery, many people would put off seeking help for their stomachaches until they could not function because of the pain. Many people put off seeking help for their alcohol problems because they see the treatment (total abstinence) as worse than the pain they are experiencing when they use alcohol. Treatment programs tend to promote this attitude because of the two major premises underlying the therapeutic approach to alcoholism: (1) excessive drinking is maladaptive, and (2) there are ultimate causes that lead to alcoholism. These concepts cause therapists to use uniform treatment techniques for all alcoholics and to focus attention on the maladaptive behavior. Such attempts often lead to short-term improvement, but relapse is likely in the long term, leading to frustration for both the alcoholic and the therapist. Each alcoholic or problem drinker presents unique challenges. Each requires an individually tailored treatment plan based the drinker's unique biochemistry, personality, family history, and current situation (Esterly & Neely, 1997).

The focus should be on the adaptive consequences that reinforce drinking. People drink inappropriately or behave inappropriately under the influence of alcohol for definite reasons. For example, some people may not feel comfortable having sex without being under the influence of alcohol. If they give up drinking they think they will also have to give up sex. For the purposes of treatment and prevention, it is important to determine how drinking and behavior under the influence of alcohol serves an adaptive function in individual and in the family. Therapy should then be structured around helping the alcoholic to manifest necessary behaviors while sober as well as to learn alternative behaviors for the inappropriate drunken behavior. In many cases, these results are most effectively achieved through family therapy.

AA is a wonderful program for those who accept it, but many people who need treatment find AA unacceptable. Sample cases are presented to show why AA works for some alcoholics and not for others. These cases indicate how an understanding of etiology can help determine a treatment approach.

Suppose Individual A, a person in treatment, has answered high and low risk questions as presented in chapter 4. Also consider that they have risk levels as shown in Figure 5–1. The treatment task then involves moving the person down on the risk chart where possible. Not much can be done in the physiological area, except to prescribe Antabuse and medical aid. In this hypothetical case, the individual has refused this form of treatment, and so the two other risk levels must be reduced.

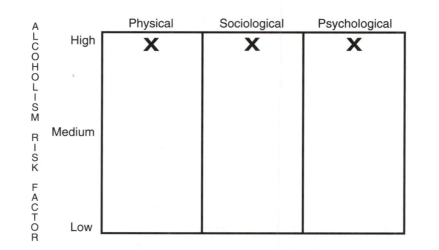

**Figure 5–1** Alcoholism Risk Factors for Individual A.

For this person, AA can reduce both risk levels. In the sociological area, AA removes this person from a circle of friends who abuse alcohol and places him among friends, fellow AA members, who all have a desire to quit drinking. This moves the person from a high to a low risk level in the sociological area.

In the psychological risk area, the person's self-image must be improved. The individual needs someone to love and someone who loves him, and he must feel he has something worthwhile to contribute so his self-image will improve. From the moment the person walks into the AA meeting, the feeling that "I'm not alone with this problem" begins to improve his self-image. Later, as this person becomes more involved in the program and experiences successes, he feels even better about himself. The individual finds support when he gets a sponsor who is available 24 hours a day. Between meetings and the relationship with the sponsor the individual has a chance to develop positive relationships, something that may have been missing in his life. The final push toward a genuine feeling of self-worth comes when the individual begins to do 12-step work and helps others with their alcohol problems. Many recovering alcoholics find this activity so rewarding that they become full-time alcoholism counselors, sometimes at a salary scale lower than their previous employment.

The results of Individual A's contact with AA are shown in Figure 5–2. All effective treatment and prevention programs generally bring about the results illustrated in this exhibit. However, these risk levels cannot be changed in a matter of minutes. Permanent changes take a great deal of effort on the part of the individual and perhaps carefully planned treatment on the part of the therapist.

In some cases, AA may be antithetical to rehabilitation. The individual in such a case may have a profile similar to Individual B in Figure 5–3.

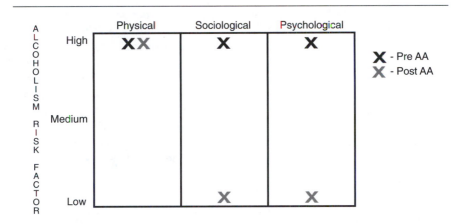

**Figure 5–2** Effect of AA on Alcoholism Risk Factors for Individual A.

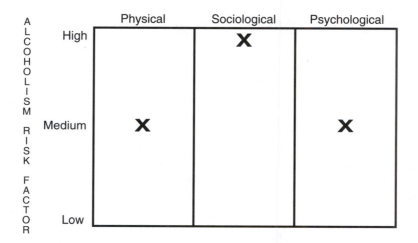

**Figure 5–3** Alcoholism Risk Factors for Individual B.

This person is from a social subgroup that drinks a great deal. She has self-esteem that could be improved but could also be worse. Therefore, this person is approximately in the middle of the psychological risk area. Suppose this person received a citation for driving under the influence of alcohol, and part of the court's recommendation included participation in AA. At the first meeting, this person sees no one with whom to identify. Most members are older, and the individual drinking histories that are recounted by the members sound nothing like this person's drinking pattern. As a result, this person's self-image begins to drop, and she may think "Can my drinking really be as bad as these people's?" After the AA meeting this person meets friends at a bar, and they end up drinking, which causes guilt and more self-doubt. After the AA experience, the individual's psychological risk level may increase as shown in Figure 5–4. This result may explain why many people do not return to AA and many never go initially.

Other interesting case histories provide insights into the dynamics of alcoholism. The risk profile of a woman, Individual C, is shown prior to her alcoholism in Figure 5–5. Because her father was alcoholic, she was at high risk physiologically. Socially, she was at medium risk because, although most of her friends drank, none abused alcohol openly. Psychologically, she was at medium to low risk because of her high self-esteem that came almost solely as a result of her role as a mother. Most of her positive self-image came from being needed by her children.

Shortly after her last child left home her risk factor chart looked like Figure 5–6. Her sociological risk factor changed because she began to drink alone and was no longer subject to the controls of her social group. Psychologically, her self-image deteriorated when she was no longer needed by her children, and her

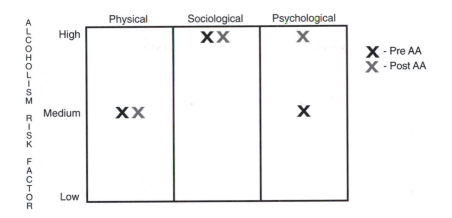

**Figure 5–4** Effect of AA on Alcoholism Risk Factors for Individual B.

husband was no help because he had always been independent. Treatment for her involved altering her environment to help make her feel needed. In this case, the goal was accomplished when she became an alcoholism counselor. If this problem had not been solved, her treatment would have been unsuccessful.

This example indicates that there are two distinct types of alcoholics. For simplicity's sake, they will be referred to as Type A and Type B. The Type A alcoholic never had a positive self-image due to a family background that restricted this person's psychological development. Such a person may say "I was alcoholic from my first drink." The profile of a Type A alcoholic is shown in Figure 5–7.

Adolescents often fall into this category. They never develop a positive self-image, and alcohol helps them cope with the resulting pain and anxiety. Treatment initially focuses on building their self-image from scratch and is often more difficult than working with the Type B alcoholic, who at one time had a positive self-image. In order to determine why the Type A alcoholic's self-image is so poor, it is often useful to examine the role this person played in his or her family of origin. Examine how his parents treated him while he was growing up. Sometimes, if clients understand how they were controlled by a situation, they can break the hold of the past. The therapist should help patients understand how sometimes their problems are a natural consequence of early life experiences. A person may say, "I am no longer going to let my overdemanding mother or overprotective father make me feel bad about myself." This is a significant beginning for successful treatment. However, if the client is an adolescent and must return to the family, it is imperative that the entire family receive treatment. In fact, there are very few cases in which family therapy is not useful with alcoholic clients and their families.

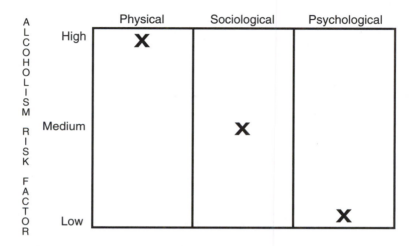

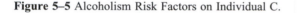

**Figure 5–5** Alcoholism Risk Factors on Individual C.

Type B alcoholics at one time in their lives had positive self-images. The role of the therapist is to reestablish these alcoholics' sense of worth. The following is a case example of a Type B alcoholic. Originally from a small town, this man played football in high school and was popular with his peers. Even though there was drinking in his high school, he did not partake because the coach said anyone caught drinking would be kicked off the team. In college, he also had a positive self-image because of his achievements in sports, and he was at low risk for alcoholism in all areas. When he left college, he joined the Air Force and went to pilot training. He began to drink but with no significant problems. During his 10-year career in the Air Force, he became a major, a fighter pilot, a husband, and the father of two children. All experiences kept his self-image high, although he did eventually drink regularly, as is the custom among many military personnel.

He subsequently left the Air Force, hoping for a job that would provide more time with his family. The job market was not what he expected; the only position he could obtain was as a traveling salesman. He spent four nights each week on the road, and he made less money than he had as a pilot. After six months or so, he began a pattern of sitting in his motel room each night watching television after visiting the bar for a few drinks. His sales were not good, and he started drinking more to cope with discouragement. This routine caused him to get a later start in the morning and sell less. Soon he quit earlier each day and drank more. This evolving pattern, as well as family problems, caused him to go from feeling generally good about himself to feelings of depression and despair. He felt guilty about his drinking, yet it continued unabated. For this person, treatment should include a reevaluation of his employment and therapy for his family problems.

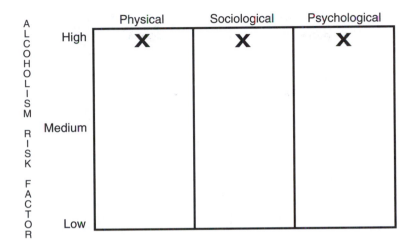

**Figure 5–6** Alcoholism Risk Factors for Individual C after Children Left Home.

Abstinence from alcohol (at least for a period of time, maybe for life) should be suggested. In this case, the job change put this person in a high-risk category sociologically and psychologically, and this factor should be taken into consideration in his treatment.

Although there are thousands of reasons people become alcoholic, they all fit into the three areas covered in the etiology chapters. First, a person's body may handle alcohol so that it becomes easy to become addicted. This information should be used in prevention work to identify high-risk individuals in this area. The prevention task involves keeping people at low risk levels in the other two areas. The role that society plays in the etiology of alcoholism can no longer be ignored. No major public health problem has ever been prevented by treating only the individual who has contracted it. Schools, public policies, and, most importantly, individual families all play a part in both the sociological and psychological risk development for the individual. In the family, the individual develops values condoning alcohol abuse and fails to learn that there is an acceptable and an unacceptable way to use alcohol. Vitally, families teach individuals to feel good or bad about themselves.

If this model of etiology is correct, the key to both prevention and treatment is understanding the family. This is the natural place for parents to gain feelings of self-worth by helping the system grow and develop and move in a positive direction. If the parents are doing this, the children develop positive feelings of self-worth as well. They learn to help each other and to exist in harmony with their environment. Many alcoholics can regain a sense of positive self-worth and a positive attitude from AA, but AA does not and should not replace the family as

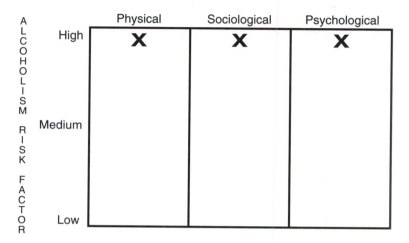

**Figure 5–7** Profile of a Type A Alcoholic.

the primary source for the fulfillment of the basic needs of being loved and needed. If the AA member is meeting those needs both in the family and in AA, fine. But if only AA meets those needs, something is wrong; the family is not functioning effectively.

The remainder of this book addresses the methods, problems, and advantages of treating and preventing alcoholism through a family systems model. The key to alcoholism treatment is understanding and working with the family.

## REFERENCES

Esterly, R.W., & Neely, W.T. (1997). *Chemical dependency and compulsive behaviors.* Mahwah, NJ: Lawrence Erlbaum Associates.

Fingarette, H. (1990). Why we should reject the disease concept of alcoholism. In R. Engs (Ed.), *Controversies in the addictions field.* Dubuque, IA: Kendall/Hune.

Hearings before the United States Senate Committee on Labor and Human Resources, (1994) (testimony of Senator Harold E. Hughes, Ret.).

Levin, J.D. (1995). *Introduction to alcoholism counseling: A bio-psycho-social approach* (2nd ed.). Washington, DC: Taylor & Francis.

Miller, W.R., & Munoz, R.F. (1982). *How to control your drinking: A practical guide to responsible drinking.* Albuquerque, NM: University of New Mexico Press.

Peele, S., & Brodsky, A. (1991). *The truth about addiction and recovery.* New York: Simon & Schuster.

Vogler, R., & Bartz, W. (1982). *The better way to drink: Moderation and control of problem drinking.* Oakland, CA: New Harbinger Publications.

Walters, G.D. (1992). Drug-seeking behavior: Disease or life-style? *Professional Psychology: Research and Practice, 23,*139–145.

# PART III

## Treatment

Part II covered theories of etiology of alcoholism. Although many factors contribute to the development of abusive drinking, there is no single cause for alcoholism. Family system theorists focus on "what happened, how it happened, and when and where it happened" during the treatment process, without concern for *why* it happened (Bowen, 1978, p. 261). Every member of the family plays a part in its dysfunction.

Part III focuses on treatment of the alcoholic family. It presents family therapy techniques that may be unfamiliar to the alcohol counselor and includes techniques for family therapists who are inexperienced in working with alcoholic families. Many alcoholic families receive no treatment, and many family therapists tend not to deal with alcohol problems. In the United States, 15.3 million adults and their families are affected by alcoholism, and numerous other families have at least some alcohol-related problems (Eighth Special Report to the U.S. Congress on Alcohol and Health, 1993). Alcohol has become the drug of choice for teenagers, making it difficult for family therapists to ignore this maladaptive side of family functioning.

Although physiological, psychological, and social factors lead to the development of self-destructive drinking patterns, they should not be viewed by the family therapist as causal. Berenson (1976) believed that looking for the ultimate cause for alcoholism makes the therapist incapable of effectively treating alcohol problems. He stated, "At the same time, he(/she) must be willing to allow clients to accept cause-and-effect thinking, such as the disease model of alcoholism, if that will assist them in helping to resolve their drinking problem. The therapist must therefore not commit himself(/herself) to any causative notion of alcoholism but act as if he(/she) had one" (Berenson, 1976, p. 285).

The focus of treatment, therefore, should be on the aspect of the system that perpetuates the drinking behavior. This factor is unique in each family and should be evaluated without preconceived notions of typical behavior patterns.

Bailey (1963) estimated that 15–20 percent of the cases seen at family service agencies are alcohol related, and if therapists were motivated to look further for symptoms of alcohol abuse, the figures could be greater. Some sources estimate 40 percent of cases in outpatient clinics have some substance abuse problem. Steinglass (1976) said that there are several reasons counselors avoid alcohol-related issues in therapy: (1) they are concerned about their own drinking behavior and are reluctant to diagnose others, (2) they are used to dealing with symptoms in children and not in the parental subsystems, and (3) they are afraid of confronting and experiencing intoxicated behavior. Berenson (1976) also stated that a lack of knowledge of alcoholism causes avoidance of therapy with alcoholic families. This avoidance is further perpetuated by the doctrine that only those who have experienced alcoholism can understand it or help others.

French (1987) listed three reasons she believed that family therapists avoid treating alcoholism: (1) Publications in family therapy literature suggest that alcohol abuse is linked to individual neuroses that are outside of their expertise, (2) empirical data to dispel cultural myths concerning alcoholics have not often appeared in marriage and family therapy literature, and (3) a greater emphasis on family structure over process may suggest that problems of alcoholic families are more effectively resolved by reorganization and elimination of alcoholics from families.

Family therapists also lack formal graduate training in treating drug and alcohol problems. In a follow-up survey of graduates from accredited degree-granting marriage and family therapy (MFT) training programs, Hines (1996) found this to be a weak area of training. The respondents at the masters level reported an estimated 9.25 mean hours of training in alcoholism treatment and 5.59 hours in the treatment of other substances/drugs. The doctoral-level students estimated 15.18 hours of training in alcoholism treatment and 7.89 hours of training in working with substance/drug abuse. The top two presenting problems for which masters and doctoral graduates most strongly recommended increased emphasis in the MFT training programs were alcoholism and other substance/drug abuse (Hines, 1996).

Another recent study (Lim, 1997) attempted to quantify factors influencing marriage and family therapists' willingness to treat alcoholics. Lim wondered if the therapists' willingness to treat alcoholism was related to: (1) beliefs about alcoholics and alcoholism, (2) education in issues of chemical dependency, (3) experience in working with alcoholics, and (4) personal experience with alcoholism or alcoholics, such as having an alcoholic parent or spouse or being in recovery. In her survey of 283 clinical members of the California division of the American Association for Marriage and Family Therapy she was surprised to learn that 40 percent of the respondents had experience working primarily with alcoholic clients, 35 percent had done so for more than five years, and 15 percent had done so for 10–25 years. There was a positive relationship between experience and these therapists' willingness to treat alcoholism.

Beliefs about alcoholism were not, however, predictive. Therapists who believed in the disease model, the free will model, or a mixture of both were equally willing to treat alcoholics. Less than half of the respondents had ever received classroom education in chemical dependency; however, 92 percent had sought out chemical dependency education through seminars and workshops. Almost one third had gained 50 hours of such training. This training was related to the therapists' willingness to treat alcoholism, as was a therapist's personal experience with alcoholism or alcoholics. Therapists who had an alcoholic parent or spouse, or were themselves in recovery, were more willing to treat alcoholics. When therapists, however, had no experience in working with alcoholics, no amount of education or type of personal experience positively influenced their willingness to work with alcoholics. This suggests that a combination of experience and education does encourage marriage and family therapists to treat alcoholics.

Alcohol counselors avoid family therapy for several reasons as well: (1) They may not have training in family therapy, (2) they may believe that it is opposed to Alcoholics Anonymous, (3) they may see it as incompatible with the disease concept of alcoholism, (4) they may be unsupported in their efforts to use family therapy by their employers, and (5) due to the traditional model of inpatient treatment of alcoholism, the family may be unavailable or unwilling to participate. Family members may scapegoat the alcoholic to wash their hands of the problem.

Another reason that family therapy is avoided by some alcohol treatment providers is found in the history of alcoholism treatment. Originally this treatment was provided, in a great part, by recovering alcoholics. It was easy for them to relate to their patients; however, they saw their goal as getting their patients sober, and they were not concerned with other family members. In fact, they may even have developed a belief that the family was the cause of the problem. The other potential problem for alcohol counselors is the opposite belief—that focusing on the family problems is nothing more than a justification for the alcoholic to drink. They believe that "he doesn't drink because she nags"; he drinks because he is an alcoholic.

During the 1980s and through the 1990s counselors in alcohol treatment centers have been broadened in scope to include spouses, adult sons and daughters of alcoholics, and counselors with no family history of alcoholism. Alcoholism has clearly been identified as a family disease and the majority of treatment programs include some type of family program. Too often these family programs are an add-on and the family systems theory is not incorporated into the philosophy of the treatment center. Valentine (1994) explained, "These 'family programs' fail to address the systems issues and view treatment as an individual process: The alcoholic/addict learns how to stay sober and the partner learns how to be less co-dependent" (p. 3). These programs fail to make the needed second-order change, the change of the family rules governing the system.

Although family therapy is more cost-effective than treating each member individually, and even more cost-effective if multifamily therapy groups are utilized, it is not a mainstream treatment approach in the addiction field. One reason: It is generally not reimbursable by insurance companies. It is, however, often covered as a treatment for family members seen by a mental health professional. Managed care has also made an impact on substance abuse treatment. The trend is to limit inpatient treatment to detoxification only. Treatment providers have shifted to outpatient and day treatment programs to save on hospital expenses. This move allows patients to stay on their jobs and continue living with their families if it is feasible. This provides a great opportunity to involve family members in the treatment and aftercare of the alcoholic/addict family member.

Part III should further encourage both family therapists and alcohol counselors to consider a family approach to the treatment of alcoholism and problem drinking.

## REFERENCES

Bailey, M.B. (1963). The family agency's role in treating the wife of an alcoholic. *Social Casework, 44,* 273–279.

Berenson, D. (1976). Alcohol and the family system. In P. Guerin (Ed.), *Family therapy: Theory and practice.* New York: Gardner Press.

Bowen, M. (1978). *Family therapy in clinical practice.* New York: Jason Aronson.

Eighth Special Report to the U.S. Congress on Alcohol and Health. (1993). Rockville, MD: National Institute on Alcohol Abuse and Alcoholism.

French, S. (1987). Family approaches to alcoholism: Why the lack of interest among marriage and family professionals? *Journal of Drug Issues, 17,* 359–368.

Hines, M. (1996). Follow-up survey of graduates from accredited degree-granting marriage and family therapy training programs. *Journal of Marital and Family Therapy, 22*(2), 181–194.

Lim, D. (1997). Correlates to family therapists' willingness to treat alcoholics (Doctoral dissertation, United States International University, 1997). *Dissertation Abstracts International* (in press).

Steinglass, P. (1976). Experimenting with family treatment approaches to alcoholism, 1950–1975: A review. *Family Process, 15,* 97–123.

Valentine, D.R. (1994, February). Family systems approaches in chemical dependency treatment. *Family Therapy News,* 3 & 12.

# CHAPTER 6

# Diagnosing the Alcoholic Family

This chapter covers three processes involved in family evaluation: (1) observations by the therapist, (2) reports from the family, and (3) assessment of the family structure by the therapist. The diagnosis determines if a family is a candidate for therapy and should have as its outcome a treatment plan that involves every family member. This plan should include goals for treatment and an evaluation of the potential for change within family structures. Diagnoses are not conducted to label individual pathology.

Clarken, Frances, and Moodie (1979), in reviewing family therapy literature, listed instances when family evaluation is essential. First of all, family evaluation may be needed to understand such situations as:

- The identified patient is a child or adolescent.
- The problem is sexual difficulty.
- The family or marital problem is serious enough to jeopardize relationships, job stability, health, or parenting ability.
- The family is experiencing a developmental or accidental crisis.
- The family defines the problem as a family problem.

Second, whenever psychiatric hospitalization is considered, family evaluation is essential in order to gain historical information and discover the influences of the family on the illness as well as to encourage family involvement in treatment. Third, family diagnosis is important when family treatment is found necessary due to such factors as obvious family interactions around the problem, failure of other therapies, the number of family members affected by the problem (a parent and child in the same family may both be alcoholic), and when secondary gains of symptoms are linked to family pathology.

On the other hand, family evaluation should not be done when a family member insists on a private session in order not to reveal a valid family secret that would jeopardize another family member (for example, an adolescent who has just left home). But even when the family is divorcing without hope of reconciliation, family evaluation can be done with the custodial parent and children. Sessions with both of the divorcing parents and the children can greatly improve the painful process of restructuring the family and keeping the children from being caught in the marital conflict. However, when repetitive intrapsychic conflicts occur outside of the family structure, individual treatment may be more beneficial. Family treatment is also contraindicated when a client has a history of sabotaging treatment alliances or when a client has extreme schizoid or paranoid pathology.

The therapist may come in contact with alcoholic families that require family evaluation in a number of ways.

First, the symptom bearer may be a child in a family in which one or both parents have drinking problems. However, these problems may be hidden from the therapist, and the child may experience the pain of the family dysfunction. Although these alcoholic families appear to be much like other dysfunctional families, certain clues may expose a hidden drinking problem. Therapists should inquire about drinking patterns and complete a drinking history of the spouses if the following conditions exist:

- A pattern of alcoholism is evident in either family of origin.
- The children are protecting their parents.
- There is a role reversal with a child appearing in a parental role.
- Denial or isolation is a family pattern.
- There is a report of physical abuse or incest.
- There is obvious scapegoating of the child.
- Parents have an irrational fear of teenage alcohol and drug abuse.

It is possible that the presenting problem in the child is alcohol and/or drug abuse. Although these symptoms may not be caused by alcoholism in the family, they can alert therapists to the possibility that the symptoms in the child may be a response to addiction in one or both parents.

The second type of family views drinking behavior as incidental to other family problems. Berenson (1976) believed these families occasionally have a pattern of alcoholism that is characterized by slight or infrequent behavior changes when drinking. The relationship between the spouses is symmetrical on the surface, with a feeling of "we-ness." Also, in this type of family the amounts and patterns of drinking are variable; alcohol problems tend to be secondary and recede if other problems are resolved.

The third type of family seeks therapy with alcohol as the major presenting problem. This family is organized around alcohol and its meaning in the family; the drinking behavior is part of the family structure. The drinker may or may not be physically addicted. Berenson (1976) said the members of these families agree that alcohol is a problem, and there may be intense conflict about it. In addition, alcohol consumption in these families increases the severity of other problems. Behavior changes during intoxication are generally intense and common, and the relationship between the spouses fluctuates and is immersed in overt conflict. This type of family is not always distinguishable from the second type by the amount of drinking but rather by the behavior change in the drinker, the quality of the spouses' relationship, and the longer history and duration of the problem.

The fourth way an alcoholic family appears for therapy is during a period of aftercare. One or both spouses in this category may have completed inpatient or outpatient (individual) alcoholism treatment, and the family homeostasis may be out of balance. The marital relationship could be threatened, or a new symptom bearer could emerge. Families often describe themselves at the time as "walking on eggshells." Family therapy may be viewed here as a prevention of further difficulties or as a second stage of treatment. Families may resist treatment if they feel the alcoholic member has a special relationship with the therapist, and alcoholics may resist having their families scapegoat them in front of their therapists. It is difficult for the alcohol counselor who has developed a relationship with the alcoholic to be impartial. Family therapy with this type of family should be conducted by a therapist other than the alcoholic's primary counselor, or the counselor should bring in a cotherapist who is unfamiliar with the alcoholic (especially if the alcohol treatment is continuing simultaneously). This is also a good way to involve alcoholism counselors in family therapy and educate family therapists about alcohol problems.

Recovering families may also come for treatment many years after they have established a stable sobriety. They may come into treatment with marital problems; behavior, emotional, or substance problems in the children; or problems related to arrested family life cycle development. Frequently these families have not learned to function as a healthy system and are continuing to produce symptoms in other members or subsystems. They may have never talked about the alcoholism or the recovery process as a family and the rules about not talking about the alcoholism may still be operating.

Kaufman (1984) described four types of family reactivity patterns: (1) the functional family system where family members have the ability to wall off and isolate alcoholic behavior (similar to type 2 above), (2) the neurotic, enmeshed family system where drinking behavior interrupts normal family tasks, causes conflict, shifts roles, and demands new adaptation (similar to type 3 above), (3) the disintegrated family system where the alcoholic is separated from the family but members are still available for family therapy, and (4) the absent family system that is marred by total loss of family. Although all of these family types react to the alcoholism, the first two are different degrees of reactivity, while the second two are more a function of family structure.

Kaufman (1984) further stated, "There is now substantial evidence to conclude that family systems play a significant role in the genesis of alcoholism, as for example in the transmission of marital and family roles of alcoholism from one generation to the next" (p. 7). In his article "Myths and Realities in the Family Patterns and Treatment of Substance Abusers," Kaufman (1980) rejected myths about substance abusers' family patterns. He pointed out that families of drug abusers are very similar to families of alcohol abusers; however, the drug abuser may be a child, while the alcohol abuser may be the adult. In over half of the families with an identified patient with a drug problem there is also a parent who is alcoholic. He felt that the family plays an important part in the onset and perpetuation of substance abuse, yet it may not be the cause of all substance abuse. He also cautioned about overgeneralizing about alcoholic families and added that they vary according to ethnic background, sex of the alcoholic, and life cycle stage of the family.

Kaufman (1991) later reviewed his 1980 article on myths and realities in the field and concluded that counselors are learning more and more about the importance of the family in the root and maintenance of substance abuse. The field is acknowledging there is more to the family system than the mother-son relationship; the fathers are not all distant, the mothers are not all enmeshed, and there are unique dynamics in the family systems of various ethnic groups. Siblings are also incredibly important in family therapy.

Kaufman (1991) also updated his subgroups of alcoholic/addict families, thinking that there are far fewer "functional family systems" than he first believed. These functional families were able to wall off and isolate alcoholic behavior.

It is important to remember that families often change categories or fall somewhere between them. A family whose presenting problem is incest may see a serious alcohol problem as secondary.

Families in category three and possibly category one, in which drinking continues to be a major issue, must be treated differently than families in the other categories. The drinking behavior is the primary issue. The cooling-off of emotional tensions and separation of the enmeshed spouses must precede other family work. All families in conflict tend to search for blame either within or outside the family. In general, the family evaluation process is entered with one of four orientations:

1. There is nothing wrong with any of us, but nothing is right in the family.
2. There is a problem with someone in the family.

3. There is a problem with everyone, according to everyone else.
4. Nothing is wrong with the family or any member, but someone outside of the family believes there is and sent us here.

This general framework may color family responses to the evaluation and diagnosis process. Motivation and receptivity to family therapy can be reviewed with reference to the events that led up to the initial contact with the therapist. In other words, was the family coerced into therapy? Were they responding to symptoms in a child? Was there a family developmental crisis, such as a death, a birth, a midlife crisis, a divorce, or a change in a member of the family from drinking behavior to sobriety?

In the beginning of a family evaluation, care should be taken not to develop a therapeutic alliance with the family representative who calls for the appointment. Demographic information and a brief statement of the problem are all that is necessary. This information should later be shared with the rest of the family so that special secrets do not exist between the therapist and one family member. Also, the family should be involved in treatment as soon as possible and before the alcoholic is further scapegoated and labeled as the problem.

Therapists disagree as to the feasibility of working with a drinking alcoholic or problem drinker. Berenson found that the key to understanding consequences and behavior patterns built around drinking is often to observe drunken behavior. "Drunken behavior . . . can be seen as a clue that will help to resolve the problem, rather than being a problem that must be rigorously suppressed" (Berenson, 1976, p. 288). Berenson also stated that in the family where alcohol is a chronic problem, the drinking behavior must stop before family change can occur. However, in families where drinking is less chronic, family therapy techniques may change the system enough to reduce or eliminate excessive drinking. Other therapists insist on sobriety or at least an absence of drinking prior to the family sessions. Kaufman (1979) stated that "most therapeutic changes in dysfunctional families cannot be initiated until the regular use of chemicals is interrupted" (p. 255). However, individual work with the alcoholic may increase his or her drive for recovery but increase resistance to treatment in the spouse.

The issue of sobriety appears to be a matter of therapist preference and depends on the pattern of drinking behavior in the family. If, however, the therapist takes a rigid stand on sobriety for all families, some who could have been helped may be lost. In some cases chronic relapsers have been drinking for years to numb the pain of family issues, such as a parent's suicide. Until these issues are addressed, sobriety may seem too painful for them. For several years an arbitrary rule existed in the alcohol treatment profession that required counselors to avoid family issues until the alcoholic had a year of sobriety. Many alcoholics, however, may never reach that year if they do not resolve their family issues.

The evaluation of the family may be limited in time, with a recommendation for family therapy accompanied by a treatment plan. On the other hand, evaluation may be part of the ongoing process of therapy and may represent a continuously changing view of the family as information and observations lead to a more complex diagnosis than is possible in an initial assessment. Therapists not only gather information for an evaluation but also help the family experience abusive drinking behavior as a family problem.

Another way of evaluating families was proposed by Steinglass and his colleagues (Steinglass, Bennett, Wolin, & Reiss, 1987). This approach involves a model based on a developmental construct they call *systemic maturation*. That is, all families proceed through a developmental process that can be divided into early, middle, and late phases. The second major construct of the model is *developmental distortion*. This refers to the changes and alterations of the usual developmental process that are results of experiences with which a family has to deal such as chronic alcoholism.

A family may come to therapy in any of the three phases. The first or early phase of family development is focused on identity formation. The newlywed couple is creating a new family based on their past history and what they have learned from their families of origin and their other life experiences. The couple may be influenced by one family of origin more that the other. The amount of influence of the families of origin is related to how they left their families. Adults who never really left or who cut themselves off from their families are more likely to repeat destructive patterns. At this stage the newly formed family may be laying the groundwork for establishing a family identity that involves alcoholism as a central organizing force, especially if one or both of the spouses grew up in an alcoholic family. Although alcoholic drinking may not be present at this stage, rules and attitudes toward alcohol use are established at this time, setting up the potential for the transmission of alcoholism into this new family (Steinglass et al., 1987).

In the middle phase the family has developed some regulatory mechanism and behavior sequences and specializes in its areas of concentration. One of these areas can be chronic alcoholism. The more the alcoholism disrupts the regulatory behaviors the family uses to order itself and grow, the more distortion will occur in this development. The homeostatic mechanism operates in this family to keep the status quo in the face of the disruption or unpredictability of the alcoholic behavior. This reduces the potential of individual or family growth. Steinglass et al. (1987) suggested focusing on three types of regulatory behaviors: (1) short-term problem-solving strategies, (2) daily routines, and (3) family rituals. In a diagnostic interview with the entire family it is determined how these behaviors are altered during periods of heaviest drinking. This helps the therapist decide if the alcoholism has become a central organizing force (an alcoholic family) or if this is a family with an alcoholic.

Steinglass et al. (1987) described two critical issues for families in the late phase of development: (1) the final distillation and clarification of the family's unique identity, and (2) the process of transmission of this identity to future generations. The late-phase family attempts to transmit its identity to the beginning of the new early-phase family as the children leave to start their own families. Steinglass and his colleagues found two common presenting problems that these families bring to therapy. The first is the drinking behavior of a child of a "recovered" dry alcoholic family. The second is the need of the children who are leaving to get some resolution to the alcoholism before they go. This is an excellent opportunity for prevention work with these high-risk young adults. The more aware they are of the patterns that encouraged and perpetuated the alcoholism and related problems for family members, the more likely they will be able to stop the intergenerational transmission process.

## OBSERVATION OF BEHAVIORS

Observation of behaviors is done in the here and now. Family therapists must have all of their senses tuned to the behaviors and actions of the families they are evaluating. Both verbal and nonverbal clues are present in family functioning patterns in every interaction. From the onset of contact with the family, therapists begin to formulate impressions. If it is possible to see the family enter the clinic, the therapist should note such behaviors as who is walking next to whom, who announces to the receptionist the arrival of the family, where they sit in the waiting room, how the children are controlled, and who fills out application forms.

When the family enters the therapy room, particular attention should be paid to the way the seating arrangement problem is solved. It is useful to have a sofa or combination of chairs that provide for close seating of the marital couple so that they may choose to sit together or obviously sit far apart. If the spouses sit together, note whether one spouse begins to lean away from the other, pulling the other spouse with him or her. This clue is often useful in determining which spouse is less satisfied with the marital relationship. When extra chairs are provided, more combinations are possible, and distancing can be observed more accurately. If the office is small and seating is limited, some of the observations are contaminated by the limitations of the environment. Sometimes children tend to move during the interview toward a parent or sibling. They may insist on being between the spouses or jump in the mother's lap if the anxiety level rises.

### Communications

As soon as a family member begins to speak, the therapist is experiencing the content of the message and the process of the communication. The way the family communicates is important for evaluating alliances, boundaries, and family roles. For the therapist, observing the process may be more valuable than the content. Who does the most talking? Who speaks for whom? Does a child defocus the conversation if anxiety is high? How do the parents communicate? Does nonverbal behavior contradict the verbal message? Are the children in any double binds? Is anyone reading someone else's mind? Do the family members take turns, interrupt, or all talk at the same time? Family communication patterns are very important in therapy and often reflect the very structure of the family as well as the areas of difficulty and the resources of the family.

**Family Roles**

The therapist observing communication patterns begins to identify family role behaviors. "One of the most common ways for a family to reduce stress is to assign specific roles to individual members to have them acted out in the conflict situation" (Walsh, 1980, p. 13). Chapter 3 defines Satir's four basic role models: (1) placating, (2) blaming, (3) irrelevant, and (4) superresponsible (Bandler, Grinder, & Satir, 1976). Similarly, Wegscheider (1979) developed role categories for the alcoholic family that he called *survival roles*. These are emotional masks worn by family members to cover their true feelings in an effort to maintain the family's balance. As a crisis develops in the family system or anxiety about drinking becomes high, each member clings to his or her respective role tightly to brave the storm.

Wegscheider described the person in the family who is projecting low self-worth and is unable to deal with crises (because of defensive behavior) as the "victim." Victims feel shame, inadequacy, guilt, pain, loneliness, and fear, but they wear masks of anger, aggression, denial, perfectionism, charm, blame, and manipulation that are similar to Satir's blaming role. "The victim believes that if his or her pain were allowed to emerge full force, the balance of the family system would be destroyed catastrophically" (Wegscheider, 1979, p. 33). "In the family with alcoholism, family members soon learn they cannot expect the usual behavior from the alcoholic person in terms of family roles. To compensate, nonalcoholic members shift their role performance in an effort to keep the family functioning" (Hanson & Estes, 1977, p. 71).

The person who is the closest to the victim cannot escape this process. Wegscheider called this role the "protector." The protector is angry but, like other roles, does not show this openly. To keep stability, the protector manipulates the victim and derives a sense of importance by keeping the victim in need of protection. It is difficult for the protector to change this behavior or see it as dysfunctional. The protector sees the demand of this role to be superresponsible. He or she is passive and powerless and deserves rewards such as excessive eating or control of family functioning and money. If these roles exist in the parental subsystem, this didactic relationship will seek a third side to the hypothetical triangle, possibly one of the children. This child will work to give dignity and meaning to the family by achieving and putting the needs of others above his or her own. Wegscheider labeled this role the "caretaker." It has also been called the "family hero" and the "fixer" by other authors. A special achiever mask is worn by this person, but he or she never reaches personal success. These people have a special role, yet they never feel important or never feel the closeness they wish from their families. The children often continue this pattern throughout their lives, sometimes entering the helping professions in order to perpetuate the role.

The other children also develop roles to save the family. The "scapegoat" volunteers to be "the problem" and may get the family into therapy. A child may also pull out of the family and allow family members not to worry about him or her. The youngest child often plays the "irrelevant" role and defocuses by becoming a comic. "For the sake of balance in the family, the system needs to have someone fulfill each role. So in small families one person may have to play several roles alternately" (Wegscheider, 1979, p. 34). These roles are not the focus of therapy nor are they diagnoses, but they provide a perspective for viewing the family interaction that causes maladaptive behavior in every member. All families have role behaviors. It is the rigidity of these roles as survival strategies that creates problems for family members.

## Family Sculpting

As the family role pattern emerges, triangles, alliances, and emotional relationships appear. The technique of family sculpting is a way of observing these patterns more clearly and is useful with families who are skilled in verbal manipulation and who resist the traditional interview process. Family sculpting was developed by Papp (Papp, Silverstein, & Carter, 1973) to demonstrate to families the systems concept and the role of each member in the evolution, maintenance, and resolution of family problems. It is a useful technique to help the family experience the "familiness" of the problem.

To do this, one of the family members assists the therapist(s) in arranging and shifting family members in a tableau of emotional relationships. The therapist may recognize a family member who makes a good family sculptor. "Adolescents usually make excellent sculptors because of their insight into family truths, and their natural relish in manipulating their elders. Latency children are also good natural sculptors, though what they produce may be somewhat idealized and stereotyped" (Simon, 1972, p. 51).

When the sculpture is complete, according to one member, all others are asked to report their perspective and their feelings about their placement. Marital difficulties often are portrayed by children placed between the parents. Often the children are attached to the mother while the father is alone in a corner of the room. People can be placed at the top of chairs to indicate an authoritarian position or power. They may be under tables to represent a protected position or unawareness. Members may face toward the family or look away.

When a sculpture is achieved that everyone agrees represents the family's current position, goal setting can begin. This step is approached by asking each person where he or she would like to be and asking him or her to experience that position. The emphasis of sculpting is to gather information about individual family perceptions, to activate silent members, and to increase emotional intensity. This often allows family members to experience their reactions to the moment. Care should be taken not to overinterpret the sculpture or believe it is a true picture of the family. "Some sculptors represent their ideal family, others are the fulfilling of a special wish; others are a deception, with some family-political purpose" (Simon, 1972, p. 55).

Virginia Satir used sculpting to help family members experience the roles she had identified (Bandler, Grinder, & Satir, 1976). She put the placater on one bended knee (an unsteady position) looking up with a plea to a blamer. The blamer stood firmly and pointed his or her finger at the placater. During the process of therapy, as family members triangulated a third person into a dyadic conversation, Satir had them physically experience this. For instance, if a mother was talking to her upset husband about why she continued to give money to their drug-abusing son, Satir had the mother stand between her husband and son with her arms stretched and pulled by them. She wanted the mother to experience the stuckness of the position and the family to see her position. This led to helping the mother find a way to get out of being pulled in two opposite directions. The evaluation technique was also a therapeutic intervention.

### Family Puppet Interview

A technique that uses the drama of family sculpting but further removes the family from the direct experience of their problems is the family puppet interview. Families who are unskilled in putting thoughts and feelings into words or who manipulate others with intellectualization can use the puppet drama to cut through defenses and examine family dynamics in a nonthreatening way. This technique is most useful for families with children ages five to 12 who may find it difficult to talk to the therapist directly about family problems. The therapist who uses this technique can observe decision making, family patterns, and symbolic communications that help members experience the family nature of the problem.

To begin the interview, the therapist explains the process and rationale for using puppets as a family activity and as an aid to the children. Twenty or more puppets are made available with a stage to further shelter an anxious or resistive family.

The puppets represent an assortment of real-life people of all ages, including role characters, policemen, and doctors, or fantasy figures such as princesses, kings, queens, fairies, witches, and devils. Animals can take on both tame (dogs and cats) and ferocious (lions and alligators) characteristics.

Each family member is asked to select one puppet and introduce it, making a statement about what it represents. The therapist at this point should observe which puppets are selected and rejected as well as who makes the decisions and for whom. Family members may select a puppet to represent themselves and how they wish to be or fear to be, for example, or to represent someone else.

The family is then asked to make up an original story to act out with the puppets. This process should be observed, and the therapist should not take part at this stage. Roles, alliances, and subgroups should be observed. Who takes the roles of organizer, dominator, disciplinarian, scapegoat, victim, and pacifier?

The therapist can set up the drama by announcing the play and calling for the action to start. If the family begins to narrate the story, the therapist can ask to be shown by the puppets how that would look. If the family becomes stuck without a solution, as families in real life do, the therapist can help them explore alternatives.

At the conclusion of the play, the therapist can make use of the established puppet roles by engaging in dialogue with the puppets and encouraging them to speak to one another. Themes and conflicts can be further explored and clarified. Often the issue that brought the family into therapy is played out.

At the end of the drama, a discussion is held to connect the experience with real-life happenings. Family members are asked to think of a title for the play and talk about the moral of the story or the lesson learned. Each member is asked to pick the character he or she would most like to be and least like to be. Finally, the family members are asked if this play was in any way like their own family or experiences they have had. They are encouraged to talk further after the session.

The family puppet interview provides many opportunities to observe the visible as well as the covert ways that family members communicate with each other. "The puppet choices, the conflicts expressed in the fantasy, the post-play discussion when members are invited to associate the story with real life, and the inquiry about the relationship of the story to the family's functioning all give important clues about the family and the available ego strength for confronting problems" (Irwin & Malloy, 1975, p. 190).

## Structured Task Performance

Another technique that elicits observable diagnostic information and does not rely totally on verbal reports involves the assignment of tasks for the family to complete during the assessment period. Minuchin, Montalbo, Guerney, Rosman, and Schumer (1967) devised a number of tasks that family members were asked to carry out while the therapist observed family interaction patterns. For example, families were asked to plan a menu using their favorite foods or decide how they would spend 10 dollars. (Today that would have to be 100 dollars.) This elicits information about the family hierarchy—who is in charge—problem-solving style, communication patterns, and family rules.

Watzlawick (1966) developed a structured family interview based on the assumption that human behavior is patterned. In the interview, solutions to tasks are requested by the therapist, and observations are made to discover patterns of behavior in the family.

Watzlawick began the interview by asking each member individually what he or she saw as the family's problems. These responses remained confidential. This process defocused the attention from the identified patient and allowed each member to feel that his or her input was valued. The family members were then assembled in one room and told that there were discrepancies in their perceptions of problems and that they should discuss these and come to consensus on their main problem. This procedure also allowed early observation of family communication patterns.

The second assignment was for the family to plan something in five minutes that they could do together. The importance of this assignment was not what the family planned but whether or not they could make a decision in the time allotted and how it was done.

The third task focused on the parents and asked them to explain how the couple met and got together. Patterns of marital interaction, methods for handling discrepancies, and current patterns of interaction became apparent.

The fourth item began with the parents discussing the meaning of the proverb "A rolling stone gathers no moss." After five minutes the children were returned to the room and the parents taught the children the meaning of the proverb. Watzlawick listed 16 possible interpretation patterns and 10 typical responses to this proverb. Marital communication patterns could be observed as well as teaching patterns. If disagreement occurred in the parental subgroup, children were often pulled into the argument, which pointed out coalitions and decision making by the children.

The fifth task was entitled "Blame." The seating arrangement for this task placed the father to the left of the therapist, followed by the mother, and then oldest to youngest children. Each person was asked to write on a card the main fault of the person on their left, excluding the therapist. No identifying marks or names were included. The therapist collected the cards and added two cards to the pile reading "too weak" and "too good" to stimulate controversy. The therapist then read out each card, asking the family to make a forced choice as to whom each statement applied. "Each family member is thus forced to blame somebody, and by so doing implies automatically that in his opinion this criticism was leveled by the person sitting on the right of the victim" (Watzlawick, 1966, p. 263). This task provided data on scapegoating, self-blame, and favoritism.

This interview can be done in one hour. It gives the therapist a wealth of information about the process of family interaction and allows the family to experience the family philosophy.

A similar family task interview (FTI) was developed by Kinston, Loader, and Miller (1985). The interview is conducted by audiotape without the therapist present, which reduces family efforts to draw the therapist into the process. The therapist observes the family interaction via a one-way mirror. There are seven tasks:

1. Plan something together that will take at least one hour. (4 minutes)
2. Build a tower with a box of blocks. (4 minutes)
3. Discuss likes and dislikes of each family member. (4 minutes)
4. Sort a deck of cards in a pattern. (9 minutes)
5. Complete the following story: A family is at home. One member is missing and late returning. The phone rings and the family is asked to come to the hospital urgently. (9 minutes)
6. Parents choose a well-known saying and explain it to the children. (9 minutes)
7. Discuss the interview.

The interview is coded and scored on a scale from 1 to 6 in the areas of affective status, communication, boundaries, alliances, adaptability and stability, and family competence.

**Family Art Evaluation**

The family art evaluation was developed by Kwiatkowska (1967) at the National Institute of Mental Health. The use of art media in the family interview allows for an alternate mode of expression for families who are defensive, manipulative with words, or unskilled in verbal expression. Alcoholic families are often thus described. The initial model of the family art interview takes two to three hours and includes six drawings. The process has been adapted, shortened, and modified by many other family and art therapists (Bing, 1970; Landgarten, 1981; Rubin & Magnussen, 1974; Sherr & Hicks, 1973; Callaghan, 1993). In art evaluation, the family is assembled in a room with easels set in a semicircle. Because many people become anxious when asked to create artwork, it is necessary for the therapist to reduce initial resistance by assuring the family that the quality of the artwork is not the focus and that only the process of family interactions is important.

Initially, family members are asked to make a free picture—a drawing of anything they wish. Kwiatkowska found that people introduce themselves in this drawing or illustrate the family problem. Second, the family members are asked to draw a picture of the family. These portraits may show isolation of family members or a close togetherness. The third drawing is an abstract composition of the family. This is the most difficult assignment, and it stirs discussion among family members about symbols used for each member. In the fourth task, family members make scribbles on paper with their eyes closed. They must then find something in the scribble that will help them make a composition by ignoring or adding lines. The next assignment is a joint family scribble. Each person again makes a scribble, and the family decides which one they will use to complete as a picture. In this effort, the entire family works on one composition. The final work is, again, a free drawing that may express feelings about the process of the art evaluation. At the completion of each piece of artwork, the family members are asked to give their pictures a title and to then sign and date them.

It is extremely helpful to have a cotherapist or observer (Kwiatkowska's term) to help observe the wealth of verbal and nonverbal behavior elicited by this process. Similar observations can be made in the art evaluation as in any task assignment, but in addition, symbolic art productions confront the family with expressions that cannot be denied.

Rubin and Magnussen (1974) adopted four of these techniques and established a two-hour art evaluation session at the Pittsburgh Child Guidance Center. Family members were first asked to make individual pictures from a scribble and title them. Next they were asked to make family portraits and view and discuss these simultaneously. Finally they were asked to create a joint family mural and free drawings if time allowed. Rubin and Magnussen found that "family members could communicate maximal information about individual and family characteristics with minimal stress" (p. 190). Observations of behavior that correlated with the content of the drawings strengthened diagnostic impressions.

Landgarten (1981) adapted similar techniques to develop her initial family interview. She asked each family member to draw his or her initials on the page and then make a composition or design incorporating the letters and give it a title. This is similar to the scribble technique, but Landgarten thought that it was less threatening to deal with a familiar symbol. The second assignment called for the family to divide up into two teams to make a nonverbal mutual drawing. Each person selected a different color so that each contribution could later be evaluated. No talking was allowed, and the family decided what they would draw and how it would get done without words. The third task was a verbal family task-oriented art product. Each member was given a different color of plasticene clay or construction paper and decided on an artistic product to create. Therapists could observe decision-making processes, such as who the leader was, how the artwork got started, who initiated communication, who was ignored, and how much discussion occurred. In addition, it could be determined if the family members worked in teams, individually, or at the same time. How was the space of the room used? Who chose the title? Who wrote it down? When the family members were finished they were asked to state how their perceptions of the experience could be matched with the actual happenings.

Bing (1970) used an art evaluation technique in part of a structural family interview. She used Watzlawick's tasks and added a conjoint family drawing at the end of the session, when the family felt less threatened by an art assignment.

Each family member was asked to choose a colored marker that he or she would use throughout the drawing so it would be obvious exactly what each person had drawn. The instructions were:

> I'd like for you as a family to draw a picture as you see yourselves now as a family. You can draw the picture any way you want to, but I'd like to encourage you to be as creative and original as you can in representing yourselves as a unique family. You can draw the persons any size and place them in any position on the paper. They may be drawn touching each other, or separately. You can draw yourselves or each other, whichever way you think best describes your family. (Bing, 1970, p. 176).[1]

Bing observed specific processes to allow comparison with other families:

- the organizing role
- the sequence of who draws first, second, and so on
- the relative size of the person represented, which depends in part on who drew whom, and in what order
- choice of which family member was drawn by whom
- isolation of persons
- specific content and unusual themes.

Bing found that families in which nearly all family members draw themselves rather than someone else are less cohesive than families in which members draw mostly each other.

A conjoint family drawing was used in the case of Sally, whose case history appears in chapter 3. When the task of a family portrait was presented to this family, they became quite anxious and resorted to stress-coping roles. To ease the anxiety, Sally, the identified patient, jumped up and began drawing the mother safe in her kitchen. She then drew the withdrawn father under the car, working in the garage. After some time, the mother drew Sally in the picture, sitting at her desk in school. The mother stated that she wished Sally could go to school and be

---

[1]Reprinted with permission.

happy. This drew attention to the presenting problem and the notion of the "sick" child. The teenage girl drew herself going to a movie alone, without her mother worrying—a wish that put the focus back on the mother. Finally, the middle boy got up and drew the whole family together watching television, the ultimate wish of family unity. Sally continued to draw members of the family all over the page, causing confusion, with each member of the family represented more than once. The father never drew anything or gave any input into the process (Figure 6–1).

In alcoholic families it is interesting to have each member draw his or her perception of the family without looking at the others. Often common themes will occur when the family views the drawings together even though they were drawn separately.

Callaghan (1993) used an art evaluation process with alcoholic families to determine how the family symptom of alcoholism was maintained. In this process family members are asked to draw a picture of the family problem. Members then discuss their picture. The therapist uses circular questioning, asking one member about the behaviors between two others, to obtain diagnostic information about

**Figure 6–1** Conjoint Family Portrait

the family. The family is asked what they have done about the problem and if it worked. The family members are then asked to draw a picture or make a collage about how they expect therapy to change the problem. Differences are discussed and treatment goals can then be set.

To evaluate roles, the therapist asks family members to choose one or two pictures cut from magazines that tell something about each of them. They then glue their pictures on a single sheet of paper in any order they want. The therapist watches who goes first, who places their pictures next to whose, and how this got decided. The family then discusses the images they selected and their order and placement on the paper.

The second assignment to evaluate roles is a nonverbal conjoint family drawing. This is followed by a discussion of how and where family members represented themselves. The therapist asks if there were any rules broken, such as talking or changing colors. Next the family does a verbal family drawing and the two processes are contrasted.

In another case, an art evaluation was done on a family who came to a child guidance center to work on issues of parenting and adding a new family member. Jean, age 34, had been a practicing alcoholic and drug addict for 20 years before going through inpatient alcohol treatment. When her first child was born, she was a member of a Hell's Angels group and did not wish to parent her daughter, Joan. Joan was given to the paternal grandparents to raise, and Jean was denied permission to see her. When Jean's son was born, she kept him with her. Jean divorced her alcoholic husband, remarried, and had a third child, a son. Some years later she divorced her second husband.

At the time of the evaluation, Jean was living with her fiancé. Joan, age 16, had left her grandparents and came to live with her mother for the first time in her life. When the family was asked to draw family portraits, an unmistakable theme of isolation became apparent. The mother's (Jean's) family drawing (Figure 6–2) used compartments to divide the family. She was at the Holiday Inn working, while Joan was shown in a room of the house watching television. A messy kitchen and living room separated her from her mother. This untidy house was the source of arguments between the mother and daughter. The two boys were pictured playing ball, but they had a tree between them. Mother's fiancé was drawn in another square representing his job, which took him out of town during the week. Joan's picture (Figure 6–3) showed all of the family in a neat row divided by a line separating her and her boyfriend from the rest. She saw herself as the only one who was isolated. The teenage boy, Bob, (Figure 6–4) drew lines between each member of the family except between himself and his brother. However, he placed his brother's friend between them. The youngest boy, Tim, (Figure 6–5) drew family members as being busy doing something on their own. The teenagers were involved with their respective boyfriends and girlfriends; the mother was leaving; and the mother's fiancé was taking his parrot inside the

**Figure 6–2** Jean's Family Drawing

**Figure 6–3** Joan's Family Drawing

**Figure 6–4** Bob's Family Drawing

**Figure 6–5** Tim's Family Drawing

house, while the boy's friend was playing with someone else. There was little emotional connectedness in this family.

A wealth of family information can also be gained from the artwork of an adolescent when the entire family is not available. The Parents-Self-Centered Drawing (PSCD) is a projective drawing technique developed by Burns (1990) to depict parents-self relationships and parental introjects. The adolescent is asked to draw him/herself and his or her parents inside the form of a circle and surround the figures with symbols. Burns suggested the following introduction: "Draw your parents and yourself inside the circle. Try to draw a whole person, not stick people; surround the figures with symbols or drawings, also inside the circle, that you associate with each person" (Burns, 1990, p. 3). Art therapy has been criticized because little systematic research exists to validate the ability of art therapy criteria or techniques as diagnostic tools. A recent study (Thomas, 1997), however, was able to show significant differences in family drawings of hospital-ized, depressed adolescents and nondepressed, non-hospitalized adolescents. Experienced art therapists rated these PSCDs and were able to significantly discriminate between the two groups on cohesion, expressiveness, and conflict in the family drawings. The same adolescents completed the Moos Family Environ-ment Scale (Moos & Moos, 1981), a highly reliable and valid instrument, which discriminated significantly between the two groups on the same variables.

The richness of one drawing was evident in the family drawing of one of the depressed, hospitalized adolescents. She used a pencil to draw her mother on the left side of the circle with stars and a diploma, a bust of herself at the top of the circle, her father on a hospital gurney on the right, and on the far right was a black heart surrounded by a line of red with the word abandonment. Her comments were: "That's my mom, me and my dad. That's a diplopma by my mom. She is very smart, but we don't talk much. We don't communicate. She tries, but I reject her. My father left me two weeks before I was born. I only saw him seven times. They called me when he was dying and I went to the hospital and I saw him die. The black heart is for abandonment. He chose drugs over me" (Thomas, 1997, p. 165).

Family art evaluation offers direct observations of family behavior as well as graphic creations full of visual symbols that can be useful in family therapy. It provides a record of the evaluation process that can be referred to later or can be compared with similar compositions at the completion of therapy. The therapist should use caution in interpreting the artwork and should place more value on the process of its production and the interaction patterns of the family than the pictorial content.

The purpose of directly observing family behavior is to gain information about family patterns that may be largely outside of the family's awareness and thus not be obtainable by questioning. In forcing situations in which family members must solve problems and interact with each other, behavior patterns, structure, boundaries, and alliances can be noted. The therapist's observations are not shared with the family at the time of the evaluation. Rather, they are stored with the therapist for future reference and matched with other information to formulate treatment plans. The family cannot tolerate dealing with anything other than the presenting problem at the time. Although they are aware of some of the dynamics, they may not wish to have these pointed out.

## FAMILY REPORTS

The two categories—direct observations and family reports—are not mutually exclusive. Whenever a family is relating a historical report, there is observable behavior and emotion, and whenever a task is being observed, there is a content element present that gives historical information about the family.

Family reports describe then-and-there behaviors that may provide information about family interaction outside of the therapy setting. Reports can come from the family or from outside sources, such as in-laws, neighbors, teachers, ministers, and previous mental health records. If the family was referred for therapy by someone in the community, this person's report can be valuable. Often families with drinking problems are connected to public and private agencies such as alcohol treatment centers, Alcoholics Anonymous, Al-Anon, Alateen, welfare agencies, child protective services, juvenile court, public schools, day care centers, child guidance centers, and public health nurses and physicians. These people play a large part in the social existence of the family and should not be overlooked by the therapist; they may exert considerable influence on the family and the therapy. If a release of information can be obtained from the family, it is helpful to consult with other community members who are involved so that a uniform approach can be developed. Some families are adept at using gossip to get two service providers fighting with each other over treatment planning while they conveniently slide out of therapy or out of the focus. If many agencies are involved with a family, it is helpful to have periodic conferences, which include the family, to set goals and communicate clearly and directly.

### Personal Reports

In initial interview processes, it is helpful to get personal reports from all family members about their current and historical family situation. Personal reports include information such as job histories, educational histories of both parents, drinking histories of the spouses and families of origin, and educational histories of the children (including number of schools attended, academic abilities, behavior problems, and special skills and abilities).

Satir (1967) initiated her conjoint family therapy with a family life chronology. She began by asking the family as a whole what their perceptions of the problem were. Then she asked the spouses how they met, when they decided to marry, and what attracted them to each other. She divided the spouses to look at their respective families of origin and asked each spouse how he or she viewed his or her parents, siblings, and family life. Following this, a comparison of the past histories of the spouses was made, including how they met. Then the spouses were asked about their expectations of marriage.

This structured interview gives comfort to family members, who see the therapist as being in charge. It gives the therapist information about the families of origin of both spouses and points out strengths of the marital relationship while also giving observations of current difficulties. Satir began with a positive time period, when the spouses met and fell in love. This reminds the couple of a time that may have been more positive than the present and gives them hope. It also gives a more balanced picture than just taking a history of the presenting problem.

Continuing in the chronology Satir asked about the early married life of the spouses and connected it to past functioning in the families of origin. She explored the married couple's expectations of parenting and linked this with the rearing styles of their parents. Turning to the children, she asked about their views of the parents. Satir finally addressed the family as a whole, stressing the need for clear communication and giving a note of hope for the family with closing remarks.

**Family Genogram**

Another form of taking a life chronology involves drawing a structural diagram of a family's three-generational relationship system called a *genogram*. "A genogram is a format for drawing a family tree that records information about family members and their relationships over at least three generations" (McGoldrick & Gerson, 1985, p. 1). They display family information graphically that provides a quick gestalt of complex family dynamics and how the presenting problem may be connected to the family context and its evolution over time (McGoldrick & Gerson, 1985). It is generally accepted that alcoholism can be a three-generational problem. The genogram is a visual diagram of this process.

The genogram is valuable to the therapist and to the family. It puts the presenting problem in a historical context and allows the family to see itself in a new way. It reduces scapegoating, gender power imbalances, and anxiety by providing a structured process of gaining known family history. Each member is valued and included without judgment. Genograms "enable an interviewer to reframe, detoxify, and normalize emotion-laden issues, creating a systemic perspective which helps to track family issues through space and time" (McGoldrick & Gerson, 1985, p. 2).

Genograms are helpful to therapists as tangible maps of the family history, structure, and relationships. They provide an excellent clinical record that can be used for case presentations and allows therapists unfamiliar with the case to quickly understand the family. The genogram is especially useful in tracking multigenerational patterns, triangles, cross-generational alliances, and coalitions.

Genograms are most often associated with Bowen therapy and theory, which uses the technique to track the multigenerational transmission of the family emotional system (Bowen, 1978). However, they have also been used by many other therapists who have adapted them to their methods (Carter & McGoldrick-Orfanidis, 1976; Guerin & Pendagast, 1976; Brandt, 1980).

Guerin & Pendagast (1976), Bowen (1978), and McGoldrick and Gerson (1985) used the symbols shown in Figures 6–6 and 6–7 to illustrate the relationship graph.

> Once the names and ages of each person, the dates of marriages, deaths, divorces and of births are filled in, other pertinent facts about the relationship process can be gathered, including the family's physical location, frequency and type of contact, emotional cutoffs, toxic issues, nodal events, and open/closed relationship index. (Guerin & Pendergast, 1976, p. 452)

The third level of genogram construction involves delineating the relationships between family members. McGoldrick and Gerson (1985) added different types of lines to symbolize different types of relationships between two members of a family (see Figure 6–7). These relationship patterns include very close or fused, fused and conflictual, poor or conflictual, estranged or cut off, close, and distant. As these are added to the genogram, triangles become evident and repeated intergenerational triangles may also appear. It is also helpful to draw a dotted line around those parts of the family living under the same roof. A double circle (female) or a double square (male) is used to indicate the identified patient or the person giving the genogram information. A circle or square with the bottom half colored in can represent an alcoholic. This is useful in tracking alcoholism in a family with multiple alcoholic members over several generations.

Other information that is useful for the genogram includes medical history of chronic illnesses and causes of death, ethnic background and migration date, religion or religion change, education, occupation, unemployment, military service, retirement, difficulty with the law, physical abuse, incest, obesity, alcohol and other drug abuse, smoking, dates of family members leaving home, and current location (McGoldrick & Gerson, 1985).

It is useful to note the physical location of the families of origin to determine if either spouse is using physical distance to avoid emotional issues. Questioning can include the type and frequency of contact. This may demonstrate whether the family is cohesive—remaining close to the original location of the family of

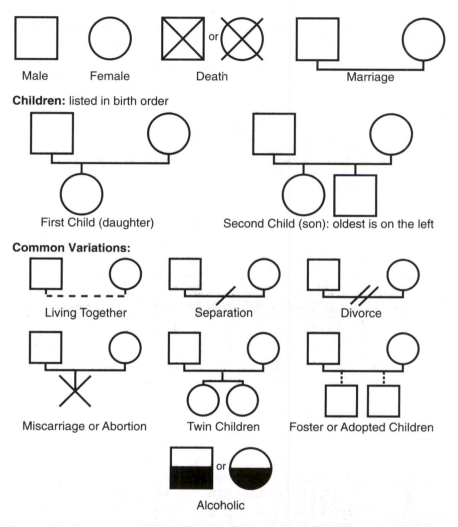

Male    Female    Death    Marriage

**Children:** listed in birth order

First Child (daughter)    Second Child (son): oldest is on the left

**Common Variations:**

Living Together    Separation    Divorce

Miscarriage or Abortion    Twin Children    Foster or Adopted Children

Alcoholic

**Figure 6–6** Genogram Symbols. *Source:* From GENOGRAMS IN FAMILY ASSESS-MENT by Monica McGoldrick and Randy Gerson. Copyright © 1985 by Monica McGoldrick and Randy Gerson. Reprinted with permission of W.W. Norton & Company, Inc.

origin—or explosive—with family members tending to move far away from one another. Information about the frequency of phone contacts is important, as are insights into communications roles such as the "family switchboard," who keeps everyone connected and informed. Places and times of family gatherings can point to ritualistic visitation patterns. Notations can be made about each member's

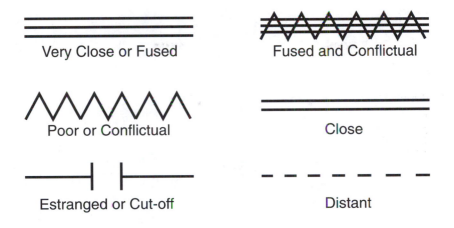

**Figure 6–7** Relationship Lines. *Source:* From GENOGRAMS IN FAMILY ASSESS-MENT by Monica McGoldrick and Randy Gerson. Copyright © 1985 by Monica McGoldrick and Randy Gerson. Reprinted with permission of W.W. Norton & Company, Inc.

personality, occupation, and quality of interpersonal relationships. Information can also be gathered to determine both the emotional pursuers and distancers. Family issues that cause conflict or disruption should be noted. Religion, educational level, an early death of a child or parent, serious physical illness, death of an only child, marriages due to pregnancy, and alcohol abuse can also be discovered. Dates of marriage, death, and divorce can be included, as well as ages of family members shown inside of the symbols.

Patterns of intergenerational alcoholism can be traced. Often alcoholism will skip a generation in the bloodline but occur in a spouse of a child from an alcoholic family and then recurr in their children. Figure 6–8 is a genogram of a family with alternating alcoholism and nondrinking patterns. The etiology section addresses the parenting style of the teetotaler, which produces children with alcohol problems. In this family, the nondrinkers appear moralistic, and the alcoholic parent produced nondrinking moralistic children whose offspring then became alcoholic.

The genogram can be useful in connecting current crises to unresolved issues in the families of origin. The genogram in Figure 6–9 shows a family who requested therapy after their daughter attempted suicide with an overdose of medication.

This history-taking session was uneventful until a comment was made by the mother, Sharon, that when she was 10 years old her mother took a job outside the home, and she had never forgiven her for that. It had taken her 23 years to get enough courage to tell her parents how much this hurt her. Sharon felt that her mother saw money as more important than her daughter, and she vowed never to

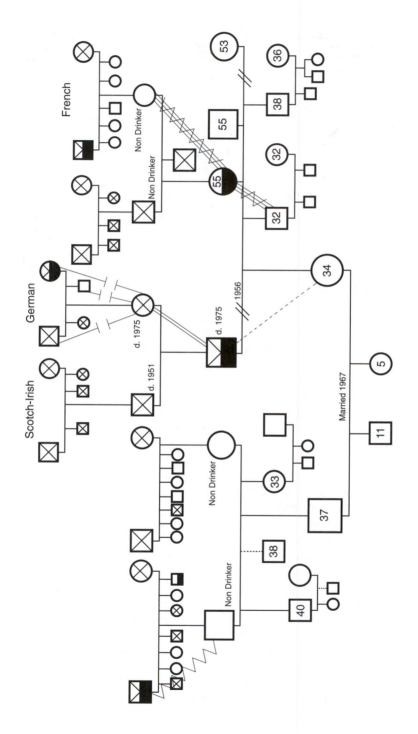

**Figure 6–8** Genogram.

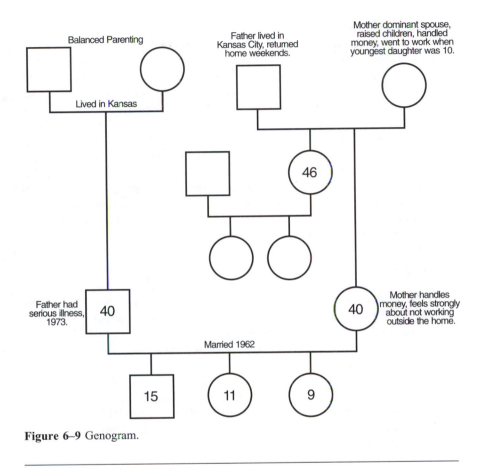

**Figure 6–9** Genogram.

convey this to her own children. Sharon and her daughter had repeated arguments over issues involving money. Every time her daughter asked for something special and Sharon had to turn her down, Sharon felt in a bind. On one hand, she was not able to give her children all they wanted, and on the other hand, she was angry at her daughter for making her sound just like her mother who, as Sharon perceived her, was always preoccupied with money. As hard as Sharon tried not to choose money over her children, the limitation of money and her daughter's demands set up this situation. The daughter interpreted her mother's irritation as a rejection and felt unloved by her family. This issue of money handling was unresolved by the spouses, and although Sharon was uncomfortable handling the money, her husband was unable to accept this responsibility.

Genograms are useful for eliciting a clear picture of the extended family and also may provide the family with insights into unconscious behavior patterns.

## Family Photographs

An interesting variation of history taking is an analysis of selected pictures from the past. Family members are asked to select a set number of photographs they think say something important. All take turns telling why they chose the photographs, what meaning the photographs have for them, and their feelings about the pictures.

The therapist can observe many important behaviors, such as which pictures were shown first and last, who in the family was left out, how quickly or slowly they are presented, how much interest or anxiety is aroused, and how much joking and laughing accompanies the presentation. Pictures can be observed for closeness and distance of each family member to others and the general atmosphere of the photographs. "Usually, alignments, splits, role behaviors, boundaries, communication processes, and family structures are thrown into sharp relief in this process" (Anderson & Malloy, 1976, p. 262).

## Family Evaluation Instruments

As the field of family therapy developed, a need arose for valid and reliable instruments for measuring family systems. There are two types of instruments: observations of families, and paper-and-pencil self-reports. Two of the latter type that have been developed and revised to measure family functioning are particularly useful with alcoholic families.

The first is the Family Environment Scale (FES) (Moos & Moos, 1981). The FES uses a 90-item true-false self-report questionnaire with 10 subscales that measure the social and environmental characteristics of a family. The instrument was normed on more than 1,100 normal families and 500 distressed families. The subscales are divided into three categories:

1. Relationship dimensions
   - *Cohesion*—the degree of concern and commitment of family members and the degree of help and support they give to one another
   - *Expressiveness*—the degree family members are allowed and encouraged to act openly and to express their feelings directly
   - *Conflict*—the degree of open expression of anger and aggression and generally conflictual interactions of the family
2. Personal growth dimensions
   - *Independence*—the assertiveness, self-sufficiency, and ability of family members to make their own decisions and to think things out for themselves
   - *Achievement orientation*—orientation toward achievement (for example, school and work) and/or competition
   - *Intellectual-cultural orientation*—the degree of interest in political, social, intellectual, and cultural activities

- *Active-recreational orientation*—the degree of participation in social and recreational activities
- *Moral-religious emphasis*—stress on active discussion of ethical and religious issues and values
3. System maintenance and change dimensions
   - *Organization*—importance of order and organization and planning of family activities, and explicitness and clarity of family rules and responsibilities
   - *Control*—the use of family rules and procedures to run the family and the extent to which family members order each other around (Moos & Moos, 1981)

The FES was found to significantly differentiate between 42 alcoholic families, of which 59 percent were families in which the male spouses were alcoholic, and 285 "normal" families (Filstead, McElfresh, & Anderson, 1981). The alcoholic families perceived their family environments to be much less cohesive and expressive *(p < .001)* and perceived less emphasis on independence of individuals, intellectual-cultural activities, active-recreational concerns *(p < .001)*, and organizational tasks *(p < .05)* than the "normal" families. The alcoholic families also reported much higher levels of conflict than did the "normal" families (Filstead, McElfresh, & Anderson, 1981).

The FES can be used as part of an initial evaluation or as a pre- and posttest to evaluate treatment progress. The 10 subscales can be graphed once the raw scores are converted to standard scores. This allows the therapist and the family to see how similar or different they are from the normative families. It is an excellent vehicle for goal setting. For instance, a family that is much higher on the conflict subscale and much lower on the cohesion subscale than the norms might want to work on reducing fighting and improving their abilities to help and support one another.

The second instrument is the Family Adaptability and Cohesion Evaluation Scales III (FACES III) based on the circumplex model (Olson, Portner, & Lavee, 1985). The circumplex model of marital and family systems was first conceived by Olson, Sprenkle, and Russell (1979) and further refined by Olson (1986). This is a double-axis model, with one continuum (horizontal) being cohesion and the other (vertical) being adaptability. *Cohesion* is defined as the emotional bonding and the degree of individual autonomy that family members experience (Olson, 1986). This definition includes emotional bonding, supportiveness, family boundaries, time with friends, and interest in recreation. There are four levels of cohesion that are similar to Minuchin's boundaries: disengaged, separated, connected, and enmeshed. *Adaptability* refers to how flexible family systems are and whether or not they have the ability to change. This is the ability of the system to change its power structure, role relationships and relationship rules in response to situational stress (Olson, 1986). The dimension involves leadership, control, discipline, roles, and rules. It also has four levels: chaotic, flexible, structured, and rigid. The model thus creates 16 possible family systems—four balanced on both dimensions, four extreme on both dimensions, and eight mid-range.

FACES III is a 20-item paper-and-pencil scale. Each question has a five-point response option. The inventory is given twice. The instruction for the first administration is, "Describe your family now"; then the family is asked to respond to, "Ideally, how would you like your family to be?" The difference between the two scores measures the level of satisfaction. These scores can be charted in a family profile for interpretation (Fredman & Sherman, 1987).

Killorin and Olson (1984) evaluated chemically dependent families using FACES. They found that chemically dependent families fell into all 16 types of family systems. They included disengaged as well as enmeshed systems and chaotic as well as rigid systems. Olson and Killorin (1987) also compared chemically dependent families with nondependent families using FACES. On the scale of cohesion, about one third of the chemically dependent families perceived their families as disengaged (30 percent of the identified patients and 37 percent of their spouses) compared with 6 percent of the nondependent. In terms of family adaptability, 26 percent of chemically dependent patients and 20 percent of their spouses saw themselves as chaotic, whereas only 5 percent of the nondependent families rated themselves as chaotic. Adolescent chemically dependent patients rated 44 percent of their families as disengaged compared with 8 percent of nondependent adolescents. On the adaptability dimension, 52 percent of these adolescents rated their families as chaotic compared with 20 percent of the nondependent. These adolescents were three times more likely to come from extreme-range families than nondependent adolescents (30 percent versus 10 percent). Both parents and adolescents from chemically dependent families saw their families as more disengaged and more chaotic than nondependent parents and adolescents (Olson & Killorin, 1987).

The purpose of these reports is to gain additional information from outside the family and from the family itself to support observations of current behavior. Evaluations usually contain components of both processes. "The choice of a particular method for evaluating a family depends upon the ideology of the therapist and the state of the family when it enters therapy" (Guerin & Pendergast, 1976, p. 450). Therapists should choose techniques that are compatible with their personal styles. They should pick the method that will get the most information from the family while causing family members the least amount of stress. Therapists should be sensitive to the needs of the family and willing to listen to their pleas for help with a crisis. Families in crisis may need a cooling-off period before being given assignments that might seem unrelated to their immediate needs.

## THERAPIST ASSESSMENT OF FAMILY STRUCTURE

At the completion of the evaluation process, the therapist has assembled impressions about the family's structure, communication patterns, boundaries, alliances, triangles, subgroups, and intergenerational patterns. Role patterns are apparent, and levels of involvement between family members can be assessed.

## Family Relationships

A cognitive map can be formed to delineate the overinvolvement or under-involvement in each subgroup. One technique applies a rating scale for relation-ships with indications for treatment planning. For instance, if marital partners are distanced and underinvolved, if one parent is in charge while the other abdicates the parental role, and if there is overinvolvement between a mother and a daughter, the relationship chart would look like Table 6–1. Involvement is rated on a 1 to 10 scale, with 1 representing no involvement and 10 extreme overinvolvement.

In the alcoholic family, a typical pattern consists of an underinvolved marital relationship (except around the issue of drinking), an unbalanced parenting load, an alcoholic spouse underinvolved with children (except in the case of an incestuous relationship), a nonalcoholic spouse in a strong alliance with the oldest child (the fixer), an overprotected youngest child, and a middle child isolated from all members.

Often the pattern of underinvolvement or isolation of family members occurs, as in the family drawings in Figures 6–2 through 6–5. The mother may abdicate her role as a parent because of her preoccupation with the drinking behavior of her husband and the daughter may become parentified (take on adult behaviors) to help maintain stability and protect the other children. The daughter may become angry at her mother for not being more loving to her father, causing distance between mother and daughter. This daughter then becomes overly concerned with the father and may begin to believe that she can cure alcoholism with love. Eventually, she may seek an alcoholic to marry and cure. Drinking behavior itself sets up isolation in the alcoholic family. The father drinks away from home by himself or with his friends and returns home to nurse his hangover in private. The mother drinks at home but isolates herself to hide it. If both parents drink together, they shut out the children, and both become underinvolved. These children may become symptomatic to gain attention or decide that their needs are unimportant.

**Table 6–1** Relationship Chart

| Relationship | Score | Therapy Goal |
|---|---|---|
| Husband-Wife | 2 | increase involvement |
| Father-Mother | 2 | mutual parenting responsibility |
| Father-Son | 4 | slight increase |
| Father-Daughter | 1 | increase involvement |
| Mother-Daughter | 9 | decrease involvement |
| Mother-Son | 2 | increase involvement |
| Brother-Sister | 2 | increase sibling support |

These children focus on the problems of the parents and others outside of the family. If this rigid role behavior continues, these children may marry alcoholics or go into helping professions to perpetuate the pattern. They have difficulty caring for themselves or achieving emotional closeness when they believe their needs are unimportant.

Families with long-standing, chronic drinking problems may not show isolation in the marital couple. They are often violently overinvolved around the issues of drinking, and their personal identities may have meshed into the "we-ness" that Bowen (1978) refered to when people lack a sense of differentiation. If this intense emotional involvement can be cooled off, Berenson (1976) found, isolation may then occur, and the second stage of therapy may involve reducing the isolation.


## Mapping

Minuchin (1974) developed a process of making a therapeutic map of the family structure. The map is a working hypothesis of family interactions and leads to possible restructuring techniques and therapy goals. The map can be graphed on paper and revised during the therapy process. It might be shared with the family or it may exist only in the therapist's head.

The therapist looks for information in six areas to construct the map:

1. the family structure as a whole, and its transactional patterns
2. the system's flexibility and capacity for change
3. internal relationships—for example, enmeshed or disengaged
4. sources of stress and support available
5. developmental stages of the family
6. how individuals' symptoms are used or reinforced

Minuchin used symbols in his mapping to indicate clear, diffuse, and rigid boundaries. He also mapped affiliation, overinvolvement, conflict, coalitions, and detouring. He used letter symbols for mother, father, children, boy, girl, therapist, and adolescent in graphs of parental, marital, and sibling subsystems or of the entire family. The diagrams can become complicated but can be a useful short-hand for charting family structure and goals for change. See Minuchin (1974) for a complete list of mapping symbols.


## Adaptive Consequences

In evaluating an alcoholic family, the therapist must not only look for the maladaptive consequences of the drinking behavior but also must define the adaptive consequences of drinking. Davis, Berenson, Steinglass, and Davis

(1974) described this process: "Postulate that alcohol abuse has adaptive consequences that are reinforcing enough to maintain the drinking behavior, regardless
of its causative factors. These adaptive consequences may operate on different
levels including intrapsychic, intracouple, or to maintain family homeostasis" (p.
210).

Drinking may be tied to fun and recreation and symbolize a time when
individuals can set aside depressive behaviors and enjoy themselves. The notion
may be, "If I'm drinking, I'm having fun, and I can only have fun if I'm drinking."
Asking this person to give up alcohol is asking him or her to give up fun. The
adaptive consequences may be more subtle and difficult to determine. For
instance, alcohol consumption may maintain physical distance to avoid sexual
contact. Intoxication may be the only state that allows couples the intensity to
make contact by fighting or that decreases inhibitions enough to allow for sexual
activity. Drinking may inadvertently allow for stabilization of the family or
maintenance of social isolation.

The concept of adaptive consequences was derived from a research project in
which couples were videotaped in wet (drinking) states and dry states (Davis,
Berenson, Steinglass, & Davis, 1974; Steinglass, Davis, & Berenson, 1977). The
couples were then videotaped watching the videotapes. In an interview, Steinglass
(1991) reflected on this research and described a vignette of what happened.

> Two couples were sitting on a couch with the VCR and monitor in front
> of them watching a tape. At one point the husband in family A turns to
> husband in family B and says, "Did you see that exchange that just
> happened between you and your wife?" And husband B says, "What
> exchange?" Husband A stops the video tape, rewinds it, says "Well, let's
> watch it again, and really watch it this time." So he watches again. And
> again husband A says, "Now watch the way you were physically
> behaving with your wife and the physical affection you're showing her.
> Just watch your arm around her and the way you were stroking her neck,
> . . ." So they replay the tape and sure enough they see it very clearly. And
> then husband A says to husband B, "You never do that when you're
> sober." (Steinglass, 1991, p. 5)

Determining the adaptive consequences of alcohol consumption is important
because the goals of treatment are to produce adaptive behaviors during sobriety
and to develop effective ways to achieve positive consequences without alcohol
consumption.

Steinglass, Davis, and Berenson (1977) further developed a model to demonstrate how drinking behavior is maintained (Figure 6–10). It is based on three
concepts: "interactional behavior cycling between the sober state and the intoxicated state; patterning of behavior that has reached steady state; and the hypoth-

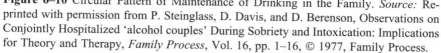

**Figure 6–10** Circular Pattern of Maintenance of Drinking in the Family. *Source:* Reprinted with permission from P. Steinglass, D. Davis, and D. Berenson, Observations on Conjointly Hospitalized 'alcohol couples' During Sobriety and Intoxication: Implications for Theory and Therapy, *Family Process*, Vol. 16, pp. 1–16, © 1977, Family Process.

esis that alcohol use in the alcoholic family has become incorporated into family problem-solving behavior" (Steinglass, 1979, p. 167). Figure 6–10 demonstrates the circular pattern of the alcoholic family, beginning with three ways a family can experience a problem. These parallel the patterns families present with for family therapy. The first problem is pathology in an individual family member, the second difficulty is interactional conflict between family members, and the third area involves the family's inability to adjust to the social environment.

When any of these problem areas threaten to destabilize the family, the family seeks an equilibrium that is associated with changing from sober to intoxicated behaviors. Steinglass believed that intoxication adds stability because of the rapid change in behavior due to the physiological effect of alcohol and the predictability of the intoxicated behavior.

**REFERENCES**

Anderson, C.M., & Malloy, E.S. (1976). Family photographs: In treatment and training. *Family Process, 15,* 259–264.

Bandler, R., Grinder, J., & Satir, V. (1976). *Changing with families.* Palo Alto, CA: Science and Behavior Books.

Berenson, D. (1976). Alcohol and the family system. In P.J. Guerin (Ed.). *Family therapy: Theory and practice.* New York: Gardner Press.

Bing, E. (1970). The conjoint family drawing. *Family Process, 9,* 173–194.

Bowen, M. (1978). *Family therapy in clinical practice.* New York: Jason Aronson.

Brandt, J. (1980). *The family diagram.* Washington, DC: Groome Center, 5225 Loughboro Road.

Burns, R. (1990). *A guide to family-centered circle drawings*. New York: Brunner/Mazel.

Callaghan, G.M. (1993). Art therapy with alcoholic families. In D. Linesch (Ed.), *Art therapy with families in crisis: Overcoming resistance through nonverbal expression*. New York: Brunner/Mazel.

Carter, E.A., & McGoldrick-Orfanidis, M. (1976). Family therapy with one person and the therapist's own family. In P.J. Guerin (Ed.), *Family therapy: Theory and practice*. New York: Gardner Press.

Clarken, J.F., Frances, A.J., & Moodie, J.L. (1979). Selection criteria for family therapy. *Family Process, 18,* 391–403.

Davis, D.J., Berenson, D., Steinglass, P., & Davis, S. (1974). The adaptive consequences of drinking. *Psychiatry, 37,* 209–215.

Filstead, W.J., McElfresh, O., & Anderson, C. (1981). Comparing the family environments of alcoholics and "normal" families. *Journal of Alcohol and Drug Education, 26,* 24–31.

Fredman, N., & Sherman, R. (1987). *Handbook of measurements for marriage and family therapy*. New York: Brunner/Mazel.

Guerin, P., & Pendagast, E.G. (1976). Evaluation of family system and genogram. In P.J. Guerin (Ed.), *Family therapy: Theory and practice*. New York: Gardner Press.

Hanson, K.J., & Estes, N. (1977). Dynamics of alcoholic families. In N. Estes & Heinemann (Eds.), *Alcoholism: Development, consequences and interventions*. St. Louis, MO: Mosby.

Irwin, E., & Malloy, E. (1975). Family puppet interview. *Family Process, 14,* 179–191.

Kaufman, E. (1979). The application of the basic principles of family therapy to the treatment of drug and alcohol abusers. In E. Kaufman & P. Kaufman (Eds.), *Family therapy of drug and alcohol abuse*. New York: Gardner Press.

Kaufman, E. (1980). Myths and realities in the family patterns and treatment of substance abuse. *American Journal of Drug and Alcohol Abuse, 7*(3 & 4), 257–279.

Kaufman, E. (1984). Family systems variables in alcoholism. *Alcoholism: Clinical and Experimental Research, 8*(1), 4–8.

Kaufman, E. (1991). Interview: Edward Kaufman, M.D. *Family Dynamics of Addiction Quarterly, 1*(3), 1-11.

Killorin, E., & Olson, D.H. (1984). Chaotic flippers in treatment. In E. Kaufman (Ed.), *Power to change: Alcoholism* (pp. 99–129). New York: Gardner Press.

Kinston, W., Loader, P., & Miller, L. (1985). *Clinical assessment of family health*. London: Hospital for Sick Children, Family Studies Group.

Kwiatkowska, H.Y. (1967). Family art therapy. *Family Process, 6,* 37–55.

Landgarten, H.B. (1981). *Clinical art therapy*. New York: Brunner/Mazel.

McGoldrick, M., & Gerson, R. (1985). *Genograms in family assessment*. New York: W.W. Norton.

Minuchin, S. (1974). *Families and family therapy*. Cambridge, MA: Harvard University Press.

Minuchin, S., Montalbo, B., Guerney, B., Rosman, B., & Schumer, F. (1967). *Families of the slums*. New York: Basic Books.

Moos, R.H., & Moos, B.S. (1981). *Family Environment Scale manual*. Palo Alto, CA: Consulting Psychologists Press.

Olson, D. (1986). Circumplex model VII: Validation studies and FACES III. *Family Process, 25*, 337–351.

Olson, D.H., & Killorin, E.A. (1987). *Chemically dependent families and the circumplex model*. Unpublished research report, University of Minnesota at St. Paul.

Olson, D.H., Portner, J., & Lavee, Y. (1985). FACES III: Family adaptability and cohesion evaluation scales. In D. Olson, H. McCubbin, H. Barnes, A. Larsen, M. Muxen, & M. Wilson (Eds.), *Family inventories* (revised edition). St. Paul, MN: Family Social Science, University of Minnesota.

Olson, D.H., Sprenkle, D., & Russell, C. (1979). Circumplex model of marital and family systems I: Cohesion and adaptability dimensions, family types and clinical applications. *Family Process, 22*, 69–83.

Papp, P., Silverstein, O., & Carter, E. (1973). Family sculpting in preventive work with well families. *Family Process, 12*, 197–212.

Rubin, J., & Magnussen, M. (1974). A family art evaluation. *Family Process, 13*, 185–200.

Satir, V. (1967). *Conjoint family therapy*. Palo Alto, CA: Science & Behavior Books.

Sherr, C., & Hicks, H. (1973). Family drawings as a diagnostic and therapeutic technique. *Family Process, 12*, 439.

Simon, R. (1972). Sculpting the family. *Family Process, 11*, 49–59.

Steinglass, P. (1979). Family therapy with alcoholics: A review. In E. Kaufman & P. Kaufman (Eds.), *Family therapy of drug and alcohol abuse*. New York: Gardner Press.

Steinglass, P. (1991). Interview: Peter Steinglass. *Family Dynamics of Addiction Quarterly, 1*(4), 1–9.

Steinglass, P., Bennett, L.A., Wolin, S.J., & Reiss, D. (1987). *The alcoholic family*. New York: Basic Books.

Steinglass, P., Davis, D., & Berenson, D. (1977). Observations of conjointly hospitalized "alcohol couples" during sobriety and intoxication: implications for theory and therapy. *Family Process, 16*, 1–16.

Thomas, R.J. (1997). A comparison of depressed, hospitalized adolescents and non-depressed, not hospitalized adolescents on the Family Environment Scale and the Parents-Self-Centered Drawing (Doctoral dissertation, United States International University, 1997). *Dissertation Abstracts International* (in press).

Walsh, W.M. (1980). *A primer in family therapy*. Springfield, IL: Charles C. Thomas.

Watzlawick. P. (1966). A structural family interview. *Family Process, 5*, 256–271.

Wegscheider, D. (1979). *If only my family understood me*. Minneapolis: Compcare Publications.

# CHAPTER 7

# A Prescription for Family Treatment

This chapter introduces the process of family therapy. Volumes have been written on the theory and techniques of family therapy, and it is a popular subject for research and innovation in programming.

This chapter discusses possible treatment strategies to use with the four types of alcoholic families discussed in chapter 6. These include approaches for the family with chronic alcohol problems and techniques for families in which alcohol problems are secondary or not chronic. The chapter is structured in the chronological order in which the treatment methods are used in family therapy. That is, chronic emotional issues are covered first, followed by a discussion of Haley's (1976) model of family therapy with the nuclear family. The chapter then follows the course of family therapy as it leads to marital therapy and marital couples groups. The final stage is family of origin work. Additional stage models for treating the alcoholic family address working with the family from a drinking state through reorganization of the family and finally to intimacy.

Because families with an adolescent substance abuser pose unique issues, some models that have been developed and tested for adolescents are also covered in a short section.

The last section of this chapter is a brief overview of treatment approaches used by five major theories of family therapy: structural family therapy, strategic family therapy, Bowen therapy, experiential family therapy, and behavioral family therapy.

First, the therapist must decide which treatment mode is most appropriate for the client. Clarken, Frances, and Moodie (1979), in reviewing the literature, listed guidelines for discriminating between cases appropriate for family/marital therapy and those that would be more successful in individual treatment. Family or marital treatment is recommended when individual treatment has not been successful or has involved family issues. Family and/or marital treatment is also recommended if improvement in the identified patient leads to symptoms in another family member.

Individual treatment is indicated when "the presenting problem of the individual does not have a significant etiology or an effect upon the family system" (Clarken et al., 1979, p. 395). This is unlikely in an alcoholic family. Individual treatment is also indicated in the following situations:

- when family therapy is misused to deny personal responsibility for a major personality disorder
- when psychopathology of a family member would be prevented by individual work
- when there is massive unworkable pathology in a parent that would point to working with the child individually to teach him or her to cope with the parent
- when parents are deceitful in treatment
- when individuation would be enhanced (This is disputed by authors who believe family work is the best way to individuate.)
- at the end of family treatment, if individual pathology remains
- if detoxification or medication is needed before family therapy

Once the decision is made to engage family members in treatment, an assessment should be conducted to determine the family's motivation for treatment and to decide which treatment method would be most appropriate.

Chapter 6 lists four types of alcoholic families that ask for therapy. First, a family may require therapy when there is hidden alcoholism in one or both parents and a child is the symptom bearer. These families may give clues to alcohol abuse through reports of alcoholism in the families of origin; overfunctioning in one parent and underinvolvement in the other; role reversals; attempts by children to protect their parents; children's fear of talking about the family; denial or isolation; reports of physical abuse or incest; scapegoating of a child; or irrational fear of teenage alcohol or drug abuse. The symptom in the child might be alcohol or drug abuse. Because the parental alcohol abuse is hidden, it is difficult to assess the chronicity of the problem. The therapist must initially focus on the presenting problem while looking for ways to incorporate the drinking problem into therapy. If the family leaves therapy before the parental alcoholism is discovered, the scapegoated child will be angry that his or her efforts failed and may progress to worse symptoms. The therapist should begin with Haley's (1976) approach (described later in the chapter) or a similar family therapy approach. If the alcoholism surfaces, a shift to Berenson's (1976b) chronic approach may be necessary.

In a second type of family, members may openly talk about drinking but are more concerned about other family problems. The history of alcoholism in these families is not very significant. The drinker usually does not have a marked behavior change when drinking. The spouses' relationship is symmetrical at first impression. Alcohol problems in these families seem to result from other problems and will recede if the contributing problems are solved. Because it is unlikely that alcohol is a chronic emotional factor in these families, the therapist should focus on the presenting problems and follow the Haley model.

The therapist should not ignore the issue of drinking and should connect the family difficulties to the excessive drinking at every opportunity. What looked like a family with an alcoholic or problem drinker in the beginning of therapy may turn out to be an alcoholic family chronically organized around the alcoholism.

In the third type of family, alcohol abuse is a major problem because the family is organized around the alcoholic's drinking. There is intense conflict, and the drinking makes other problems worse. The alcoholic may be physically addicted to alcohol and have definite behavior changes when drinking. If the spouses are in intense conflict and the emotionality of the family is high, an initial cooling-off period may be required, with the therapist taking control of the sessions. These families would probably respond to Berenson's chronic family model, discussed later in this chapter.

The fourth type of alcoholic family may seek help when an alcoholic member has completed treatment and is sober. These families are often out of balance. Marital problems may revolve around issues of control of the family, or a new symptom bearer may be produced. If the child's behavior is the presenting problem, the family may have realigned in a negative way. The therapist should assess the family system and look for the adaptive consequences of past drinking. Families referred after the alcoholic member has received individual treatment may have family members who resist looking at their own limitations or the part they play in the problem. These families need to view drinking behavior as only one part of family interaction and allow the alcoholic to get rid of this label and reenter the family with new interaction patterns. The family members must also recognize that they played a role in the drinking behavior.

In all four of these family styles, the issue of drinking must be squarely faced, at some point, by the therapist. It must be understood that the drinking problem will be dealt with and not ignored. This does not mean that the therapist will allow the family to blame all of their problems on the drinking of one member, nor must every session include work on this area.

In a fifth kind of family, the alcohol problem occurs in an adolescent. These families may have hidden parental alcoholism, no parental problems, or parents who are recovering alcoholics. Treatment methods for working with these adolescents are covered later in the chapter.

*Self Help &*

## FAMILY THERAPY AND ALCOHOLICS ANONYMOUS

A further decision by the therapist should be made about the involvement of families in Alcoholics Anonymous (AA) or Al-Anon. This issue is similar to the decision about sobriety discussed in chapter 6. Some therapists insist on attendance of AA meetings as a prerequisite for therapy. Others make distinctions in which clients are encouraged to attend AA. Because attendance at AA meetings may not be appropriate for all problem drinkers, a rigid position on the subject may rule out help for families who might benefit from family therapy alone. Also, many alternatives to AA may be more appealing to some alcoholics. These include Rational Recovery, SMART groups, Women for Sobriety, Secular Organization for Sobriety, and many more specialized self-help groups.

Family therapy and AA may seem to be working at cross-purposes, with AA and Al-Anon "focusing on the alcoholic person as the 'patient'—the antithesis of the family systems approach which identified alcoholism as a family dysfunction and directs treatment at the entire family" (Hindman, 1976, p. 7). Actually, these self-help groups and family therapy have five common factors. They agree that: (1) family members other than the alcoholic suffer, (2) change can occur when significant others are engaged in the process, (3) family members can resist change by the alcoholic, (4) if the alcoholic recovers emotionally and the other family members do not, a crisis may occur, and (5) the individual is responsible for personal change. Davis (1980) saw the commonalties as: (1) both approaches make light of willpower as a necessary motivation for change, (2) they recognize that family members suffer, (3) they make use of contact with significant others to make change in the drinking behavior, and (4) family members can be a source of resistance to change on the part of an alcoholic.

Davis (1980) also listed differences between AA and family therapy. In family therapy the family is the primary treatment medium, while AA uses a group process. There is no direct work with relationships in AA or Al-Anon, where the focus is on personal detachment and reducing reactivity. Although Bowen therapy will work with one person on reducing reactivity to the family of origin, the supportive agent is different in that family therapy involves family members, while self-help groups utilize peers. Observations of how the family operates are available to the family therapist and self-help groups have only reports.

Davis (NIAAA, 1978) warned of a pitfall that can occur when both approaches are used simultaneously: "As family members begin working on a thorny problem in either the therapy or self-help group and there is a resulting rise in anxiety, they may attempt to avoid facing the problem by escaping to the other treatment approach" (p. 4). This problem can be avoided by coordination efforts between the therapist and the AA sponsor. If the family therapy shifts away from the drinking issue to reduce anxiety, AA may be avoided in favor of family sessions. While other problems are appropriate to address in family situations, the connection with alcohol should continue to be a main concern. A choice of family therapy as the sole treatment may be flattering to the therapist, but the decision to change treatment methods should be made on a therapeutic basis and as a joint decision between the family and the therapist.

Another difficulty can arise if the alcoholic creates a triangle between the therapist, his/her AA sponsor, and himself/herself. Alcoholics may block the family therapist by reporting that their sponsor said just the opposite of what the therapist says. Family therapists can reduce this rigid triangle by asking the alcoholics to bring in their sponsors for a session. This can reduce the splitting of the helpers and give more power to the process of change.

Family therapy and AA are, however, incompatible if family therapy is applied to multiple problems of the alcoholic family without a commitment from all concerned to work toward eliminating the drinking behavior as the first priority (Davis, 1980). Changing communication patterns or improving expression of feelings alone will not, by itself, stop a chronic alcohol problem.

Berenson (1976b) believed that "continuation in AA and Al-Anon is up to the client, with the therapist being careful that an early decrease in attendance may be a warning of an impending resumption of drinking, and that continued and frequent attendance for many years may become a stress in the marriage" (p. 292).

Schroeder (1991) suggested that AA and family therapy are compatible from early recovery through reorganization of the family and even in late recovery. She saw AA as helping the alcoholic to take responsibility for self, which is a differentiation move. It is like Bowen's idea of taking an "I position." Family therapy can then promote cohesion and help the family balance between having a sense of belonging while allowing individuation of its members. Schroeder (1991) also suggested that the family therapist can design ways for the family to see that the 12-step group is a metaphor for the healthy family. The cohesiveness and loyalty of the group allows for trust. This same process can be built in the family.

## THE CHRONIC ALCOHOLIC FAMILY

If the therapist is working with a family that has a chronic, ongoing drinking problem (in one or both spouses) and a high degree of emotionality about drinking, treatment initially should focus on drinking management. Berenson (1976b) developed a two-phase treatment approach for families organized around alcohol consumption. Such families may have: (1) a drinker who consumes a moderate amount of alcohol but whose spouse is angry and accusing, (2) a drinker who consumes alcohol intermittently but has severe arguments with family members, or (3) a situation in which both spouses drink excessively with much related conflict. This treatment approach is based on Bowen's (1974) theory, the concurrent use of Alcoholics Anonymous and Al-Anon, and Berenson's clinical experience (Berenson, 1976a).

The initial phase involves management of drinking and setting up conditions that will terminate drinking. The evaluation portion of this treatment should note changes in behavior of the drinker and the other family members when intoxication occurs. Adaptive consequences of this behavior should be noted and a history of drinking patterns in the families of origin included. Care should be taken in this phase to avoid blame (which can lead to nonproductive arguments) and a continuation of the existing family system. Each family member must view his or her behavior as a part of the total problem. History taking is a neutral process that allows an overly emotional system a chance to cool off and begin emotional distancing. Berenson believed drinking may continue in these families but that work on family dynamics cannot occur until drinking stops. This is achieved by encouraging an emotional distance in the marriage. By working with the person who is most motivated (usually the nondrinking spouse), the emotional involvement is toned down and the family helped to detach from the alcoholic. Al-Anon can be used in this phase as support, and it is suggested that the nonalcoholic move toward the Al-Anon sponsor emotionally while distancing from the alcoholic.

In this stage, "the focus is on the nonalcoholic becoming more responsible for self, rather than attempting to control the alcoholic" (Berenson, 1976b, p. 292). In Fogarty's (1976) terms, the spouse, who is the emotional pursuer, must learn to stop chasing the distancer, who is, typically, the alcoholic. This advice applies to the therapist as well. It is useless to pursue alcoholics in treatment if they are using their drinking behavior to distance themselves emotionally. In systems terms, it is better to focus on the family by facilitating changes in the motivated spouse.

To stop the nonalcoholic from pursuing, Fogarty (1976) suggested the pursuer must resolve the emptiness he or she is trying to fill through pursuit. He said, "The therapist should take the pursuer into his (her) own inner emptiness by asking questions like, 'What would it be like inside of you if you lost your spouse?'" (p. 326). Nonalcoholics must learn to achieve for themselves what they are trying unsuccessfully to get from their spouses. Distancing may be a new behavior, but these techniques can be learned if the nondrinker observes the drinker. When the distancer is no longer pursued, loneliness may begin to occur. This can be very helpful to the alcoholic, who may become interested in self-examination and change. "The more a spouse takes a position for herself, the more likely the alcoholic is to stop drinking; the more the spouse takes a position in order to get the alcoholic sober, the more likely such a move is going to be a failure or transient success; or, if successful, the more likely there will be other family problems when the drinking stops" (Berenson, 1976b, p. 293).

If the therapist is able to work with both the alcoholic and the spouse, the therapist must maintain control of the sessions and reduce the affective content of treatment. In these emotionally charged families, defensiveness and blame can spark a conflict that is difficult to stop. Discussions should avoid the relationship between husband and wife, if it is volatile, and move toward problems that both persons brought with them from their families of origin. This discussion takes the attention away from the spouses and cools the system. It also provides a view of how each member contributed to the drinking. The discussion can lead to an examination of marital expectations and periods of history that were happy times for the marital couple. Work and children are also safe subjects and can provide ways of discussing the family structure without direct conflict. If these techniques do not cool down the marital subsystem, the therapist may need to see the couple in individual sessions.

When emotional distance has been achieved, Berenson (1976b) found that a state occurs that he referred to as "walking on eggs" for fear the drinking will resume. At this point, the second phase of treatment attempts to decrease the emotional distance without the resumption of drinking. An attempt is made to reproduce in the sober state adaptive behaviors that were present during intoxicated states.

A good example of this form of treatment was presented by Carter (1977). It involves a case study of a family who came for therapy with a 14-year-old son with school problems. Carter (1977) approached this issue with what she called a "Minuchin-Bowen sequence." She "begins work by focusing on the presenting problem and recommending tasks around that problem, as Minuchin does, and then will either glide into extended family work, or make an explicit second contract with the family to go on in that direction, i.e., coaching parents in work on their families of origin as taught by Bowen" (p. 50).

In this particular case, it became evident that a parental separation was contributing to the son's school problem. In working with the parents, Carter constructed a family genogram that included questions about drinking patterns. She discovered that both families of origin were from Ireland. All of the grandparents were born in Ireland, and the families lived within blocks of each other in the Bronx. The proliferance of alcoholism in both families was astounding. The father came from a family in which both parents were alcoholic, and they had come from alcoholic families as well. The maternal grandmother had six brothers who were all alcoholics and seven sisters who "drank a lot," except for one who became a nun. The mother's family of origin included an alcoholic father, a mother from an alcoholic family, and eight older brothers and sisters, all of whom drank problematically.

Although this was clearly a family with a chronic, long-standing history of alcoholism, neither parent saw alcohol as a problem, and both vehemently refused to have anything to do with Alcoholics Anonymous. The father refused to stop drinking completely, and the mother defined alcoholics as "falling down drunks" or "skid row bums" that had nothing to do with any of her drinking behaviors.

Carter abandoned her usual approach of insisting on AA attendance and used Berenson as a consultant and support person while attempting a new approach to family therapy.

With this approach, the adaptive consequences of drinking were identified, and Carter found that alcohol allowed this family to have a good time. While drinking, they were able to express tenderness and affection (a rare occurrence while sober), have sex (with which they otherwise had difficulties), and to express anger and bitterness that they otherwise avoided. These adaptive consequences certainly did not get problem areas dealt with functionally, but it did get them expressed. Simply stamping out drinking, in this framework, would also be stamping out good times, affection, sex, and emotional release. Carter's goal was to transfer the (drunken) behavior that was serving a functional purpose to the repertoire of sober behaviors.

This treatment lasted two and a half years and was successfully completed when new roles and behaviors eventually replaced old ones. Predictions were made that efforts to change would fail if the drinking continued. A videotape of the mother's drunken behavior was used to help produce the adaptive part of the drunken behavior when she was sober. Extensive family-of-origin work was done with the mother that restructured family relationships and allowed her to shed her victim role.

David Treadway (1989) also developed a model for working with chronic families. His therapy process was adapted from Bowen's model for working with couples with active alcoholism. He chose this model because of the extreme emotional reactivity in these couples and their inability to take personal responsibility for their behavior. He outlined a six-stage model for working with these couples.

1. **Disengagement.** The goal of this stage is to shift the responsibility back to the drinker and to help the spouse change standard responses to the substance abuse that help maintain it. Treadway believed that the chemical abuse is inextricably intertwined with the couple's behavior pattern. This reflects the strategic notion that families develop a circular pattern of behavior around a problem, the pattern itself often becoming part of the problem. He also believed that the spouse may be the most motivated person to change and that a change in his or her behavior will force a shift in the alcoholic's behavior. Another goal of this stage is to get the drinker to stop by changing the spouse's behavior, referring him or her to Al-Anon, or creating an intervention. In a way, the approach is to fire the spouse from trying to get the drinker

to quit; the therapist takes on this role, freeing the spouse to take responsibility for his or her own recovery.

One of Treadway's favorite techniques is telling the nonalcoholic spouse to not demand that the alcoholic not drink over the weekend. Instead he or she is to clip a sale coupon from the paper advertising the alcoholic's favorite alcoholic beverage and present it to the alcoholic, saying, "If you are going to drink this weekend, be sure to shop at this sale." This changes the expected communication pattern: The pursuing spouse backs off and surprises the alcoholic. The nonalcoholic spouse should then go to an Al-Anon meeting.

2. **Differentiation.** The goal of this stage is to help family members tolerate the discomfort and confusion surrounding sobriety and to reduce their unrealistic expectations about early recovery. Treadway acknowledged that couples whose relationship is organized around the substance are destabilized by the removal of the substance from the balance. Spouses also become more aware of the pain and hurt associated with the struggle with the substance abuse. Treadway used a Bowen model at this stage to lower the reactivity in sessions by becoming the third point of the triangle: All of the conversation ran through him. He did not allow the spouses to attack one another and worked to break the fusion of the couple. This is similar to doing individual therapy with the spouse watching. He hoped to develop empathy in each spouse for the other.

3. **Negotiation.** Usually, couples in early recovery have difficulty negotiating and problem solving because one spouse has been overfunctioning in most areas and the other has been subordinated and treated like a child. Because the overfunctioning spouse has developed some sense of worth, if not martyrdom, from the overfunctioning, he or she may be reluctant to give up this hierarchical position. However, the other spouse has to find something to do in the family besides drink. Treadway taught such couples how to put their feelings aside and work effectively together. He acted as an arbitrator in this process.

4. **Conflict management.** One of the most common dynamics of alcoholic or addict families is the everpresent conflict. Conflict can occur during dry stages and wet stages. Substance abuse either dampens conflict or fuels it. Couples in early recovery try to avoid open conflict at all costs because they fear it will lead to drinking or using. Couples need to learn how to tolerate conflict without letting it escalate out of control. Treadway helped couples learn to tolerate unresolved conflict and to fight fairly.

5. **Resolution of the past.** Couples who have been struggling with substance abuse for years have a large storage vault full of hurt, anger, and resentment. As they begin to acknowledge the wasted years of dealing with addiction, unresolved pain from childhood may also emerge in this grief process. Treadway's goals for this stage are to unite the spouses around the shared

pain and loss, instead of allowing the typical adversarial blaming of each other, and to help the couple come to a position of acceptance. Acceptance is not necessarily forgiveness, because some things may not be forgivable, especially physical abuse, sexual abuse, affairs, or refusal to participate in sex.

6. **Intimacy.** Intimacy and sexual behaviors are just as intertwined with substance abuse as is conflict. Sexual dysfunction and sexual abuse are problems commonly coexisting with chemical dependency. Intoxication may be connected with intimate behavior or avoidance of intimacy, and fear of intimacy can be a problem for adults who were raised in chemically dependent families. It is possible that neither spouse has ever seen a positive model of intimacy in a couple relationship. Treadway helped couples "separate reasonable expectations for intimacy from attempts to make up for unresolved family-of-origin needs. Coming to terms with their old grief in relationship to their original families is often a prerequisite to setting realistic expectations for their couple relationships" (p. 96). During this last stage of the treatment model, Treadway removed himself as the third point of the triangle and empowered the couple to take more leadership in the therapy and to become more self-reliant.

Couples may not go through all of the stages of the model or may come and go in therapy over a several-year period. This is, however, a good example of how Bowen theory and a focus on intergenerational issues can be used in treating chemical dependency.

## FAMILY THERAPY WITH NONCHRONIC ALCOHOLIC FAMILIES

In families of recovering alcoholics and in families in which alcoholism or problem drinking is not the presenting problem, alcohol may not be the central issue of the early family sessions. If the therapist redefines the problem as alcohol abuse, the family may become anxious or may feel unheard and pull out of therapy. It is important to begin with what the family identifies as the problem. If the therapist can remain flexible and spontaneous, an initial solvable problem can be a good starting point.

This beginning period allows family members to experience the family nature of their problems. The entire family should attend the early sessions, and the network of support people who are involved with the family are useful for the initial interview.

Haley (1976) developed a structure for the first family interview. He defined four stages: (1) social, (2) problem, (3) interaction, and (4) goal setting.

The *social stage* establishes a comfort level and provides a naturalizing of the social environment. Family members are allowed to sit where they wish. The therapist has a greeting exchange with family members to get their names, ages, and additional innocuous information. The idea is to demonstrate that each person is important and can contribute to the session. At this point it can be determined who is missing from the family and if any members of the extended family would be important contributors.

The issue of blame may arise at this time with the alcoholic family. Either the family is uncomfortable with the unstated alcohol problem and blames a child for their presence in therapy, or family members continue to scapegoat the alcoholic and remain uninterested in their own contributions to the family problems. The therapist should focus on the here and now and avoid discussion of specific problems initially. The family will present a dominant mood that the therapist should attempt to match.

With parents and children all in one room, parent-child interactions, discipline modalities, and sibling relationships may also be noted. This, however, represents only how family members act in front of others and may be different from behavior at home. Also, at this time the parents may be openly in disagreement, in agreement, or in over-agreement about the child's problems. One of the spouses may be reluctant to participate in the session.

Additionally, the therapist can observe the seating arrangement to see if the identified patient is isolated or sitting between the parents or if the parents have an allied child near them.

It is best at this time to keep all conclusions about the family interaction tentative, and therapists should not share their observations with the family. At some level the family is aware of these dynamics and sees this as an invasion. Haley says, "To point out something like a seating arrangement is asking the family to concede something they might prefer not to concede, and thus that action could arouse defensiveness and cause unnecessary difficulties in the therapy" (p. 19).

The second stage is the *problem stage*, and it begins with an inquiry about the family's view of the problem that brought them in for therapy. It signals the end of the social atmosphere stage and indicates that it is time to get down to business. It may be very confusing to the alcoholic family to be in family therapy when it is obvious to them who has the problem. The therapist must clarify why the entire family is asked to participate. The problem orientation can remain, but the therapist may state that it is important to get everyone's opinion of the problem. Usually the therapist has some prior knowledge of the family from a referral source or from the family member who called for the appointment. If the family seems secretive, it is beneficial for the therapist to share this information with the family.

During questioning about the problem area, the therapist needs to decide who to ask and in what way. If the family is simply asked what the problem is, the therapist may receive a long history of all the negative behavior of the identified patient. The therapist instead can offer hope for change and ask questions such as, "What do you want changed in your family?" To assess what caused the family to ask for help, the therapist may ask, "How did the decision get made to call for this appointment?" or "What has happened recently that motivated you to call for the appointment?" Haley suggested, "As a rule, the more general and ambiguous the inquiry of the therapist is, the more room there is for the family members to display their point of view" (p. 21). The therapist should avoid being overly specific because the family may focus on one area such as problems of the child or the alcoholism. This focus simply reinforces the notion that only one person has problems.

It is difficult to present questions to the family as a whole, and usually the therapist is biased in selecting who is addressed. If the therapist is an alcohol counselor, her sympathies may be with the alcoholic, who seems victimized by a nagging spouse. If the therapist is child oriented, he may be angry at the parents, who have neglected and hurt the children. A decision about who to address can best be made by first examining the family hierarchy of power and influence. Usually one parent is more motivated to work than the other, and one parent has more power to get the family to return for further sessions. Haley believed the person who can get the family back to therapy should be treated with respect, but the underinvolved parent should be engaged first.

Sometimes the most detached family member is a child. In this instance, it is best to start talking with the person who is least involved and sits farthest away and work through the family to the most involved member. It is inadvisable to begin with the identified patient, as it may look like the therapist is blaming him or her. Identified patients are used to getting attention when the family is anxious, and this pattern must be broken by the therapist. Haley wrote, "Every therapist must watch out for a tendency to turn to, or on, the problem person in a benevolent way when he or she (the therapist) is anxious and under stress" (p. 25).

In addition, the problem that brought the family to therapy must be clearly stated and not minimized. If the tendency is to extend the social stage and not deal with issues, the family will be confused. If alcohol abuse is the presenting problem and a direct discussion of this issue is skirted, the problem will grow in magnitude and take on the aura of being unmentionable. Even if the therapist does not agree that the presenting problem is the main issue of the family, it can be used as a lever to create change. For instance, if the presenting problem is child oriented but the therapist is certain of marital conflict, the marital relationship can be approached by addressing disagreement on parenting issues. Haley stated, "Usually family members say that one person is the problem. The therapist's job is to think of the problem in terms of more than one person. By thinking that way he is most able to bring about change" (p. 33).

As the problem is being presented, the therapist should simply listen to the family and observe behaviors. The therapist should avoid making interpretations, giving advice, and encouraging emotional reactions with inquiries about feelings and not facts. One member of the family must not be allowed to monopolize the discussion. The therapist must have enough control of the session to allow everyone to speak. If the therapist is not in control, things will go on as they have in the past, and change will not occur.

If the family requested therapy because of a problem with a child, the chances are good that the parents are talking metaphorically about marital problems. If the mother says her daughter is unaffectionate, it is possible that she is also saying her husband is not affectionate. These hypotheses should not be shared with the family. There is a reason that things are not talked about directly, and the child's behavior should not be outwardly connected with the marital situation. If the problem statement is left open and ambiguous, these dynamics can be expressed to the therapist indirectly through safe subjects.

Alcoholic families have many areas that have become forbidden to discuss, and the children may be protecting the parents by withholding information or taking the blame for family troubles. The alcoholic couple may be unable to talk about certain subjects in a sober state but can let the therapist know indirectly that they exist. The therapist can observe all the levels of communication and interaction and can begin to think about the family's problems in a systems context. The therapist does not have to convince the family of this approach; the family will experience it in the process of treatment.

The third stage Haley described is the *interaction stage*. Here the therapist begins to direct individuals to speak to one another, rather than having all comments directed to the therapist. At this stage family members may be able to act out some of their problems. A role-play situation of family interaction around a problem can be set up, allowing the therapist to observe the structure of the family and interaction patterns.

The fourth stage is the *goal-setting stage*, which requires a more detailed definition of the problem. The desired changes are defined and a clear therapeutic contract is negotiated. In order for the family to begin change, it is necessary to put the problem into terms that are solvable, observable, and measurable. This is important for observing therapy outcomes and for giving the family a clear direction for working. At this stage the therapist can ask specific questions about the symptoms, such as when they occur, if they are constant or periodic, if they come on quickly or gradually, or how intense they are. It is useful to find out what everyone does in reaction to a problem. If the problem is drinking, questions can be asked about shifts in everyone's behavior and how it is different from behavior around sober states. In families that present a problem in an area other than alcohol abuse, the goal of the family may not be to stop the drinking of one member. If the therapist insists on abstinence instead of the family's goal, the family may leave treatment. But if abstinence *is* the goal, it is easily observable and can be defined in terms of family behavior.

The alcoholic may also be in the victim or scapegoat role in the family, and it would be dangerous to try to convince the family otherwise at this stage. If the therapist has been involved with the individual treatment of the alcoholic, the temptation may arise to defend the alcoholic and fight the rest of the family. If the therapist works too hard to free the alcoholic from this negative position, the family may have to make the alcoholic worse to show the therapist they were correct. This is also true of a family who has a scapegoated child the therapist wants to save.

In this initial session, the therapist is working to join the family by making everyone feel at ease, allowing everyone to contribute, involving all family members with each other, and including everyone in the decision-making process. If done in a genuine manner, this joining allows the therapist to enter the family and to begin to bring about change from within.

If the family seems hesitant about committing to a course of therapy, it may relieve their anxiety to set a certain number of sessions after which an assessment of progress will occur and a decision to continue can be made.

## Giving Directives

When the therapist has a good idea of the family structure and functioning he or she can begin to give directives or assignments for the family to do in the session and between sessions. These directives are designed to break a rule or pattern in the family interaction in order to bring about change in the system. Every interaction the therapist has with the family has some impact and can be seen as a directive. The behavior of the family around these assignments gives the therapist additional information.

Directives can be stated in two ways. The therapist can tell family members what to do, or the therapist can tell them the opposite of what to do, assuming they will rebel against the directive and do the opposite.

In the first case, it is difficult to tell individuals to do something and have them obey without a great deal of therapist credibility. Haley (1976) said, "If someone drinks too much, sometimes it is a good idea to tell him not to drink. He might stop. But if the problem is severe, he is likely to drink more, and a therapist does not usually have the power to enforce the directive" (p. 52). If the directive comes in the form of good advice, it is not likely to be useful in making change. Directives that are used to change a sequence of behaviors are more helpful and are carried out more often if the family members can see gains for themselves. The therapist and family need to agree on a task that will achieve movement toward the goal that was agreed on. In this direct approach, the therapist must use what has been learned about the family as encouragement to complete the task.

Similarly, it is beneficial to find out what unsuccessful means the family attempted to use in the past to solve the problem. If family members can be made to see how desperate their situation is, they will be more motivated to change. Predictions of worse problems in the future can motivate the family to take action.

If family members are not desperate and they believe they are improving or if they are in aftercare and are looking for maintenance of sobriety, the therapist can promote continuation of this improvement and design a directive that will continue progress.

In stating the directive, the therapist must make precise task assignments and make sure everyone understands the tasks. If the purpose of the directive is to demonstrate unity, everyone must be included. If boundaries need clarification, the subsystems may need to be divided and directives given only to members of the subset. For instance, to increase marital involvement, an assignment can be given to the parents that excludes participation of the children.

If the family seems resistant or excessively stuck in patterns, it is helpful to predict that the family will think the assignment is silly and useless or that they will be unable to do the task. If the task is not done, the therapist should not excuse this disobedience but should help family members see they have failed themselves. If the family wishes to have a second chance, the same directive should not be used. The family should experience the loss of a chance for improvement by their reluctance to carry out the directive.

The second form of directive is referred to as a *paradoxical directive* and should be used carefully with families that are resistant to change, that gain from drinking, or that are practiced at causing the therapist to fail. When the family homeostasis is in a stable state, members are comfortable and less motivated to try a different way to behave. Even if the alcoholic continues to drink, the family may feel more comfortable staying in a predictable pattern of behavior and resist a direct approach from the therapist. Families in aftercare may be unstable due to the change in one person and easy to motivate, or they may be stable in their pattern of interaction with the alcoholic in the role of the victim or scapegoat. By using this rebellious, resistant stance, the therapist can assign a behavior opposite to the desired behavior and can predict failures or assign a directive that involves a request for an increase in the symptom.

When the therapist predicts difficulties, the outcome is usually positive. The idea is to gain the family's compliance whether or not they follow the directive. By predicting that therapy goals will not be achieved if drinking continues, the therapist will be correct if problems occur, and a connection will have been made between drinking and problem behavior. But if there are no problems, then the therapeutic goals have been achieved.

Similarly, if a task assigned in a paradoxical way is carried out, the therapist and client are working together even if the therapeutic goal is not achieved. If the task is not done or the opposite of the directive is carried out, the goal is achieved. Whichever way the family chooses, positive change occurs. The family follows a directive or resists and changes for the better.

In stating paradoxical directives, the therapist must show how these actions will benefit the family members or they will see the therapist as sarcastic. For example, the therapist might say, "It would be too unsettling for this family for Dad to discipline, so he should continue in not correcting the children's misbehavior." Such a statement confronts the family's need to maintain homeostasis at all costs and presents the maladaptive behavior in positive terms.

The successful use of paradox requires much skill and practice and an ability to think of serious problems in a gamelike way.

Haley (1976) listed eight stages of paradoxical intervention:

1. Establish a relationship that can bring about change.
2. Define the problem clearly.
3. Set goals clearly.
4. Offer a plan or a rationale to make the directive seem reasonable.
5. Disqualify the person in the family who has become the authority on solving the problem.
6. Give the paradoxical directive.
7. Observe the response to the directive and continue to prescribe the symptom.
8. As improvement occurs, avoid taking credit for the change, because the family or person is doing the opposite of what is being requested; act puzzled by the improvement.

When assigning direct or paradoxical tasks, the therapist should be certain that they are easy enough for the family to carry out within the existing time and financial limitations, so that if they are not completed the therapist can assume resistance to direct attempts to change the system. In setting the tasks, the therapist should combine what the family thinks is important (the presenting problem) with what the therapist thinks is important (organizational change).

## TRANSITION TO A MARITAL FOCUS

Once improvements have been made in the presenting problem (e.g., reduction in symptoms in a child or reduction in abusive drinking in a family member), the focus of therapy should shift to the underlying problems that were producing the symptoms. If the family leaves therapy without making a major shift in structure, it is likely that the identified patient will return to the original symptomatic behavior or gain new symptoms. Furthermore. another family member may become symptomatic.

If the family is in therapy due to a problem with a child, it is likely that the child is acting out the marital difficulties of the parents. When improvement in the child is created by separating the generational subgroups, the marital issues may surface. These issues may be very difficult for the couple to discuss. Haley (1976) said, "In most therapy with disturbed children, it can be assumed that if parents could easily concede their marital difficulties the child would not be the problem" (p. 155).

If the family initiated therapy because of alcoholism in a parent and the symptoms have been reduced or the alcoholic has achieved sobriety, the marital issues will most likely surface. Haley stated, "Whenever a married person has a severe symptom it inevitably has a function in the marriage, and there will be consequences in the marriage when a symptom is cured" (p. 155). Some families in long-term recovery may still be passing symptoms from one member to the other because the marital issues have never been resolved.

If the marital issues are acknowledged and openly talked about, a contract can be negotiated with the couple to work on them. If the family is unable to directly confront marital problems, these issues may be discussed indirectly by the use of analogies and metaphors.

As the parents begin talking about the presenting problem, the therapist will be able to detect subtle differences of opinion between the spouses. They may talk about their issues in global terms—the problems of all men or all women—or they may talk about another relationship that is similar to theirs. The therapist should respond to these analogies in the same context and not make the interpretation that the spouses are talking about themselves. As family members talk about their problems, the therapist can connect the problems to the relationship of the parents. When the couple is able to admit the difficulties in the marital relationship, a contract can be developed to work in this area.

## Marital Work

When the couple identifies issues in the marital relationship that need intervention, the marital stage of family therapy begins. This phase of treatment may also be the first stage of treatment. Esterly and Neely (1997) preferred to begin with the couple, unless one or more children were exhibiting symptoms or behavior problems, and brought the children into the family sessions after the marriage has been stabilized. It is most productive in marital therapy to work with both spouses so that the therapist does not take sides or have a distorted view of the relationship, although individual sessions may be necessary at times. Haley stated, "Often a marital therapist may feel like a labor negotiator, or a diplomat, involved in conflictual issues. If he joins one side against the other, he becomes part of the problem rather than part of the solution" (p. 161). Remaining impartial is very difficult and the therapist's bias cannot be entirely eliminated. Therapists should be aware of their sex role biases, their attitudes about marriage, and their own struggles with marital relationships.

If possible, the therapist's values in these areas should be kept under wraps in the course of marital therapy, and the therapist should resist joining in a coalition with one spouse against the other. The focus of marital work should be on interpersonal issues and not on individual problems of the spouses. Fogarty (1976) stated, "In dealing with these situations, it is important for the therapist to remember that there is no such thing as an emotional problem in one person, no matter how it looks" (p. 147).

To begin to bring about change in the system, the therapist must determine which spouse will be easier to change. Berenson (1979) felt that the spouse of the alcoholic is suffering more and therefore is more motivated to change. Bowen (1974) stated, "Those family members who are most dependent on the drinking person are more overtly anxious than is the one who drinks" (p. 116). Spouses of alcoholics are often overfunctioning and respond more quickly to attempts to tone down their overinvolvement than the underinvolved alcoholics respond to efforts to increase their involvement. In terms of Fogarty's theory of the pursuer and distancer, the spouse becomes the pursuer in an attempt to change the alcoholic, and the alcoholic becomes the distancer, moving away from the spouse. Alcoholics often focus more on the behaviors of the pursuing spouses than their own behaviors.

The therapist can, if deemed appropriate, see the spouse alone as a way to stop the pursuing or overfunctioning. If both spouses are willing to attend, they can be treated as a unit. Bowen (1974) believed that families in which both spouses attend therapy have better outcomes. Berenson (1979) saw a further advantage in working with both spouses if the alcoholic attends a therapy session drunk.

Berenson wrote, "In the session, the therapist defines it as the spouse's problem rather than his (her) own and may proceed to do a session while the alcoholic is drunk, pointing out either in the session, or by means of videotape after the session, how the drinking affects the interaction within the couple" (p. 235). The pursuing spouse gains the opportunity to establish a feeling of self-determination and responsibility for his or her own behavior, rather than blaming someone or something else. Bowen (1978) referred to this as taking an "I-position."

The next step in working with an alcoholic family is building an emotional support system. These supports can be connections with friends, extended family members, social agencies, vocational training, and the self-help groups of Al-Anon and AA. However, Berenson (1976b) noted, "AA may be a problem if the alcoholic has an impression that he can only share his thoughts and feelings at AA meetings or with his sponsor, not with his spouse" (p. 294). Instead of alcohol, the alcoholic may use the AA meetings as a distancer from the spouse.

In the past 10 years many studies have indicated that marital therapy has a positive outcome when it is part of the treatment for alcoholism. In a review of some of these studies, O'Farrell (1989) found that marital therapy alone or in combination with individual alcoholism treatment produced better marital and/or drinking outcomes during the six months following the beginning of treatment than methods that did not involve the spouse.

Couples therapy is used with alcoholics during three broadly defined states of recovery: (1) initial commitment to change, where it is recognized that there is a problem that needs help, (2) the change itself, in which the abusive drinking is stopped and the couple stabilizes this change for a few months, and (3) the long-term maintenance of change (O'Farrell, 1991). The studies that evaluate these couple models are presented in chapter 11.

A promising model is *behavioral marital therapy* (Holtzworth-Munroe & Jacobson, 1991; McCrady & Epstein, 1995). This model combines a focus on the drinking with work on marital relationship issues through the use of positive couple activities and teaching communication and conflict resolution skills.

McCrady and Epstein (1995) hypothesized four factors that contribute to therapeutic change:

1. **Intensive assessment**. This consists of an assessment of drinking and its consequences, including feedback from the nonalcoholic spouse, and the increased knowledge about the drinking problems. The information is collected to facilitate motivation to engage in new behaviors that support change.
2. **Enhancement of self-efficacy**. This is done by introducing a series of small, successful changes in the behavior of each partner. This encourages self-efficacy in making larger, more difficult changes.
3. **Increase in positive reinforcers**. The positive reinforcers are increased for abstinence and the overall value of the relationship. This is done to provide a strong incentive to maintain the changed drinking behavior.
4. **Learning new cognitive and behavioral coping skills**. This gives the couple an expanded repertoire for dealing with high-risk situations that may lead to relapse.

Wetchler, Nelson, McCollum, Trepper, and Lewis (1994) reported testing the efficacy of using a brief, couple-focused therapy model with couples where the wife is the alcoholic/addict. These women have a sustained substance abuse problem and are involved in an ongoing dyadic relationship. This relationship is defined as marital or cohabiting, heterosexual or lesbian. The model, *systemic couples therapy* (SCT), is an integrated model combining aspects of structural, strategic, and Bowen therapies (McCrady, 1990; O'Farrell, 1991). It is an abstinence-based model that was designed for use in conjunction with individual substance abuse treatment.

From the strategic model comes the idea that a woman's substance abuse is maintained by present interactional behaviors. Wetchler et al. (1994) believed that a woman's ongoing substance abuse is maintained by the couple's relationship and that the substance abuse stabilizes this relationship. It can be a way of avoiding problems that cannot be solved.

Because traditional gender roles give men greater power in relationships, this model integrates concepts of power and hierarchy from the structural approach (Goldner, 1991). This issue of power is very important in treating women substance abusers. Traditional treatment is based on men's desire to control alcohol; thus, men must admit they are powerless over alcohol in order to gain this control. This paradoxical notion is often not useful for women, and it may just increase the general feeling of powerlessness they already experience in life and in their relationships (Johnson, 1990). SCT attempts to develop more egalitarian relationships that support recovery.

Bowen's influence on this model is the concept that relationship patterns are repeated across generations. This concept puts the substance abuse in a multi-generational context that gives the couple more control over and choices about their drug use.

SCT is a 12-session model with three broad stages (Wetchler et al., 1994). Stage 1 is concerned with creating a context for change, assessment, and contracting for treatment. Joining, from the structural model, is used to connect with the couple. The assessment involves evaluation of individual issues, couple interactions, and multigenerational dynamics. This is followed by a contract for both individuals to be involved in the therapy.

Stage 2, challenging behaviors and expanding alternatives, attempts to change the process of the couple's relationship. The therapist tries to alter the destructive sequence of behaviors around the drug use and improve the couple's problem-solving ability and communication skills. Family-of-origin issues that involve repeated patterns of alcohol use and couple interactions are reviewed. A Bowen coaching intervention is used to help the women respond in a new, more differentiated way to their families of origin.

Stage 3, consolidation, focuses on consolidating the change that has occurred in the couple during therapy. The therapist helps the couple review the changes they have made and helps them develop a strategy for solving future problems.

It has only been in the past 15 years or so that treatment providers have recognized the differences in men and women alcoholics. Women develop alcohol problems later than men but progress faster toward problem drinking. They metabolize alcohol differently. They frequently are victims of sexual abuse of various kinds. They have a higher incidence of depression and low self-esteem, and lack role identity. They often have partners who abuse substances and may move from abuse to no use or social use after a divorce (Wilsnack & Beckman, 1984). The strength of the SCT model is its integration of aspects of several marital and family therapy schools to specifically address the unique needs of women alcoholics.

## Marital Couples Groups

An alternative to working with an individual spouse or marital couple is a marital couples group. This approach combines marital therapy, based on a family treatment approach, with group theory, which has been found useful in working with alcoholics. The combination of these two approaches is a popular family-level therapy approach to alcoholism, and several research studies of this method have been reported (Cadogan, 1973, 1979; Gallant, Rich, Bey, & Tevanova, 1970; Steinglass, 1979; Steinglass, Davis, & Berenson, 1977). Cadogan (1979) found that the "very existence of a group of people with similar life circumstances and similar problems coming together for the purpose of resolving their difficulties, and sanctioned by the authority of a professional therapist, lends hope to its members" (p. 189).

Cadogan used group dynamics and problem-solving principles with groups composed of four to six alcoholic couples. These groups focused on interpersonal relations and linked human relations problems with emotional difficulties. By making the group more homogeneous, Cadogan found that marital, childrearing, and in-law problems can be worked on that are relevant to all members. Also, the effect of alcoholism on the marital relationship lends itself to group cohesiveness.

Cadogan (1979) also found these groups to be useful in reestablishing a homeostatic level based on factors other than problems in the family. The groups are additionally beneficial in restructuring interpersonal relationships both within marriages and with other group members. Social isolation, common to alcoholic families, is reduced by participation in the group, and there is pressure on the couples to extend their social contacts outside of the group members. A couple's communication skills are improved because repressed feelings are expressed. Another important function of these groups is to identify and change pathological family interactions. Cadogan (1979) stated:

> Some marital unions are formed by immature individuals who are not ready for a meaningful and adult relationship. These marriages are based on a desire on the part of both members to parentify each other. As a result, the anxiety-producing features of the original parent-child relationship are often reproduced and reexperienced, and the self-defeating coping mechanisms used in childhood are again utilized. (p. 194)

The group is particularly useful in helping individuals see these pathological relationships in other group members and thus acknowledge responsibility for difficulties in their own relationships.

Bowers and Al-Redha (1990) studied 16 couples to evaluate the efficacy of individual therapy versus couples group therapy. There were no differences found at the termination of treatment, but differences were noted six months and one year after treatment. The couples group subjects reported significantly lower alcohol consumption and better marital adjustment than those in the individual treatment condition.

Couples groups can also be used as a transition to family-of-origin work. Framo (1991) used a couples group to assess which problems couples bring to therapy can be solved in marital therapy and which are projective identifications from their families of origin. At the beginning of his couples group he contracted with each group member for a family-of-origin session as part of the marital work.

**Family-of-Origin Work**

If dysfunctional patterns originating from the couple's families of origin are not addressed, they will eventually be repeated. Framo (1976, 1991) used a marital couples group to examine these intergenerational carryovers. He found that spouses' irrational demands are often caused by voids never filled in their family of origin. Framo (1976) found that when couples reach a point in therapy when marital issues have been fully explored and they are unable to reconcile further differences, they are in what he refers to as the "dirty middle" of therapy, where someone must change. He suggested the families-of-origin sessions be included as part of the work on the marital problems. This is almost always met with resistance and refusal, but the marital couples group is used to encourage couples to involve their families. Although the resistance is very strong, Framo was so convinced of the strength of this method that he eventually persuaded 60 percent of his clientele to comply.

Sessions are composed of the husband or wife and his or her family of origin, including siblings. In order to avoid discussion about the marriage, the other spouse is not included. The goal of the sessions is to establish an adult-to-adult relationship between the spouse and his or her respective parents. The sessions center on the life cycle of the family, the key events, happy times, traumatic occurrences, and family structure. The process is similar to working with the nuclear family and often leads to the discovery of information about the family of origin that was previously unknown. Clarification of misunderstandings and misinterpretations of childhood perceptions can occur. Parents become real people to their children and patterns of the past are broken. Framo (1976) stated,

"The client, by having sessions with his or her family of origin, takes the problems back to where they began, thereby making available a direct route to etiological factors" (p. 197). Once these issues have been cleared up with the family of origin, the need to make irrational demands on the other spouse is gone, and the nuclear family can continue at a new level.

If clients' parents are dead, Framo suggested they bring in siblings, aunts, uncles, or any close friend of their parents. Work is done to bring back the memory of the parents, and similar changes can be made with interaction patterns. Satir used group members in a technique she called *family reconstruction* to act the parts of the family members in order to produce a simulation of the family of origin (Satir, 1988).

Similarly, Julius and Papp (1979) developed a technique called *family choreography* with alcoholic families during work on a project funded by the National Institute on Alcohol Abuse and Alcoholism (NIAAA). The focus is prevention of alcoholism in children of families that have a history of drinking. The process is similar to psychodrama and requires several therapists to play the parts of the family. The client becomes the director, and family scenes are acted out. First the family of origin is portrayed, and then a similar scene is created that depicts the nuclear family. Julius and Papp stated:

> This is particularly useful in the alcoholic family system, since it enables the people taking part to perceive the drinking problem across multigenerational family lines, to observe and experience the similarities of behavior of those surrounding the alcoholic in times past and present, and to realize that while the actors may have changed from grandfather to father to husband to brother to son, the roles and situations have remained exactly the same. (p. 202)

When a scene is repeated many times, participants begin to see their own part in the patterns and can begin to change their own behavior instead of blaming others. Problems can be resolved instead of perpetuated.

Bowen (1978) developed a theory of working with families and individuals that involves differentiating from families of origin. He did not bring the families into the session, as Framo did, but coached family members in reconnecting with their families of origin and developing an improved sense of self. He taught his theory and promoted differentiation in the face of chronic anxiety. The specifics of this therapy are covered in the last section of this chapter.

In this final stage of family therapy (working on family-of-origin issues), changes can be made in the interaction patterns of both spouses. This is designed to halt the multigenerational process of alcohol abuse.

## A Stage Model of Family Therapy with Active Alcoholics

Not all family therapy with substance abusers goes through the above stages of family, marital, and family-of-origin work. Some models focus on getting the alcoholism out of the system and then restructuring the family into a healthy system.

This model was designed by Usher and her colleagues for working with families with active alcoholism. The model is divided into four phases: (1) treatment initiation, (2) learning, (3) reorganization, and (4) consolidation (Usher, Jay, & Glass, 1982; Usher, 1991). The initial stage of treatment initiation includes the engagement of the family in treatment, removal of the alcohol from the system, and then treating the family system without the alcohol. This involves an assessment process of making clinical judgments about the level of functioning of the couple or family and the homeostasis of the family that maintains that drinking. The alcoholism is clearly defined as the problem. The therapist contracts with the family for the alcoholic to stop drinking and for each member to participate in either AA or Al-Anon. The goal of this stage is engagement of the entire family in therapy.

The second phase is the process of learning. When the alcohol is removed, the family is left to deal with the "emotional desert" of finding themselves without the skills to relate to one another (Usher, Jay, & Glass, 1982; Usher, 1991). Couples and families discover how to communicate with one another and to solve problems.

The third phase, reorganization, is involved with growth and change. This involves examining how the couple and/or family has made changes, facilitating the process of repair, and evaluating the alcoholic's ability to maintain abstinence and the involvement of the individual and family in AA and other support groups.

The fourth phase is consolidation. Here the goal is empathic family interactions and the process of developing intimacy. The family at this stage is no longer organized around the drinking or the nondrinking. The alcoholic has maintained sobriety and the family begins to take risks in creating a sense of renewal and intimacy.

## The Therapist's Family of Origin

When therapists are working with families it is easy for them to identify with those who have similar life experiences or values. Once a family therapist starts to side with one member or begins to treat a client like someone in his or her own family of origin (or nuclear family), he or she can no longer be an agent of change (NIAAA, 1979). When a therapist becomes the third side of a triangle through being biased in an issue between two others, family members are likely to blame the therapist for their troubles and avoid dealing with the issues between themselves. This is much like the projection process with two parents and a child. Therapists need to examine their own relationships and the dynamics of their families of origin so that they can recognize when they are being pulled into a family, are playing out their own family role, or are failing to keep a therapeutic perspective on the family. For instance, therapists should examine how they feel about father figures because when they are working with a family that has a father like theirs, it will affect their therapeutic decisions. Bowen (1978) believed that clients could not go beyond the level of self-differentiation of the therapist. He recommended a lifelong process for all therapists of working on self-differentiation.

In working with alcoholic families, therapists need to further examine their feelings and thoughts about alcoholism and alcoholics. Therapists' perceptions in this area come from their experiences with their own family systems. Therapists from families where there was no alcoholism or strict abstinence see these issues differently from those who are alcoholic or whose parents or spouses are alcoholic. Therapists who have not examined their perspectives are at risk of joining the family system of their clients and impeding family change. They can become rescuers or persecutors of alcoholics or other family members.

Therapists should evaluate the possibility of overinvolvement with the family if they are taking sides or are rescuing a family member or are confused after a family session. Another warning sign is a feeling of pride in the family's accomplishments. Therapists should beware of telling someone in the family how to act, failing to record certain information in the case records, and viewing members of the family as either victims or villains.

To combat these tendencies, therapists must evaluate their feelings, beliefs, and biases about alcohol, alcoholics, and their roles in the dynamics of their families of origin and their nuclear families. Relationships with parents and siblings and their own birth order should all be examined. Therapists should receive feedback and supervision from other professionals or work in pairs if they are being enmeshed in family dynamics. Videotaping of family sessions can be extremely valuable to the therapist and can be used for supervision and self-analysis.

## ADOLESCENT ALCOHOL AND OTHER DRUG USE AND ABUSE

Families with alcohol problems or those in therapy because of symptoms in a child may be concerned about the drinking habits of their teenagers. If the teen is brought to family treatment as the identified patient, a family history of the drinking patterns of all family members should be taken.

In terms of treatment, Berenson (1976b) divided adolescents with drinking problems into two categories: (1) teenagers from families in which there is no significant history of drinking problems, and (2) teenagers from families in which drinking problems exist in the parental and/or sibling subgroups.

In the first instance, Berenson used contingency and behavioral or reciprocal social contracting, similar to that of Malout and Alexander (1974) and Stuart (1971), whose work was primarily with juvenile delinquents and their families. Often families are concerned with drug use, truancy, and misbehavior as equally disturbing problems.

It is important to note that the major "drinking problem" among youth today is not alcoholism, not problems associated with heavy drinking over a long period of time, but the negative consequences of intoxication, including impaired driving performance, accidents, aggression and violence, disturbed interpersonal relationships, property damage, and impaired school and/or job performance. In youth, alcohol problems are more often associated with episodic and binge drinking than with either physical or psychological addiction to alcohol (U.S. Department of Health and Human Services, 1981, p. 6).

Alcohol is also related to other serious problems of adolescents. "The teen-aged driver is responsible for 44% of all fatal crashes at night where alcohol is involved. Drunk driving accidents are the leading cause of death in people aged 16 to 24. Alcohol was found in the blood of 58% of teens killed in traffic accidents, and 43% of those were legally drunk" (Archambault, 1992, p. 17).

In Berenson's treatment of this first category of teen drinkers (no family history), observable, acceptable behaviors are rewarded and unacceptable behaviors are punished by withholding privileges. Parents are advised that controlling the teenager's drinking outside of the home is not possible but controlling behavior, whether it involves drinking or not, is within their reach. Berenson (1976b) stated, "The goal is to diminish the over concern about drinking, set effective limits, and allow the teenager an opportunity to grow up and become a social drinker, someone whose behavior is seen as coming from within himself, not from a bottle" (p. 295). If the parents are put in charge of the adolescent's behavior, they may feel more able to make changes than with an approach that tries to change the teen's thoughts and feelings.

Alcohol abuse, drug abuse, and adolescent delinquency should be viewed as symptoms of possible family maladjustment. The teen may be using these behaviors to attract attention to a family with a severe alcohol problem in one or both parents.

When the history of the adolescent uncovered alcohol abuse in the parents or a history of problems in several family members, Berenson (1976b) focused first on the alcohol problems in the parental subgroup. He began by working with the more motivated spouse, and this often encouraged the other spouse to enter therapy. If both spouses are alcoholic, the problem is compounded. The therapist can begin by working with the spouse who is sober at the time and switch to the other spouse as the drinking pattern shifts. By connecting the drinking behavior to presenting problems and predicting difficulty in change, the therapist can avoid jumping in to save the family and can simultaneously allow the family to take responsibility for changing.

It is valuable to stop the multigenerational transmission of alcoholism with the parents so that abusive drinking by the adolescent can be controlled (by the parents) and turned around before becoming chronic in adulthood.

There are times when adolescent drug abuse needs to be addressed directly because it is interfering with the adolescent's educational and social progress. In the past, adolescents who were diagnosed as chemically dependent were put into inpatient treatment programs in hospitals. Very few of these programs involved the families in any significant way. Often it was a relief to the family to have someone else "fix" the child. These programs have ceased to exist for two reasons: (1) chronic relapsing of adolescents on return to their families, and (2) refusal of insurance companies to pay for this treatment.

These problems, however, fostered the development of new models of treatment that are designed to intervene in adolescent drug abuse and the related problems. Todd and Selekman (1991a) further defined the issues and problems with chemical dependency treatment of adolescents. They stated that although there is much concern about drug use in adolescents, alcohol is the most commonly abused chemical substance. About 90 percent of teens drink before they finish high school and one in seven high-school seniors drinks to inebriation on at least a weekly basis. Forty percent of these seniors use other drugs such as cocaine, amphetamines, and look-alike drugs. These teens see their use as social, being influenced by peer and parents use (Todd & Selekman, 1991a). Although this amount of alcohol and other drug use may seem alarming, most drug use by adolescents can best be understood as transitional behavior that occurs within normal development from adolescence into adulthood (Jessor & Jessor, 1977). In fact, in another longitudinal study, Shedler and Block (1990) found that adolescents who had engaged in some drug experimentation (primarily with marijuana) were the best adjusted in adulthood compared with adolescents who used drugs frequently or who had never used drugs. It is, however, difficult to determine what drug abuse is transitional and what is an addiction that needs intervention.

Traditional treatment for adolescent chemical dependency is not very successful with 10 percent of the adolescents maintaining sobriety for six months beyond treatment. Todd and Selekman (1991a) saw as a major treatment problem the failure to involve the family in a substantial way. They recommended engaging the family early in treatment, normalizing drug abuse, reframing it in a system context, and complimenting the parents for bringing the adolescents to treatment. They actively involved families in the treatment plan and gave them choices.

Another failure of standard treatment is to not involve other systems that affect the adolescent. Adolescents are influenced by schools, probation departments, peers, coaches, and a variety of potential helpers. Todd and Selekman (1991a) normalized relapses as part of the recovery process for adolescents, reframing them as inevitable but also as opportunities for comeback practice. They involved the family in a fire-drill-like response to the relapse and practiced this in sessions. Selekman (1991) even used the adolescent's peers in family therapy to facilitate trust between parents and adolescents, to act as a consultation team, and to provide a natural relapse-prevention support system.

The National Institute on Drug Abuse funded studies to assess the usefulness of family therapy as a treatment for adolescent drug abuse. This led to several models of family therapy designed specifically for this purpose. The Purdue brief therapy model, created and evaluated at Purdue University, was one of the family therapy models that integrated family therapies that have previously demonstrated their effectiveness, which was applied to adolescent substance abuse (Lewis, Piercy, Sprenkle, & Trepper, 1991; Piercy & Frankel, 1989). The model included theory from Stanton and Todd (1982), who demonstrated the effectiveness of structural-strategic family therapy with adult heroin addicts; Szapocznik, Kurtines, Foot, Perez-Vidal, and Hervis (1983, 1986) at the University of Miami School of Medicine, who found strategic therapy effective in decreasing adolescent drug abuse; Minuchin, Rosman, and Baker (1978), who found that structural family therapy decreased symptoms of psychosomatic illnesses such as asthma and anorexia nervosa; Alexander (1974), who used functional family therapy to work with juvenile delinquents; and Patterson (1982), who repeatedly demonstrated the effectiveness of behavioral contracting with delinquent adolescents. The brief 12-session model is geared to help change the entire family into a healthier supportive environment. Its goal is to stem the current drug abuse of an adolescent and prevent the development of drug use by a younger sibling.

The treatment process has four phases:

1. Join the family and assess structure. *build rapport, trust  make assessment*
2. Implement the mode by giving directives and teaching assertiveness and refusal skills. *Set goals, education*
3. Facilitate and monitor change. *case manage, keep things going  solve issues, other problems*
4. Terminate the therapy. *summarize, provide referrel, follow up evaluating change*

The treatment goals are:

• to decrease the family's resistance to treatment
• to restrain immediate change through presenting the dilemma of change with instructions to go slow
• to establish parental influence
• to assess the presenting problem for system payoffs
• to interrupt dysfunctional sequences of behavior
• to teach assertion skills

In a study of 148 adolescents and their families, this model was compared by the Purdue researchers with a family drug education program, the Training in Parenting Skills (TIPS) program, and individual-based drug counseling of adolescents. The results indicated that the two brief, family-based drug interventions together appeared to reduce the drug use of nearly half (46 percent) of the adolescents. In commenting on this success, Lewis (1991) stated:

> We suspect that this success was due partly to the fact that both of these outpatient interventions focused on the systemic treatment of entire family groups. In contrast, however, the family therapy intervention seems to have been more effective in significantly reducing adolescent drug use for a greater percentage of the adolescents (54.6%) than the family education intervention (37.5%). An even more dramatic result of the study was this: Although more than twice as many adolescents in the family therapy condition (40%) were hard drug users at their pretest, twice as many of these had users (44.4%) moved to no use at all by the posttest time, compared to only the 25% of the hard users in the family education condition who moved to no drug use. (pp. 2–3)

This Purdue project is also analyzing data about how the model works for minorities, lower sociecomomic groups with less education, and single-parent families. Additionally, the researchers are doing a long-term follow-up to determine if this model is effective prevention of substance abuse for the younger siblings in the families.

The Purdue model was successful with roughly 69 percent of the families. However, a group of adolescents and their families did not respond (Todd, 1991). The project staff referred to them as "no-problem problem" families who were typically mandated for treatment and did not admit there was a problem (Eastwood, Sweeney, & Piercy, 1987). This group responded to the more positive approach of solution-focused therapy, which focused on their strengths and abilities to solve problems.

In another comparison study of family therapy with family education and group treatment for adolescent substance abuse, Joanning, Quinn, Thomas, and Mullen (1992) found family therapy was superior to the other two treatments. In a controlled outcome study of Anglo and Hispanic youth in Lubbock, Texas, drug users were randomly assigned to three treatment groups. The family therapy treatment was a structural-strategic model that involved 60- to 90-minute weekly sessions for seven to 15 weeks. The treatment team consisted of two therapists and one supervisor. The adolescent group therapy was a traditional outpatient group of 12 90-minute sessions that involved integrated social skills training, cognitive development, and role theory. The group process was used to encourage a drug-free lifestyle. The family education program was given biweekly in six sessions of two and a half hours. The three to four families in each group learned about the effects of drugs on the body, behavior, and the family. This included films and discussion.

The family systems therapy was superior to the other two in reducing adolescent substance abuse. At the posttest 54 percent of the family systems therapy subjects were not using drugs compared with 28 percent in the family drug education model and 16 percent of the adolescents in the group therapy. The families that benefited from the family therapy treatment included some that were highly disorganized with marital conflict and weak parental coalitions, single-parent families, and well-organized families. The families that did not respond well included those with parental chemical abuse, more chronic adolescent substance abuse, or others presenting with a variety of idiosyncratic problems (Todd, 1991). The 40 percent of families with these characteristics responded better to more constructivist methods such as the Milan systemic approach (Boscolo, Cecchin, Hoffman, & Penn, 1987), the Ackerman approach (Papp, 1983), and the Anderson and Goolishian approach from the Galveston-Houston Family Institute (Anderson & Goolishian, 1988).

Other models were also developed specifically for treating adolescent substance abuse. Liddle was the principal investigator of the Adolescent and Family Project of the University of California, San Francisco. As part of that NIDA-funded project he developed *multidimensional family therapy*. This model addresses multiple spheres of human functioning, including the affective, cognitive, and behavioral domains of each individual in the family and the subsystems of the family (Liddle & Diamond, 1991; Todd, 1991).

All the above models were based on the Stanton and Todd (1982) model of structural-strategic therapy used to treat heroin addicts. New models, however, were developed that have their roots in the Mental Research Institute (MRI) Brief Therapy approach (Fisch, Weakland, & Segal, 1982; Watzlawick, Weakland, & Fisch, 1974). The Solution-Focused Brief Therapy model was developed by de Shazer (1985) and refined by others (Berg & Gallagher, 1991; O'Hanlon & Weiner-Davis, 1989).

Solution-focused therapy had a basic assumption that "nothing always happens." That is, there are times when adolescents are not abusing substances. Berg and Gallagher (1991) believed that nagging and preaching by the therapist only replicates the family's efforts that haven't worked to halt the drug use. Instead they focused on what the adolescents are doing right and what they are good at. They constructed solutions rather than solved problems.

The interventions used by solution-focused therapists involve asking questions and searching for successes. Questions include questions to find exceptions or when the adolescent does not use drugs or have problems; scaling questions that help focus the treatment goal and assess change; the miracle question, "If a miracle happened overnight while you were sleeping and your problem is solved, how would you know?"; coping sequence questions, to search for strengths in negative clients; and pessimistic sequence questions that join the therapist with the client in acknowledging how bad the problem is while looking for some optimism (Berg & Gallagher, 1991).

Solution-focused therapists also look for past successes or days without drugs before therapy, current successes made during therapy when the adolescent was able to overcome the urge to use drugs, and future successes in the form of clear, concrete, and measurable goals. They also foster a positive attitude and a focus on change by reframing negatives positively and giving lots of compliments.

Selekman (1992) was creative in using some of Michael White's (1986) cybernetic approach to externalize the drug problem. He challenged adolescents to fight the drug monsters and asked them how long they have been carrying the problems on their backs. He also searched for strengths and interests of the adolescents and integrated them into the treatment plans. In one instance Selekman created a plan for beating the urge to use drugs in an adolescent who was a wrestler; he assigned scoring points for fighting the drug monster similar to how a wrestling match is scored. He also gave lots of compliments and award certificates to his clients.

Therapists have integrated other approaches with solution-focused brief therapy to create a more playful approach to the treatment of adolescent substance abusers. Todd and Selekman (1991b) proposed an integrated model, adding some of the new theories of solution-focused brief therapy and White's cybernetic approach (White, 1986) to a base of structural-strategic therapy. This incorporates the aspects of each model that they believed are most useful in working with families with adolescent substance abusers.

## AN OVERVIEW OF TREATMENT TECHNIQUES FOR FAMILY THERAPY

In chapter 3, the etiological and philosophical bases of structural family therapy, strategic family therapy, Bowen therapy, experiential family therapy, and behavioral family therapy were presented. This section covers specific family therapy techniques attributed to each of these models. This is only a brief overview of each theory, and further reading is recommended in each of these areas.

### Structural Model

The structural model was developed by Minuchin (1974), who saw individual symptoms as system-maintaining devices. He believed they are expressions of family dysfunction or are at least supported by the family system. Minuchin observed that symptoms are reinforced by family members and that a restructuring of the family must occur to reduce the symptoms. Minuchin thought that dysfunction in the family occurs when there are unclear levels of authority and power, when expectations are misunderstood, when there is confusion as to the functions of subgroups, or when rigid or diffuse boundaries exist in the family.

The goal of structural family therapy is to alter the family structure so that the family can solve its problems. The therapist alters boundaries and realigns subsystems to change the behavior and experiences of each of the family members (Nichols & Schwartz, 1995). A common goal is to help parents function as a single parental unit without division or conflict. Parents, also, need to be in charge of the children and not act as their buddies or peers.

Minuchin (1974) developed a highly structured process for family therapy with three overlapping parts. First, the therapist joins the family in a position of leadership and director of the therapy process. Minuchin referred to this as joining the family like a wise uncle. The second process is mapping the underlying structure of the family. Minuchin devised a system of symbols to graphically map out the family structure, boundaries, and interactions. The third process is the intervention to change the family structure.

In the initial joining, the therapist uses counseling techniques of empathy and support to adopt the family's style and blend into its world. This joining is tempered with professional objectivity so that the therapist does not become a pawn that is moved by the family rules like other members.

Joining and accommodation techniques include: (1) maintenance—that is, support of individuals, subsystems, and alliances that exist in the family, (2) tracking family communication patterns with clarification and reflection to let family members know they are understood, and (3) mimesis, or a reflecting of the mannerisms of the family and its individual members. The therapist greets each member and uses his or her position to respect the authority of the parents by asking them to describe the problem. Children are also respected and given a chance to present their perspectives. The therapist tries to match the family's tone and way of speaking, using language—even coping mannerisms and postures. This is an important part of therapy. The therapist must be accepted by the family before its members will allow him or her to change them.

The next step is working with interaction. This is a process, called *enactment*, of getting family members to talk to one another so the therapist can observe the interactions. The therapist may give a directive—for instance, for the parents to have a conversation about their concerns for their son—or may have a parent try to get a child to behave. This gives the therapist a chance to see how they behave at home, to observe boundaries and rules for behavior.

An interactional or structural diagnosis is done that focuses on family interactions. This process has six areas of evaluation:

1. family structure as a whole, including transaction patterns
2. family flexibility and capacity for change
3. sensitivity of individual members to each other in an enmeshed or a disengaged family
4. family life context, with attention to areas of stress and means of support
5. family developmental stage and ability to perform stage-appropriate tasks
6. use of individuals' symptoms to reinforce family structure

The goal of the diagnosis is to move the family from seeing only one person as having a problem to spreading the problem to all family members and then to finding a solution that will benefit all of them. The diagnosis is established in the first session but is refined and revised as more data are gathered and interventions are tried.

After the diagnosis of the family structure, the therapist creates a map or guideline for restructuring the family and establishing goals. Minuchin developed symbols for boundaries, affiliation, overinvolvement, conflict, coalition, and detouring. He used letters to denote family members and therapists in drawing out these maps. When a plan has been made for change, the restructuring process begins. The techniques of accommodation are the beginnings of the restructuring process, which attempts to move the family toward goals established in the mapping process. Restructuring is a confrontation and a challenge to the family to make a change. The therapist tries to unbalance the family and move its members toward new problem-solving methods. The following are restructuring techniques:

- **Actualizing family transactional patterns**. In this process the therapist engages the family in interactions so their patterns and structure can be observed, including nonverbal behaviors that may be incongruent with their verbal behavior.
- **Marking boundaries**. The boundaries between individuals or subsystems in a family may be too weak (enmeshed) or too strong (rigid). By changing rules or establishing specific functions for subsystems, the therapist can strengthen enmeshed boundaries and ease rigid boundaries. If boundaries are diffuse and relationships enmeshed, therapists find ways of marking boundaries. This can be done in the sessions by changing where people are sitting or between sessions by assigning tasks. Rigid boundaries can be opened up by connecting family members. During a session, the therapist might ask family members who are distant from the family to become more involved in the process of the session as well as challenge conflict avoidance by family members.
- **Escalating stress**. The therapist tries to promote a healthier resolution of stress in the sessions. Stress is created when the therapist encourages conflict,

joins alliances, and emphasizes differences. The therapist then has an example of how the family responds to stress and can work toward change in the stress-reduction patterns that are maladaptive. Unbalancing is an attempt to arbitrarily add importance or weight to one person's perspective in order to make a shift in the process and shake the homeostatic balance. The therapist shows preference to individual family members in turn to even things up.

- **Assigning tasks.** These are the homework assignments that can begin in the sessions and can be assigned for clients to work on during the week.
- **Utilizing symptoms.** The therapist may rally the family around the task of removing a symptom, may exaggerate a symptom so that the family will get rid of it, may deemphasize a symptom, or may move on to a new symptom to remove the secondary gains involved with the symptom.
- **Manipulating the mood in the family.** The therapist observes the family atmosphere and predominant mood and attempts to match it, as Haley (1976) recommended. Change can occur when the therapist exaggerates the mood and points out this pattern to family members by outdoing them. If everyone is yelling, the therapist can yell louder.
- **Providing support, education, and guidance.** The therapist becomes a teacher and instructs the family how to behave in a more appropriate way. As part of changing the family structure, structural therapists may use a cognitive or educational approach to normalize behaviors that the family may see as terrible or to reframe behavior or problems with a positive twist.

This structural method works to aid the family in building a new structure that can deal more positively with stress. Termination of therapy comes when the family can resolve its present problems via the new structure.

**Strategic Family Therapy**

This chapter has already addressed the techniques of Haley (1976), whose work in developing his strategic problem-solving theory evolved from the communication model. This section briefly outlines techniques used by other strategic therapists.

Strategic family therapy found its roots in the thinking of Gregory Bateson and Milton Erickson. It has also been influenced by the MRI group in Palo Alto where Haley worked with John Weakland and Don Jackson on the communications model. That group later developed the MRI brief family therapy model. Other influences were systems theory and cybernetics and Minuchin's structural family therapy (Nichols & Schwartz, 1995).

In strategic family therapy, the primary responsibility for change lies with the therapist, whose job it is to plan a strategy for solving the client's problems. The therapist sets clear goals that lead to this end. Strategic therapists define the problem as a type of behavior that is part of a sequence of acts between several people.

The first task is to define the presenting problem in such a way that it can be solved. Interventions involve directives about something that the family members are to do, both inside and outside of the interview. They may be straightforward requests or paradoxical.

Madanes (1991) proposed six dimensions for conceptualizing a problem. These are paradoxical ways of viewing behavior.

1. **Involuntary versus voluntary**. Individuals come to therapy believing that they have no control and that their symptoms are involuntary. The therapist reframes the symptoms as voluntary and gives the family members choices.
2. **Helplessness versus power**. Individuals with symptoms often feel helpless to change; however, the position of helplessness is often powerful.
3. **Metaphorical versus literal sequences**. The idea that a symptom is a metaphor for the problems of another family member may lead the therapist to focus on the real problem.
4. **Hierarchy versus equality**. This is related to the issues of power and helplessness. Often children are in a power position over their parents and this disturbs the hierarchy of the family. Although all family members are equally valuable as human beings, in healthy families the parents are in charge.
5. **Hostility versus love**. Individuals are often seen as being motivated mainly by hostility or love, and the same behavior can be interpreted either way. A parent's disciplinary action toward her child may be seen by others as hostile punishment or as an act of love that teaches.
6. **Personal gain versus altruism**. The symptomatic person may be motivated by altruism or personal gain. This is connected to whether the person is perceived as hostile or loving.

These ways of viewing the problem and the symptomatic person help the therapist to understand the paradoxical nature of human behavior. It is much easier to develop a paradoxical directive if the therapist can see both sides of the dichotomy.

Madanes (1991) believed all problems can be thought of as stemming from the dilemma between love and violence. The more intense the love, the closer it is to violence in the sense of intrusive possessiveness. She outlined four dimensions of family interactions and needed interventions:

1. **To dominate and control**. Power is used for personal advantage and the relationships are exploitive. The therapist needs to redistribute power and

change how power is used. The problems that these families bring to therapy are delinquency, drug abuse, behavioral difficulties, and bizarre behavior. The strategies for change are correcting the hierarchy, negotiations and contracts, changing who benefits from the symptom, and using rituals and ordeals.

2. **To be loved**. Family members are involved in a struggle to be cared for that leads to self-inflicted violence. The therapist needs to redistribute love among family members, change how love is used, and change the wish to be loved to the desire to love and protect others. Family members usually experience psychosomatic symptoms, depression, anxiety, phobias, eating disorders, and loneliness. The dominant emotion is desire and the inter-actions are excessive demands and criticism. The strategies for change involve changing the way parents are involved with children, prescribing continuation of the symptom, prescribing a symbolic act, and prescribing pretending the symptom to the family.

3. **To love and protect**. This interaction may elicit intrusiveness, possessive-ness, domination, and violence. The dominant emotion is despair. The thera-pist must change how family members protect and love each other and who takes care of whom. The therapist introduces the wish to repent for the violence. Families like this come to therapy with suicide threats and attempts, abuse and neglect, guilt obsessions, temper tantrums, and thought disorders. The strategies include reuniting family members, orienting them toward the future, and arranging reparation; changing who is helpful to whom; and empowering the children to be appropriately helpful to their parents.

4. **To repent and forgive**. The interactions are based in grief and resentment, and include lies, secrecy, deceit, self-deprecation, isolation, and dissociation, and the emotion is shame. Presenting problems are incest, sexual abuse, attempted murder, and sadistic acts. The therapist finds out who did what to whom and changes the wish to avoid responsibility to the desire to become compassionate and to develop a sense of unity with others. The strategies are to create an atmosphere of higher emotions, to find protectors for the victims, and to elicit repentance, forgiveness, compassion, and a sense of unity with others.

The goals of this therapy are to control action, control mind, control violence, encourage empathy, encourage hope and humor, promote tolerance and compas-sion, and encourage forgiveness and kindness (Madanes, 1991).

## Bowen Therapy—An Intergenerational Approach

The techniques used in this model are based on Bowen's (1978) concepts of personality. The focus of therapy is on the central triadic relationship of the parents and a child. The projection process is investigated, and part of the triangle is changed so differentiation can move to a higher level. If one part of the triangle or one of the triangles in the family is changed, the whole system changes.

In a family that is emotionally charged, such as an alcoholic family, anxiety must be reduced before change can occur. If change is requested prematurely, too much anxiety will be created in the family, which may refuse further treatment.

Initially, short-term goals are set that include all family members. However, the central figures may be worked with individually or included with other family members later in the therapeutic process. The therapist helps clients see their problems in a family orientation and facilitates communication between all family members.

In addition, a detailed diagnosis of the family system is done that includes the observation of relationship triangles, an analysis of the projection by parents onto children, and a determination of the degree of individual and family differentiation. The person who is most likely to respond is identified and is usually the one who is most differentiated. This move toward individuality will increase family tension, and the family will resist this change. The resistance may have an effect on the person trying to differentiate, and he or she may become emotionally distressed and withdrawn. But true differentiation does not necessarily occur with a physical separation, and the family may reestablish a lower level of differentiation.

The therapist encourages rationality to counter emotional responses and thus convinces the person who is attempting differentiation that he or she is doing the right thing and should resist the pull back into the ego mass of the family. The therapist must be careful not to appear to be siding with one family member against the rest, while continuing to encourage the differentiating person to respond in a less emotional way and to break old patterns. This allows the family to realign in a new manner.

The therapist should also encourage the use of "I" statements to help the individual express responsibility for his or her own beliefs, feelings, and behaviors. If the differentiating person develops a new way of speaking, the family may respond in alternative ways. This is only the beginning of change, and the family may continue to resist. Until the tension is released by the family, there is potential to revert back to the old process.

After the successful differentiation of one person, there is usually a period of tranquillity that may be followed by other family members also seeking a higher level of differentiation. Termination of therapy occurs when widespread change is established. This method of treatment can be useful in short-term symptom reduction or can involve a family in years of treatment. It is useful for chronic alcoholic families to reduce emotionality and eventually attempt marital and family-of-origin work. Bowen (1978) worked with spouses and children of alcoholics when the alcoholics refused to attend therapy and was successful in changing the alcoholic family system enough to influence change in all the members. However, he preferred working with the entire family.

Although Bowen therapy is considered to focus more on theory and to offer few practical techniques, seven techniques are prominent (Nichols & Schwartz, 1995).

1. **Genograms**. This technique is used to organize data during the evaluation of the family and to track relationship processes and triangles over the course of therapy. This evaluation process is covered in chapter 6.
2. **The therapy triangle**. The family will attempt to pull the therapist into its symptom-related triangles, but the therapist needs to stay free of the emotional entanglements and remain detriangulated. This allows the family system to calm down and begin to solve problems. In treating couples, each spouse is asked a series of process questions designed to tone down the anxiety and increase the availability of objectivity and thought. Effort is made to slow down the overfunctioner and allow the underfunctioner to become involved.
3. **Relationship experiments**. The goal here is to help family members to become aware of their roles in the system dynamics. For instance, pursuers are encouraged to restrain their pursuit and to decrease their demand for emotional connection to see what happens. Distancers are encouraged to move toward others with communication of thoughts and feelings.
4. **Coaching**. This does not mean telling people what to do. It means asking process questions to help clients figure out family emotional processes and their role in them. The goals are to increase self-understanding and self-focus and to develop functional attachments to family members.
5. **The I-position**. This is a way of decreasing anxiety and breaking the cycle of emotional reactivity. It means taking a personal stance on an issue rather than being focused on what others are doing.
6. **Multiple family therapy**. This is a model that Bowen used with multiple couples in a group (Nichols & Schwartz, 1995). He took turns working with each couple while the others watched. The purpose was for the couples to learn about the emotional process by watching others from a more detached perspective. Framo used this process in his multiple couples group (Framo, 1991).
7. **Displacement stories**. This involves showing films and videotapes and telling stories to teach families about system functioning. This approach was developed by Phillip Guerin (1971).

The goal of Bowen therapy is differentiation, which is a lifelong process of striving to keep one's being in balance through reciprocal external and internal processes of self-definition and self-regulation. This is different from individuation, autonomy, and independence. It involves taking a nonanxious stance in the face of anxious others; saying "I" when others are demanding "we"; being clear about one's own personal values and goals; and taking maximum responsibility for one's own emotional being and destiny. Differentiation is an emotional concept, not a cerebral one. It has to do with the fabric of one's integrity and the capacity to be one's own integrated aggregate-of-cells person while still belonging to or being able to relate to a larger colony (Friedman, 1991). The therapy focuses on how to be an individual in a group.

**Experiential Family Therapy**

Satir (1967) is considered a pioneer in the communication model area, which developed into an experiential family therapy model. She clearly outlined a step-by-step process for family therapy in her book *Conjoint Family Therapy*. Her approach focuses on making families aware of their communication processes. The goals of her therapy are to enhance individuals' potential for becoming more fully evolved as human beings, to gain new hope and to help reawaken old dreams or develop new ones, to strengthen and enhance coping skills, and to make individuals aware of their abilities and choices. The emphasis is on hope.

Satir's therapy is considered humanistic and experiential. She believed that dysfunctional behavior is the result of a deficit in growth, that an arrest in self-development or the self-actualization process causes psychological problems. She believed that, when left alone, humans tend to flourish and separate from societal and familial pressures. A healthy family is one that offers its members the freedom to be themselves by supporting privacy as well as togetherness.

Satir emphasized two important concepts: (1) the concept of *self*, which has eight levels—physical, intellectual, emotional, sensual, interactional, contextual, nutritional, and spiritual; and (2) the concept of *self-esteem*, whereby the ability to communicate is linked to the individual's self-esteem. Individuals with low self-esteem have never separated from their parents and individuals with similar self-esteem levels regroup together. This concept seems influenced by Bowen's thinking.

The process of therapy is in three phases: (1) gathering information, (2) transforming the system, and (3) consolidating change. The role of the therapist is to enter each session as if it were the first time with the family and explore what can be discovered. The therapist should be authentic and communicate congruently. The therapist is a teacher and a coach.

As a therapist, Satir initially helped to establish trust in each family member for the others. Confidentiality was explained, and she worked to elicit confidence in her ability as a therapist. Next, the focus was on family awareness of behaviors and communications. She used the "here and now" behavior of the family to help them face their problems. She employed techniques such as the life chronology (discussed in chapter 6), a description of a typical day, acting out an at-home conflict situation, and investigating an individual's role in the family's delivery of messages.

Her techniques included role-playing, family sculpting, role reversal, direct communication between dyads, experiencing the other's reality, visualizations, and family reconstruction, which is a blend of Gestalt therapy, guided fantasy, hypnosis, psychodrama, and sculpting.

These techniques create a new awareness in the family that can be used to change communication patterns. The new behaviors are applicable to daily life routine and may be role-played in the family therapy session.

The length of time the family is involved in this treatment depends largely on their degree of disorganization and their willingness to change. This form of treatment is useful to families who are currently operating with old role behaviors (even though the alcoholic is sober) or those families who are chaotic due to isolation, miscommunication, or misunderstanding, and who teach these processes to their children. Conjoint family therapy is popular in the alcohol field. The role behaviors that Satir defined have been adapted to the alcoholic family. This theory is covered in more detail in chapter 3.

## Behavioral Family Therapy

Behavioral family therapy is based on the theories of behavior therapy and a social learning model. A short explanation of the theory is needed to understand this model of family therapy. There are four main steps in the process of behavior therapy. The first involves gathering data to obtain a clear picture of individuals and their environment. Depending on the presenting problem, this evaluation may include questionnaires, personal histories, standardized tests, or simply an informal interview. The second step is a determination of the areas that need remediation. This decision is shared between the client and the therapist. The third step is the intervention phase, breaking behaviors into smaller units. The fourth step is a follow-up check to determine the success of the program and decide if further procedures are needed.

In the intervention step, the behaviors that need remediation are evaluated for strength. How long have they been going on and how often do they occur? Behaviors are often charted to establish a baseline of occurrence. This baseline is needed to determine progress. Next, reinforcers are applied to behaviors that are to be increased and concurrent techniques are used to decrease unwanted behaviors. If behaviors are to be increased, the therapist must pick from four kinds of reinforcing procedures:

1.  respondent conditioning—giving a reward every time a behavior occurs
2.  shaping—rewarding successive approximations of the behavior
3.  scheduling reinforcement based on time or number of behaviors
4.  modeling—the imitation of behavior that is seen in others

Once a procedure is selected, a program is set up that is closely monitored by the therapist. Early in the program, the therapist should observe the client's reactions and then make periodic evaluations until the desired behavior occurs.

If a behavior is to be decreased, the therapist selects from five procedures that will reduce the occurrence of these behaviors:

1.  extinction—the removal of all reinforcers
2.  saturation—the overloading of reinforcements to make the reinforcements noxious
3.  punishment—a negative response to behavior such as a slap
4.  time out—the removal of the person from the reinforcing situation
5.  systematic desensitization (developed by Wolpe, 1973)—working with phobic reactions through pairing an anxiety-producing situation with a relaxed state

The model is described in more detail by Patterson (1971).

Therapists in this model begin with families by asking what members are teaching each other and how they reinforce behaviors. The therapists also establish what the family is willing to do.

The steps of working with the family parallel those of behavior therapy. First, family members are asked what behavior they want changed and what behavior they would like substituted for it. In the second step, the family is asked to count and record the target behavior to establish a baseline. In step three, a program is established by selecting goals and techniques that use social reinforcers. Respondent conditioning is the first choice of procedures, but if that is not possible, a schedule of reinforcement is established. If the behaviors to be changed are complex, shaping is used. Patterson used contracting between family members and reported these contracts to the therapist as a social reinforcer. Once new behaviors have been internalized, there is no further need for reinforcement.

This treatment is usually short-term and nonanalytical. The therapist is interested in overt, observable behaviors. Alcoholic families that exhibit predictable patterns of role behaviors are good candidates for behavioral family therapy. If the adaptive consequences of the drinking behavior could be learned during sober states, the need for the family to reinforce drinking will be reduced.

Behavioral marital therapy has been used with success in treating alcoholic couples. Related models include contingency contracting, in which one person agrees to change something if the other changes. Models used with couples struggling with alcoholism were presented earlier in this chapter.

## REFERENCES

Alexander, J.F. (1974). Behavior modification and delinquent youth. In J.C. Cull & R.E. Hardy (Eds.), *Behavior modification in rehabilitation settings*. Springfield, IL: Charles C. Thomas.

Anderson, H., & Goolishian, H. (1988). A view of human systems as linguistic systems: Preliminary and evolving ideas about the implications for clinical theory. *Family Process, 27,* 371–393.

Archambault, D.L. (1992). Adolescence: A physiological, cultural, and psychological no man's land. In G. Lawson & A. Lawson (Eds.), *Adolescent substance abuse: Etiology, treatment and prevention*. Gaithersburg, MD: Aspen Publishers.

Berenson, D. (1976a). A family approach to alcoholism. *Psychiatric Opinion, 13,* 33–38.

Berenson, D. (1976b). Alcohol and the family system. In P.J. Guerin (Ed.), *Family therapy: Theory and practice*. New York: Gardner Press.

Berenson, D. (1979). The therapist relationship with couples with an alcoholic member. In E. Kaufman & P. Kaufman (Eds.), *Family therapy of drug and alcohol abuse*. New York: Gardner Press.

Berg, I.K., & Gallagher, D. (1991). Solution focused brief treatment with adolescent substance abusers. In T.C. Todd & M.D. Selekman (Eds.), *Family therapy approaches with adolescent substance abusers* (pp. 93–111). Boston: Allyn & Bacon.

Boscolo, L., Cecchin, G., Hoffman, L., & Penn, P. (1987). *Milan systemic family therapy: Conversation in theory and practice*. New York: Basic Books.

Bowen, M. (1974). Alcoholism as viewed through family systems theory and family psychotherapy. *Annals of the New York Academy of Science, 233,* 115–122.

Bowen, M. (1978). *Family therapy in clinical practice*. New York: Jason Aronson.

Bowers, T.G., & Al-Redha, M.R. (1990). A comparison of outcome with group/marital and standard/individual therapies with alcoholics. *Journal of Studies on Alcohol, 51*(4), 301–309.

Cadogan, D.A. (1973). Marital group therapy in the treatment of alcoholism. *Quarterly Journal of Studies on Alcohol, 34,* 1187–1194.

Cadogan, D.A. (1979). Marital group therapy in alcoholism treatment. In E. Kaufman and P. Kaufman (Eds.), *Family therapy of drug and alcohol abuse*. New York: Gardner Press.

Carter, E.A. (1977). Generation after generation. In P. Papp (Ed.), *Family therapy: Full length case studies*. New York: Gardner Press.

Clarken, J.F., Frances, A.J., & Moodie, J.L. (1979). Selection criteria for family therapy. *Family Process, 18,* 391–403.

Davis, D.I. (1980). Alcoholics Anonymous and family therapy. *Journal of Marital and Family Therapy, January,* 65–73.

de Shazer, S. (1985). *Keys to solution in brief therapy*. New York: W.W. Norton.

Eastwood, M., Sweeney, D., & Piercy, F. (1987). The "no-problem problem": A family therapy approach for certain first-time adolescent substance abusers. *Family Relations, 36,* 125–128.

Esterly, R.W., & Neely, W.T. (1997). *Chemical dependency and compulsive behaviors.* Mahwah, NJ: Lawrence Erlbaum Associates.

Fisch, R., Weakland, J., & Segal, L. (1982). *The tactics of change: Doing therapy briefly.* San Francisco: Jossey-Bass.

Fogarty, T.F. (1976). Marital crisis. In P. Guerin (Ed.), *Family therapy theory and practice.* New York: Gardner Press.

Framo, J.L. (1976). Family of origin as a therapeutic resource for adults in marital and family therapy: You can and should go home again. *Family Process, 15,* 193–209.

Framo, J.L. (1991). *Family of origin therapy: An intergenerational approach.* New York: Brunner/Mazel.

Friedman, E.H. (1991). Bowen theory and therapy. In A.S. Gurman & D.P. Kniskern (Eds.), *Handbook of family therapy: Vol. 2.* New York: Brunner/Mazel.

Gallant, D.M., Rich, A., Bey, E., & Tevanova, A. (1970). Group psychotherapy with married couples; A successful technique in New Orleans alcoholism clinic patients. *Journal of Louisiana State Medical Society, 122,* 41–44.

Goldner, V. (1991). Sex, power, and gender: A feminist systemic analysis of the politics of passion. In T.J. Goodrich (Ed.), *Women and power: Perspective for family therapy* (pp. 86–106). New York: Norton.

Guerin, P. (1971). A family affair. *Georgetown Family Symposium,* vol. 1, Washington, DC.

Haley, J. (1976). *Problem solving therapy.* New York: Harper and Row.

Hindman, M. (1976). Family therapy and alcoholism. *Alcohol Health and Research World, Fall,* 3–9.

Holtzworth-Munroe, A., & Jacobson, N.S. (1991). Behavioral marital therapy. In A.S. Gurman & D.P. Kniskern (Eds.), *Handbook of family therapy,* vol. II (pp. 96–133). New York: Brunner/Mazel.

Jessor, R., & Jessor, S.L. (1977). *Problem behavior and psychosocial development: A longitudinal study of youth.* New York: Academic Press.

Joanning, H., Quinn, W., Thomas, F., & Mullen, R. (1992). Treating adolescent drug abuse: A comparison of family systems therapy, group therapy, and family drug education. *Journal of Marital and Family Therapy, 18*(4), 345–356.

Johnson, S. (1990). *Wildfire: Igniting the she/volution.* Albuquerque, NM: Wildfire Books.

Julius, E.K., & Papp, P. (1979). Family choreography: A multigenerational view of an alcoholic family system. In E. Kaufman & P. Kaufmann (Eds.), *Family therapy of drug and alcohol abuse.* New York: Gardner Press.

Lewis, R.A. (1991). Testimony before the house select committee on children, families, drugs and alcoholism. Hearing on: Adolescent substance abuse: Barriers to treatment, 101st Congress of the United States, Washington, DC.

Lewis, R.A., Piercy, F.P., Sprenkle, D.H., & Trepper, T.S. (1991). The Purdue brief therapy model for adolescent substance abusers. In T.C. Todd & M.D. Selekman (Eds.), *Family therapy approaches with adolescent substance abusers.* Boston: Allyn & Bacon.

Liddle, H.A., & Diamond, G. (1991). Adolescent substance abusers in family therapy: The critical initial phase of treatment. *Family Dynamics of Addiction Quarterly, 1*(1), 55–68.

Madanes, C. (1991). Strategic family therapy. In A.S. Gurman & D.P. Kniskern (Eds.), *Handbook of family therapy: Vol. 2.* New York: Brunner/Mazel.

Malout, R.E., & Alexander, J.F. (1974). Family crisis intervention, a model and technique of training. In R.E. Handy & I.G. Cull (Eds.), *Therapeutic needs of the family*. Springfield, IL: Charles C. Thomas.

McCrady, B.S. (1990). The marital relationship and alcoholism treatment. In R.L. Collins, K.E. Leonard, & J.S. Searles (Eds.), *Alcohol and the family* (pp. 220–243). New York: Guilford Press.

McCrady, B.S., & Epstein, E.E. (1995). Marital therapy in the treatment of alcohol problems. In N.S. Jacobson & A.S. Gurman (Eds.), *Clinical handbook of couple therapy* (pp. 369–393). New York: Guilford Press.

Minuchin, S. (1974). *Families and family therapy*. Cambridge, MA: Harvard University Press.

Minuchin, S., Rosman, B., & Baker, L. (1978). *Psychosomatic families: Anorexia nervosa in context*. Cambridge, MA: Harvard University Press.

NIAAA Information and Feature Service. No. 49, (July 11, 1978).

NIAAA Information and Feature Service. (August 6, 1979). Counselors should study own family system. No. 62.

Nichols, M.P., & Schwartz, R.C. (1995). *Family therapy: Concepts and methods*. (3rd ed.). Needham Heights, MA: Allyn & Bacon.

O'Farrell, T.J. (1989). Marital and family therapy in alcoholism treatment. *Journal of Substance Abuse Treatment, 6*, 23–29.

O'Farrell, T.J. (1991). Using couples therapy in the treatment of alcoholism. *Family Dynamics of Addiction Quarterly, 1*(4), 39–45.

O'Hanlon, W., & Weiner-Davis, M. (1989). In search of solutions: A new direction in psychotherapy. New York: W.W. Norton.

Papp, P. (1983). *The process of change*. New York: Guilford Press.

Patterson, G.R. (1971). *Families*. Champaign, IL: Research Press.

Patterson, G.R. (1982). *A social learning approach to family intervention; Coercive family process*. Eugene, OR: Castialia.

Piercy, F.P., & Frankel, B.R. (1989). The evolution of an integrative family therapy for substance abusing adolescents: Toward the mutual enhancement of research and practice. *Journal of Family Psychology, 3*(1), 5–26.

Satir, V. (1967). *Conjoint family therapy* (2nd ed.). Palo Alto, CA: Science and Behavior Books.

Satir, V. (1988). Advanced marriage and family therapy. Course presented at United States International University, San Diego, CA.

Schroeder, E.D. (1991). Family therapy and twelve-step programs: A complementary process. In I.B. Isaacson (Ed.), *Chemical dependency: Theoretical approaches and strategies*. Haworth Press.

Selekman, M. (1991). "With a little help from my friends": The use of peers in the family therapy of adolescent substance abusers. *Family Dynamics of Addiction Quarterly, 1*(1), 69–76.

Selekman, M. (1992). Taming the chemical monsters: Cybernetic-systemic therapy with adolescent substance abusers. In G. Lawson & A. Lawson (Eds.), *Adolescent substance abuse: Etiology, treatment and prevention*. Gaithersburg, MD: Aspen Publishers.

Shedler, J., & Block, J. (1990). Adolescent drug use and psychological health: A longitudinal inquiry. *The American Psychologist, 45*(5), 612–630.

Stanton, M.D., & Todd, T.C. (1982). *The family therapy of drug abuse and addiction*. New York: Guilford Press.

Steinglass, P. (1979). An experimental treatment program for alcoholic couples. *Journal of Studies on Alcohol, 40*(3), 159–182.

Steinglass, P., Davis, D.I., & Berenson, D. (1977). Observations of conjointly hospitalized alcoholic couples during sobriety and intoxication: Implications for theory and therapy. *Family Process, 16*, 1–16.

Stuart, R.B. (1971). Behavioral contracting within the families of delinquents. *Journal of Behavior Therapy and Experimental Psychiatry, 2*, 1–11.

Szapocznik, J., Kurtines, W.M., Foot, F., Perez-Vidal, A., & Hervis, O. (1983). Conjoint versus one person family therapy: Some evidence for the effectiveness of conducting family therapy through one person. *Journal of Consulting and Clinical Psychology, 51*(6), 889–899.

Szapocznik, J., Kurtines, W.M., Foot, F., Perez-Vidal, A., & Hervis, O. (1986). Conjoint versus one person family therapy: Further evidence for the effectiveness of conducting family therapy through one person with drug-abusing adolescents. *Journal of Consulting and Clinical Psychology, 54*(3), 395–397.

Todd, T.C. (1991). The evolution of family therapy approaches to substance abuse: Personal reflections on integration. *Contemporary Family Therapy, 13*(5), 471–495.

Todd, T.C., & Selekman, M.C. (1991a). Beyond structural-strategic family therapy: Integrating other brief systemic therapies. In T.C. Todd & M.C. Selekman (Eds.), *Family therapy approaches with adolescent substance abusers*. Boston: Allyn & Bacon.

Todd, T.C., & Selekman, M.C. (1991b). An integrated approach. In T.C. Todd & M.C. Selekman (Eds.), *Family therapy approaches with adolescent substance abusers*. Boston: Allyn & Bacon.

Treadway, D. (1989). *Before it's too late*. New York: W.W. Norton.

U.S. Department of Health and Human Services. (1981). *Guide to alcohol programs for youth*. (DHHS Publication No. ADM 81–437). Washington, DC: U.S. Government Printing Office.

Usher, M.L. (1991). From identification to consolidation: A treatment model for couples and families complicated by alcoholism. *Family Dynamics of Addiction Quarterly, 1*(2), 45–58.

Usher, M.L., Jay, J., & Glass, D.R. (1982). Family therapy as a treatment modality for alcoholism. *Journal of Studies on Alcoholism, 43*, 927–938.

Watzlawick, P., Weakland, J., & Fisch, R. (1974). *Change: Principles of problem formation and problem resolution*. New York: W.W. Norton.

Wetchler, J.L., Nelson, T.S., McCollum, E.E., Trepper, T.S., & Lewis, R.A. (1994). Couple-focused therapy for substance-abusing women. In J.A. Lewis (Ed.), *Addictions: Concepts and strategies for treatment*. Gaithersburg, MD: Aspen Publishers.

White, M. (1986). Negative explanations, restraints and double description: A template for family therapy. *Family Process, 25* (2), 169–184.

Wilsnack, S.C., & Bechman, L.J. (1984). *Alcohol problems in women*. New York: Guilford Press.

Wolpe, J. (Ed). (1973). *The practice of behavior therapy: Vol. 2*. New York: Pergamon Press.

# CHAPTER 8

# Related Problems:
# Abuse, Sexual Dysfunction,
# and Divorce

The family model of treatment acknowledges that alcohol abuse is only one of the problems that dysfunctional alcoholic families may bring to treatment. Family relationships, marital relationships, vocational growth, educational achievement, social relationships, and intergenerational boundaries may be suffering in these families. This chapter covers further serious problems that often accompany alcoholism in a family: spouse abuse, child abuse and neglect, incest, sexual dysfunction, and divorce. These problems can occur in any combination and do not necessarily result because of alcoholism, nor does alcoholism result from family violence. Researchers in the field of family violence believe that once a pattern of violence is established in a family, it would occur even in the face of abstinence (Gelles & Straus, 1988; Browne, 1987). Violence also tends to increase in frequency and intensity over time (Gelles & Straus, 1988; Browne, 1987). In the light of this information, violence has serious implications for the well-being of family members, and it is inadvisable to avoid dealing with the problem until abstinence is achieved (Gorney, 1989).

It is estimated that 48–87 percent of batterers are intoxicated at the time of the abuse (Gelles, 1972; Appleton, 1980). In a study of 234 abusive men who had been charged with abuse, 70.5 percent were under the influence of alcohol and/or other drugs (Roberts, 1988). Interestingly, 58 percent of this sample were not referred to counseling for their violent behavior.

Although women are often homicide victims in these violent relationships, they sometimes find themselves facing homicide charges for killing the batterers. Browne (1987) studied 250 battered women, 42 of whom killed their batterers. She found that the difference between the women who killed and those who did not was a change in behavior of the batterer. They had gone a step beyond the usual level of violence that the women had come to expect or they turned the violence toward the children. Of the two groups, 79 percent of the men killed became intoxicated every day or nearly every day, whereas only 40 percent of the other men fit this pattern. The men who were killed were also more likely to use street and prescription drugs.

In a review of research published in English, Orme and Remmer (1981) found no empirical data to support an association between alcoholism and child abuse. Although there does not seem to be a cause-and-effect relationship between these actions, many studies and articles describe alcoholic families that experience violence, incest, and neglect (Browning & Boatman, 1977; Hanks & Rosenbaum, 1977; Hindman, 1977, 1979; Sanchez-Dirks, 1979; Spieker & Mouzakitis, 1976; Virkkunen, 1974). Kempe and Helfer (1972), who were first to describe battered child syndrome, stated that alcohol is involved in one third of child abuse cases. Virkkunen (1974), while investigating 45 incest cases, found that 22 of the perpetrators were alcoholic. Often these studies are based on subjective opinions rather than hard data, and the findings are contradictory. Definitions of drinking problems vary, samples are small, and data on drug and alcohol problems are sometimes combined. Yet, the family therapist must be alert for signs of family violence and incest as possible issues in working with the alcoholic family.

## FAMILY VIOLENCE

### Abuse

For years child abuse was ignored, but in the 1960s dramatic child abuse cases stirred public awareness and encouraged research in the detection and prevention of this problem. Researchers found four factors common in families in which child abuse occurs: (1) isolation, (2) a history of abuse in the family, (3) young, inexperienced parents, and (4) greater than average complications with pregnancy (Kent, 1975; Smith, Hanson, & Noble, 1974). The connection between physical abuse and alcohol can be seen in the isolation of alcoholic families and abusive families. Many alcoholics were themselves abused as children and have physical abuse and incest as part of their family history. Alcoholics often can be described by some of the characteristics that Spinetta and Rigler (1972) found in the child abuser: low frustration tolerance, low self-esteem, impulsivity, dependency, immaturity, severe depression, problems with role reversals, difficulty in experiencing pleasure, and lack of understanding of the needs and abilities of infants and children. Cork (1969), in a study of children from alcoholic families, found that role reversals are common, with the child performing the role of the adult and the alcoholic acting childlike in a preoccupation with self.

There are other similarities in children from alcoholic families and those who are abused. Caffey (1965) found that abused children have the following characteristics: retardation, deformity, illness, behavioral problems, disobedience, delinquency, and emotional problems. Chafetz, Blane, and Hill (1971) found that children of alcoholics have emotional and behavior problems and are disobedient. Children from alcoholic families and abusive families often feel ashamed of their situation and feel guilty about their part in it.

Because disabled children are at high risk for child abuse, there may be a connection between fetal alcohol syndrome and child abuse. Children who have deformities or growth difficulties because of alcohol abuse by the mothers during their pregnancies may be at risk for physical abuse (Mayer & Black, 1977). Spieker and Mouzakitis (1976) found that the maltreatment that children receive from alcoholic parents is not so much physical abuse as neglect.

Child abuse is not a small problem. One thousand children are killed by their caretakers annually, and one in 22 children are victims of physical abuse, whereas neglect occurs twice as often (Gelles & Straus, 1988). Gelles and Straus (1989) also estimated that one in 10 girls and two in 100 boys are sexually molested before the age of 18. They also believed that emotional abuse, such as criticizing and belittling, is the most damaging of all abuse.

Family violence, however, is not limited to child abuse. The battering family is often seen by professionals working with abuse in families. The husband who beats his wife may beat his children, and this wife and the children may retaliate with violence against the husband as well as each other (Scott, 1974). This connection is often not made because the child protective services (which investigate child abuse) are not involved with spouse abuse. Conversely, the court system that has jurisdiction over marital disputes is not involved with child abuse. It is typical that spouse abuse often goes undetected or unreported. Often the spouse who is beaten is the wife, due to physical size and societal norms. The man plays out the macho role and the wife is the victim. In American society, in the past, it has been accepted that what goes on in the home is a private domestic matter, and it may even be justifiable for a husband to beat his wife. Wives in these situations feel helpless and incompetent. They are often ridden with guilt and shame and may feel unable to make a change because they believe they deserve the punishment and can do nothing to stop it. Often the wives are financially dependent and have children to support. They feel penniless and powerless.

Alcohol abuse does not cause marital violence, but the two behaviors seem to occur in family systems that look similar. These families are closed systems, isolated from the community, and they have many family secrets.

Beating does not necessarily occur during intoxication, and often violence is part of sober behavior (Roy, 1977). In families in which violence occurs during drinking episodes, beatings do not stop when drinking stops. However, men often drink when they feel like beating their wives because they are released of responsibility if they are drunk (Gelles, 1972). Coleman and Straus (1979) believed that the abuser uses alcohol for a time-out from expected behavior, and they stated, "Following this argument, individuals do not become violent because they are drunk, but get drunk so they may become violent" (p. 5).

Violence is affected by societal values. Linking spouse battering to alcohol abuse neglects the subservient role of women in society, the problems of marriage as an institution, and the use of alcohol as a means of asserting power and dominance (Sanchez-Dirks, 1979). American society accepts violence as a way to solve problems—the West was settled by those who were fastest on the draw. Physical punishment was (and is) used in schools, and the death penalty has been established as a deterrent to violent crimes.

Television and movies cash in on Americans' love for violence. As stress levels increase in our society, violence seems to become the way to solve problems. Similarly, as stress increases in the alcoholic family with alcohol abuse or sobriety, the tendency to use violence to solve problems increases. Steinmetz and Straus (1974) found that the more intimate the relationships of a group, the higher is the level of conflict. Because the family is the most intimate group in society, the level of conflict is very high. They also believed that conflict is an integral part of the family, but as long as society does not see family conflict as wrong, there will be reluctance in the family to learn nonviolent ways to solve problems.

Three out of 100 Americans—6 million people—are victims of violent crimes yearly (Gorney, 1989). These are not just attacks by criminals on the streets. Individuals are more likely to be assaulted, beaten, or killed at home by a "loved one" than in any other place or by strangers (Gelles & Straus, 1988).

The problem of abuse in the family is multicausal. Poverty, negative family circumstances, and occupational and emotional problems contribute to abuse along with drinking behavior. In looking at the alcoholic-abusive family, Flanzer (1981) identified three areas of abuse and neglect: (1) the drinker hits others, (2) the drinker is hit by others (being an easy target), and (3) children are neglected. Flanzer defined violence in the family as a stabilizing factor, much like the function of drinking behavior. He said, "Family violence works! It is initially a very effective form of conflict resolution. The abuser uses it to reinstate the 'steady state,' i.e., to ward off any attempt at change taking place within the family" (p. 30). This necessitates rigid role behavior or a reversal of roles to allow the family to survive. Role models often come from the family of origin, where abuse occurred. Parenting styles are learned from the family of origin, as well as role expectations. If the family of origin's values designed men to play a macho role or if women were seen as victims and children were beaten, the chances are great that these values and behaviors will be recreated in the nuclear family.

When parents use violence to discipline their children, they teach them to hit if they are angry or to hit if they want to control. These children learn how to hit from the individuals who teach them how to love. Flanzer (1981) wrote, "The message is clear: hitting and loving go together. If you don't hit, you don't love" (p. 31). In this situation, parenting equals hitting. Flanzer further described the potential abuser as longing to be a "big adult" and to be able to control children. If these are children of alcoholics, they learn two destructive methods of problem solving: drinking and hitting. Abusers rarely take responsibility for their actions, projecting blame for the abuse onto others. They usually have high role expectations of their victims, who never seem to meet the goals. Abusers are usually jealous and possessive of their victims and keep them isolated from others.

Flanzer described the victim as socially isolated and ashamed of the scars of the abuse. The blame projected by the abuser becomes internalized and further isolates him or her from others. The victim takes the abuse deservingly in his or her own mind and never wavers in family loyalty.

Flanzer described a third role in the abuse triangle—the rescuer. The rescuer is a person with good intentions who enjoys controlling and becomes enmeshed in the problem between the abuser and the victim. The therapist can become a rescuer and reduce tension in the relationship between the abuser and the victim. If the rescuer takes sides, he or she will get blamed for everything and will also assume the role of the victim.

This nuclear family triangle often mirrors similar triangles and ways of relating that were found in one or both of the spouses' families of origin. Abuse is intergenerational, much like alcoholism. Hanks and Rosenbaum (1977), in a study of 22 women who had lived with violent alcohol-abusing men, found three distinct types of families of origin in these women. Their histories suggest that they carried the conditions that existed in their families of origin into their marriages. The three types of family of origin are: (1) subtly controlling mother/figurehead father, (2) submissive mother/dictatorial father, and (3) disturbed mother/multiple fathers.

In the first category, the father seemed to be dominant while the mother appeared passive and supportive. With a closer look, the mother's subtle control was apparent in the way she treated the father (as childish and unable to cope). The mother was the controller but allowed the father to appear as the authority. Outwardly, these appear to be stable families. They never argue, and the daughters described these marriages as ideal and perfect. These perfect couples, however, produced daughters who became involved with violent, alcohol-abusing men and who often have serious emotional disorders themselves. These daughters married to escape their home and did not know their husbands drank before they married them. They described their spouses as perfect, except for their drinking, and rarely brought charges against them for the abuse. These women did not feel they were in danger despite personal injury and physical damage. The couples reported being closer after violent episodes and projected the blame for these episodes onto outside sources (for example, the police or friends). Violent encounters occurred when the women encouraged the men to do better, but the men saw this as criticism, which recreated situations like those in the families of origin and led to violent behavior on the part of the men.

In the women's families of origin the mothers were overprotective. The fathers overcompensated by being strict and punished the daughters severely. This situation put the daughters between their parents. The parallels between the women's families of origin and their nuclear families were striking. Both mothers and daughters married men who needed rescuing. The fathers inappropriately and severely punished the daughters, and they married husbands who continued this pattern. Their mothers drove a wedge between the daughters and their fathers, and the daughters drove a wedge between their husband and their children. The marriages in both families were stable despite chronic unhappiness. The parents wanted to present a good face, and these women and their husbands blamed the community. Both of these positions created isolation for the family; there was a difference between behavior in public and in their homes.

The second category of family of origin is the submissive mother/dictatorial father. The fathers in the families of origin of these women often deserted their families, drank, and put in long hours at work. The marriages were a series of separations and reconciliations. When at home, the fathers were verbally and physically abusive to their wives, who were dependent and unassertive; many were daughters of abusive fathers.

The daughters in this group were critical of their parents. They had either been involved in family abuse or had received excessive, unsolicited affection from their fathers. When their fathers were sober, they were irritable, harsh, and intolerant of weakness or imperfection. They were critical of the mothers who tried unsuccessfully to keep the peace. The mothers turned to their daughters for support and created a cross-generational alliance with them as their "pals." This disturbance of boundaries went further as the daughters took on adult duties to help out and so became parentified. Some of the daughters became tomboys to try to gain approval from their fathers and avoid their fathers' anger. The mothers viewed their adolescent daughters as competitors for the fathers' attention; they encouraged the "pal-daughters" to defy the fathers and then encouraged the fathers to punish the daughters for this defiance.

The daughters selected mates in an impersonal manner that was usually situational and unrelated to the men. They knew the men drank heavily. These men were hypermasculine and felt no remorse for violence. The women sheltered these men from prosecution for their crimes, and they often bragged about their husband's physical abuse and strength, which had a reinforcing effect. The children in these nuclear families were abused, and their mothers were unable or unwilling to protect them. There were many separations and reconciliations in the nuclear family as well as in the women's families of origin. These women either had no contact with their parents or maintained a hostile, dependent relationship.

If there was contact, the parents became overly involved with their daughters' marriages and were active in the violent episodes of their daughters' marital disputes.

The families of origin of the women and their nuclear families were parallel in several ways. Both mothers and daughters married men they knew were violent and abused alcohol. The lives of both families were structured around violent episodes and absences by the husbands. The women were indiscreet about sexual involvements, and their actions led to abuse from their husbands that was similar to their fathers' reactions to their adolescent sexuality. These daughters, like their mothers, were seemingly unable to terminate their unsatisfactory marital relationships.

The third group of women came from a family of origin marked by a pattern of disturbed mother/multiple fathers. In these families, the fathers were abusive to both the mothers and daughters. The families were very mobile because the mothers often left their mates and returned to their own mothers. The children were neglected and frequently left with relatives or friends. The mothers' relationships with their daughters were either affectionately smothering, intrusive, and overly close, or withdrawn, angry, and rejecting.

The daughters repressed their anger and became "good girls" who were indispensable to their mothers. They were parentified in their role behaviors and were used by their mothers as counselors and confidants. These daughters frequently had no peer relationships and dropped out of school. Although these children worked hard to be productive, parentlike girls, they were often scapegoated for family problems and abused. The daughters fantasized about their "good fathers" and were silently angry at the mothers' degradation of these absent men. The daughters frequently witnessed their mother's sexual promiscuity and were victims of incest by their fathers or stepfathers.

The relationships these mothers had with their families of origin were ones of rejection or distant, hostile dependence, but the families of origin did not become involved in the violence of the nuclear families. The women were usually resistant to treatment, less educated than those in other categories, married young, and were not motivated to change unsatisfactory relationships.

The women were mysteriously attracted to their mates, possibly in a search for the fantasized fathers. They developed quick, intense, dependent relationships and made themselves indispensable to the men (as they had done with their mothers) to keep from being abandoned. The women knew the men they married were violent alcohol abusers and were unable to list any good points about them. These couples often separated after the violent episodes, and it was the men who initiated reconciliation. The women allowed the men to return because they were lonely.

The indispensability that the women created made these relationships overly close in a conglomerate "we-ness," and violence was used to distance the individuals in an attempt to recover individual identity. Often the men in these relationships had a history of maternal rejection. The women could bring on violent attacks by recreating this pattern in their nuclear families by divulging infidelities.

The nuclear families paralleled the women's families of origin in several ways. First, both the mothers and daughters had difficulty maintaining consistent relationships. The daughters functioned as indispensable to both their mothers and their spouses and related to their own children much like they had been treated by their mothers, alternately smothering and neglectful. The mothers and daughters lived with a series of abusive men and because of their environments had come to expect violence and abuse.

The families of origin for these women influenced mate selection and the pattern of their nuclear families. The men whom they chose were parallel to those in their own families of origin. The nuclear families as a whole mirrored the families of origin. In these couples no one person seems responsible for the violence. It appears to be an intergenerational pattern that perpetuates itself.

Studies looking at the intergenerational connection between family-of-origin violence and current alcohol use or violent behavior have varied in their findings. In a study looking at the relationship of alcohol and other drug abuse and domestic abuse, Bennett, Tolman, Rogalski, and Srinivasaraghavan (1994) suggested that domestic violence is not directly related to the experience of violence or addiction in the family of origin, external locus of control, or severity of alcohol abuse. In fact, they found that the more a man drank, the less he abused his partner. They did find, however, correlations between domestic violence and early onset of drug/alcohol-related problems, low income, a history of nonalcohol drug use (particularly cocaine), and a history of arrest and outpatient counseling. This sample, however, may not be representative of the whole population of substance abusers who are violent. The pool of subjects contained a high number of men who were violent both within and outside the family.

There is also an intergenerational connection between alcohol abuse in women and physical and/or sexual abuse. All three problems have intergenerational patterns in families. In testing the hypothesis that women who were abused as children may have an increased risk for alcohol problems, Miller and Downs (1993) found a connection. In comparing women in outpatient alcoholism treatment programs, first-time offender drinking and driving classes, shelters and support groups for women who have experienced violence, outpatient mental heath centers, and women in randomly selected households who were a control group, they found the following: "Women in alcoholism treatment programs experienced higher rates of childhood victimization, significantly more severe violence by fathers, and more childhood sexual abuse than did women in drinking and driving classes and women in households" (p. 142). The same women also experienced significantly more childhood sexual abuse than did women without alcohol problems in other treatment settings. With regard to domestic violence the alcohol-treatment women experienced higher levels of violence by partners than did the control group and experienced more violence from pretreatment and lifetime partners than women in the drinking and driving group. This connection between a lifetime pattern of victimization of women in alcohol treatment is important in planning appropriate treatment plans for women that address these issues along with the alcohol problem.

In working with abusive families, the person who has been abused is often the most motivated for change. Hanks and Rosenbaum (1977) found that the degree of stability in the families of origin predicted the probability of these women entering therapy. They also found a commonality in the severe degree of isolation of the women and the families. This isolation caused these women to become depressed and further dependent on their mates, making separation difficult. The goal of therapy often is to change women's patterns of reaction to their spouses to avoid abuse and increase self-protection. If the woman has left her spouse, the goal may be to provide an understanding of patterns of her family of origin and the intergenerational process of alcohol abuse and violence in order to prevent her from recreating a similar situation.

It is also useful to look at the role of the abuser in these families. Elbow (1977) found that, in an attempt to maintain homeostasis, the usual coping mechanisms of the family may fail. When tension is not relieved, a person may find it difficult to maintain self-control, and violence may erupt. Elbow (1977) in her study of abusers in violent marriages, found that abusers tend to project the blame for their violence on others, may deny the need for counseling, and may deny their mates the freedom to seek counseling. The abusers insist that their mates conform to their definitions of role behavior, and the mates are often treated as possessions or ego extensions. The abusers see their mates as symbols of other significant relatives, often projecting attributes of their parents onto their spouses in a parentification of the mate. They usually expect their marriages to be replications of their parents' marriages or antitheses of these relationships.

It is difficult to understand why battered spouses stay in their marriages unless intergenerational familial factors are examined. Several factors can contribute to the strength of the attachment: (1) frequency and severity of abuse, (2) a childhood background of abuse, (3) the degree of the victim's power and resources, (4) low self-esteem of the victim, (5) a sense of shame in the victim, and (6) love for the spouse that provides need fulfillment in the victim (Elbow, 1977).

Elbow (1977) categorized abusers into four syndromes based on the emotional needs of each group. "Homeostasis is maintained if that basic need is met. Central, too, is the significance of the mate to the abuser" (p. 518). These four syndromes are: (1) the controller, (2) the defender, (3) the approval seeker, and (4) the incorporator.

The controller's emotional need is autonomy. These abusers project blame for their behavior onto others and have no internal controls. They are controlled by external sources, which they resent. Controllers are in charge of their mates' outside friendships and refuse to allow their spouses to enter therapy. The spouses are seen as possessions that cannot be lost. Violence occurs in these relationships when the abuser's authority is threatened. Abuse is then considered justifiable. Anxiety occurs for the controller when there is a loss of control or autonomy. The mate often symbolizes the parent who controlled the abuser as a child, leaving little room for autonomy. Mates are often attracted to controllers due to their ability to control events and make things happen.

The defender's emotional need is protection. These abusers have internal control; their conflicts stem from a difference between desires and internal limits. Because the defender fears harm, violence is often a defense—hit before being hit. Defenders are self-righteous and are attracted to mates they perceive to be less powerful. They need their mates to cling to and depend on them so they will feel strong. They are rescuers and protectors with limits and moral prohibitions. Their mates are not allowed to leave them because defenders need to protect someone.

The approval seeker's emotional need is confirmation or approval of behavior. Although approval seekers have well-internalized control, they have very low feelings of self-worth. They set high expectations for themselves and are achievers but never gain satisfaction. They go out of their way to please others and become depressed when they do not succeed. Self-esteem is based on the acceptance and approval of others and must be constantly reinforced. Violence occurs when their self-worth is threatened. These abusers are usually children of overdemanding parents who withdrew approval if their high expectations were not met. The spouses of the approval seekers are often isolated because of the insatiable demands of the abusers for constant reassurance. Withdrawal from the abusers to seek relationships with others is seen as abandonment or disapproval.

Drinking may be part of the pattern of the approval seekers. They are frightened of their anger and must reduce their inhibitions with alcohol. These abusers cannot achieve intimacy, and sexual intimacy is often unattainable because of the projection of inadequacy onto the spouses. Unlike controllers, approval seekers reject therapy for themselves but will allow their spouses to go. On the other hand, abusers may come into therapy when their spouses have left the marriage or are threatening to leave. The loss of the spouse would be intolerable to the approval seeker because it indicates failure.

The incorporator's emotional need is affirmation. Incorporators need to validate their being and gain a sense of who they are. To do this they incorporate others into their personality. Thus, having a good wife makes an incorporator feel he is a good husband. Incorporators need to incorporate the ego of another to experience themselves as whole people. In Bowen's terms, an incorporator has a highly undifferentiated sense of self (Bowen, 1978). These abusers may become desperate and cling to their mates. Often heavy alcohol and drug abuse occur. Incorporators come from families where children were dependent on their parents and not allowed to develop their individuality. Their mates are attracted to them by their strong desire for a close family. This closeness can become a prison for these mates as the incorporators control their every move out of fear of losing them.

In working with these couples, there are several things for the therapist to remember. First, never berate the abuser in front of the victim. There is a reason for the marriage, and the victim's needs are involved as well. The victims are usually ambivalent; the therapist can work in this area of conflicting feelings. If the abuser is condemned by the therapist, the victim will feel the need to come to the spouse's defense. If emphasis is placed on a family systems approach, the battered spouse can begin to see his or her part in the familial pattern without having to feel blamed. If the couple plans to remain together, the therapist can help the spouse find a way to avoid violence and thus instill in this person a sense of mastery. Mastery can be gained by helping the spouse make a choice and finding the best way to live with that choice.

Elbow (1977) pointed out to these spouses that they have essentially three choices: (1) they can leave, (2) they can choose to stay and hope for change, and (3) they can stay and give up hope for change. Most often, battered spouses will choose one of the last two options. There are many reasons for maintaining these marriages, and therapists who push victims of violence to prematurely leave their spouses may lose their clients. Therapists should be aware of three indicators that may signal a victim's readiness to leave an abusing spouse: (1) planning, (2) investment in self as a person, and (3) coming to grips with the reality of the situation (Elbow, 1977). Only after victims search out shelter and community help, develop self-worth, find a job or decide on ways to gain financial support, and recognize that the pattern of abuse will continue are they ready to change situations. More women are killed leaving a batterer than staying with him.

Although there has been some feminist criticism of conjoint treatment of violent couples, successful couple treatment models do exist. The fear of the feminists is that marriage and family therapists, approaching the couple from a systemic, noncausal perspective, will give the battered woman the message that she is equally responsible for the violence and her victimization. Further, battered women who are asked to converse freely in sessions in an equal way with the batterer may be in danger after the session. Family therapy, in general, has been criticized for not making overt in therapy what is a distinct power inequity in society.

The Gender and Violence Project at the Ackerman Institute, in focusing on this issue, studied couples in therapy for domestic violence (Goldner, Penn, Sheinberg, & Walker, 1990). The thinking of Goldner et al. involved gender, violence, men, and women from both a feminist and a systemic stance. They believed that these couples exemplified extreme stereotypes of gender arrangements that structure intimacy. They think there is a taboo against the collapse of gender differences that operates in all relationships between men and women. Men experience humiliation and loss of power when the gender divisions blur and women are at risk for punishment if they claim male prerogatives. Goldner et al. stated, " Indeed we have come to think about battering as a man's attempt to reassert gender differences and gender dominance, when his terror of not being different enough from 'his' woman threatens to overtake him" (p. 348).

The assumptions that the project staff made about these couples were:

1. Gender inequality is a social reality and women who are beaten by men are victims, while at the same time reciprocities and complementary patterns are part of the cycle of violence.
2. Ethically, the batterer is responsible for the violence and intimidation, and the woman is responsible for protecting herself as much as possible.
3. Social control is sometimes necessary to stop violence and battering is a crime.

Goldner et al. qualify this by stating that the staff try to separate their work from social control.

The project used a multitheoretical approach including psychoanalytic aspects, social learning dimensions, sociopolitical issues, and systemic thinking. A cocreating approach was used with the couples to develop an understanding of the violence and how to intervene with it.

Goldner and her colleagues (1990) found three parts to the couple relationship: the man's side, the woman's side, and the alliance. The man's side involves gender ideas about masculinity, rigidly adhered to, and denial of dependence, fear, sadness, and a need for protection. They also believed that the fathers of these men gave love contingent on the son fulfilling a particular definition of masculinity. These fathers were often brutal and the sons felt so disconnected that they developed an intense but deeply buried longing for male connection. These feelings are often carried and expressed by the woman in these relationships. The project staff wrote, "It is when he is most close to recognizing the feeling as his own that, we believe, he is most tempted to be violent" (p. 352).

Instead of finding self-defeating victims in the women, the staff found they were women of substance who had strong opinions and conveyed a sense of personal power. They found that women "form a sense of self, of self-worth and feminine identity, through their ability to build and maintain relationships with others" (p. 357). These women saw their husbands as hurt children and thought they had to build them up and make them feel better about themselves. They could sense their batterers' fragile dependency and believed that leaving was betraying the terms of the relationship. Staying with the batterer protected the women from the guilt of giving up their caretaker role; staying was what gender pride and self-respect demanded (Goldner et al., 1990). The women's families of origin were similar to the men's in their excessive patriarchal structure. The belief was that men should be stronger than and in charge of women. Women were undervalued.

The alliance is the aspect of the relationship that preserves reconnection after a violent episode. The alliance is experienced by both the man and the woman as a bond that is secret and hidden because it is seen by others as shameful, sick, and regressive (Goldner et al., 1990). This bond is important for the therapist to know about because it is a secret coalition against the outside world, which includes the therapist. The "more outside forces try to separate the couple, the more the bond binds them together" (Goldner et al., 1990, p. 359). Often the couple fled the families of origin, clung to each other, and felt rescued by each other. This works until a split occurs between the loyalty to the bond and the loyalty to the family of origin. This is seen as an either-or decision in which the partner is good as long as the family is seen as bad. If the partner disappoints or the family supports, the shift to the family of origin may occur, resulting in a violent confrontation of the partner. These dynamics are important to understand for family therapists who want to treat the couple.

Another project focusing on violent, alcoholic couples studied the occurrence of violence in couples after alcohol treatment using behavioral marital therapy (BMT) (O'Farrell & Choquette, 1991; O'Farrell & Murphy, 1995). This study looked at the prevalence and frequency of marital violence of 88 male alcoholics and their wives as they entered treatment and one year after completing BMT. The alcoholics and their wives had a significantly higher amount and frequency of marital violence than a matched nonalcoholic comparison group. The researchers found that the frequency and prevalence of the violence decreased in the year following treatment; however, it was still high compared with the nonalcoholic controls. The extent of violence was, however, related to the drinking outcome status of the alcoholic. The alcoholics who were still sober after one year no longer had higher levels of marital violence, whereas the relapsed alcoholics did. These findings provide initial support for the hypothesis that recovery from alcoholism can reduce the risk of marital violence to a level that is similar to the nonalcoholic population.

## Intrafamilial Sexual Abuse—Incest

Another form of child abuse seen in conjunction with alcoholism is intrafamilial sexual abuse or incest. Justice and Justice (1979) stated, "Incest is any sexual activity—intimate physical contact that is sexually arousing—between nonmarried members of a family" (p. 25). This can range from fondling of erogenous areas to mutual masturbation, oral-genital relations, and sexual intercourse. The most common form of incestuous relationship is father-daughter. However, incest occurs in mother-son, brother-sister, uncle-niece, grandfather-granddaughter, stepfather-stepdaughter, and any other combination of family relationships. Because this discussion is limited by the nature and scope of this book, its remainder focuses on the most common form of incest, father-daughter.

Families that become involved in incest are not very different dynamically from abusive families. Justice and Justice (1979) stated, "In both types of families, the parents are turning to the child to get their needs met. In the physically abusive family, the parent tries to beat the child into meeting his or her needs. In the incestuous family, the parent uses sex and seduction" (p. 256).

Barnard (1983, 1984, 1990) has studied the family dynamics of alcoholic families and the dynamics of families in which incest has occurred. He found the following similarities between these families:

- Generational boundaries are blurred.
- The marital dyad is dysfunctional and the parental dyad fragmented to nonexistence.
- The marital sexual relationship is deteriorated.
- Normal inhibitory anxieties are short-circuited or muted.
- Family affect is muffled and distorted.
- Denial is rampant and "secrets" predominate.
- Family roles are pathologically assigned and calcified.
- The family is isolated, emotionally and otherwise.
- A profound state of pathologically rigid homeostasis or "stuckness" exists.
- Sibling relationships come to be pathologically disturbed.
- An excess of belongingness or separateness develops to the detriment of another person.
- Intimacy and trust problems persist.
- Dependency issues are unresolved.

There is no one cause of incest in a family. However, some similarities exist among families in which father-daughter sexual relationships occur. Usually there is an authoritarian, powerful father and a weak and helpless mother, who often suffers from depression. The daughter is in a role reversal with the mother and thus assumes her sex-role position. This family is a closed system, socially isolated from the community, and family members have a low level of differentiation. Family values are religiously conservative and moralistic. Family members see the world in black and white, and this view eases their uncertainty and low sense of self-worth by supplying definite answers to unsolvable problems.

The mother in these families is often the keeper of the secret. She refuses to choose between her husband and her daughter and allows the relationship to continue. The mother in many cases was abused herself. There are also instances in which the mother is not aware of the sexual abuse of the daughter by the father. Summit and Kryso (1978) stated, "Just as abused children are at risk of becoming abusing parents, sexually abused girls are at risk of selecting an abusive partner and failing to protect their children from intrusion" (p. 245).

In such families, the marital relationship may be in a fixed distance emotionally and sexually. Both spouses are unable to meet their needs in the marital relationship because of serious emotional cutoffs with their parents in terms of inadequate affection and nurturance (Brown, 1978). The mother tries to get the nurturance from her daughter that she did not receive from her mother, and their roles reverse. The marital couple frequently is not at home together during the time the children are there. The mother may be doing shift work or working at night as a nurse or hospital aide to avoid the dysfunctional emotional and sexual relationship. If the father remains home with the daughter, a pseudomarital relationship is set up so that the father's nurturance needs can be met. Often these fathers feel such low self-worth that they are unable to go outside of the family to have their needs met due to fears of rejection.

Brown and Tyson (1978) listed 14 characteristics of incestuous families:

1. availability of victim—mother works at night
2. role confusion
3. sexual dysfunction in marriage
4. inability of father to meet unresolved sexual needs outside of the family
5. recent changes in the family pattern, stressors
6. extreme overprotection or overrestrictive involvement of the father in the daughter's social life
7. heightened fear of separation or abandonment by all family members
8. overprotection of younger siblings by the incest victim
9. acting-out behavior of the victim
10. a child who is frequently victimized
11. male children who molest other male children; female children who molest other female children
12. unrealistic attitude of the child that the happiness and well-being of the family is her responsibility
13. parents sexually abused as children
14. a mother who spontaneously sacrifices the children's emotional or physical well-being to protect the marital relationship

If a family has some of the above characteristics and no incest is occurring, this is probably because: (1) there is a weak attachment between the father and the daughter, (2) the father has adequate inner defenses, (3) the father can meet his sexual needs outside of the family, or (4) there is a good sexual relationship between the father and the mother (Brown, 1978).

If a family comes to therapy with no previously reported incestuous relationships, yet some of the cues that signal incest are present in the family dynamics, a further check can be made of the individual members. Justice and Justice (1979) stated, "One of the most obvious signs that incest is taking place can be seen in the mood and behavior of the daughter" (p. 155). The daughter is often depressed, withdrawn, and suspicious of others. In school, she may feel isolated and may fear that others will stare at her. As previously stated, the daughter may act as a parent, taking on adult roles and blurring generational boundaries. There is also an aura of secretiveness surrounding the daughter that may stem from the father threatening harm if their secret is not kept. This secretiveness can resemble withdrawal. These cues are common in preadolescents or adolescents, whereas more somatic cues are typical in younger children. Justice and Justice stated,

> The behavioral cues in a small child may include enuresis (bedwetting), soiling, hyperactivity, altered sleeping patterns (sleeping a lot or little at all), fears, phobias, overly compulsive behavior, learning problems, compulsive masturbation, precocious sex play, excessive curiosity about sexual matters and separation anxiety. (p. 158)

These symptoms in isolation are not sufficient to indicate sexual activity but should be coupled with family dynamics, observations, and factual data before any accusations are made. The father may also supply cues that can support assumptions. The most obvious cue is the crossing of generational boundaries by the father who behaves impulsively, irrationally, and immaturely. Another possible paternal behavior is romantic pursuit of the daughter. The father may appear to be acting more as his daughter's peer than her parent. In the same vein, the father may become jealous of his daughter's social contacts and become so authoritarian that he restricts all social contacts outside the house. The daughter may feel trapped and hopeless and may run away from home. These families often seek therapy to get help in setting limits with their daughter.

Running away is a behavior that alerts youth service systems and police departments to potential family difficulties. However, this is not a guarantee that the incest will be uncovered unless someone working with the family is skillful enough to recognize the potential for incest and can support the family enough to allow a member to report the occurrence of an incestuous relationship.

Other family members exhibit behaviors that can give these hypotheses support. For instance, the mother may become both a rival and a childlike person dependent on her daughter. The roles are reversed, yet there is still competition between the mother and the daughter for the father's affection. If the daughter (who is engaging in the incestuous relationship) is gaining special favors from her father over the other siblings, the mother may be angry at this daughter for occupying her special position.

Alcoholism is a possible indicator of incest if it is coupled with other cues. Browning and Boatman (1977), in a study of 14 incest cases, found, "There was a strikingly high incidence of alcoholism among the fathers, and almost all were described by their wives as being prone to emotional outbursts and physical violence" (p. 71). Virkkunen (1974) studied 43 cases of incest, of which 22 involved alcoholism. His findings indicated that the alcoholics had been involved with criminal activities and violence prior to the incest more than had the nonalcoholic group. Virkkunen stated:

> In the study it was clearly discernible that alcoholized subjects experienced more often than others sexual rejection on the part of their spouse, and, thus, this could be regarded as a contributing factor in the evolution of the incest offense. . . . The cause of this appeared to be mainly disgust at the abuse of alcoholic drinks and its consequences, as well as the result of a large family and/or poor living conditions. (p. 127)

If this is the case, alcohol abuse may be a contributing factor in deteriorating marital and sexual relationships that set up a family pattern leading to incest between the father and daughter. Another possibility is that the poor marital relationship may have existed prior to the alcohol abuse. But from a systems perspective, it is not important which came first, but rather how one symptom perpetuates another in a circular pattern. The family therapist needs to evaluate the abusive family system and be aware of the possible existence of alcohol abuse, physical abuse, and sexual abuse within that system.

To prevent sexual abuse or keep it from recurring once it has been reported to the proper officials and social control agents, the therapist must break the cycle and remove a piece of the interaction that sets up the atmosphere for sexual abuse. To do this, the therapist can: (1) work for reduction of overinvolvement of the father and daughter, (2) improve the marital and sexual relationship of the parents, and (3) draw a boundary between the parent and child generations. This may be accomplished by reducing inappropriate role behaviors of the father and daughter or the role reversal of the mother and daughter and by encouraging the mother to assume a parental role. A further option is to work with the abusing father on family-of-origin issues. These are the roots of his inability to get nurturance and sexual satisfaction in an appropriate way and the source of his extreme insecurity and low sense of self-worth.

In working with a sexual abuse family it is important to reduce the dysfunctional role behaviors used by family members. Abusive fathers cover their insecurity and fear with hostility and play out their roles as they imagine the world sees them—as the monsters. It is most difficult for therapists to help individuals they view as monsters; they can only punish. The view of the parent as a monster denies that children are sexual beings and that the parents have sexual feelings for them (Justice & Justice, 1979). It also denies the strength of the circular, behavior-producing family system.

Likewise, it is dangerous to treat the mother and daughter as victims. If the mother was a victim of incest, this may have precipitated her depressed behavior that contributes to the atmosphere that allows incest to occur. The victimization of the daughter may be the beginning of a lifelong role that she perpetuates by placing herself in similar positions, such as by marrying an abusive man.

The literature on the treatment of incest has changed the word *victim* as a description of someone who has experienced incest and replaced it with the word *survivor*. There is some danger here. The connotation could be that the person survived the abuse and thus is not in need of help. The purpose of the change in terminology is to cause a shift in the thinking of all those involved with incest, including those in the helping profession, to see abused children as strong and resilient who can get better with treatment. They should not be viewed as or see themselves as lifelong victims. Although theorists disagree on the severity of the problems of children who experience incest, there is potential for various consequences for both the child and the parents.

Justice and Justice stated, "Incest does not affect every child to the same extent. Since people are unique, so are their responses to stressful and traumatic events" (p. 181). The consequences may be resolvable in a short time, or the incest may leave scars that never completely disappear. These consequences may occur at three different times: (1) during the incest, (2) at the discovery of the incest, and (3) when participants later have difficulties in their life functioning and suffer long-term consequences for themselves and their children (Justice & Justice, 1979). Because incest occurs in families on an intergenerational basis, lack of attention to the children who experience incest may sentence the next generation to reexperiencing the family pattern.

Although sexual abuse affects the entire family, possibly the most traumatic event is the discovery of the incest by someone outside the family system. Justice and Justice (1979) noted, "Although in our experience the most lasting consequences usually come from the disturbed family relationships that give rise to the incest, we agree that the discovery can produce a traumatic effect" (p. 174). At the time of the discovery a gaping hole is opened in the closed family structure; others have discovered the inner workings of the family. Outside persons or agencies need to continue to call attention to these issues to stop the family from closing ranks and resisting change. At the time of the report of incest, the family mobile that was in a delicate balance is blown by a strong wind, causing a great disturbance in the system. The family is easier to change in this state of flux than when the wind dies down and the family regains a static balance.

Justice and Justice (1979) outlined one form of working with the incestuous family in their book *The Broken Taboo*. They believed, "The whole family is a 'victim' and steps must be taken to strengthen and support the family, not traumatize it further" (p. 241). To help the child, they stop the child's feelings of self-blame by giving the child support; explaining that incest does happen, it is not supposed to happen, and it will stop; and stating that the child is not responsible. The position they take with parents is one of understanding, without condoning or dismissing the incestuous behavior. They support the family and confront their problems. Three important points are made: (1) legal charges must be dealt with, (2) incest is not acceptable and must stop, and (3) the role reversal in the family is harmful.

Justice and Justice (1979) found that during the first therapy session the family may be angry, resentful, distrustful, and frightened. They began with all of the family members and asked them what happened and what family problems exist. Next, they asked what had happened since the discovery of the incest. During the session the therapist observed how the family related and began to teach them new ways of interaction. The parents were encouraged to take responsibility verbally for the occurrence of the incest and to express their regrets for this exploitation to the child.

The next therapeutic step was to place the parents in a couples group to work on marital issues. The children were added later. Justice and Justice (1979) stated, "The typical problems we work on with each parent include symbiosis, marital relationship, stress reduction, sexual climate, isolation and alcoholism" (p. 246). They make three-month contracts with each couple to work on:

- reducing symbiosis—a parent turning to the child to meet the needs of the parent
- strengthening the marital relationship by exchanging complaining and angry ways of communicating for active listening and the use of "I" messages that contain no blaming, defending, or judging
- improving the sexual climate by strengthening generational boundaries as the sexual relationship of the marital couple is improved
- reducing stress by eliminating stressors and using relaxation techniques
- reducing isolation through contacts with couples in the group
- curbing alcoholism by making contracts with alcohol-abusing members to stop drinking either with the help of Alcoholics Anonymous or by using the group in conjunction with family therapy

The adults in the couples groups work through their old feelings of depression, guilt, shame, and anger. They improve their self-image and receive information on how incest occurs in a family. Marital couples rejuvenate their sexual relationship and obtain help for sexual dysfunctions.

A second method of working with incestuous families was developed at the Child Sexual Abuse Treatment Program (CSATP) in California by Giaretto (1976), who found that family members must receive separate counseling before family therapy is useful. The Giaretto team first worked individually with the child, mother, and father. They then saw the mother and daughter together, then the husband and wife. After the marital counseling, the family was seen as a unit.

In 1972, some parents from this program created a self-help group for incestuous families called Parents United; the group employs a professional mental health worker and a paraprofessional as coleaders. The daughters of the families formed a teen group called Daughters United. These self-help groups are still available across the United States and are a useful adjunct to therapy for breaking down the isolated family. However, they can become an isolated refuge that allows the family to maintain isolation from the remainder of the community. Families need treatment even if the incestuous relationship is no longer in existence.

A multimodal program for treating sexually abused children was developed at the Ackerman Institute (Sheinberg, True, & Fraenkel, 1994). This program includes individual, group, and family therapy. Information in one therapy context is transferred to another and back again. The project staff stated, "We find that this circulation of issues, conflicts, and dilemmas between modalities generated a more comprehensive understanding of each family member's unique experience" (Sheinberg, True, & Fraenkel, 1994, p. 263). This supports the therapist's effort to help the abused child reconnect with trustworthy family members in more positive ways. The treatment modalities include a children's group, a mothers'/caretakers' group, family therapy, individual therapy, and an art program for the children. The children's group draws on traditional child play-therapy approaches that combine role-play, open-ended stories, games, and drawing designed to help children express their thoughts and feelings. This allows the children to talk metaphorically, which feels safer to them.

Families leave treatment after varying lengths of time. The recommended criteria for a child to terminate treatment are: (1) she has someone in the family with whom she can share her feelings when she is upset, (2) she can express a range of feelings in therapy and out, (3) her school performance is as good as before the abuse, and (4) she does not have symptoms such as nightmares and bed-wetting (Sheinberg, True, & Fraenkel, 1994). The group and individual/family sessions meet on alternating weeks and are conducted by one or two specific therapists who work with each family.

## SEXUAL DYSFUNCTION

A brief discussion of sexual dysfunction is included in this chapter because of the frequent occurrence of poor sexual relationships in alcoholic and abusive marriages, and the potential for sexual abuse of children in families in which there is sexual dissatisfaction between the spouses. O'Farrell, Choquette, and Cutter (1995) compared 26 married couples with an alcoholic husband to 26 marital-conflicted and 26 nonconflicted couples without alcohol problems on both sexual dysfunction and a wide range of sexual satisfaction variables. They found that male alcoholics and their wives experienced less sexual satisfaction and more sexual dysfunction than nonconflicted couples. These problems included the husbands' diminished sexual interest, impotence, premature ejaculation, and wives' painful intercourse. When compared with the conflicted couples the only problem that occurred more with the alcoholic groups was impotence. The researchers suggested that most of the sexual adjustment problems suffered by male alcoholics may be a function of marital unhappiness, and the physical effects of alcohol may account for the increased impotence.

Although sexual dysfunction is a problem that should not be overlooked, it is a subject that cannot be addressed in earnest while the issue of alcohol abuse is unresolved and family dynamics maintain the dysfunction. One of the adaptive consequences of drinking may be to avoid sexual relations, or drinking may be psychologically connected to sexual intercourse. Thus, if the alcoholic gives up drinking that has been connected to sexual activity, sexual intimacy may be sacrificed when sobriety is achieved. The nonalcoholic spouse may have a fear of intimacy. Sobriety of the alcoholic may raise the anxiety of the spouse about dealing with intimacy issues and may lead to a relapse of the alcoholic to reduce the tension. Further, a spouse who has given up her power in the family when her husband sobers up and regains the authority position may withhold sexual favors as her last hold on power. This perpetuates sexual dysfunction in the marriage after the alcohol abuse stops.

There are further connections between alcohol and specific sexual dysfunctions in both men and women. However, except for the unique interaction of alcohol and sex, sexual dysfunction in alcoholic marriages is no different from sexual dysfunction in the general population. Although there are connections between alcohol abuse and sexual dysfunction, the most pervasive etiological factor of sexual difficulties in alcoholic marriages is the inability to form intimate relation-ships (Forrest, 1978; Howard & Howard, 1978).

Before working with couples on their sexual relationship, therapists should evaluate their own comfort level with sexual problems and their own values and feelings of sexual adequacy. Prior to making a decision to work with the couple on sexual problems or to refer to a sex therapist, an assessment should be made with the couple to evaluate their readiness to work on sexual difficulties. Clarken, Frances, and Moodie (1979) established criteria for deciding on sex therapy or marital therapy. They found that sex therapy is indicated when: (1) the marital problem is clearly focused on sexual dysfunction, (2) there is a willingness and ability to carry out the sexual functioning tasks that would be assigned during treatment by the therapist, and (3) there is a strong attachment to the marital partner and both partners are interested in reversing the sexual dysfunction. If one of these factors is missing, the couple will probably sabotage efforts by the therapist to reverse the problematic behaviors, and task assignments will not be carried out due to a fear of being hurt (in both spouses) and a lack of trust in the relationship.

Marital therapy is indicated prior to sex therapy if: (1) sexuality is not an issue, or it is just one of many issues in marital dysfunction, (2) anger and resistance are too intense to carry out the extra session tasks around sexual functioning, and (3) the participants are not committed to each other or there are covert or overt behaviors to dissolve the marriage (Clarken, Frances, & Moodie, 1979). If sex therapy is the choice, the therapist should work with the relationship between the couple and not allow one spouse to blame the other for sexual difficulties. In the alcoholic marriage, problems are perpetuated by blame and projection of inadequacies onto the spouse. Barnard (1981) gave an example of this relationship interaction in the maintenance of alcohol-sexual difficulty:

> The more alcohol is consumed the more difficult it becomes to perform adequately. As the male experiences erectile failure, more and more, he becomes more and more anxious, which lessens the likelihood of his developing and maintaining an erection. In order to protect his own fragile and threatened sense of masculinity he cuts his wife with hurtful remarks, and she becomes angry and likewise feeds into his anxiety and anger, which makes it unlikely either of them are going to be able to be sexually responsive. (p. 113)

Renshaw (LoPiccolo & LoPiccolo, 1978) proposed a circular theory of the three A's—anger, anxiety, and alcohol, which are all connected in a circular fashion (Figure 8–1). Anger and hurt interfere with the relaxation that is necessary to experience sexual pleasure. This results in fear of failure and anxiety. Alcoholics have often learned that anger and anxiety can be reduced by alcohol, and they turn to the old problem solver when they are worried about sexual performance. Alcohol consumption, however, interferes with sexual functioning, producing further frustration, anger, and anxiety over performing adequately.

In treating the sexual relationship and attempting to break this self-destructive cycle, the therapist must not view the relationship as having an isolated sexual dysfunction that can be cured by a prescription of task assignments but rather must view the relationship as made up of two individuals whose life experiences have brought them to the point of a self-perpetuating dilemma. The relationship is composed of two sexual beings who view their sexuality as more than just sexual intercourse. It also involves intimacy or the affective part of the relationship, the sharing, caring, and risk taking between two individuals. It involves reproduction

**Figure 8–1** Anxiety, Anger, Alcohol Cycle

and family planning, sexual identity, self-concept, role identity, and sexualization, the use of sexuality to gain a better position. All areas must be examined in the course of sex therapy.

A relationship is more than the sum of its two parts, and each member must be seen as having a unique contribution. Society and families of origin set up sex role and sex performance expectations for men and women, yet keep factual sexual information hidden, producing misconceptions and faulty ideas.

Men who abuse alcohol frequently are acting out the macho role by being aggressive, and they may appear to be without emotion or concern for the feelings of others. They are expected to be sex experts. If they fail sexually, their self-images are damaged, and they become anxious and fearful of further failure. This leads to avoidance of sexual contact or reduction of anxiety by the use of alcohol. When the condition achieves problematic proportions, men are silent and do not talk to others about an unacceptable weakness. Men from alcoholic families usually have had no model of intimacy and affection and do not know how to discuss the issue with their wives. This silent suffering can lead to loneliness, fear, despair, low self-esteem, and alcoholism (Barnard, 1981).

Women are confused about their sex role and societal expectations for their sexual functioning. They may not be certain if they are supposed to enjoy sex or participate only for purposes of reproduction and to please men. If these women are from alcoholic families, they can be playing out roles from their families of origin, or they may have negative opinions of sex if they were sexually abused by their alcoholic fathers. Because women tend to talk less about sex than men, they may have more misconceptions and believe that their self-worth is defined by the degree men value them. Self-worth, then, becomes dependent on another. Women also make a cognitive connection between alcohol and sexual functioning and may be unable to differentiate the two (Barnard, 1981).

Books are available that contain specific techniques for working with sexual dysfunction (Allgeier & Allgeier, 1995; Fleit, 1979; LoPiccolo & LoPiccolo, 1978; Masters & Johnson, 1970; Masters, Johnson, & Kolodny, 1995; Sager, 1974). When working with motivated families, Masters and Johnson (1970) and Sager (1974) found that many sexual dysfunctions have extremely high cure rates: vaginismus, 100 percent; premature ejaculation, 98 percent; ejaculatory incompetence, 82 percent; orgasmic dysfunction in the female, 83 percent; secondary impotence, 70–80 percent; and primary impotence, 55 percent. Sex therapy can be very rewarding for marital couples who had previously resolved issues such that working on sexual dysfunctions was precluded. This area should not be overlooked by therapists working with alcoholic or problem drinking families. The therapist should uncover the client's/couple's sexual problem, freely examine the issues, and clarify problem areas. The therapist should also provide insights and interpretations as to how these problems affect the client's chemical dependency; provide emotional support and reduce anxiety and hostility; and educate and give permission, when necessary, in an effort to reduce guilt and increase positive feelings of self-worth in the clients (Lawson & Lawson, 1996). If the therapist is uncomfortable in working with a couple on their sexual dysfunction, a referral should be made to a sex therapist.

## DIVORCE

A therapist who works with alcoholic, abusive families frequently must address the issue of divorce. Families may see divorce as a solution to unresolvable difficulties, they may need help in making a decision to stay together or to separate, or they may already be in the process of divorce. Although marital issues are best worked out if children are not involved, divorce is a family issue. The children are affected and should not be ignored by the therapist. This does not mean that the children should share in making the parents' decision about divorce. Once this decision is made, however, it should not be kept a secret from the children.

Divorce is a major stress for the family. Even if it means an end to the violence, it is still a broken promise of "till death do us part" and may be seen as a failure to play out the husband and wife roles. The parents can be so involved in their own adjustment and grieving that they overlook the children's reactions. Children have different reactions to divorce according to their developmental levels and the amount of anger and fighting that continues between their parents after the divorce (Wallerstein & Kelly, 1980).

Divorce does not necessarily cause pathology in the parents or the children. In fact, divorce can improve the functioning of family members who have been living in a chaotic environment. Gardner wrote two books to help families get through this stressful time with the least amount of problems—*The Parent's Book about Divorce* (Gardner, 1977) and *The Boys' and Girls' Book about Divorce*

(Gardner, 1970). These books give information and practical solutions to common problems and dispel irrational ideas that children often develop during this stressful period. Children tend to blame themselves for their parents' divorce or think they can behave in certain ways to cause the parents to get back together. Children in alcoholic families can be especially vulnerable to these misconceptions because of the family's secretiveness. Children's own role behavior is also tied to their parents' behaviors.

Spouses of alcoholics may have a difficult time resolving the divorce and fully cutting the ties with the alcoholic person and the drinking behavior. The confusion can slow down the grieving process after the divorce. This process is the reverse of grieving over a death. In death, the survivor tends to view the deceased as perfect, initially, but as resolution proceeds, imperfections are remembered until the memory of the person becomes the reality of the person. In divorce, the spouse views the mate as all bad with no redeeming qualities, and as resolution proceeds positive attributes begin to surface until this mate is remembered as a real person with both good and bad traits. To help with this resolution process, the therapist can ask the spouse of the alcoholic to make two lists of characteristics of his or her mate. One column consists of the characteristics of the person, the other the features of the drinking behavior. The spouse can then recognize the positive qualities of the mate that he or she has disregarded due to the negative alcohol abuse. This step begins a healthier grieving process that can lead to resolution.

The children in an alcoholic family's divorce can have resolution difficulties as well. If the father is alcoholic, the mother may feel justified in restricting visitation of the children, so they will not be hurt as she was. This is a painful game that the wife can use to further punish her husband in the name of security for the children. However, this tactic deprives the children of a parent. With the increasing prevalence of joint custody and court-mandated visitation for noncustodial parents, these power plays can be curtailed by the court. It is, however, important to take the children's safety into account if the alcoholic parent is still drinking and driving with the children in the car or if the alcoholic parent is a perpetrator of child physical or sexual abuse, even if the alcoholic is no longer drinking.

Children need to have a realistic picture of their parents as well. If the custodial parent denigrates the noncustodial parent or excuses his or her behavior, the children are robbed of their own opinions. In an alcoholic family, the children may be told their father or mother is sick or has a disease called alcoholism, and so the parents are getting a divorce. This can confuse the children who already have opinions about the parent and may now feel guilty about being angry at a parent who is sick or may feel deserted by a parent with whom they are aligned. Children can become angry and confused by the logic of the parents divorcing because a parent is "sick."

Therapists working with alcoholic families in the process of divorce should educate the parents and the children about potential problems and misconceptions. They should help all of the family members express their ideas and feelings about the divorce. After the divorce, attention should be paid to communication processes so that the children are not used as messengers or spies between parents and triangulation of children into unfinished parental issues is stopped. Parents should speak directly to each other and not burden children with negative statements about each other or ask children to take sides.

## REFERENCES

Allgeier, A.R., & Allgeier, E.R. (1995). *Sexual interactions* (4th ed.). Toronto: D.C. Heath & Co.

Appleton, W. (1980). The battered woman syndrome. *Annals of Emergency Medicine, 9*, 84–91.

Barnard, C. (1981). *Families, alcoholism and therapy.* Springfield, IL: Charles C. Thomas.

Barnard, C. (1983). Alcoholism and incest: Improving diagnostic comprehensiveness. *International Journal of Family Therapy, 5*, 136–144.

Barnard, C. (1984). Alcoholism and incest: Similar traits, common dynamics. *Focus on the Family, 27*–29.

Barnard, C. (1990). *Families with an alcoholic member.* New York: Human Science Press.

Bennett, L.W., Tolman, R.M., Rogalski, C.J., & Srinivasaraghavan, J. (1994). Domestic abuse by male alcohol and drug addicts. *Violence and Victims, 9*(4), 359–367.

Bowen, M. (1978). *Family therapy in clinical practice.* New York: James Arnoson.

Brown, A. (1978). A family systems approach to incest victims and their families. *The Family, 6* (1), 9–11.

Brown, A., & Tyson, C. (1978, January). *Fourteen characteristics of incestuous families.* Workshop presentation to the Graduate School of Social Work, University of Utah, Salt Lake City, UT.

Browne, A. (1987). *When battered women kill.* New York: Free Press.

Browning, D., & Boatman, B. (1977). Incest: Children at risk. *American Journal of Psychiatry, 134* (1), 69–72.

Caffey, J. (1965). Significance of history in diagnosis of traumatic injury to children. *Journal of Pediatrics, 67,* 48–53.

Chafetz, M., Blane, H., & Hill, M. (1971). Children of alcoholics. *Quarterly Journal of Studies on Alcohol, 32,* 687–698.

Clarken, J.F., Frances, A.J., & Moodie, J.L. (1979). Selection criteria for family therapy. *Family Process, 18,* 397.

Coleman, D.H., & Straus, M.A. (1979). *Alcohol abuse and family violence.* Paper presented at the annual meeting of the American Sociological Association, New York.

Cork, M. (1969). *The forgotten children.* Toronto: Paperjacks, in association with Addiction Research Foundation.

Elbow, M. (1977). Theoretical considerations of violent marriages. *Social Casework,* 515–526.

Flanzer, J. (1981). The vicious circle of alcoholism and family violence. *Alcoholism*, 30–32.

Fleit, L. (1979). *Alcohol and sexuality*. Arlington, VA: H/P Publishing.

Forrest, G. (1978). *The diagnosis and treatment of alcoholism*. Springfield, IL: Charles C. Thomas.

Gardner, R. (1970). *The boys' and girls' book about divorce*. New York: Bantam Books.

Gardner, R. (1977). *The parents' book about divorce*. New York: Bantam Books.

Gelles, R.J. (1972). *The violent home: A study of physical aggression between husbands and wives*. Beverly Hills, CA: Sage.

Gelles, R.J., & Straus, M.A. (1988). *Intimate violence*. New York: Simon & Schuster.

Giaretto, H. (1976). The treatment of father-daughter incest: A psychosocial approach. *Children Today, 5*, 2–5.

Goldner, V., Penn, P., Sheinberg, M., & Walker, G. (1990). Love and violence: Gender paradoxes in volatile attachments. *Family Process, 29*(4), 343–364.

Gorney, B. (1989). Domestic violence and chemical dependency: Dual problems, dual interventions. *Journal of Psychoactive Drugs*, 21(2), 229–238.

Hanks, S., & Rosenbaum, P. (1977). Battered women: A study of women who live with violent alcohol-abusing men. *American Journal of Orthopsychiatry, 47*(2), 291–306.

Hindman, M. (1977). Child abuse and neglect: The alcoholic connection. *Alcohol Health and Research World, 1*(3), 2–7.

Hindman, M. (1979). Family violence. *Alcohol Health and Research World*, (4)1–11.

Howard, D., & Howard, N. (1978). Treatment of the significant other. In S. Zimberg, J. Wallace, & S. Blume (Eds.), *Practical approaches to alcoholism psychotherapy*. New York: Plenum Press.

Justice, B., & Justice, R. (1979). *The broken taboo: sex in the family*. New York: Human Sciences Press.

Kempe, H.C., & Helfer, R.E. (1972). *Helping the battered child and his family*. New York: J.B. Lippincott.

Kent, J.T. (1975). What is known about child abusers? In S.B. Harris (Ed.), *Child abuse, present and future*. Chicago: National Committee for Prevention of Child Abuse, 1975.

Lawson, G., & Lawson, A. (1996). *Essentials of chemical dependency counseling*. Gaithersburg, MD: Aspen Publishers.

LoPiccolo, J., & LoPiccolo, L. (1978). *Handbook of sex therapy*. New York: Plenum Press.

Masters, W.H., & Johnson, V.E. (1970). *Human sexual inadequacy*. Boston: Little, Brown.

Masters, W.H., Johnson, V.E., & Kolodny, R.C. (1995). *Human sexuality* (5th ed.). New York: Harper Collins.

Mayer, J., & Black, R. (1977). The relationship between alcoholism and child abuse/neglect. In F. Seixas (Ed.), *Currents in epidemiological studies*. New York: Grune & Stratton.

Miller, B.A., & Downs, W.R. (1993). The impact of family violence on the use of alcohol by women. *Alcohol Health and Research World, 17*(2), 137–143.

O'Farrell, T.J., & Choquette, K. (1991). Marital violence in the year before and after spouse-involved alcoholism treatment. *Family Dynamics of Addiction Quarterly, 1*(1), 32–40.

O'Farrell, T.J., Choquette, K.A., & Cutter, H.S.G. (1995, June). *Sexual satisfaction and dysfunction among alcoholic, maritally conflicted and nonconflicted couples.* Paper presented at the International Conference on Treatment of Addictive Behaviors, Leevenhorst, The Netherlands.

O'Farrell, T.J., & Murphy, C.M. (1995). Marital violence before and after alcoholism treatment. *Journal of Consulting and Clinical Psychology, 63*(2), 256–262.

Orme, I., & Remmer, J. (1981). Alcoholism and child abuse. *Journal of Studies on Alcohol, 42*(3), 273–287.

Roberts, A.R. (1988). Substance abuse among men who batter their mates: The dangerous mix. *Journal of Substance Abuse Treatment, 5*, 83–87.

Roy, M. (1977). Current survey of 150 cases. In M. Roy (Ed.), *Battered women* (pp. 225–244). New York: Van Nostrand Reinhold.

Sager, C.J. (1974). Sexual dysfunctions and marital discord. In H.S. Kaplan (Ed.), *The new sex therapy.* New York: Brunner/Mazel.

Sanchez-Dirks, R. (1979). Reflections on family violence. *Alcohol Health and Research World, 4*(1), 12–16.

Scott, P.D. (1974). Battered wives. *British Journal of Psychiatry, 125*, 433–441.

Sheinberg, M., True, F., & Fraenkel, P. (1994). Treating the sexually abused child: A recursive, multimodal program. *Family Process, 33*, 263–276.

Smith, S.M., Hanson, R., & Noble, S. (1974). Social aspects of the battered baby syndrome. *British Journal of Psychiatry, 125*, 568–582.

Spieker, G., & Mouzakitis, C. (1976, September). Alcohol abuse and child abuse and neglect: An inquiry into alcohol abusers' behavior toward children. Paper presented at the 27th annual meeting of the Alcohol and Drug Problems Association of North America, New Orleans, LA.

Spinetta, J.J., & Rigler, D. (1972). The child abusing parent: A psychological review. *Psychological Bulletin, 77*, 296–304.

Steinmetz, S.K., & Straus, M.A. (1974). *Violence in the family.* New York: Harper & Row.

Summit, R., & Kryso, J. (1978). Sexual abuse of children: A clinical spectrum. *American Journal of Orthopsychiatry, 48*(2), 237–251.

Virkkunen, M. (1974). Incest offenses in alcoholism. *Medicine, Science and Law, 14*, 124–128.

Wallerstein, J., & Kelly, J. (1980). *Surviving the breakup: How children and parents cope with divorce.* New York: Basic Books.

# CHAPTER 9

# Children of Alcoholics and Adult Children of Alcoholics

## INTRODUCTION

Chapter 8 addressed the impact of violence, sexual abuse, and divorce on children living in alcoholic families. These are extreme circumstances and should not be ignored in the treatment of such families. However, simple exposure to a parent who is alcoholic or life in a family in which alcohol abuse is a central dynamic in itself can be equally damaging to children. Children of alcoholics have been ignored by alcohol treatment agencies in favor of working with the alcoholic individually or working with the alcoholic and his or her spouse. Agencies that treat children are often unaware of the alcohol abuse in the family, or they believe that only individuals with special information can treat alcohol problems. It is typical to refer such families to alcohol treatment agencies as soon as alcohol becomes an issue in treatment. This would be logical if treating the alcoholic produced positive change in the children. However, in a study of alcoholic families in Pennsylvania, Booz-Allen and Hamilton (1974) found that "the treatment and recovery of the alcoholic parent does not appear to reduce the problems experienced by the children" (p. 63).

The family system is often out of balance and unable to adjust, and the children do not give up their coping roles. Cork (1969) did a study of 115 children between the ages of 10 and 16 who lived in alcoholic homes. She found that the home situations of the abstainers were not much different from those in which the alcoholic continued to drink. Children did not, in the absence of therapy, report that family life became significantly better when drinking stopped. One child described the impact of his father's sobriety in this way:

> Dad's changed now that he's not drinking. He's friendlier, and he talks more. Sometimes he even tries to act like a father and makes some rules,

but he never sticks to what he says. I think he's afraid we won't love him if he does. My parents don't fight quite as much now but they're not really happy. Mom never lets Dad forget about his drinking days. She's still the one who runs things. Dad seems more like one of us kids. (Cork, 1969, p. 53)

This family continued to operate with a poor marital subsystem and a parent who crossed generational boundaries. The child who spoke these words was still affected by the marital fighting and lack of consistent parenting.

Children living in homes where alcohol abuse is occurring or has occurred total 30–40 million (Booz-Allen & Hamilton, 1974; Rivinus, 1991). This is one of every six Americans. Six and one-half million are younger than 18 years (Woodside, 1988). These children are at high risk for developing social and emotional problems, and they are twice as likely to develop alcohol-related problems as are children of nonalcoholics (Bosma, 1975; Goodwin, Schulsinger, Hermansen, Gruze, & Winokur, 1973). The alcoholic parents who are raising these children, in 52 percent of the cases, came from homes where one or both of the parents had a drinking problem (Fox, 1968). In the light of this information, it does not seem appropriate to exclude children from the treatment process. Children need to develop new channels of communication within the family, and they should have an opportunity to explain their perspective on the family process.

## PROBLEMS OF THE CHILDREN

Many studies and reports have found various problems in children who live with alcoholics. Sloboda (1974) found that parents often do not live by society's rules; discipline is inconsistent and the children become confused and unable to predict parental behavior. Chafetz, Blane, and Hill (1977) compared 100 alcoholic families with 100 nonalcoholic families that were seen at a child guidance center. They found that marital instability, poor marital relationships, prolonged separations, and divorce were considerably more prevalent in the alcoholic families (41 percent versus 11 percent). Family theory views marital disruption as a major contributor to children's symptoms. Additionally, these researchers discovered more serious illnesses and accidents (possibly as a result of neglect) as well as more school problems in children in alcoholic families compared with those in nonalcoholic families. Children from alcoholic homes externalized conflict and were more often involved with police or the courts. According to Chafetz et al., "This suggests that children of alcoholics have a difficult time becoming socially mature and responsible adults" (p. 696).

Hindman (1975–1976) wrote that alcoholic families are chaotic, confusing, and unpredictable to the children, who often experience neglect, abuse, and inconsistent discipline and rarely experience structure. As a result, they become isolated, develop adjustment problems, and have difficulty with peer relationships.

Booz-Allen and Hamilton (1974) reported, "Having an alcoholic parent is an emotionally disturbing experience for children. If children do not resolve the problems created by parental alcoholism, they will carry them the rest of their lives" (p. 73). The most frequent disturbances they found were emotional neglect of the children and family conflict, defined as violence, aggression, fighting, arguments within the home, and spouse abuse. Emotional neglect occurred when the alcoholic withdrew from the child, building a wall that did not provide the child with communication, affection, or parenting. These families also experienced the full range of other family problems, including nonfulfillment of parental responsibilities, instability, divorce, separation, death, physical abuse, and inappropriate physical behavior to meet the needs of the parent.

The children in this study expressed strong feelings about living with an alcoholic parent. Most frequently they resented their situation, particularly the parental duties they had to perform and not having "normal" parents. Often they expressed embarrassment about their parents' inadequacies and lack of responsiveness. They did not bring their friends home because they did not want them to witness the chaos there. They also expressed a full range of feelings, including love, admiration, respect, fear, anger, hate, guilt, and loneliness. The children had the need to love their parents, but they had ambivalent feelings that caused them confusion.

As the children grew up in these families they experienced various problems. Young children developed school problems, delinquency, and fighting. A high percentage of the children had difficulties in developing relationships with peers. Less common problems included alcohol and drug abuse, depression and suicidal tendencies, repressed emotions, and a lack of self-confidence and direction.

Children were at a higher risk of developing problems when they:

- belonged to a lower socioeconomic group
- witnessed or experienced physical abuse
- were six years old or younger at the onset of the parental alcohol abuse
- were an only or oldest child
- lived in a nonsupportive family situation

These are the children who gain the least from parental treatment and need to be included in a family treatment process. Although children's personalities, attributes, and personal internal resources determine the degree of difficulties they will have, the researchers felt that "the nuclear and extended family had the greatest potential for positively affecting the child" (Booz-Allen & Hamilton, 1974, p. 76).

Hecht (1973) focused on the alcoholic family and concluded that communication was often incongruent, unclear, and led to the isolation of family members. Children observe their parents saying one thing and doing another and do not know which message to respond to. If these messages become double binds, the children cannot win with either choice. Spouses of alcoholics often protect the child with half-truths about the alcoholic, but unfortunately the children come to believe that parents cannot be trusted. To survive in this environment, children learn to ignore verbal messages and watch for actions and deeds. Similarly, they imitate the parental communication style of fighting and hostile sarcasm, often acting out their impulses. Children living in these systems feel alone and have difficulty trusting others.

These families have further difficulties with role behavior. The parents do not perform parental duties, and sex role models are distorted or nonexistent. Children also cross generational boundaries and function as parents in many areas. Also, family members take on survival role behaviors when the alcoholic was drinking.

Inconsistencies in discipline make it difficult for children to see clearly the connections between cause and effect. Family rules are not clear-cut and frequently change. It is axiomatic that, when parents are overly involved with alcohol, it is difficult for them to understand their children's dilemma.

Hecht (1973) reported that children, on the other hand, have a great need to love their parents, but when their parents are abusing alcohol or neglecting them, they become angry. This anger is not directed at their parents but turned inward. The children also are afraid that matters will worsen and their home disappear. If the children live in a single-parent family, this fear often becomes reality if the parent enters inpatient treatment or is incapable of providing a home for the children. The children may be placed in a foster home or institution until the parent is capable of parenting again. This need to love a parent and have that love returned causes children distress when the parent is drinking. They then become ashamed of the parent. Their anger and resentment translate into rebellious behavior. Ironically, this behavior may be the very thing that leads to the placement of children away from their parents. The child often becomes the "bad" person while the alcoholic is hidden and protected by other family members.

Clinebell (1968) reported four factors that produce damage in the lives of children of alcoholics. The first factor is role reversal. Children may undertake parental duties because the parent is unable or because responsibilities are forced on them. Also, the alcoholic may be treated as a child and, in return, act helpless. In incestuous families, the daughter and mother switch roles. Second, an inconsistent and unpredictable relationship with the alcoholic is emotionally depriving to the child. Third, the nonalcoholic inadequate parent struggles with major problems, and because his or her own needs are unmet, he or she is unable to attend to the needs of the children. The fourth damaging factor is social isolation of the family as protection from further pain and suffering. Due to embarrassment, the family builds a wall of defenses around itself that leaves no room for social relationships or adequate peer relationships for the children. Although these conditions do not occur in all alcoholic families, they are damaging when they do exist.

Cork (1969) interviewed 115 children who lived in alcoholic families to gain an understanding of the child's perspective. She found that these children became so absorbed in family problems that they were unable to develop a sense of responsibility or an ability to solve problems. They were dealing with adult problems and had not expressed their feelings about this with others. As Cork interviewed them, they enthusiastically talked about a subject that was ordinarily taboo.

The following is a list of some of the children's concerns:

- They would not go to a friend's house because they would not dare reciprocate and invite friends to their own homes due to the unpredictable and embarrassing behaviors of their parents.
- They were angry at everybody.
- They were preoccupied at school with worry about what would happen when they returned home.
- They envied their friends who seemed to have fun with their families.
- Children without siblings felt alone.
- When both parents were drinking, the children felt neglected.
- The children believed they had to be parentlike, especially if the mother was drinking.
- If the parents were separated, the children worried about each parent's loneliness. They wished for their parents to reunite even if the home was calmer during the separation. The children seemed to feel an even deeper loss of the alcoholic parent if this person moved out of the home.
- Adolescents were unable to separate and individuate from their parents. They did not experience a sense of responsibility or control over their lives. It was difficult to break away from somebody with whom they had no ties. One child said poignantly, "I want to be somebody, but I feel like a nobody."
- The children often excused the alcoholic for his or her behavior and condemned the nonalcoholics for being hostile and angry, deducing from this that love and caring would cure alcoholism. Research unfortunately indicates that many such children do marry alcoholics to try out their hypothesis.
- These children experienced multiple separations and reunions of their parents and learned not to depend on any consistent state.
- Even when the alcoholics stopped drinking, the children continued to have problems.

The study also surveyed children's focus of concern in their family life, how they thought they were affected by having an alcoholic parent, their views about drinking, problems caused by drinking, and their attitudes about their own future use of alcohol. Interestingly, the children's primary concern about their family was not alcohol consumption. The main concerns were parental fighting and quarreling and a lack of interest in them by both parents (Table 9-1). Children felt affected in many ways by parental alcoholism, and the largest group made a choice not to drink because they were afraid of being like their alcoholic parents. Approximately two thirds said they would never drink for various reasons, and one third said they would drink in moderation. Five children were already drinking. Ironically, if previous research is correct, 25–30 percent of these children who have decided not to drink or drink moderately will become alcoholic (Wolin, 1993). If this is the case, simply making a decision about drinking, without further therapy to eliminate the child and family problems, is not enough to prevent alcoholism in these children. Cork was distressed by the fact that the children she rated as most disturbed were the children who planned to drink moderately or were already drinking.

Cork also looked at the grandparents of these children and found that two thirds of the fathers of the alcoholic parents were alcoholic and 10 percent of their mothers were alcoholic. One half of the fathers and 7 percent of the mothers of the nonalcoholic parents were alcoholic. This seems to substantiate theories of an intergenerational process and makes the third-generation children truly at high risk, even though they have cognitively decided not to drink like their alcoholic parents.

Although this could point to a genetically inherited problem, many other characteristics of interpersonal relationships and interpersonal problems may be contributors as well. Cork deduced from her work that "the key to alcoholism lies in the interpersonal relationships within the family" (p. 79). She believed that the

---

**Table 9–1** Children's Focus of Concern in Their Family Life

| Concern | No. of Children |
|---|---|
| Parental fighting and quarreling | 98 |
| Lack of interest of alcoholic parent | 96 |
| Lack of interest of nonalcoholic parent | 73 |
| Unhappiness of parent | 35 |
| Drunkenness | 6 |
| Drinking | 1 |

Note: Some children responded with more than one answer.

Source: Reprinted with permission from the Alcoholism & Drug Addiction Foundation, Toronto, Ontario, Canada. December, 1981.

major environmental stresses of the parents and grandparents in this study were difficulties in marriage and family life.

Studies of the children of alcoholics have revealed a wide range of child and family problems that occurs in alcoholic families, depending on the nature of the study and the questions asked. There appear to be two focuses, an individual focus on the problems of children and a second focus on family relationship problems. Exhibit 9–1 is a grouping of the reported problems of the child who lives in an alcoholic family. These problems were reported by families identified as problematic either by social services or by self-referral to therapy and do not necessarily represent all families with alcoholic members. Not all children of alcoholics have these problems, and some children without alcoholic parents exhibit them anyway. It is possible that all these individual problems are a result of living in a family system that is not functioning in the best interests of its members.

When the mother is alcoholic, children experience more of these problems than when they live with an alcoholic father. When both parents are alcoholic, the child is without a parental resource (Cork, 1969; Fox,1968). Exhibit 9–2 is a list of family problems divided among the dyadic marital relationship, the parental

---

**Exhibit 9–1** Problems of Children Who Live in Alcoholic Families

*Physical Neglect or Abuse*
  serious illness
  accidents
*Acting-Out Behaviors*
  involvement with police and courts
  aggression
  alcohol and drug abuse
*Emotional Reactions to Alcoholism and Chaotic Family Life*
  suicidal tendencies
  depression
  repressed emotions
  lack of self-confidence
  lack of life direction
  fear of abandonment
  afraid of future
*Social and Interpersonal Difficulties*
  family relationship problems
  peer problems
  adjustment problems
  feeling different from norm
  embarrassment
  overresponsible
  feel unloved and unable to trust

**Exhibit 9–2** Problems of the Alcoholic Family That Affect More Than One Person

---

*Marital*
  marital instability and fighting
  prolonged marital separation
  divorce
  death of a spouse
  physical abuse of a spouse
*Parental*
  inadequate parenting
  lack of structure
  inconsistencies
  emotional neglect of children
  inability or unwillingness to perform parental duties
*Cross Boundaries—Parent and Child Relationships*
  physical and sexual abuse of children
  parentification of a child
  role reversal
  family conflict
  isolation of family from society
  isolation of individual family members with the family
  incongruent communications
  lack of trust between family members
  family secrets

---

relationship, and triadic parent-child relationships. Family therapy treats dysfunctional family relationships, separates overinvolved coalitions and joins underinvolved members, reduces family tension, and creates a new family balance at a higher level of functioning. This allows for each member to feel more fully centered and self-determined. As a result, the adaptive consequences of alcoholism are reduced or eliminated, and problem symptomatology in the children and parents often disappears. Family conflicts produce persons with a high degree of inner tension who may reduce anxiety with alcohol consumption (McCord, McCord, & Gudeman, 1960). If this family conflict is reduced, the inner tension of the alcoholic and the drinking may also be reduced or eliminated. With a reduction of family tension, individual members are able to survive in the family without using rigid role behavior to try to solve the family problems and can pursue self-determination.

### Role Behavior in Children of Alcoholics

Satir (Bandler, Grender, & Satir, 1976), a pioneer in family therapy, identified roles that family members play when they are under stress. Family members work hard at these roles to save the family system at the expense of their own emotional and physical health. Satir identified these roles as:

- the *placater*, who agrees with everyone, appears helpless, and feels worthless
- the *blamer*, who disagrees and blames but feels lonely and unsuccessful
- the *superreasonable* or computer, who is logical and computes in a calm way but feels vulnerable
- the *distractor* or irrelevant, who makes no sense, is obtuse and off the subject, and thinks nobody cares

These roles hide the actors' true feelings and interfere with clear, congruent communication. When the role behaviors fail and the stress continues, family members change roles in a desperate attempt to cope.

Wegscheider (1981a, b), a student of Satir's, identified six roles specific to the alcoholic family. These are seen as defenses that cover the true feelings of the person and make communication difficult. These roles are:

1. the *dependent*, who is angry, rigid, perfectionist, charming, righteous, and grandiose but feels guilt, hurt, shame, fear, and pain
2. the *chief enabler*—a spouse, parent, or coworker who provides responsibility but feels hurt, angry, guilty, and afraid
3. the *family hero*, usually the oldest child, who provides self-worth for the family with hard work, achievement, and success, but feels lonely, hurt, and inadequate. The achievement is for others and the family; the hero is not rewarded with self-worth.
4. the *scapegoat*—the child who acts out, abuses alcohol and drugs, and takes the focus off the seemingly unsolvable family problem of alcoholism. The scapegoat volunteers for this position but feels lonely, rejected, hurt, and angry.
5. the *lost child*—the child who offers relief by not being a problem. This child withdraws and is quiet and independent but feels lonely, hurt, and inadequate.
6. the *mascot*, often the youngest child, who provides fun and humor and distracts family members. The mascot is protected from what is really happening but senses the family tension and feels insecure, frightened, and lonely.

Wegscheider observed individuals play out these roles to survive in their families in her years of work with alcoholics. She used a family approach to help all the family members recover and reestablish a functional family system.

These role behavior descriptions have often been used almost as pathological diagnostic categories for children of alcoholics (COAs) and adult children of alcoholics (ACAs) instead of viewed as role behaviors that can be found in any family. When stress is high, family members revert to these behaviors to solve problems. The difficulty comes when the stress is constant and the role behaviors become rigid. They have even been described by Wegscheider and others as survival roles.

The important thing for therapists to know is that individuals can become more flexible. The goal of therapy with a family hero, therefore, is not to make him or her a scapegoat, but to broaden the repertoire of behaviors of the individual within his or her chosen role. Wegscheider (1981b) distinguished the children's roles by describing what will happen in adulthood to these children if they get help or do not. She believed that family heroes without help may become workaholics, take responsibility for everything, and marry a dependent person. With help, they can learn to relax, accept failure, and take responsibility for only themselves. The scapegoat without help may develop delinquency, have trouble at school or the office, or have an unplanned pregnancy. With help, scapegoats can accept responsibility for their behavior, learn to see reality, and may become good counselors. Lost children without help have little zest for life, develop sexual identity problems, suffer from bedwetting, have difficulty with long-term relationships, and often die young. With help, they learn to be independent, talented, creative, and imaginative. Family mascots without help are compulsive clowns, have difficulty with stress, may marry a hero, and are at risk for chemical dependency. With help, they can give up being clowns, learn to handle stress, and develop a good sense of humor that makes them fun to be with.

Black (1979, 1981a) defined the role behavior of children of alcoholics in two categories: (1) the misbehaving, obviously troubled children, and (2) the mature, stable, overachieving, behaving children who Black believed are the majority. These behaving children develop survival roles to provide their own stability. They learn the family rule—don't talk about what is happening. They detach from others, repress feelings, and organize to take care of others. In the alcoholic family, the children learn to trust only themselves, and in school they are self-reliant and set short-term goals that lead to accomplishment. Consequently, these children develop a good self-image through their successes outside of the home. This process works well until long-term life decisions have to be made. Such children of alcoholics find themselves in their mid-20s unable to cope with adulthood. Alcohol provides a reduction of loneliness and pain that these children have learned to be sensitive to. They repeat the stress-reduction process that worked in their family of origin. Another option these children select is to find an alcoholic spouse with whom to perpetuate their role behavior and take care of someone again.

In her research, Brown (1979) found that adult children of alcoholics are unable to trust their own feelings and are afraid of not being in control. They have problems with intimacy, responsibility, identification, and expression of feelings. As children, these people learned to avoid upsetting their parents by holding in their feelings at all costs. Their parents were unpredictable, and the children never could be certain of the reactions to their outward expression of feelings.

As long as these children get some secondary gains for their role behaviors, they maintain a positive self-image. However, when the easily achievable, short-term goals disappear and are replaced by long-term adulthood goals, there is no foundation of self-worth to fill the gap. Lack of self-worth, in the cases of these achieving children, often leads to alcohol abuse as a pain reliever.

Black (1979) divided these young children of alcoholics into three types of role behavior that they rigidly play and bring with them into adulthood:

1. *Responsible ones* are usually the oldest children who feel responsible for everyone. They provide structure for the family and become angry at themselves if they cannot control. These children are adultlike, serious, rigid, and inflexible. They have little time for play or fun. Their self-reliance leads to loneliness, and they often marry alcoholics. This role is very similar to Wegscheider's family hero.
2. *Adjusters* follow directions and must be flexible to adjust to the fighting, separations, and multiple life changes of the alcoholic family. They think they have no power over their own lives.
3. *Placaters* are emotionally sensitive children. They take care of others first to reduce their own pain and make life easier. They believe they do not deserve to have their own needs met. They smooth over conflicts and are rewarded for their help. They work too hard at taking care of others and neglect their own feelings and needs. Placaters can become empty-nest alcoholics when their own children grow up and no longer need care.

An example of one of these roles is shown in the following case study seen by one of the authors in a therapy situation. An 11-year-old girl, an adjuster, lived with an alcoholic father who was divorced when his daughter was less than one year old. His transient lifestyle took the two of them throughout the country, and his daughter had never gone to the same school for a whole year until she was placed in a foster home (after it was discovered that she had been sexually abused by her father for five years). This child explained to a child protective services worker that she did not mind the lifestyle except for the sexual abuse. When her father was not making progress in treatment, she explained this by saying, "You can't expect a lot from him, or you'll be disappointed." Her acceptance and adjustment was a desperate attempt to hold on to the only family member she had ever known.

Adjusters work hard at taking care of others and deny any feelings of their own. They are adaptable and adjust to many situations, but they are manipulated by others and can lose their self-esteem.

Although there are rewards for these role behaviors (responsible ones are successful, adjusters are adaptable, and placaters are appreciated), there are negative consequences as well. These children have difficulty expressing feelings, especially feelings with a negative connotation. Anger and sadness go unnoticed or are punished in their family.

The role does not change when the child leaves the alcoholic family or when the alcoholic achieves sobriety without a positive change in the family system. The children relate to the behavior and attitudes of their parents and not their drinking (Cork, 1969). They learn to deny their feelings because they are unable to tolerate their strong reactions to the family situations. They protect themselves with denial and continue to do so even when the drinking stops.

In their report, Booz-Allen and Hamilton (1974) identified four coping mechanisms that parallel the role behaviors of children:

1.  *Flight*—These children avoid the alcoholic by not being at home, hiding in their rooms, running away, becoming involved in activities outside of the home, going to college, getting married, getting a job, emotionally withdrawing, blocking memory, or turning to religion.
2.  *Fight*—These are the aggressive, rebellious, acting-out children who are seen as behavior problems. They sometimes end up in court or are placed out of the home.
3.  *Perfect child*—These children never do anything wrong. They mind their parents and excel in school. Parents bring them out of the shadows to show them off as examples to the others.
4.  *Supercoper*—These children usually are the oldest children and can become confidants of nonalcoholic spouses. They are parentified children who feel responsible for the other family members.

These role behaviors of children of alcoholics are not separate categories. Children have blends of several of these behaviors and use different ones as the occasion warrants. A family hero who goes off to college and is influenced by his peer group to drink abusively (and fails at school) can quickly become the scapegoat. If a scapegoat leaves home and the family is still in need of one, the next oldest may fill the scapegoat position.

Figure 9–1 is a chart that compares the child behavior roles described by Black, Wegscheider, and Booz-Allen and Hamilton. The Satir role behaviors that pertain to all the family members parallel the role behaviors of alcoholic children.

## TREATMENT TO HELP CHILDREN

Children who live in alcoholic families may be identified as "the problem" or may seem like perfect children. Both of these roles take the focus off the central

| Black | Booz-Allen and Hamilton | Wegscheider | Characteristics | Satir |
|-------|------------------------|-------------|-----------------|-------|
| Adjuster | Flight | Lost Children | loneliness, isolation, escapes, never complains, will not cause further problems | irrelevant (no place for me) |
| (no role) | Fight | Scapegoat | hurt, anger, rejection, feelings are close to the surface, takes the focus off of the alcoholic | Blamer (lonely and unsuccessful) |
| Placater | Perfect Child | Mascot | provides relief, emotionally isolated, makes others feel good | Placater (worthless) |
| Responsible One | Super Coper | Family Hero | loneliness, over-achiever, parentified | Super-Responsible (vulnerable, no feeling) |

**Figure 9–1** Coping Roles

problems of the family dynamics, the marital stress, and the tension around the abuse of alcohol. The best way to help children who live in alcoholic families is to improve the functioning of the nuclear family. Improvement in family communication patterns, rebuilding of marital and parental relationships, reestablishment of trust and respect, and facilitation of emotional contact change the environment that is damaging to children.

If the alcoholic is still drinking, work with the nonalcoholic spouse could lead to establishing one parent who can protect and care for the children. The spouse must stop taking responsibility for the alcoholic's drinking or sobriety. It is difficult for anyone to solve a problem when someone else has taken responsibility for it. The spouse can then begin to take care of himself or herself and begin to structure the home environment as well as consistently parent the children. Hecht (1973) stated, "The spouse, as much as possible, must avoid assigning tasks to the children that they are not ready to undertake, and avoid directing toward them the anger the nonalcoholic parent feels toward the alcoholic" (p. 1767).

In addition to the family work, children can benefit from group therapy with other children. The group provides them with a place where they can express feelings without fear of reprisal and where role behavior is not necessary. Children also learn that they are not alone in their experiences and that they can establish relationships with peers. Ackerman (1978) noted, "Helping children of alcoholics to work through their feelings and establish effective relationships with others will be very helpful in overcoming the impact of an alcoholic parent" (p. 109). When children develop self-confidence, they believe they can control themselves and have an influence on the outcome of their lives. These feelings are preventive medicine for children at high risk for turning to alcohol as a problem solver.

Black (1981b) used group work with children to let them know that they are not alone, that their parents' alcoholism is not their fault, that addiction is hard to stop but the parent can get help, and that the children need to take care of themselves. She used art therapy in her children's groups to help participants talk about difficult subjects. Black (Patterson, 1980) said, "Asking youngsters to draw pictures of their family life and their views on alcoholism helps reverse a tendency in the children to deny the existence of a problem."

## Treatment Programs

In looking at treatment programs for children from alcoholic families, it is impossible to avoid the idea of prevention. Treating the behavioral or emotional problems of children who have lived with an alcoholic parent is surely a major step in preventing these high-risk children from becoming alcoholics themselves.

Although children have been overlooked in alcohol treatment in favor of working individually with the alcoholic or with the marital couple, they need to become a target population for prevention efforts. In the 1980s some treatment centers pioneered support groups with structured activities for children of their clients. For example, Black (1979, 1981) used art therapy with groups of children in a California treatment center. However, the direct treatment of young children of alcoholics diminished with the advent of the powerful adult children of alcoholic social movement, which shifted the focus to the problems that these children had as adults.

A model of a program of prevention and treatment designed specifically for children of alcoholics can be seen in the Children from Alcoholic Families Program, developed in the early 1980s and still funded by the Nebraska Division on Alcohol and Drug Abuse. This program is based on the theory of prevention through reduction of risk in the physiological, sociological, and psychological areas. There is little that can be done to move children from high risk to low risk in the physiological area. Genetically, some individuals may be unable to drink without problems. However, children can be educated about this high-risk factor and taught warning signals if they should choose to drink. Changes *can* be made, though, in the sociological and psychological factors that make children high risk.

Sociologically, high-risk children live in an environment where alcohol is used abusively. One parent models drinking to get drunk and to avoid reality. Often the other parent drinks abusively as well, or abstains and is morally critical of the spouse. Neither of these positions models a responsible approach to alcohol. In the Children from Alcoholic Families Program, parents become more aware of the model they set and talk about appropriate and inappropriate drinking with their children. They can educate their children about alcohol and begin to open up communication processes in the family so that the children can come to the parents when they need answers to difficult questions. Parents are also taught new parenting strategies. Improvement in parenting skills can lower the risk factors of the children. Children who learn to make good choices, who feel responsible for their behavior, and who can control their environment are children who grow up with more self-assurance and tolerance for stress. Ethnic factors are examined, and the family history of alcoholism for three generations is charted in a genogram. Generally, an effort is made through education and family therapy to improve the family system, including communication patterns, parenting skills, and drinking-related values, all of which affect the child.

Psychologically, prevention of alcoholism in the children of alcoholic families involves improving self-esteem and allowing them to believe that they can make good decisions and be capable individuals. Chemically dependent persons are low in self-esteem, unable to cope, unable to relate to others, and lack decision-making ability. They also have unhealthy dependencies and a low tolerance for tension (Glenn, 1981).

To decrease risk factors, work is done to promote positive self-image and to give children enough life skills to create successful life experiences. Group work is used to improve their ability to relate to peers, enhance their ability to make decisions, increase their independence, and develop positive techniques to help them deal with stress.

Another prevention-treatment strategy is Albee's model for preventing problems that are multicausal (Albee, 1981).

Figure 9–2 is an equation that can be viewed as a fraction. Prevention occurs when the numerator is reduced or the denominator is increased. Children of alcoholics can do little about the organic factors of inherited genetic predispositions to alcoholism, and it is impossible to eliminate stress from the environment. It seems more possible to increase the denominator by teaching coping skills to children and their families, increasing the competence and self-esteem of all the individuals involved in the program, and connecting them with support networks in the aftercare portion of the program.

The Children from Alcoholic Families Program works in three areas to increase the denominator of the prevention fraction.

$$\frac{Organic\ Factors\ +\ Stress}{Coping\ Skills\ Competence\ +\ Self\text{-}Esteem\ +\ Support\ Networks}$$

**Figure 9–2** Prevention Fraction

1. The *children's groups* increase the coping skills of the children, give them competence, and improve self-esteem.
2. The *family therapy* improves the communication skills, enhances family relationships, and increases problem-solving abilities.
3. The *aftercare* component provides support groups and connects families and individuals with community agencies and resources that build support networks for children and their families.

The Children from Alcoholic Families Program is housed in a child guidance center, the Lincoln/Lancaster County Child Guidance Center, and is not affiliated with any alcohol treatment program, nor does it support any one treatment philosophy for alcoholism. It was created to prevent alcoholism by interrupting the intergenerational processes of alcoholism. The focus is on the children.

The program has five components:

1. **Intake component**. The goal of the intake component is to screen and evaluate children and families to determine family goals, degree of risk, and areas in need of modification. Families are eligible if at least one parent has had a drinking problem or currently is drinking abusively. Families may include a parent with long-term sobriety, a parent who recently entered or completed chemical dependency treatment, or a chemically dependent parent without sobriety.

   At the intake, children are referred to an age-appropriate group, parents are placed in the parents' group, and a case manager/family therapist is assigned to the family. The groups are closed and time limited (six weeks). Family therapy occurs once a week in addition to the groups.
2. **Parents' component**. The parents are offered a two-pronged approach—a psychoeducational group and individual treatment for stress management. The parents' group is a forum for discussion of prevention strategies, role behaviors, family systems, and parenting education. Individual treatment includes biofeedback for increased control of automatic functions that mediate and affect levels of bodily tension and progressive relaxation. Clients are taught how to obtain more complete relaxation in the bodily musculature most vulnerable to tension buildup.

   At least one parent is required to attend the parents' group. If the alcoholic will not attend, work is done with the spouse to improve the family environment and possibly change the family system.
3. **Children's component**. The children experience alcohol education, socialization, and treatment for emotional and behavioral problems through a peer group modality. Therapists attempt to induce a level of comfort conducive to the spontaneous expression of feeling. The intent of the group is that

reasonable freedom of expression should exist without fear of reprisal. Rigidified role behavior should be unnecessary.

The goals of these groups are:

- to let the children know they are not alone
- to inform children that it is not their fault that their parents are alcoholics
- to teach the children about the nature of addictions and the difficulty their parents have in achieving and maintaining sobriety
- to reassure children that alcoholism is treatable
- to help children learn about themselves and how to take care of themselves
- to allow for expression of positive and negative feelings
- to foster improved peer relationship skills
- to teach problem-solving techniques
- to evaluate children's levels of coping skills, social skills, and overall function in conjunction with the family. This diagnostic information is needed to determine a reasonable plan for aftercare or continued treatment involvement.

4. **Family component**. Each family has a family therapy session once a week for six weeks. Unique family therapy goals are established for each family. The goal of this component is to allow the family to view the effects of alcoholism on each member and the system as a whole. The family can then view the problem existing within the family system and begin to move from an unhealthy system to a healthy one. That is, they can move from a family with secrets and limited intimacy, a family with hidden rules in which only performance has value, to a healthier family system. The healthy state allows open communication and can accept differences, negotiates rules openly, and values the feelings of its members.

Because each family is unique, the type and degree of change needed varies. However, the overall goal is movement toward a healthy system that produces children who are emotionally strong.

5. **Aftercare component**. When the family members have completed the six weeks of group and family sessions, an aftercare assessment is accomplished by gathering information from each counselor who is familiar with a family member, results of formal evaluations, and contacts with other sources in the community capable of providing a measure of social and emotional coping. The results of this assessment determine if the family member would benefit from further family therapy, inclusion in a long-term aftercare group, referral to self-help groups (such as Al-Anon, AA, Alateen, and Alakid), referral to the Child Guidance Center's Children of Divorce Project, or a networking of family members to outside supports and recreation facilities.

The long-term support groups are an extension of the children's groups with less intensity. Therapeutic camping experiences for these groups are being developed in conjunction with the YWCA.

Some of the families in the program are remaining beyond the six-week period and are establishing an Adult Children from Alcoholic Families Group to lessen the intergenerational impact of alcoholism.

Due to the varying range of problems and coping skills, each family is assessed individually as is risk estimation for the children. The aftercare plan reflects the needs of the family. Booz-Allen and Hamilton (1974) determined that:

> Parental alcoholism is not equally disruptive in all families. In some cases, alcoholism is a relatively minor characteristic in the total fiber of family life; the family functions well with a basically positive atmosphere, whether in spite of or because of the alcoholism of a parent. If the situation is not seriously uncomfortable, the child need not take extreme measures to defend himself against it; he simply accommodates the alcoholism as a limited problem. (p. 41)

The Nebraska program focuses on the strengths of families and gives them concrete methods for reducing the risk of their children. Families and children are not kept in the program indefinitely. They are given realistic projections for the success of their family and are encouraged to develop their own support networks and leave the program without further need for intervention.

Children of alcoholics are at high risk for developing behavioral and emotional problems as well as alcoholism. These problems can be displayed in aggressive, acting-out behavior or hidden behind achieving, mature, perfect behavior. These seemingly perfect children can have difficulties in relationships as they grow older and are at risk for abusing alcohol. Even children who make a decision to avoid alcohol may turn to it when they can no longer cope. Also, these children develop resiliencies and strengths as they learn to cope with destructive family environments. This field of thought is covered more thoroughly in the section on adult children of alcoholics.

Treatment methods for alcoholism must include the children if these problems are to be eliminated and if the intergenerational transmission of alcoholism is to be halted.

## ADULT CHILDREN OF ALCOHOLICS

As alcoholism moved from being seen as the problem of an individual to one that affects family members and others around the alcoholic, the scope of treatment widened to include family members, even children. There was a group, however, that was ignored until the early 1980s, when it was recognized that adults who were raised in alcoholic families did not escape unharmed. They often brought a variety of problems with them into adulthood and played out in their own families what they learned or did not learn in their families of origin.

Jacobson (1991), in chronicling the ACA movement, reported that the term *adult children of alcoholics* was first used in 1979, and that this naming was pivotal in the rise of the powerful ACA movement. Black (1987) reported that:

> The term "Adult Children of Alcoholics" was one that Stephanie Brown and I coined as we described our work to *Newsweek* magazine in 1979. ... We thought that within the adult today who was raised in an alcoholic home, there is a child that continues to need nurturing. That same child still needs to learn skills that many others learned in childhood. (p. xxvi)

Although this sounds like a simple statement that children of alcoholics missed out on some of their child development processes, the label soon became a lifelong diagnosis of pathology that spawned shelves of self-help books aimed at ACAs. The publication of Claudia Black's *It Will Never Happen to Me* (1981) and Janet Woititz's *Adult Children of Alcoholics* (1983) shook to the core the 21 million ACAs in the United States, many of whom began to seek help for themselves. The acknowledgment of the long-range consequences of living in a chaotic alcoholic family began the drive to make treatment for this population legitimate. This brought with it, however, a trend to pathologize all adult children of alcoholics.

As the popular literature concerning ACAs grew, a pathological profile developed with a long list of problems attributed to ACAs. Most of these problem lists came from therapists working with an ACA population who came for therapy, but they were often falsely generalized to the entire population of ACAs. Common problems found in the literature include:

- difficulty with intimate relationships
- lack of trust in others
- fear of loss of control
- conflicts over personal responsibility characterized by superresponsible and/ or superirresponsible behavior
- denial of feelings and of reality
- harsh and relentless self-criticism
- low self-esteem and lack of identity
- denial of personal needs
- black-and-white thinking
- inability to relax or have fun
- fear of abandonment

This is only a partial list of problems attributed to ACAs. Vannicelli (1989) made a list of 30 problems she found in the popular literature but noted that many were problems that the general public bring to therapy; they were not unique to ACAs. Vannicelli further pointed out that ACAs themselves are not all the same and don't have the same profile of problems. Factors she found that differentiate the type and severity of problems ACAs bring into therapy include:

- whether one or both parents are alcoholics
- the age of the child at the onset of the parent's alcoholism
- the economic stability of the family
- the availability and use of external support
- the duration and severity of the alcoholism
- the number of generations of addiction in the family
- the recovery status of the alcoholic
- the presence of psychiatric illnesses in the family
- the presence of physical or sexual abuse in the family
- the abilities of the nonalcoholic spouse

There is also a difference between ACAs who enter therapy and those who do not. Barnard and Spoentgen (1986) compared college-age ACAs who went to the campus clinic for therapy and ACAs at the same college who did not. They found that those who sought treatment had more parental loss, lower financial resources, lower innerdirectedness, lower self-regard, lower self-acceptance, lower capacity for intimate contact, and more reactivity. This is important to understand so that research done with a clinical population is not generalized to the population as a whole. Barnard and Spoentgen also found the eight-week group therapy for ACAs to be effective in improving innerdirectedness, self-regard, and capacity for intimate contact with others.

When ACAs are examined in the general population (nonclinical), some of the problems they are believed to share as a group are not validated. Boye-Beaman, Leonard, and Senchak (1991), in a longitudinal research project examining alcohol use and marital functioning of newlywed couples, discovered an interesting pattern of assortative mating. They found that daughters of alcoholics, who have been thought to tend to marry alcoholics, were no more likely to marry frequent heavy drinkers than those not raised in an alcoholic home. The same was true of sons of alcoholics, who were no more likely to marry a heavy drinker. The children of alcoholics were, however, twice as likely to marry each other as those not from alcoholic families. Heavy drinkers, as well, were more likely to marry other heavy drinkers than expected by chance. Another important point made by the research team was that many of the children of alcoholics did not marry spouses who were raised in alcoholic families. Nearly 70 percent of women from alcoholic families married men from nonalcoholic families, and 59 percent of men from alcoholic families married women from nonalcoholic families. This may reflect a resilient group of ACAs who deliberately select spouses from well-functioning, nonalcoholic families. Bennett, Wolin, and Reiss (1988) found this deliberateness to reduce the transmission of alcoholism across generations. This research is discussed in the section on intergenerational transmission of alcoholism.

To confuse the issue of accuracy of problems attributed to ACAs, a more recent study of assortative mating found that nonalcoholic daughters of alcoholics were more than twice as likely to marry an alcoholic as nonalcoholic daughters of nonalcoholics, regardless of the gender of the alcoholic parent (Schuckit, Tipp, & Keiner, 1994). Sons of alcoholics, however, did not marry alcoholics more frequently than sons of nonalcoholics.

In trying to understand the etiology of ACA problems, it is most useful to view those problems that children of alcoholics bring into adulthood as developmental problems that are solvable. This does not eliminate the possibility that ACAs may also have severe mental illnesses that may require more treatment. A developmental view helps to clarify why some ACAs seem problem-free while others seem to struggle with life.

Depending on the time of the onset and the severity of alcoholism in the family, children of alcoholics arrive at adulthood having missed out on a normal childhood development. If the alcoholic parents are consumed by their illness early in the child's life, care may be inadequate, inconsistent, and rejecting. Infants learn that they cannot depend on their parents and do not develop the sense of trust that is necessary to move to the next step in the development of a healthy child. This failure to develop a sense of trust interferes with adult interpersonal relationships and intimacy (Beletis & Brown, 1981).

As children move into their second and third years they begin to explore their world. In alcoholic families children are often stifled in many ways so they won't upset the drinking or hung-over parent. If this restriction is excessive, children develop a sense of shame about their natural inquisitiveness. At this stage children may be overprotected from the negative environment and limited in a way that denies them a sense of self-control. Adults who experience these restrictions as children feel a sense of shame and a lack of control. As children become more involved with the environment, motor skills develop. In alcoholic families curiosity is often treated as inappropriate. Feelings and play are shut down and children are blamed for their parents' problems. Children can develop a sense of guilt and blame that lasts throughout life.

As children go off to school they begin to separate from their parents. This is accomplished when children know that they can return back to the nurturing home. The child of the alcoholic is often unequipped to navigate this separation. However, the child may be pushed to take on adult responsibilities. In school the child can become an excellent student, driven to perfection that is never achieved, while other children give up before they even start. The child of the alcoholic may reach adulthood with a sense of helplessness and inferiority.

The adolescent children of alcoholics find themselves trying to develop an identity and to separate from their families. Those children who mastered the earlier developmental tasks have the self-esteem and confidence required for these difficult tasks. In the alcoholic family, needs, feelings, and true identity are denied. "In fact the driving need to deny feelings and needs is a denial of self" (Beletis & Brown, 1981, p. 204).

The pull to remain in the alcoholic family system either doesn't allow children to leave or pushes them to rebellion. The rebellion takes the form of early marriage (sometimes to alcoholics or dependent spouses) or leaving under negative circumstances. The child may leave adolescence with the façade of an identity that covers fear of autonomy and confusion about life direction.

Early adulthood for the ACA is a time of denial of personal problems, a denial of personal needs, and a feeling of having escaped the chaos of the alcoholic family. It is not until the late 20s, nearing Levinson's (1978) Age-Thirty Transition, that children from alcoholic families begin to recognize their emotional attachment to the struggles of their childhood. Individuals often find themselves approaching 30 alone, after several disastrous relationships, overly devoted to their career, unsure of their goals, unable to trust, obsessed with controlling everyone and everything, and terrified of intimacy, yet desperately wanting it. This identity crisis may include a discovery that they have been acting all their life and they don't know who they are. This may lead them to seek therapy.

Those ACAs who do not respond at this time may find themselves at 40 still emotionally tied to their families of origin. They are still trying to fix things, but as they approach the midlife transition of the 40s, they may be forced to look closely at themselves. There is a strong possibility that they will find themselves repeating the patterns and dynamics of their families of origin. They may be alcoholic themselves, married to alcoholics or divorced from several, and they may be raising children in the same environment in which they were raised. This is the time that they can take steps to break the intergenerational chain of alcoholism or they can conclude that there is never going to be any hope for them as they slide into self-pity and stagnation. Many ACAs seek therapy at this time.

ACAs who miss this chance may find themselves in later years looking back on their lives as full of missed opportunities and disastrous relationships; they feel a sense of despair. If the chain of alcoholism was not broken, they may experience the repetition of the same problems in their children and grandchildren.

The importance of looking at ACA problems from birth to old age lies in the understanding of the etiology of the common problems experienced by ACAs. The problems that exist for ACAs in adulthood may be directly linked to the years that were disrupted by the alcoholism of their parents. For instance, ACAs with intimacy problems may have been deprived of a nurturing parental relationship early in life. Seeing the ACA problems of lack of trust, obsession with control, fear of intimacy, fear of feelings, lack of self-identity, fear of conflict, inability to relax, overresponsibility, and black-and-white thinking as nothing more than developmental lags gives therapists a new perspective on them.

Just as children and adults pass through stages of development, ACAs pass through stages of recovery. Gravitz and Bowden (1984, 1990) observed from a clinical perspective that adult children of alcoholics present clearly delineated patterns of issues that develop and unfold sequentially. They grouped them into six developmental stages: (1) survival, (2) emergent awareness, (3) core issue, (4) transformation, (5) integration, and (6) genesis.

ACAs in the survival stage still operate with the role behaviors learned in childhood to survive the turmoil of their alcoholic families. Although these behaviors may have been adaptive at one time, they limit choices and spontaneity in adulthood. ACAs in this stage experience a varying amount of psychological stress, but they do not connect it to their parents' alcoholism or the family disruption this caused. They often remain in this stage unless an event such as reading a newspaper story or attending a lecture on ACA issues breaks their denial, and they begin to make the connection between their present nonproductive behavior and their parents' alcoholism. Those ACAs who remain in this stage are at high risk for becoming alcoholic or marrying an alcoholic.

The denial-breaking event marks the beginning of the emergent awareness stage. These individuals begin to identify themselves as ACAs and become aware of their physiological and psychological vulnerabilities. They often seek education about the syndrome, attend lectures, and read incessantly on the subject. They discover that they are not alone and begin to see the connections between their past and present behavior. Along with the excitement of these discoveries comes the guilt with breaking the long-standing family rule of silence.

Stephanie Brown (1988), who pioneered a program of long-term ACA groups at the Stanford Alcohol Clinic, described ACAs who decide to join the groups as being in this stage. This decision represents a conscious choice to break the denial, look at the myths, and tell the family secrets. They join the groups so they can separate from their families of origin by joining the substitute family of the group. The decision to join an ACA group poses a paradox. These ACAs are concerned whether the decision to join will allow them to finally separate from their families of origin or if it will only intensify their involvement. They see the joining process as admitting their parents are alcoholic, which they see as abandonment of a family in need. They have to work hard in group to work less on their family.

There is relief for ACAs in knowing that their current dilemma exists for a legitimate and external reason. In fact, they are not alone with these feelings. Others have similar problems and there is hope for change. The emergent awareness stage is not complete until ACAs recognize they have not been able to will themselves free of their families and their emotional baggage. They need to surrender to the belief that they have done so.

Although identification of commonalties and understanding the connection between past and present provide some relief for ACAs, awareness does not cause deep changes in behavior, emotions, or relationships. This requires longer, individualized therapy. "With the break in denial and acquisition of the label ACA, individuals begin a process of recovery that centers on a transformation in identity. . . . The process of recovery is a process of new knowledge construction, including a revision of core beliefs about the self and the family leading to ultimate differentiation and emotional separation from parents and the family of origin" (Brown, 1988, p. 7).

Although ACAs may enter group therapy at the beginning of the emergent awareness stage, it may be beneficial for them to attend a time-limited psychoeducational group for help in identifying core issues and working through feelings of guilt that come with the new identity. It is important for therapists leading these groups or working individually with ACAs in this stage to avoid giving them core issues or labels that do not fit. ACAs often have denied their sense of self and, in their rush to gain their own identity, adopt the core issues they have read about in the ACA literature.

Once the process of identification and owning the influences of the past on their present thoughts, feelings, and behaviors is in progress, ACAs move into the core issues stage. In their work at the Stanford Alcohol Clinic, Cermak and Brown (1982) identified five core issues common to their ACA group members: (1) control, (2) trust, (3) personal needs, (4) responsibility, and (5) feelings. Of the five issues, control was the most pervasive, and involved in all the other core issues. Group members either feared they were trying to control the group too much or that someone else would control it and thus control them. Silence was used by group members as passive resistance or to keep others from controlling them by not allowing opportunities for either response or rejection. Group process was filtered through the control versus lack-of-control stance. The ACAs wanted to be "good" group members and speak when appropriate, yet they felt controlled and forced to do so. Expression of feelings was tightly controlled because group members defined it as "bad." Members feared that if they ever began to express their anger, they would lose total control. Denial, suppression, and repression of feelings allowed them to survive their chaotic families and they had built a dam to hold back the flood of emotions. Depression, loss, and joy were all seen as out-of-control states accompanied by anxiety and vulnerability. The intense need to control was tied to the ACAs' desire to will themselves different from their alcoholic parents. Strong emotions were equated with out-of-control drunkenness and neediness.

For some ACAs, trust was a problem since infancy. As adults, these ACA group members showed their distrust of others by controlling their emotions and not trusting the genuineness of others' expressions of feelings, assuming they were using this expression for the effect it had on others. If a group member trusted someone, it was the same as giving them control.

In the ACA groups at the Child Guidance Center in Lincoln, Nebraska, which were modeled after the Stanford groups, we observed confusion exhibited by group members about the concepts of control, trust, and understanding. Control was expressed as making people do what you want them to do. Trust was expecting people to do what you want them to do, and understanding meant knowing why people do what they do. These group members had spent a lifetime trying to find out why their parents acted the way they did. Unless they could answer the question "Why?" they could not trust, nor could they stop controlling. Their thinking went like this: "I can't trust them, because I can't control them, because I don't understand them." This kind of thinking leads to the desire to read everything written that might provide a clue to the puzzle. If they could just fix their parents, the ACAs believed, then they would be rewarded or loved or successful.

Group members also had difficulty expressing personal needs. For many ACAs, their personal needs as a child had not been acknowledged or met by their parents. The needs were suppressed to avoid embarrassing the parents and to avoid further hurt. As adults, acknowledging the existence of personal needs was equal to admitting vulnerability—which gives others control. It was also connected to dependence on others—which, again, gives others control, or leads to guilty feelings of imposing on others whom they are controlling.

The issue of responsibility was also an echo of the past. Responsibility and blame are passed around like hot potatoes in the alcoholic family. The alcoholic does not take responsibility for his or her drinking, and other family members are willing to accept blame for what is not their responsibility. From the perspective of children, who are unable to control their environment and who feel dependent on their parents, the acceptance of blame for the alcoholic's drinking and for other family problems gives them the hope that if they can just change themselves they can control or change their family—if they can just make better grades, clean their room, be less of a problem, or become the problem, then maybe the craziness will go away. Boundaries between children and parents are confused via role reversals and lost sense of self. ACAs spend much of their time other-focused, and it is easy for them to become preoccupied with another group member's problem, take responsibility for it, and avoid the painful job of self-examination and taking responsibility for their own behavior.

The feelings that the group members tried to control had many negative connotations. When they were able to squarely place the blame for their loss of childhood and the trauma that resulted from the alcoholism on their parents, they were overwhelmed with anger. Because feelings were seen as bad and potentially overwhelming, it was difficult for the group members to express them directly or respond to another's expression of feelings.

Gravitz and Bowden (1984) identified another core issue that they found pervasive in their work with ACAs. This is the issue of all-or-none functioning that is characterized by black-and-white or polarized thinking. This is a prevalent thinking style of the alcoholic and is learned by family members. Children cope with their divided loyalties to their alcoholic parent by splitting them into the "good-sober parent" and the "bad-drunk parent." This helps them understand their continuing love for their parents in the face of drunken and often violent behavior. In their effort to control their family, children take on the family blame and allow themselves to see only their bad qualities. As adults, they have difficulty acknowledging and using their resources and strengths.

Although the role behaviors of the child often stifle adult growth, they also can be strengths and competencies. A group member in the Lincoln, Nebraska, groups shifted her rescuing, other-focused behavior into one of being naturally therapeutic and able to help others help themselves.

The all-or-nothing stance retards progress in group. Members believe that they are either all wrong or all right. If they disagree with someone, especially the group leader, they must be all wrong. They see their mistakes as value-laden. Therefore, if they are wrong, they are bad. Perfection has its roots in this thinking process. A group member in Nebraska explained her need for perfection in herself and her demand of perfection in others as her only option. For her the only other choice was "averageness," a totally unacceptable state.

Adult children bounce back and forth between extremes with little knowledge of the option in between. This is especially true in relationships in which they demand total smothering loyalty, which often leads to rejection and abandonment, or they never ask for anything out of fear of rejection or dependence.

Another issue identified by Gravitz and Bowden (1984) is dissociation, the separation of emotion from awareness. Young children of alcoholics do not have words for their feelings but can tell stories about emotional happenings. As adults they protect themselves from this flood of emotion by dissociating themselves from the pain. It is common for ACAs to have childhood memory losses, especially losses of painful events such as sexual abuse or a time of extreme fighting in the family.

As group members begin to confront their core issues, they can learn strategies that allow them to function in a better way, as they enter the transformation stage. The connection between present circumstances and the past gives ACAs energy to change. Gravitz and Bowden (1984) devised a technique called "chunking it down" to attack the core issues by breaking them into small, managable problems that ACAs want to work on. This method foils the black-and-white thinking process and prevents ACAs from jumping from trusting no one to trusting everyone, or missing all the choices that are available to them. The method allows ACAs to feel successes and rewards as small steps are accomplished.

Group members in this stage develop personal rights. This allows for boundary setting between themselves and others. This is especially important for those ACAs whose parents still drink. A group member in Nebraska made a deal with his actively alcoholic father. He informed his father that their relationship was very important to him, but he was not willing to spend time with him when he was intoxicated. He let him know that he would leave his father's house or ask him to leave his house if the father started to drink. This is a good option, especially for ACAs who have children of their own who they do not want to expose to the trauma of their alcoholic families of origin.

The integration stage is marked by the synthesis of thought, feelings, and behavior into a congruent identity. The byproducts of this integration are increased relaxation and joy. Growth is seen as a process of small changes. Mistakes are acceptable and can even be viewed as part of the risk of learning. ACAs are taught that if they are making mistakes, they must be taking risks and thus making progress. Relationships are characterized by negotiation rather than control, with appropriate boundaries between individuals. Self-trust occurs at this stage and allows for trusting others, even at the cost of potential hurt. Life becomes more pleasurable, and setbacks are experienced with new skills and confidence that they can be overcome. Black-and-white thinking mellows to allow for many possibilities and a new openness to ideas.

The final stage, genesis, is the process of transcending the recovery from past trauma to develop a sense of harmony and balance. It is not the absence of dysfunction alone but the presence of a new and varied responsiveness to life (Gravitz & Bowden, 1984). ACAs at this point find their unique strengths that were developed in the trauma of the past and integrate them into their senses of self. They are able to access all their resources and enjoy life. They are no longer Adult Children of Alcoholics—they are adults who belong to a larger world, who have learned from their pain how to be whole human beings. They achieve this not by denying their past or their problems but by understanding them and using them for their benefit.

ACAs may enter group or individual therapy at any point on this continuum. Crawford and Phyfer (1988) developed counseling strategies for each of the stages. For ACAs in the survival stage, public education helps to break their denial. Involvement with the community by providing workshops and lectures to civic organizations and school or writing stories for newspapers or newsletters creates interventions at this stage. Group and/or individual counseling sessions may be appropriate for ACAs in the emergent awareness and core issue stages. Gestalt techniques are recommended for exploring unfinished business and residue left over from the alcoholic family. The expression of feelings in therapy is painful but necessary. Cognitive restructuring and behavioral rehearsal are techniques recommended for ACAs in the transformation stage. These techniques examine self-defeating behaviors and beliefs. The integration stage requires recognizing that recovery is a continuing process and not an event. "Acquiring new, more functional living styles is a gradual process, a recovery continuum, rather than a unidimensional occurrence" (Crawford & Phyfer, 1988, p. 108). Plans for ongoing recovery and support are emphasized. The maintenance of gains made in counseling is the primary goal of this stage.

Group therapy with ACAs is a way of doing family-of-origin work without sending ACAs back home (Bowen, 1978) or having them bring the family in (Framo, 1991) when it may be dangerous or counterproductive, as when there is active alcoholism and/or violence in the family of origin. Models for conducting group therapy with ACAs identify the healing process as coming from the transference relationships between group members and group leaders (Lawson, 1990; Vannicelli, 1989). The group becomes a surrogate family and the leaders substitute parents. In this safe environment group members can explore painful issues and try new behaviors without fear of activating a drinking episode or instigating violence.

Because alcoholism in the family doesn't affect children equally and 70–75 percent of children of alcoholics do not become alcoholic, researchers are interested in how alcoholism is transmitted from generation to generation, who is at most risk, and why some seem immune. This is important for developing prevention strategies aimed at breaking the intergenerational pattern.

## THE INTERGENERATIONAL TRANSMISSION OF ALCOHOLISM

A consistent finding in the field of families and addiction is the multigenerational aspect of the addictions. The most important question for the field of addiction prevention is: How do alcoholism and other addictions transmit from generation to generation or even jump generations in families? Families that seem to function in the face of addiction and do not transmit these addictions to the offspring are important to prevention and treatment.

In an attempt to determine how the family environment may be a transmitter of alcoholism, several researchers investigated the importance of family rituals (Wolin & Bennett, 1984; Bennett, Wolin, Reiss, & Teitelbaum, 1987; Steinglass, Bennett, Wolin, & Reiss, 1987). Wolin, Bennett, and Noonan (1979, 1980) studied a group of 25 families of middle- and upper-class background and European origin. All families included at least one parent who met criteria for identification as an alcoholic or problem drinker. Structured individual interviews that covered personal history of the interviewee and the continuity of family heritage from the grandparents' generation into the current nuclear family provided information on seven areas of family rituals: (1) dinnertime, (2) holidays, (3) evenings, (4) weekends, (5) vacations, (6) visitors in the home, and (7) discipline. The investigators defined family rituals as patterns of behavior that have meaning beyond their practical outcome or function—"patterned behavior is behavior that is repetitive, stable with respect to roles, and continues over time" (Wolin et al., 1979, p. 590). They believed that these rituals are important because they "stabilize ongoing family life by clarifying expectable roles, delineating boundaries within and without the family, and defining rules so that all family members know that 'this is the way our family is' " (p. 590). Steinglass et al. (1987) stated, "Family rituals are, in effect, condensed, prepackaged training modules intended to convey to all family members the important facts about family identity" (p. 309).

Wolin et al. (1979) identified three types of families:

1. *distinctive families*, in which rituals did not change during drinking episodes
2. *intermediate subsumptive families*, which rejected intoxicated behavior when it was present
3. *subsumptive families*, in which drinking changed the fabric of the family and highly disrupted the family life

They found that families whose rituals were disrupted or changed during the period of heaviest drinking by the alcoholic parent were more likely to transmit alcoholism to the younger generation than were families whose rituals remained intact. The more that alcoholism was a central organizing force and a disruption to the family rituals, the more the children were at risk for developing alcoholism. The nontransmitter families had one outstanding quality in common: "rejection of the intoxication of the alcoholic parent openly or privately, or talking about his or her behavior disapprovingly" (Wolin et al., 1979, p. 591).

To follow up this study, Bennett et al. (1987) interviewed 68 married children of alcoholic parents and their spouses regarding dinnertime and holiday rituals in their families of origin and in the couples' current generations. They identified 14 predictor variables that contributed significantly ($p < .01$) to the couples' alcoholism outcomes. The children of alcoholics who remained nonalcoholic had limited attachments to their families of origin or selective disengagements, and the families of origin had been able to separate the rituals from the alcoholism. Specifically, they found the couples who were most resistant to transmission lived 200 miles away from their families of origin and visited them two times per year.

In summation of these ritual studies, Steinglass et al. (1987) said,

> We believe that the transmission of alcoholism from one generation to the next involves the whole family system over time. The context for transmission is the sum total of interactions, attitudes, and beliefs that define the family. The process is ongoing and dynamic and has no particular beginning, end, or pivotal event. And it often goes on outside the awareness of the participants involved, the "senders" as well as the "receivers." (p. 304)

Another concept that Bennett, Wolin, and Reiss (1988) proposed as a risk-reducing factor is deliberateness. They argued that families with serious problems, such as parental alcoholism, that impose control over those parts of family life that are central to the family's identity, communicate important messages to the children regarding their ability to take control of present and future life events. These messages, in turn, can play an important role in the extent to which the offspring are protected from developing problems in childhood, as well as alcoholism in adolescence and adulthood (p. 821).

Deliberate spouse selection, establishment by the couple of their own family rituals and heritage, participation in institutions of the community, and selective disengagement from the families of origin are strategies proposed by this group of researchers to reduce the transmission of alcoholism across generations. This is important information for family therapists working with newly constituted families who are concerned about their own risk for addictive disorders and transmission of these disorders to children.

A common theme in research on intergenerational transmission of familial alcoholism is that a supportive other or cohesion in the family is less often reported as present by those children of alcoholics who become alcoholic (Booz-Allen & Hamilton, 1974; Lawson, 1988; O'Sullivan, 1991; Simmons, 1991). Booz-Allen and Hamilton (1974) listed "having a supportive person" in the family as a risk reducer for children of alcoholics. Lawson (1988) found that adult children of alcoholics who were not alcoholic perceived their families of origin as more cohesive and supportive than adult children of alcoholics who were alcoholic. In looking at these supportive others, O'Sullivan (1991) related the presence of a childhood mentoring relationship to resiliency in adult children of alcoholics. Even in families with alcoholic fathers and families with psychiatrically disturbed fathers, the presence of a "healthy" mother produced young adults who appeared as well adjusted as the control group of young adults whose parents had neither alcoholism nor psychiatric problems (Simmons, 1991). Healthy mothers were defined in this study as having no diagnosis of substance abuse or psychiatric disorder. The common message of these studies seems to be that children can emerge from dysfunctional, substance-abusing families with some degree of resilience if they receive nurturing and guidance from someone in the family or even someone outside of the family system. From a prevention standpoint, cohesion and support in families seems to provide a buffering effect against the damage done to children in dysfunctional families.

Another group of investigators (Jacob, Seilhamer, & Rushe, 1989) observed intact families under a broad range of conditions, including laboratory observations involving experimental drinking procedures and naturalistic home observations focused on dinnertime interactions. They were interested in the impact of alcoholism on the process and structure of family life, the degree to which varying patterns of family interactions served to potentiate or inhibit the development of alcoholism in children of alcoholics, and the degree that patterns varied in relation to alcoholism versus depression. In observing episodic versus steady and in-home versus out-of-home drinking behaviors, they found that steady, in-home drinkers seemed to have a positive impact on family life. The steady, in-home drinkers and their wives engaged in more productive problem solving during the drink condition than during the nondrink conditions. This is consistent with the adaptive consequences theory of alcoholism. Jacob et al. admitted that causality cannot be determined, but the study did underscore how the interplay of familial stressors associated with alcohol abuse, parental psychiatric status, and the mother's ability to mediate negative effects affects the child.

In viewing adult children of alcoholics' responses to parental drinking styles, Tarter (1991) found that the same drinking style that Jacob et al. (1989) found to be a productive problem-solving style for the alcoholic couple was the most problem-creating style for the adult child of an alcoholic who grew up in this type of family. As compared with adult children of alcoholics from binge drinker at home, binge drinker away, and daily away drinker groups, daily at-home drinkers produced adult children of alcoholics who rated their families of origin as the most unhealthy of the four groups (on the Family of Origin Scale). These adult children of alcoholics who had daily at-home drinking parents reported that they had more alcohol problems (MAST) and depression (Beck Depression Scale) than members of the other three groups.

The family system studies add another dimension to the nature-versus-nurture controversy in the etiology of alcoholism. It is quite possible that there is no one etiological prescription for alcoholism. Genetics may play a major role in the father-son transmission of alcoholism, whereas family environment may have more of an impact on women's alcoholism. The importance of finding family environment patterns that predispose children for alcoholism is that it may be possible to prevent alcoholism in these children by changing the patterns through family therapy and parent training.

## RESILIENT CHILDREN OF ALCOHOLICS

It is clear that all children of alcoholics are not the same. Some suffer greatly from living in substance-abusing families and others from similar families appear much less scared. Wolin and Wolin (1993) and Jacobs and Wolin (1991) identified those children who are less affected as *resilient children*, who as adults work well, play well, and love well. They call the model of resiliency the *challenge model* because these children see the adversity of a troubled childhood as a challenge. This is in contrast to the *damage model*, on which so much of mental health is based and which says that a troubled family damages the child, who then has childhood pathologies and succumbs to pathology in adolescence and adulthood. The challenge model says that the troubled family creates damages and challenges that lead to both child pathologies and resiliencies. The child both succumbs to and rebounds from having both pathologies and resiliencies in adolescence and adulthood.

The idea that some children of alcoholics are resilient is not new. Werner (1986), in a longitudinal study, focused on child characteristics and the qualities of the caregiving environment that differentiated children of alcoholics who developed serious problems by the age 18 and those who did not. The study consisted of 49 subjects of multiracial backgrounds born in 1955 on the island of Kauai, Hawaii. They were evaluated at ages one, two, 10, and 18. Werner found that males and offspring of alcoholic mothers had higher rates of psychosocial problems in childhood and adolescence than females and the offspring of alcoholic fathers. Children of alcoholics who did not develop serious coping skills were different from those who did in characteristics of temperament, communication skills, self-concept, and locus of control. These resilient children also experienced fewer stressful life events that disrupted the family unit in the first two years of their lives.

Wolin and Wolin (1993) developed a list of seven resiliencies that they believed develop out of the challenge to maintain self-esteem in the face of the troubled family's neglect, criticism, physical abuse, denial, and pull to engulf its members in the emotional turmoil. These resiliencies may be innate. "Early signs of these resiliencies can be found in the first memories of successful survivors and can be traced in progressive stages through their childhood, adolescence, and adulthood" (Jacobs & Wolin, 1991, p. 9). The seven resiliencies are: insight, independence, relationships, initiative, creativity, humor, and morality. Each resiliency has a child, adolescent, and adult manifestation.

1. **Insight**—This is a psychological sophistication, an early sensing that something is wrong with the troubled parent(s). By adolescence this *sensing* becomes a *knowing*. The children understand the family dynamics and attribute the family's problems to factors outside of themselves. In adulthood the knowing becomes *understanding* about themselves and others.
2. **Independence**—This is the ability to live apart yet relate to others without pressures or demands. The early sign of independence is *straying* away from the family. Adolescents realize that distance feels better than closeness and they move from straying to *disengaging* emotionally from their families. As adults they are *separating* from their families in a freely chosen, rational way. This is reminiscent of Bowen's ideas of a healthy differentiation from the family of origin.
3. **Relationships**—This is a connecting, selective process in which children can bond with parents or others. Early in life children with this resiliency begin *interacting* with the healthier parts of their families. As they get older

they begin *connecting* with neighbors, teachers, coaches, and other substitutes for parents. As adults, they are *bonding* with friends, spouses, children, and siblings. The two resiliencies of independence and relationships can be seen as a common goal of all the family therapy theories. Family therapists try to help families develop a sense of belonging or cohesion, while at the same time allowing for independence and individuality of their members.

4. **Initiative**—This is the ability to recover from adversity, a deep sense of self-trust and personal control—survivor's pride. These children love a challenge. This resiliency begins with optimistic *exploring* and grows in adolescents to *working* and, in adulthood, becomes *generating*.

5., 6. **Creativity and humor**—These resiliencies are linked and share common processes. Creativity is the ability to express and resolve inner conflicts in symbolic form through the arts or in ways that have aesthetic value. Humor is the ability to laugh at oneself and use play as an emotional healer. Young children are *playing* with their imagination to protect them from the trauma of their family life. *Shaping* is the refinement of playing in adolescence. It adds discipline and effort to the art production. The adult version of creativity is *composing* and the adult version of humor is *laughing*. Wolin and Wolin (1993) described creativity as making nothing into something and humor as something into nothing. Children with this resilience can greatly benefit from creative arts therapies.

7. **Morality**—This is the activity of an informed conscience. Young children want to know why and begin *judging* the rights and wrongs of daily life and their parents. In adolescence this changes into *valuing* decency, compassion, honesty, and fair play. In adulthood these survivors are *serving* others even though they did not receive what they deserved in their families. They restore themselves by helping others.

Wolin (1993), in a presentation, outlined challenge model therapy. The goal of the therapy is to change a survivor's view of him/herself from damaged goods to one who prevails. This is a five-step process:

- *Step 1:* Begin with damage. This stage begins with building trust and empathy and allowing the damage to be discussed and felt. The therapist takes a complete history of the damage story and helps the survivor see how the consequences are experienced in adulthood.
- *Step 2:* Select one resiliency. The therapist identifies the most easily accepted resilience, returns to the history of damage and questions the resilient behavior in detail, and acknowledges both the damage and the strength. The therapist should expect resistance to acceptance of the resilience and compliment appropriate behavior.
- *Step 3:* Explore remaining resiliencies. The therapist should know all three stages of each resilience and try to reframe all seven to fit with the survivor's

story. The therapist should work with the resistances and accept areas of moderate to little resilience.

- *Step 4:* Build a new narrative. At this stage the therapist offers explanations of the resiliences and the damage. The therapist teaches that the survivor had a false mirroring of blame from his or her family, yet somehow he or she has been inoculated against contracting all the problems of the family. Therapists need to foster the survivor's pride and observe the shifting balance between damage and resilience.

- *Step 5:* Apply resiliencies to current problems. The therapist can use the "chunking down" technique of Gravitz and Bowden (1984) to break problems into smaller components. Therapists at this stage apply insight to the weakest areas of resilience, help survivors attempt more or less independence and create healthy relationships, and instruct survivors how to initiate and establish family rituals.

## REFERENCES

Ackerman, R.J. (1978). *Children of alcoholics: A guide book for educators, therapists and parents*. Holmes Beach, FL: Learning Publications.

Albee, G. (1981, October). *Primary prevention*. A workshop presented at Kellogg Center, University of Nebraska, Lincoln, NE.

Bandler, R., Grender, G., & Satir, V. (1976). *Changing with families*. Palo Alto, CA: Science and Behavior Books.

Barnard, C.P., & Spoentgen, P.A. (1986). Children of alcoholics: Characteristics and treatment. *Alcoholism Treatment Quarterly, 3*, 47–65.

Beletis, S., & Brown, S. (1981). A developmental framework for understanding the adult children of alcoholics. *Focus on Women: Journal of the Addictions and Health, 2*, 187–203.

Bennett, L.A., Wolin, S.J., & Reiss, D. (1988). Deliberate family process: A strategy for protecting children of alcoholics. *British Journal of Addiction, 83*, 821–829.

Bennett, L.A., Wolin, S.J., Reiss, D., & Teitelbaum, M.A. (1987). Couples at risk for transmission of alcoholism: Protective influences. *Family Process, 26*, 111–129.

Black, C. (1979). Children of alcoholics. *Alcohol Health and Research World*, 23–27.

Black, C. (1981). Innocent bystanders at risk: The children of alcoholics. *Alcoholism*, 22–25.

Black, C. (1981). *It will never happen to me*. Denver: M.A.C. Publishers.

Black, C. (1987). Introduction. In V. Rachel (Ed.), *Family secrets* (pp. xxvi–xxxviii). San Francisco, CA: Harper & Row.

Booz-Allen & Hamilton, Inc. (1974). *An assessment of the needs of and resources for children of alcoholic parents*. Report PB-241-119. Prepared for National Institute on Alcohol Abuse and Alcoholism, Rockville, MD.

Bosma, W. (1975). Alcoholism and teenagers. *Maryland State Medical Journal, 24* (6), 62–68.

Bowen, M. (1978). Alcoholism and the family. In *Family therapy in clinical practice*. New York: Jason Aronson.

Boye-Beaman, J., Leonard, K.E., & Senchak, M. (1991). Assortative mating, relationship development, and intimacy among offspring of alcoholics. *Family Dynamics of Addiction Quarterly, 1*(2), 20–33.

Brown, S. (1979, May 28). Kids of alcoholics. *Newsweek,* 82.

Brown, S. (1988). *Treating adult children of alcoholics: A developmental perspective.* New York: John Wiley & Sons.

Cermak, T., & Brown, S. (1982). Group therapy with adult children of alcoholics. *International Journal of Group Psychotherapy, 32*(3), 375–389.

Chafetz, M., Blane, H., & Hill, M. (1977). Children of alcoholics: Observations in a child guidance clinic. *Quarterly Journal of Studies of Alcoholism, 32*, 687–698.

Clinebell, N.J. (1968). Pastoral counseling of the alcoholic and his family. In R. Catanzaro (Ed.), *Alcoholism: The total treatment approach.* Springfield, IL: Charles C. Thomas.

Cork, M. (1969). *The forgotten children.* Toronto: Alcoholism and Drug Addiction Research Foundation.

Crawford, R., & Phyfer, A. (1988). Adult children of alcoholics: A counseling model. *Journal of College Student Development, 29*, 105–111.

Fox, R. (1968). Treating the alcoholic's family. In R.J. Catanzaro (Ed.), *Alcoholism: The total treatment approach.* Springfield, IL: Charles C. Thomas.

Framo, J. (1991). *Family of origin therapy: An intergenerational approach.* New York: Brunner/Mazel.

Glenn, S. (1981, April). *Steven Glenn on prevention: A summary of Glenn's comments.* A seminar on drug and alcohol abuse prevention, Omaha, NE.

Goodwin, D.W., Schulsinger, F., Hermansen, L.G., & Winokur, G. (1973). Alcohol problems in adoptees raised apart from biological parents. *Archives of General Psychiatry, 28*, 238–243.

Gravitz, H., & Bowden, J. (Summer 1984). Therapeutic issues of alcoholic children of alcoholics. *Alcohol Health and Research World*, 25–36.

Gravitz, H.L., & Bowden J.D. (1990). Therapeutic issues of adult children of alcoholics. In D.A. Ward (Ed.), *Alcoholism: Introduction to theory and treatment.* Dubuque, IA: Kendall/Hunt.

Hecht, M. (1973). Children of alcoholics. *American Journal of Nursing, 73*(10), 1764–1767.

Hindman, M. (1975–6). Children of alcoholic parents. *Alcohol Health and Research World*, 2–6.

Jacob, T., Seilhamer, R.A., & Rushe, R.H. (1989). Alcoholism and family interaction: An experimental paradigm. *American Journal of Drug and Alcohol Abuse, 15*(1), 73–91.

Jacobs, J., & Wolin, S.J. (1991, October). *Resilient children growing up in alcoholic families.* Paper presented at the National Consensus Symposium on Children of Alcoholics and Co-Dependence, Warrenton, VA.

Jacobson, S.B. (1991, October). *The recovery movement: From children of alcoholics to codependency.* Paper presented at the National Consensus Symposium on Children of Alcoholics and Co-Dependence, Warrenton, VA.

Lawson, A. (1988). *The relationship of past and present family environments of adult children of alcoholics.* Doctoral dissertation, United States International University, San Diego, CA.

Lawson, A. (1990). Group therapy with adult children of alcoholics. In D.A. Word (Ed.), *Alcoholism: Introduction to theory and treatment* (3rd ed.). Dubuque, IA: Kendall/ Hunt.

Levinson, D. (1978). *Seasons of a man's life.* New York: Ballantine Books.

McCord, W., McCord, J., & Gudeman, J. (1960). *Origins of alcoholism.* Palo Alto, CA: Stanford University Press.

O'Sullivan, C. (1991). Making a difference: The relationship between childhood mentors and resiliency in adult children of alcoholics. *Family Dynamics of Addiction Quarterly, 1*(4), 46–59.

Patterson, R. (1980, March 31). Children of alcoholics: Focus for social worker. *The Oregonian.*

Rivinus, T.M. (Ed.). (1991). *Children of chemically dependent parents: Multiperspectives from the cutting edge.* New York: Brunner/Mazel.

Schuckit, M.A., Tipp, J.E., & Keiner, E. (1994). Are daughters of alcoholics more likely to marry alcoholics? *American Journal of Drug and Alcohol Abuse, 20*(2), 237–245.

Simmons, G.M. (1991). *Interpersonal trust and perceived locus of control in the adjustment of adult children of alcoholics.* Doctoral dissertation, United States International University, San Diego, CA.

Sloboda, S. (1974). The children of alcoholics: A neglected problem. *Hospital and Community Psychiatry, 25* (9), 605–606.

Steinglass, P., Bennett, L.A., Wolin, S.J., & Reiss, D. (1987). *The alcoholic family.* New York: Basic Books.

Tarter, J. (1991). *The effects of parental alcohol drinking patterns on adult children of alcoholics.* Doctoral dissertation, United States International University, San Diego, CA.

Vannicelli, M. (1989). *Group psychotherapy with adult children of alcoholics.* New York: Guilford Press.

Wegscheider, S. (1981a). From the family trap to family freedom. *Alcoholism,* 36–39.

Wegscheider, S. (1981b). *Another chance: Hope and health for the alcoholic family.* Palo Alto, CA: Science and Behavior Books.

Werner, E.E. (1986). Resilent offspring of alcoholics: A longitudinal study. *Journal of Studies on Alcohol, 47*(1), 34–40.

Woititz, J. (1983). *Adult Children of Alcoholics.* Hollywood, FL: Health Communications.

Wolin, S. (1993). *The resilient self.* A workshop presented at the United States International University, San Diego, CA.

Wolin, S.J., Bennett, L.A., & Noonan, D.L. (1979). Family rituals and recurrence of alcoholism over generations. *American Journal of Psychiatry, 136,* 589–593.

Wolin, S.J., Bennett, L.A., & Noonan, D.L. (1980). Disrupted family rituals: A factor in the intergenerational transmission of alcoholism. *Journal of Studies on Alcohol, 41,* 199–214.

Wolin, S.J., & Bennett, L.A. (1984). Family rituals. *Family Process, 23,* 401–420.

Wolin, S.J., & Wolin, S. (1993). *The resilient self: How survivors of troubled families rise above adversity.* New York: Villard Books.

Woodside, M. (1988). Research on children of alcoholics: Past and future. *British Journal of Addiction, 83,* 785–792.

# CHAPTER 10

# When Words Fail:
# Art Therapy

Much of this section on treatment has dealt with verbal techniques used in family therapy, with the exceptions of the art and movement techniques covered in chapter 6 on evaluation and diagnosis. This perspective can be limiting because people think in images as well as words. Adding the dimension of artistic expression to therapy is useful for those clients who are not masterful with words and for those who are skilled at verbal manipulation. Clients often make statements such as, "I can't put it into words," or "Do you see what I mean?" Some clients have difficulty finding words or allowing themselves to talk about abstract subjects, emotions, or dilemmas. Their clarity of expression can be improved by giving them an additional mode of communication. Other people are so skilled at manipulating words that they can con their way out of receiving help in a therapeutic situation with rationalization and intellectualization. Alcoholics who have spent many years covering up their drinking and finding excuses for their behavior and absenteeism at work and in family life are often very skilled at excusing themselves from making change or clearly viewing themselves as needing to change. Art therapy has been used in alcohol treatment centers with positive outcomes (Albert-Puleo & Osha, 1976/77; Callaghan, 1993; Foulke & Keller, 1976; Schleicher, 1978). Albert-Puleo and Osha (1976), in their experience in using art therapy with people dependent on alcohol and drugs, found that:

> Few addicts had previously participated in artistic activity. For them it is a novel form of expression offering opportunities for new kinds of mastery and it is not felt to be threatening. Because it is outside the scope of their customary manipulations, art does not readily lend itself to the intellectualization and rationalization on which addicts rely to justify their feelings and behaviors. (p. 29)

Art as a communication method can be beneficial for the other family members, who have learned the family rule that if they talk about alcohol abuse, things will get worse. Springer, Phillips, Phillips, Cannady, and Kerst-Harris (1992) evaluated a 12-week prevention program for children of alcoholics that used art and play therapy. The program involved simultaneous peer group sessions and family interaction groups that included parents. Springer et al. found highly significant gains in competencies and reductions in identified behavior problems of the children. Art therapy is useful in breaking silence and exposing family secrets. There may be no family rules to prevent family members from drawing the family as they view it. Sometimes it is easier for family members to talk about what they have drawn than what is happening within themselves.

Kwiatkowska (1978) described working with a family whose presenting problem was an 18-year-old adolescent diagnosed as schizophrenic. After working with the family in art therapy for several sessions, she used an evaluative technique to determine the family members' views of one another. Each family member was asked to use a symbol for family members to create an abstract family portrait. Kwiatkowska stated, "It introduced the problem of the father's drinking" (pp. 145–146). The teenager, Donnie, had used a bottle of beer to represent his father in his picture. Kwiatkowska reported, "Donnie was bitter, contemptuous and accusing; he spoke with disgust of his father's falling when drunk and his sleeping on the floor" (p. 146). This, incidentally, was the first time a family member was able to talk about the family secret of the father's drinking.

Children find art therapy helpful in expressing the powerful emotions they have about the parents' alcohol abuse and their own emotional and physical abuse (Black, 1979). Children can represent their feelings in their drawings and talk about how figures in the pictures are angry without having to identify themselves as those children. Ginott (1961) stated, "Clay and paint allow fearful, fragile children to state feelings one moment and erase or negate them the next. They can commit acts that are reversible, acts than can be taken back, refined, and redefined to make it safe to explore their inner and outer world" (p. 70).

Children often lack the verbal skills to express themselves and to solve problems with words. From birth, much of the way they learn about the world is visual. Children are expert observers and store mental pictures of their world and their observations of those in it, but they are not skilled in logical thinking and may draw incorrect conclusions. They may carry these misperceptions into adulthood if their family environment does not allow for open discussion of all subjects. Drawing is a process that allows images to be reexamined, clarified, and confronted and helps the family and therapist to correct mistaken ideas such as self-blame for a parent's drinking.

Art therapy is a valuable treatment technique to use with families, children, and individuals. Denny (1969) stated that it is a "professional encounter between counselor and client where art materials and expression are introduced into the relationship in order to facilitate the release of feelings, to promote understanding of the self, to strengthen personal resources, and, most importantly, to help the client take constructive action" (p. 119). In other words, art therapy is a form of psychotherapy that uses artistic creation as a means of communication rather than relying primarily on verbalization.

Thus, the artwork of clients must be treated with as much unconditional positive regard as their verbal statements. The art must be viewed as a true expression because the persons involved created the work as an extension of themselves. The artwork should not be evaluated in terms of artistic merit but be genuinely accepted for its value as a form of communication between people. The therapist is not an art teacher. Therapy is not a place for critical remarks about the quality or correctness of the artwork. Thus, if a child paints the sky with red and white stripes, the therapist will damage the therapeutic relationship by declaring that the sky should be blue. Often, writing becomes part of the artwork. If children misspell words, they do not need to be corrected.

The therapist does not need special skills in art to be able to use it in therapy. The therapist must, however, be open to any and all forms of artistic expression and have a desire to facilitate this expression in others. Artwork should be taken seriously, and drawings should be filed away for future reference. Clients should be discouraged from destroying their creations.

## MATERIALS

Art therapy can be done with a minimum of supplies. However, it is helpful to have a variety of materials to fit various situations and to have a selection for clients to choose from. It is important to have several sizes of paper. A good selection might include typing paper, 8 1/2 by 11 inches; manila paper, 24 by 36 inches; white school drawing paper, 18 by 24 and 24 by 36 inches; an assortment of colored construction paper; and paper rolls. Paper rolls can be purchased at school supply stores, or newsprint end rolls can be purchased very cheaply from newspaper printing plants. These are used for large wall murals. A small expenditure covers a wide variety of media. Felt pens or markers are ideal because they are ready for use immediately and create brightly colored pictures. Cray-pas and oil pastels also give rich color and can be blended to achieve soft tones. Poster paints and brushes can be added as well. In addition to art supplies, magazines should be provided so that images and words can be cut and used for collages. These can be supplemented with wallpaper books, catalogs, comic books, scraps of cloth, yarn, and assorted items that can be glued to the collage. Clay is a refreshing departure from two-dimensional art. Plasticene is useful for including color in three-dimensional work, but red earth clay and gray clay put individuals more in touch with the earth and can be kept indefinitely if stored in airtight containers and water is added when the clay begins to dry.

If a large variety of materials is offered, clients may identify intuitively with a material that can express something they would otherwise not have considered. However, visual material can be introduced into therapy with any kind and size of paper and any drawing medium. It is helpful to use adult materials (oil pastels, inks and pens) with adolescents and adults instead of media such as crayons that are reminiscent of childhood.

## TECHNIQUES

Many art therapy techniques and assignments have been reported (Callaghan, 1993; Denny, 1969; Kwiatkowska, 1978; Landgarten, 1981: Schleicher, 1978). However, the techniques selected must incorporate the needs of the client, must be compatible with the therapist's theoretical orientation, and must be relevant to the situation.

Techniques chosen for the early sessions should be exploratory and nonthreatening because resistance may have to be overcome. In early sessions, techniques should be used to develop the therapeutic relationship. Following sessions can be used to define problems, express feelings, set goals, and make behavioral changes.

Techniques can be used to promote exploration, the building of rapport, the expression of inner feelings, self-perception, and improved interpersonal relations.

### Exploration

For the purposes of exploration, techniques such as automatic drawing, free drawing, and color exploration can be used. In automatic drawing or scribble drawing, the clients are encouraged to relax and make free-flowing scribble lines on paper. They may be asked to close their eyes. They make a series of drawings and then look for a pattern or design and finish by making a completed picture.

In free drawing, the choice of subject matter, material, and manner of expression are left up to the clients. They are told to express themselves freely. Clients may be asked to select a free drawing that they like least, best, or is most puzzling and then talk about it. When the clients are allowed to make choices, information can be gained by observing the process. For instance, if clients choose the same medium each time, they may fear loss of control.

In color exploration, the clients may be asked to choose the colors they like least and best and make a composition with them. They are then asked to discuss how these colors relate to each other and why they chose them. Clients may also paint or draw with colors that they think express their moods, or they may be asked to explore one color. Figure 10–1 is a drawing done by an 11-year-old incest victim who used the color black to express her anger and the phrase "leave me alone" to refer to her anger at being sexually abused.

**Figure 10–1** Black Used To Represent Anger

## Rapport Building

Rapport building involves techniques such as conversational drawing and pairs projects. In conversational drawing, group members pair off and share a piece of paper between them. On this paper they conduct a conversation with visual images. When they are finished, they discuss the process.

The technique of pairs projects requires partners to create an art object together. When they have finished, they examine the final product and talk about the interactions that occurred between them during the creation.

## Expression of Inner Feelings

Inner feelings can be expressed through such techniques as affective words; feelings X-rays; drawings of problems and feelings or dreams and fantasies; the road of life; life on a line; and paper bag masks.

Affective words are used as stimuli for painting. They can be chosen by the client or the therapist and may consist of one feeling or a combination of opposite feelings such as love and hate.

Feelings X-rays are used with children to help them identify how feelings can affect parts of their bodies and assess their impressions of where these feelings occur. The children are laid on a large piece of paper from a paper roll a little longer than their body. The therapist traces around them, hangs the paper on the wall, and says, "If I had an X-ray machine that could see inside of you that would see your feelings and not your bones, what would I see?" The children usually identify heart feelings, head feelings, and stomach feelings and can give clues to psychosomatic tendencies (Figure 10–2).

Clients may be asked to draw problems and feelings. They may draw a recent or recurring feeling or mood. This technique requires people to become aware of their feelings and to put them into a concrete form. Figure 10–3 shows a drawing done by an incest victim who was describing her anger and sadness when she was taken from her family and placed in a foster home because the incest was discovered.

Dreams and fantasies techniques can be used with children and adults. Dreams can be drawn in a sequence like a story or a cartoon. Dialogue can be added, and the interpretation should be elicited from the client. Figure 10–4 is the drawing of a 10-year-old daughter of an alcoholic. She had dreamed that a skeleton with raw meat for eyes had kidnapped her and had tricked her by being able to change into her father. In discussing the drawing, she was able to talk about her ambivalent feelings about her father and the monster he could become.

In the road-of-life technique, clients are asked to paint the road or path they have been following for the past several years or the road they see in the future.

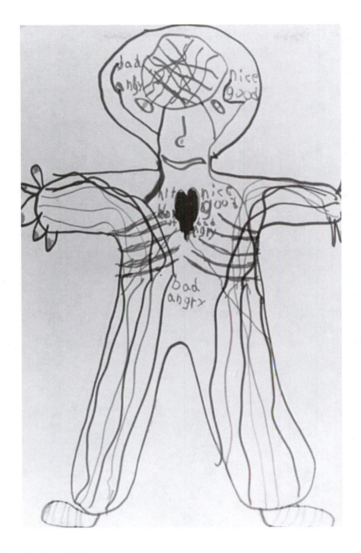

**Figure 10–2** Feelings X-Ray

This allows the client to look at the directions of their lives in perspective.

In the life-on-a-line technique, each person is given a piece of paper and asked to draw a line representing his or her life from birth to the present. The highs and lows should be shown and identified with a word or age. On the same page, the client is asked to draw another line showing his or her drinking history. This can be helpful in connecting the increase in drinking with a decrease in life functioning (Schleicher, 1978).

**Figure 10–3** Sadness and Anger

**Figure 10–4** Dream

Paper bag masks or paper plate masks can be used to help clients express how they feel inside or would like to feel (Figure 10–5). Clients are simply told to draw a face on the bag or plate. These masks can also represent the various "faces" people wear at different times with different people. Clients can become more aware of the façades they use to protect or cover their real selves.

## Self-Perceptions

Clients' perceptions of themselves can be shown in exercises such as self-portraits, "my bag," and "two animals." Self-portraits can be done in a number of ways. Clients can be asked to simply draw themselves or their ideal, or the image they believe they present to others. Other versions are one-minute full-length self-portraits that force quick decisions. Clients may also represent the self-image as an animal they identify with. These self-portraits can be used throughout the therapeutic process to assess self-image or to set goals. It is interesting that incest victims often draw themselves with no bodies as if to reject their sexuality.

The "my bag" exercise is used in a group setting after the introductory stage, when group members have some information about each other. Each person is instructed to bring a bag to the following session. On the outside is a collage of

**Figure 10–5** Paper Plate Mask

pictures and words that the person assumes everyone knows about them. On the inside are the secrets that no one in the group knows. The bags are then discussed in the group, and feedback is given by the other group members. This exercise can also be used in individual therapy as a homework assignment. Clients put images and words on the outside of the bag that describe how they believe others see them, and put pictures, phrases, and objects inside the bag that represent things about themselves that few, if any, individuals know.

In the "two animals" exercise, before the session a string covered in black tempera paint or ink is dropped onto a white paper. The string can be lifted off or dragged on the paper to create a pattern. Clients are allowed to select a paper and are instructed to find two animals in the string pattern. These animals can be real or fantasy. Clients then use markers or chalks to indicate the animals or parts of animals to create a composition. They are then asked to write four statements about each animal. This experience draws on the polarities of the personality. Figure 10–6 shows a drawing of an 11-year-old girl whose alcoholic father sexually abused her for several years. Her first animal was a kangaroo who was learning how to hop. She described it as being different colors, cute, nice, and

**Figure 10–6** Two Animals

generous. The second animal was a crab arm that she described as pinchy, hard, sassy, and likely to pinch people's toes. A major difficulty for her was social relationships and her dilemma between accepting others and lashing out at them.

## Interpersonal Relationships

Interpersonal relationships can be determined from family portraits. Each member of a family is given a piece of paper and is asked to draw the family. An alternate method is to give the family one piece of paper and ask them to make decisions about how the family will be drawn and who will be included. This can also be done with clay so that the figures can be arranged in different settings and in different proximities to one another.

Abstract family portraits in which symbols are used for the family members can be revealing (Kwiatkowska, 1978). These drawings can give a wealth of information about the relationships of family members, coalitions, and boundaries. They are extremely useful with blended families who may be having difficulties integrating all the members.

The family drawings of the Brown family (Figures 10–7 through 10–10) pointed out an extreme division between the parental subsystem and the sibling subsystem. This was evident in the separation of the two groups in each drawing. In two of the drawings, the parents were sitting at their bar drinking while the children watched television. This excessive drinking behavior was contributing to the inaccessibility of the parents by the children. In the stepfather's drawing (Figure 10–7), a tree was between the parents, and the children were working as a unit to "make waves." Mr. Brown explained that the children often stirred things up, and there were problems (the dead tree) between the parents. Goals for marital and family therapy were derived from this exercise.

A technique for gathering information about children's or adolescents' perceptions of their families is the Parents-Self-Centered Drawing developed by Burns (1990). This projective technique assesses the parents-self relationship and parental introjects. Clients are asked to draw themselves and their parents inside a circle and then surround them with symbols that represent the family and family members. The therapist instructs, "Draw your parents and yourself inside the form of a circle. Try to draw a whole person, not stick people; surround the figures with symbols or drawings, also inside the circle, that you associate with each person" (p. 3).

## ART THERAPY SESSIONS

In the art therapy sessions, clients are made to feel at ease, and the therapist explains that the art productions are not judged on their artistic value but are used

**Figure 10–7** Stepfather's Family Drawing

**Figure 10–8** Mother's Family Drawing: Parents Drinking at Their Bar; Children Watching Television Upstairs

**Figure 10–9** Teenage Daughter's Family Drawing: Parents at the Bar; Children Watching Television. Very Similar to Mother's Drawing

**Figure 10–10** Oldest Daughter's Drawing: Similar to Stepfather's Drawing

to enhance the therapy process. Landgarten (1981) stated, "Clients are introduced to clinical art therapy by being informed that this method is used to help them better understand themselves and how they function as individuals and/or part of a family or a group system" (p. 4). Directives given to the clients can be in the nature of evaluation exercises, expressions of emotions, wishes, dreams and fantasies, future plans, self-images, and family constellations.

It is best to start with simple directives that require little artistic ability to reduce resistance and give the clients a positive experience. All directives should have some relevance to short- or long-term goals so that the clients are encouraged to make progress toward changing in a positive direction.

Clients are encouraged to discuss their artwork while they are creating it and after its completion. This reduces the chance the symbols will be misinterpreted by the therapist. People tend to have their own individual symbolism. Red may symbolize anger for one person while black is more descriptive of anger for another. It is logical that clients are in the best position to make interpretations about their own work. The therapist may have opinions about interpretations; these can be expressed as questions to the client about the work. When therapists make direct interpretations of clients' work, the perspective and values of the therapist become projected onto the drawing and contaminate the interpretation. It is not necessary to convince clients of the correctness of an interpretation. It is more productive to use the artwork to stimulate communication, build rapport, encourage emoting and self-evaluation, and work toward change in a positive direction.

Drawings can be kept in files and brought to sessions to review progress and set future goals. This allows clients to review their work and take responsibility for their own change. This record of therapy is helpful for therapists. They can review the drawings for common themes and patterns that may be repeated, and the drawings can be used to confront the clients if incongruities exist.

Art therapy is especially useful for group work. The art products provide stimulation for group interaction. Quiet members can be brought into the group process when they make a statement with a drawing or sculpture that other group members respond to. Cooperative art tasks can be assigned to promote socialization and reproduce a situation that parallels social encounters outside of the group. Clients can then try out new behaviors in a structured environment. Group murals or conjoint sculptures demand cooperative efforts, leadership, and coordination among group members. Art therapy has been used successfully in multifamily therapy groups where families take turns focusing on their problems and receiving feedback from the other families in the group.

**Family Art Therapy**

Art therapy can be used in family therapy sessions for more than evaluation purposes. Art tasks can be used in the sessions in a here-and-now interchange approach. This can encourage a family to work together in new ways and develop more adaptive patterns of communication and interaction. Assignments are designed to impact on the areas that need change. If alcohol abuse is the subject of the artwork, its effect on family functioning can be examined. If alcohol abuse is absent from the work but present in the family, this contradiction can be brought out to allow the family secret to be openly confronted and discussed.

Landgarten (1981) noted, "As one or more family members begin to change, the established family system is weakened" (p. 23). When the family is in this state of movement, the therapist can have an impact on the family to push the movement and help the family achieve a higher state of functioning. Often, when one member changes, the family system renews efforts to resist change. The therapist can support the member who is changing in continuing even against the pressure of the entire family.

Family art therapy is different from family therapy only in the addition of another mode of communication into the process. Instead of talking about goals, family members draw them or create them from clay. This forces a fresh examination of the family and its interactions by all members and allows them to experience each other in a unique way. When families begin to talk about experiences that occurred outside of the sessions, these can be translated into the present by assigning the family the task of recreating the scene with movable clay figures. The scene can be acted out by moving the clay figures, and alternative problem-solving and interaction techniques can be attempted by the clay family.

Family functioning can be quickly scrutinized by observing the interactions of the family. Family coalitions, boundaries, and rules can be observed and tasks designed to impact on areas that need change. To increase empathy and under-standing between generations and to identify projection of the parents onto the children, a drawing assignment can be made. Family members are asked to draw themselves at a time when they were younger. The parents must portray them-selves as they were when they were the age of one of their children (Landgarten, 1981). This exercise gives information about alliances between parents and children. Often the father's drawing of himself as a child is very similar to his perception of his son. This assignment brings this projection to the family's awareness.

Drawings are harder to deny or ignore than verbal expressions. When a family has to draw its problems, they must begin to face them. Landgarten (1981) wrote, "Laying out the family problems gives the children a sense of relief and the parents a greater awareness of the messages which they convey to the children" (p. 27). When the problems have been clearly stated, the children do not have to hide them and protect the family.

Often symbols recur in drawings, and the family does not acknowledge their presence. The therapist can bring these symbols to the awareness of the family, and family secrets can be uncovered.

In alcoholic families, members are unpracticed at expressing emotions directly, especially negative feelings. Direct expression of anger may be difficult for all the members of the family. They may fear that direct expression of feelings will prompt a return to drinking by the alcoholic or result in an unpredictable negative response. Family members can be asked to draw their anger and give it to the family member it belongs to. This promotes direct channels of communication

**Figure 10–11** Volcano Doodle

**Figure 10–12** Digging through the Wall

**Figure 10–13** Anger

**Figure 10–14** Dealing with Anger

and eliminates triangulation of a third person. If Mother is angry with Dad for coming home late and not calling, she can direct it at him instead of yelling at her son, who has forgotten to wash his hands before dinner.

Children who have withheld anger while their parents were drinking may have difficulty risking direct communications. Special assignments can be given to the

**Figure 10–15** "Let's go, Daddy!"

children to work on between sessions. This method was used with the Peterson family. Both parents had been through alcohol treatment and were attending several therapy groups. However, their 12-year-old daughter, Susan, was not achieving in school, was socially isolated, refused to bathe, and spent a lot of time at home in withdrawal. Shortly after the family entered therapy, Mrs. Peterson asked her husband for a divorce. Susan became more withdrawn and rarely remembered to do her household chores, and this infuriated her mother. Susan would not talk directly about her anger toward her mother for fear of the physical abuse Susan received from her while she was drinking or her anger about the divorce. The Petersons had each aligned with one of their children and used them to intensify their own conflict. Susan had a close alliance with her father and had been compared in a negative context with her father for years. When her father moved out of the house, he left Susan alone to fight with her mother and sister.

Task assignments were used to help Susan work on repressed feelings between sessions. Figure 10–11 is an exploding volcano that Susan doodled during the

**Figure 10–16** Stop Drinking

initial family session while her parents were talking. Figure 10–12 is the visualization of Susan's discussion, during a family session, of her struggle to communicate openly. She described herself as coming from the left side of the picture, a dark, scary place where she had to hide her real self. She envisioned herself digging a hole in a wall, bit by bit, in an attempt to reach the other side, which she portrayed as a fairytale world with a castle. The wall, she said, was the wall she had built around herself to keep from getting hurt. It was frightening to think about digging a hole in this wall because it allowed access to her from the outside world.

In later sessions, Susan began to identify her anger. Figures 10–13 and 10–14 show her anger as a black blob with a cutoff valve. Susan had chosen to keep this valve closed and knew that the hand in the picture that was turning the valve was hers. When the anger came out of the faucet it changed colors and looked different from the stored anger. Figure 10–13 includes her list of behaviors that would allow the anger to be released: "hit, yell, tell them I'm mad, questioning, argue, disagreement, tell friends, draw, beat pillow."

**Figure 10–17** Scold-Cry

Susan was encouraged to practice these behaviors. Her mother was aware that her reaction to these expressions would be important for encouraging or discouraging Susan's efforts. Susan had difficulty in talking about her parents' drinking and her feelings about it. She was asked to write down these feelings and bring them to the next session.

Susan wrote:

I felt pretty scared when my parents were drinking. Everyday I would get snapped at for the tiniest little things, even things I didn't do. I was scared of my mom especially because she was home when I got home and she would get mad and hit me for what I thought was nothing, like leaving the cap off the toothpaste. When Dad came home things didn't change much. I would probably be at a friend's house. When I came home, usually at 5:00, dinner would be ready to eat, so we would eat dinner. After dinner we would go into the family room and watch T.V. or

**Figure 10–18** Crying

whatever. When I went to bed I could lay awake and listen to them fight. I would wonder about what was going to happen and when. I would wonder if they would ever quit drinking.

A lot of nights I would stay out late and come in secretly or I would spend the night at a friends (with permission, but they were just too drunk to remember). But I would come home. There was one time that I was told that if I was not home by 8:00, I should not come home for the rest of the night. So, I did just as I was told. I was out at Michelle's house past 8:00 and I wouldn't go home. I left her house about 8:30 and stayed outside in our yard for a while. I finally came in at about 8:45.

I guess things have changed since then. I only get hit when I need it (at least that's what Mom says. I think she does it just to make me mad). I don't get hit for just anything, but my Mom says that I still have a lot of my Dad's and Mom's bad qualities. The only thing I think is still bad is that I'm 12 years old and still can't stay out past dark, even in our own neighborhood.

**Figure 10–19** Too Young To Understand

Susan's writing allowed her to express some feelings she had held for a long time and pointed to further work to be done in the family. Both parents were projecting their own negative attributes onto Susan, and Susan was willing to assume them to maintain her place in the family structure.

Homework tasks were useful for another preadolescent girl, Nancy, whose mother divorced her alcoholic husband and moved her children thousands of miles away. The children had not had a chance to express their feelings about Dad's drinking and had a negative experience the previous summer when Dad came to visit and took the daughters shopping. He was intoxicated and passed out in a store. Nancy was asked to draw some of her memories of what it was like living with her father. The following is Nancy's description of her drawings, shown in Figures 10–15 to 10–21.

For the drawing in Figure 10–15, she said, "When the drinking of someone affects a person that cares, that person reacts back and tries to stop him from drinking." She explained Figure 10–16 as, "When someone is concerned about someone else's drinking problem they try to stop them from drinking." Figure 10–17 she explained

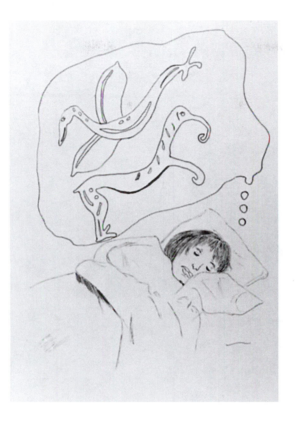

**Figure 10–20** Nightmare

as "when someone is drunk they naturally scold or beat on someone else (not knowing what they're doing), sometimes causing that person to cry."

For Figure 10–18, she said, "When children are hurt by words or actions they often scream or cry."

She explained Figure 10–19 as "the reactions of someone who is too young to understand what's going on and how it's affecting the other members (or friends) of the family."

About Figure 10–20, she said, "When children see or hear things that they do not like it builds up in them and when they go to sleep it forms a nightmare. Sometimes they dream what they saw—or heard—but often their mind makes up scary figures to frighten them."

About Figure 10–21, she said, "Children that have parents that drink don't like for them to drink, and all thoughts of their friends, family and how happy they appear to be, causes that child to dream of a happy family it'd like to be part of. Children with drinking parents tell themselves that when they're older they're not going to even go near a drink."

**Figure 10–21** Wish Dream

Nancy was able to express anger, fear, and confusion and to wish for the happy family that she believed her friends had. Nancy could not claim the child in the picture as herself and needed to use general terms in her descriptions. These were her first contributions to the family sessions after many weeks of refusing to participate.

## Individual Art Therapy

When it is not possible to work with families, children can benefit from individual art therapy. Changes in the family can occur through the way one family member responds to another. The following case studies are similar in that both girls were 11 years old and had been sexually abused by their fathers for several years. Only one father was alcoholic, but the family dynamics of both cases were similar. Both girls had taken on a parental role and were worried about their parents but were unable to admit or communicate negative feelings.

### Cheryl

When Cheryl entered therapy, she had been living in a foster home for two weeks. A police officer had questioned her at school about her sexual abuse by her father and taken her to child protective services. She was placed in a foster home away from everything she knew. She had a new school, different friends, and only saw her family once a week for supervised visits. During her initial art therapy session, she stated that she was happy on the left side of the paper and that she was sad on the other (Figure 10–22.)

The girl who was sad had no body. After several sessions Cheryl drew her feelings as shown in Figure 10–23. The gray background represented her loneliness and her expression was the emptiness and homesickness she was finally admitting to. Cheryl worked for a year making drawings about her feelings and Figure 10–24 is the face she used most—one that expressed love. Figure 10–25 represents a face she hardly ever used, a face that expressed anger and blame. At this time, Cheryl was participating in family sessions in addition to her individual work. She was encouraged to take all her drawings to her next family session to help her express these feelings to her parents. This attempt was successful and was the beginning of a more direct communication pattern between Cheryl and her parents.

Figure 10–26 is the illustration of a story that Cheryl told about a princess and a wicked queen.

Cheryl was angry at her mother because she thought her mother was emotionally isolating herself from Cheryl. Cheryl wished to teach her mother to share her feelings as well. The princess in the story left the queen, who was cold and did not care about the feelings of her subjects. The princess traveled through the forest of problems to the land where they needed a queen (the foster parents had two sons and saw Cheryl as the daughter they never had). The people of the kingdom loved the princess and made her queen and gave her a large crown because she loved them and could express her feelings. One day the young queen invited the old queen to visit her in her new kingdom so she could learn how to be happy. The old queen came but only learned a little and then returned to her kingdom relatively unchanged. The young queen was sad but realized she might not be able to teach the old queen what she had learned. This story helped Cheryl realize she could be responsible only for her own feelings and not those of her mother.

In one of the last art therapy sessions, Cheryl took a piece of paper and spontaneously drew Figure 10–27. She said, "Now that I don't have to hide my feelings, I feel as free as a bird who has flown out of the clouds."

### Lee

Lee was living in a foster home when she entered therapy. Most of her life she had moved around the country with her alcoholic father. The father had taken her

**Figure 10–22** Happy—Sad

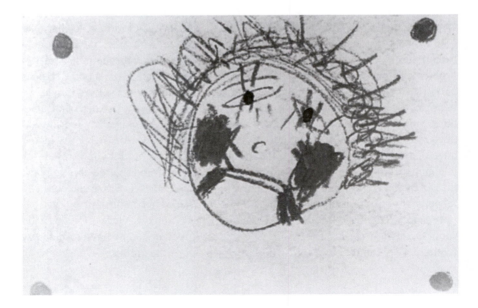

**Figure 10–23** Loneliness

**Figure 10–24** Used Most

**Figure 10–25** Seldom Used

**Figure 10–26** Fairytale

**Figure 10–27** Free as a Bird

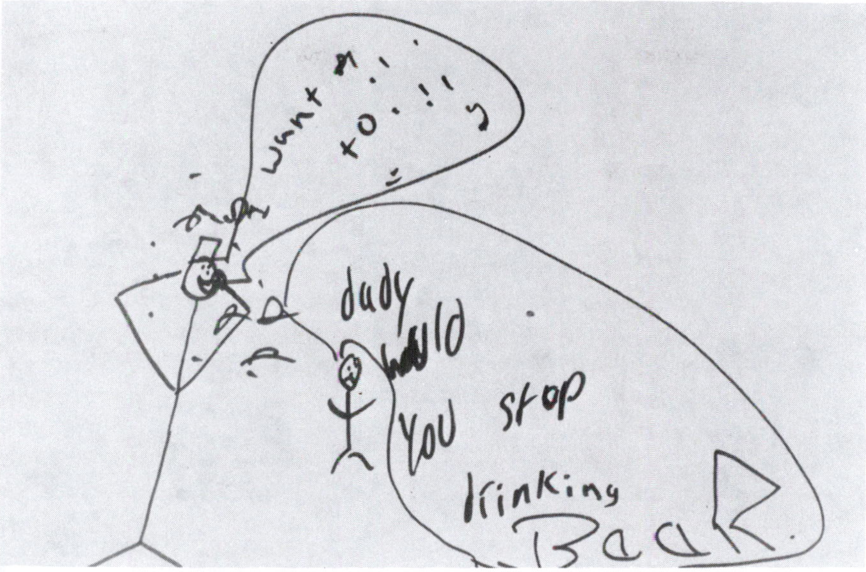

**Figure 10–28** "Daddy, would you stop drinking beer!"

**Figure 10–29** "I was scared when my dad was drinking. It made me think he was gonig to get in a car accident."

**Figure 10–30** Collage

**Figure 10–31** Jealousy

**Figure 10–32** Foster Family and Lee

away from her mother when she was a baby because the mother was beating her and was unable to care for her. Lee had never attended the same school for an entire year, and her only long-term relationship had been with her father. He was often drunk, left her alone, beat her, and sexually abused her, but she would not express any displeasure for fear of losing the only family she knew. She took on parental duties and worried constantly about her father. Once she took a six-pack of beer outside and spilled it on the driveway. This ploy, she found, was unsuccessful because he just bought more. Figure 10–28 was drawn as she talked about her frustration in being unable to convince him to stop drinking beer.

In Figure 10–29 she wrote, "I was scared when my Dad was drinking. It made me think he was going to get in a car accident."

Much of Lee's therapy was geared toward allowing her father to solve his own problems and helping her to take care of herself. Many of her artworks contained themes of wishing to be older or living on her own. Figure 10–30 is a collage of pictures from magazines. On the left is a mother-daughter picture on which she has written, "I miss my Mom." In the center is a child descending into a hole in the ground. This was a fantasy she had that if she could dig a hole in the ground, she and her Dad could live there and they would not need money. She was still taking on adult responsibilities by worrying about rent and paying bills. On the right side of the picture are the jaws of a shark and a picture of a makeup kit. She wrote, "I've always wanted makeup because it makes me feel older." Lee was worried that she would be left alone before she grew up.

After she had lived with her foster family for some time, her wish that these persons could be her real family faded as she realized she could never occupy the

**Figure 10–33** Isolated

**Figure 10–34** "Help!"

same spot as the natural children in the family. Figure 10–31 is Lee's drawing of the jealousy she felt (left) while witnessing the foster mother give her natural daughter a present from her grandmother while telling Lee there was no present for her.

Figure 10–32 shows the foster family with their children and Lee (far left) feeling left out. Lee was encouraged to share these feelings with her foster family. She took the risk and achieved a closeness with them that she had not experienced before.

Because Lee had moved so many times she was unskilled socially with her peers. She drew herself in Figure 10–33 as isolated in the world with everyone laughing at her. In Figure 10–34 she drew herself popping off the page yelling for help while others were laughing at her. Work was done in the area of social skills, and Lee was put into a group of peers to work on these issues.

## SUMMARY

The addition of art activities to the therapy process can encourage emoting in families with frozen feeling, can encourage adaptive communication and healthy problem-solving techniques, and can reach those family members who are unskilled with words or who manipulate others. Art techniques have been used successfully with alcoholic clients, in group treatment, with families, and in helping children who have experienced life problems.

## REFERENCES

Albert-Puleo, N., & Osha, V. (1976/77). Art therapy as an alcoholism treatment tool. *Alcohol Health and Research World 2*, 28–31.

Black, C. (1979). Children of alcoholics. *Alcohol Health and Research World, 4*(1), 23–27.

Burns, R. (1990). *A guide to family-centered circle drawings*. New York: Brunner/Mazel.

Callaghan, G.M. (1993). Art therapy with alcoholic families. In D. Linesch (Ed.), *Art therapy with families in crisis*. New York: Brunner/Mazel.

Denny, B. (1969). Art counseling in educational settings. *Personnel and Guidance Journal*, 119–124.

Foulke, W.E., & Keller, T.W. (1976). The art experience in rehabilitation. *American Journal of Art Therapy, 15*, 75–80.

Ginott, H.G. (1961). *Group psychotherapy with children*. New York: McGraw-Hill.

Kwiatkowska, H.Y. (1978). *Family therapy and evaluation through art*. Springfield, IL: Charles C. Thomas.

Landgarten, H.B. (1981). *Clinical art therapy*. New York: Brunner/Mazel.

Schleicher, W.R. (1978). Art therapy with recovering alcoholics. In M. Goby & J. Keiler (Eds.), *Perspectives on the treatment of alcoholism*. Park Ridge, IL: Lutheran General Hospital.

Springer, J.F., Phillips, J.L., Phillips, L., Cannady, L.P., & Kerst-Harris, E. (1992). CODA: A creative therapy program for children in families affected by abuse of alcohol or other drugs. *Journal of Community Psychology*, OSAP Special Issue, 55–74.

## SUGGESTED READINGS

*American Journal of Art Therapy,* 1976 to present.

Anderson, W. (1977). (Ed.), *Therapy and the arts*. New York: Harper & Row.

*Art Psychotherapy,* 1976 to present.

Bing, E. (1970). The conjoint family drawing. *Family Process, 9,* 173–194.

Devine, D.K. (1970). A preliminary investigation of paintings by alcoholic men. *American Journal of Art Therapy, 9*(3), 115–128.

Dilley, J. (1971). Adding a visual dimension to counseling. *Personnel and Guidance Journal 50*(1), 39–43.

Feder. B., & Feder, E. (1981). *The expressive art therapies*. Englewood Cliffs, NJ: Prentice-Hall.

Forrest, G. (1975). The problems of dependency and the value of art therapy as a means of treating alcoholism. *Art Psychotherapy, 2,* 15–43.

Gantt, L., & Schmal, M.S. (1974). *Art therapy: A bibliography. 1940–1973.* (DHEW Publication No. ADM 74–51.) Washington, DC: U.S. Government Printing Office.

Gardner, H.(1980). *Artful scribbles: The significance of children's drawings*. New York: Basic Books.

Harms, E. (1973). Art therapy for the drug addict. *Art Psychotherapy,1*(1), 55–59.

Isaacs, L.D. (1977). Art therapy group for latency age children. *Social Work*, 57–59.

Jung, C.G. (1959). *Mandala symbolism*, Bollingen series. Princeton, NJ: Princeton University Press.

Jung, C.G. (1964). *Man and his symbols*. New York: Dell Publishing.

Kellogg, R. (1967). *The psychology of children's art*. New York: CRM-Random House.

Kwiatkowska, H.Y. (1967). Family art therapy. *Family Process, 6,* 37–55.

Linesch, D. (Ed.). (1993). *Art therapy with families in crisis: Overcoming resistance through nonverbal expression*. New York: Brunner/Mazel.

Rhyne, J. (1973). The gestalt approach to experience art: Art therapy. *Journal of Art Therapy*, 237–248.

Rhyne, J. (1973). *The gestalt art experience*. Monterey, CA: Brooks/Cole.

Rubin, J., & Magnussen, M. (1974). A family art evaluation. *Family Process, 13*, 185–200.

Sherr, C., & Hicks, H. (1975). Family drawings on a diagnostic and therapeutic technique. *Family Process, 12*, 439.

*There is a rainbow! behind every dark cloud*. (1978). Millbrae, CA: The Center for Attitudinal Healing, Celestial Arts.

Ulman, E. (1953). Art therapy at an outpatient clinic. *Psychiatry, 16*, 55–64.

Ulman, E., & Dachinger, P. (1975). *Art therapy in theory and practice*. New York: Schocken Books.

Ulman, E., Kramer, E., & Kwiatkowska, H. (1977). *Art therapy in the United States*. Craftsburg Common, VT: Art Therapy Publications.

Virshup, E. (1978). *Right brain people in a left brain world*. Los Angeles: The Guild of Tutors Press.

Wadeson, H. (1980). *Art psychotherapy*. Somerset, NJ: John Wiley & Sons.

Worthings, R. (1974). Children's art: The high road to health. *Parent's Magazine, 42*, 59–60.

# CHAPTER 11

# Treatment with the Alcoholic's Spouse

The purpose of this chapter is to examine the role of the alcoholic's spouse in the recovery process. The dynamics of the spouse's relationship to the drinker and the rest of the family are discussed, as are the implications for treatment of the spouse.

In the first edition of this book, published in 1983, it was assumed when one was referring to the spouse of an alcoholic that one was referring to a woman. Women's alcoholism was still hidden at home and ignored by society. Thus, what was written in the literature on spouses described women married to alcoholic men. The other issue here, still true today, is that alcoholic women are far more likely not to have a spouse than are alcoholic men. Nonalcoholic women married to alcoholic men tend to be overly invested in and overly supportive of their husbands (Gomberg, 1986; Gomberg, Nelson, & Hatchett, 1991; Kinsey, 1966). Women stay with their alcoholic husbands for many reasons, including economic issues, childrearing issues, fear of failing their gender-mandated roles, and fear of the alcoholic's reprisals.

The other change since 1983 is the role of the codependency movement in how society views spouses of alcoholics. Spouses came to be diagnosed as coalcoholics and codependents in need of treatment. This led to a flurry of self-help books, treatment programs for codependents, and special 12-step groups called Codependents Anonymous (CODA).

## BACKGROUND OF THE PROBLEM

### The Spouse as Emotionally Disturbed

For many in the field of counseling and psychotherapy, the spouse of the alcoholic is seen not as a helpless victim of circumstances but a full contributor to a dysfunctional family unit. This is not surprising, given the large quantity of research establishing the alcoholic's spouse as stressed and in need. Whalen (1953) described four general personality types of wives of alcoholics. This work was based on interviews conducted at the Family Service Agency in Dallas, Texas. Whalen noted that husbands of alcoholic wives rarely accompany them to therapy, and she therefore focused her comments on the wife of the alcoholic man. To begin with, Whalen thought that the wife of an alcoholic, in general, has as poorly integrated a personality as her husband, even though she may appear more functional in the eyes of society. The implication here is that the wife is an equal contributor to the overall destructiveness of the alcoholic family. Whalen went on to assert that the alcoholic's wife is usually drawn to the alcoholic as a marriage partner due to her own underlying personality characteristics that are essentially negative and destructive.

Specifically, Whalen identified four personality types that recur frequently. The first she labeled the *sufferer*. This individual often chooses an alcoholic husband due to her need to be punished. She is not disappointed when the alcoholic becomes abusive, irresponsible, and incompetent. The sufferer is typically meek, apologetic, and a good homemaker. She probably comes from a family in which she was abused, and her central problem is low self-esteem. Abuse becomes a self-fulfilling prophecy. Whalen pointed out that this personality type does not always marry an alcoholic but does seek a mate who is domineering, rejecting, and cold. Her role in the alcoholic family reinforces and tolerates the behavior of her husband; she is half of a dysfunctional symbiotic relationship.

The second personality type Whalen described as the *controller*. This woman seeks a mate who needs her, an alcoholic, a handicapped person, or someone from an inferior socioeconomic or educational background. Her basic personality structure involves distrust and resentment of men in general. She wants someone weaker than herself that she can dominate and manipulate. Often her initial reason for contact with a counselor is to find an ally who will help her stop her husband's drinking. It seldom occurs to her that she has a problem—it's all his fault. The controller is often the major breadwinner and a career woman. She seldom has an active interest in the family and is hostile to and critical of her husband. In addition, she is unforgiving of and distant from her husband, denying him support or love, reinforcing his feelings of inadequacy by conveying a scolding, maternal attitude. It is obvious that this woman could undermine any attempts at rehabilitation of the alcoholic alone. She does not want a competent equal partner, even though she complains about his drinking.

The third personality type is called the *waverer*. This woman also is attracted to someone she perceives as needing her, but for different reasons than the controller. The controller wants a husband who is weak in order to control him, but the waverer seeks this kind of person due to her fear of being abandoned. If he needs her, she reasons, he is unlikely to leave her. The waverer has a great need to be loved, coupled with great insecurity. She can only feel secure in relationships with dependent people. As a mother she appears devoted, but in reality she attempts to keep her children small and needy. She is overly protective and smothering. As a wife, she may eventually become fed up with her husband's behavior and separate from him for a while. However, she can always be coaxed to return with sincere promises (which never last). She knows she is being mistreated, but she cannot resist the tender words she wants so much to hear.

The fourth personality style is the *punisher*. The punisher's relationships with people, especially men, are characterized by rivalry and aggressiveness. She is often successful professionally and has little interest in a home life. Unlike the controller, she does not demand that her husband take care of her emotionally or financially; she takes care of him. She describes her husband as cute or sweet and basically protects him. She provides her husband with almost anything and castrates him emotionally in the process. On the other hand, when he drinks and is "bad" (making a boisterous nuisance or sleeping around) he is severely punished. According to Whalen, this is also a symbiotic relationship. In this marriage, the punisher finds an outlet for her aggressive impulses in a partnership with a man who is dependent on her and who is constantly maneuvering himself into situations that justify punishment. The husband gets what he unconsciously desires—the punishment he thinks he deserves due to his low self-concept and self-hatred as a loser.

Whalen did not claim that this list of personality types is exhaustive. In reviewing this concept of the alcoholic's wife, several points need to be stressed. First, it is clear that the spouse must receive treatment concurrently with the alcoholic in order for him to have a realistic chance of recovery. Second, the effects on the children of these marriages are devastating. Both maternal and paternal roles are negative and destructive. Moreover, the stress inherent in these marriages creates confusion and anxiety in the children. Third, the children must also receive concurrent therapeutic support. And finally, Whalen emphasized that the four personality types cited are not characteristic only of alcoholic marriages. Such women often marry other types of problematic men who will be counterparts to their neuroses.

MacDonald (1956) also thought that the wife of the alcoholic male needs psychotherapy. He reported research in which wives actually developed psychiatric symptoms as their husbands' drinking decreased. Furthermore, in many cases MacDonald found that severe emotional illness occurred in the wife just at the time the husband stopped drinking. He referred to this process as *decompensation*, or the loss of ability to act as a counterbalance. What this implies, MacDonald believed, is that alcoholics and their spouses have a negative symbiotic relationship, and the cessation of drinking by the alcoholic may precipitate psychiatric symptoms in the spouse. He also believed that the wife may have long-standing emotional problems that can be disguised only while her husband is engaged in alcoholic behavior.

Another perspective on the decompensation hypothesis was forwarded by Hansen and Hill (1964), who suggested that the family has limited "emotional room" at any one time, and following a disaster the family must take turns displaying emotional disturbance. In this context, the wife of the alcoholic takes her turn by manifesting symptoms once the alcoholic appears stable and she can abandon her role as the strong one.

These studies looked at spouses who were already married to alcoholics and assumed that they had these personality disorders prior to the marriage. They sought out alcoholics for various reasons. Although these researchers spoke of an interactional pattern, theirs is not systems thinking. Another group of researchers based their study on Bowen theory (Morris, Wise, Comensky, & Loney, 1992). Bowen theory concerning substance abuse holds that substance abusers have problems with anxiety and attachments to parents and then to spouses. Substance abuse supplies a way to temporarily manage the personal and familial anxiety. This can lead to mental illness in this population. Bowen's concept of the family projection process predicts that substance abusers will select a mate with similar attachment problems and similar low levels of differentiation. This recreates the family of origin in a multigenerational transmission process that continues the substance abuse and other problems generation after generation.

Morris et al. (1992) predicted that they would find an equal level of psychopathology in both spouses and addicts. They studied 50 addicts and their spouses selected randomly from two chemical dependency treatment centers. The diagnosis of the addiction and dual diagnosis of a mental disorder were confirmed by psychological evaluation, medical evaluation, chemical dependency assessment, and social history. Minnesota Multiphasic Personality Inventory (MMPI) scores on the depression (D) scale, psychopathic deviate (Pd) scale, psychastenia (Pt) scale, and schizophrenia (Sc) scale were compared for addicts and spouses. Both groups had similar elevations on MMPI scales. The group means were considered significantly disturbed when compared with the expected prevalence in the study of the catchment area of the general population. On the depression scale the addict T-score mean was 72; the spouse T-score mean was 74. On the psychopathic deviate scale the addict T-score mean was 79; the spouse T-score mean was 79. On the psychastenia scale the addict T-score mean was 75; the spouse T-score mean was 74. Finally, on the schizophrenia scale the addict mean T-score was 76; the spouse T-score was 78. Those scores indicate that the subjects can be considered significantly disturbed when taken as a whole. "When the percentage of patients scoring at or above a T-score of 70 on the MMPI was compared with the expected prevalence rates of mental illness calculated in the Epidemiologic Catchment Area Program study, it was determined that both the spouse and the addict samples indicated a much higher prevalence of psychopathology than the general population" (Morris et al., 1992, p. 3).

The researchers contended that this is validation of Bowen's concepts of multigenerational processes and that there are similar levels of mental illness in the addicts and the spouses. From a Bowen perspective, the mental illness is created by chronic anxiety and a low level of differentiation of the individuals. The findings support the hypothosis that individuals with similar levels of differentiation marry.

### The Spouse as Not Disturbed

Up to this point, studies have been cited that describe the spouse (usually the wife) of the alcoholic as being emotionally disturbed. However, the question is whether this condition predates the alcoholic marriage or is a consequence of it (or if it exists at all). Many believe that the alcoholic's spouse is not disturbed. For example, Corder, Hendricks, and Corder (1964) used the MMPI to compare wives of alcoholics with wives of nonalcoholics. Results described alcoholics' wives as having demonstrated more psychiatric symptoms, but they nonetheless fell in the "normal" range on the test and therefore were not viewed as "sick."

Other researchers used the MMPI and found similar results. Rae and Forbes (1966) suggested that alcoholic wives are essentially normal individuals who are simply reacting to stress. Furthermore, James and Goldman (1971) concluded that the stress an alcoholic spouse experiences is in direct relationship to the intensity and frequency of alcoholic episodes. Hill (1949) presented another argument against the spouse as sick hypothesis. He suggested that the reunion of families, especially spouses, after the alcoholic's recovery is a traumatic process and does not imply that the spouse has been disturbed in the past. He pointed out that many nonalcoholic families also have readjustment problems in circumstances such as war separation. Adjustment to separation seems generally easier than adjustment to reunion for all families.

In response to the decompensation hypothesis, researchers have shown that there is no evidence that partners of addicts usually decompensate when the alcoholic/addict gets sober. Several studies reported improvement in the functioning of the spouse and other family members with the sobriety of the alcoholic/addict (Billings & Moos, 1983; Haberman, 1964; Moos, Finney, & Gamble, 1982; Moos & Moos, 1984; Nace, 1982; Preli, Protinsky, & Cross, 1990; Roberts, Floyd, O'Farrell, & Cutter, 1985; van Wormer, 1989).

Other researchers in the area also reject the theory that the alcoholic's spouse is disturbed. Paolina, McCrady, Diamond, and Longabough (1976) argued that most empirical evidence fails to differentiate spouses of alcoholics and nonalcoholics on personality variables. In this study, husbands and wives of alcoholics were compared with a norm group on the Psychological Screening Inventory (PSI) and were found not to differ significantly, with the exception of a single scale (defensiveness). However, the authors pointed out that even here alcoholics' wives' scores fell within the normal range.

A more recent study of wives of alcoholics and female spouses of incest perpetrators found, "There is no evidence to indicate that there are characterological problems with either the partners of sexual abusers or the partners of alcoholics" (Pitman & Taylor, 1992).

In summary, it is our opinion that the degree of pathology of the alcoholic's spouse must be determined individually. It is just as difficult to draw generalizations about alcoholics' spouses as about the rest of humanity. The important point here is that the spouse be assessed and not excluded from treatment. Whether the spouse contributes to alcoholism or is overstressed in reaction to it, the need for therapeutic assistance remains. It is also our opinion that the spouse of an alcoholic is very unlikely to be emotionally intact. Human beings cannot be submitted to stress and discord for long periods of time without negative psychological consequences.

## TREATMENT IMPLICATIONS

The disturbed spouse theory has several implications for treatment. First, the spouse may suffer from long-term conflicts that are independent of the alcoholic and that require therapy. Second, alcoholism may be, as Whalen (1953) referred to it, a "red herring," and not the central problem to consider in treatment. Indeed, Whalen thought that alcoholism is incidental to the four personality types discussed earlier. Therapy for these individuals involves helping them understand their core conflicts and adopt new behaviors. The third implication for treatment is that the marital unit needs assistance. Because the marriage in this situation involves the symbiosis of two essentially destructive personality types, both partners need simultaneous treatment. Consider an instance in which only half of the relationship changes. The customary expectations and responses become modified, leaving both partners confused and anxious. Finally, Whalen called for relatively long-term treatment, one year or more. She advocated a modification in the client's personality structure, accompanied by the accrual of a new behavioral set by the marital unit and the family.

In order to accomplish this task, several steps should be followed. The first is to establish trust and rapport with the spouse, who is initially seen individually. This step is important due to the inadequacy and distrustfulness that these clients exhibit. Also, Whalen specified that women who essentially dislike or are competitive with men should be seen by a female counselor. During the initial stages, the spouse is given supportive counseling. The therapist should model a noncompetitive, accepting relationship. Eventually, the core personality issues are confronted. At this stage the spouse comes to grips with her problems and drops the idea that everything is the alcoholic's fault. Behaviors are also examined, and it should be pointed out to the client how her behavior is destructive to herself and everyone close to her. Once this insight has been gained, new, healthier behaviors are suggested and attempted. In the final stage of treatment, the client understands her root personality disturbances and possible resolutions. Group therapy is recommended after the client is firmly rooted in the therapeutic process. Eventually, conjoint marital or family counseling is suggested.

Contrary to the disturbed spouse school of thought, the second theory proposes that the spouse is responding to the stress of the alcoholic marriage. The issue of whether or not the spouse's problems predated the marriage has definite treatment implications. In the latter case, long-term psychotherapy is probably not necessary. Rather, efforts should be directed toward modifying or removing the stress situation or aiding the spouse in adapting to it with less anxiety. One advocate of the wife in reaction to stress concept is Jackson (1954), who also advocated Al-Anon for alcoholic spouses. She described seven steps in family adjustment to alcoholism.

1. Incidents of excessive drinking begin and, although they are sporadic, place strains on the husband-wife interaction. In attempts to minimize drinking, problems in marital adjustment not related to the drinking are avoided.
2. Social isolation of the family begins as incidents of excessive drinking multiply. The increasing isolation magnifies the importance of family interactions and events. Behavior and thought become centered on drinking. Husband-wife adjustment deteriorates, and tension rises. The wife begins to feel self-pity and loses her self-confidence as her behavior fails to stabilize her husband's drinking. There is an attempt to still maintain the original family structure that is disrupted anew with each episode of drinking. As a result, the children begin to show emotional disturbance.
3. The family gives up attempts to control the drinking and begins to behave in a manner geared to relieve tension rather than achieve long-term ends. The disturbance of the children becomes more marked. There is no longer an attempt to support the alcoholic in his roles as husband and father. The wife begins to worry about her own sanity and about her inability to make decisions or act to change the situation.
4. The wife takes over control of the family, and the husband is seen as a recalcitrant child. Pity and strong, protective feelings largely replace the earlier resentment and hostility. The family becomes more stable and organized in a manner to minimize the disruptive behavior of the husband. The self-confidence of the wife begins to be rebuilt.
5. The wife separates from her husband if she can resolve the problems and conflicts surrounding this action.
6. The wife and children reorganize as a family without the husband.
7. The husband achieves sobriety and the family, which had become organized around an alcoholic husband, reorganizes to include a sober father and experiences problems in reinstating him in his former roles.

The wife in this case is responding to the stress of an alcoholic husband and is not seen as psychopathological herself. Instead of therapy, the spouse is first offered information about alcoholism to better understand the aberrant behaviors of the alcoholic. This is felt to be important by stress theorists. For example, up until the time of intervention, the spouse may have disbelieved the husband's memory lapses involving drinking episodes. She may discover that blackouts are a symptom of alcoholism and that the alcoholic really does forget his or her behaviors. The spouse may also believe that the alcoholic has control of his or her consumption and drinks for spite. These and other misconceptions can be cleared up and unnecessary anxiety can be alleviated. In addition to informing the spouse about the nature of alcoholism, stress theorists advocate emotional support and encourage the spouse to abandon futile attempts to make the alcoholic stop drinking, known as the "home remedy." Spouses are also given information about their enabling (the inadvertent reinforcement) of their partner's drinking. They are instructed not to cover up for the alcoholic, such as calling work and saying he or she is ill. In this way the spouse can identify his or her role in maintaining the problem and is offered new behaviors and attitudes that are healthier. Stress theorists also underline the importance of marital and family counseling during the reunion process. They point out that this is perhaps the most difficult part of recovery, and the spouse will have to give up some control of the family's affairs, among other things. Finally, Jackson (1954), Bailey (1964), and others ascribing to this theory advocate Al-Anon as an important adjunct to counseling for the alcoholic's spouse.

In assessing the impact on the spouses who are involved in the treatment of their alcoholic partners, Valentine (1995) compared a family education model with a multifamily therapy group model. He was interested in how each of these models affected the spouse. He found that both groups were effective in changing the family environment. When measuring the family environment with the Family Environment Scale (Moos & Moos, 1981) pre- and posttreatment he found the family education group significantly improved the level of independence in the spouses ($p > .01$) and the multifamily therapy group increased the spouse's perception of cohesion, expression of feelings, and organization ($p > .01$). Several other clinically significant improvements were noted in both groups. At a two-year follow-up these improvements remained.

### Al-Anon

Research by Bailey (1964) and Wright and Scott (1978) has suggested that the best treatment predictor of an alcoholic's sobriety is his or her involvement in Alcoholics Anonymous (AA) coupled with the spouse's concurrent involvement in Al-Anon. In addition, Wright and Scott researched which treatment(s), if any, were important for a spouse in order to facilitate the alcoholic's recovery. Their conclusions indicated that the more types of treatment a spouse participates in, the better. They went on to specify Al-Anon and inpatient treatment, if necessary, as the most beneficial.

Many would agree with the effectiveness of Al-Anon. But what is it, and how does it work? In many ways, its functions are parallel to AA, such as the use of the AA traditions and 12 steps as a conceptual framework for alcoholism. But Al-Anon serves the spouses and friends of the alcoholic and does not deal directly with problem drinkers. Al-Anon, like AA, is anonymous and has no governing authority. It is a self-help group that gives support, information, and encouragement to its members. Participants are helped to help themselves and give up efforts to control the alcoholic. But perhaps the most effective aspect of Al-Anon is its practical, how-to approach, offered by individuals with similar experiences. Al-Anon can serve as an important adjunct to traditional psychotherapy. Many similar goals are shared by counseling and Al-Anon (which are described in Chapter 6), and the two processes often work comfortably together.


## THE CODEPENDENCY MOVEMENT


With the broadening of the context of understanding of alcoholism from the alcoholic to the alcoholic family, many nonsystemic ideas became popular in the field. As mentioned earlier, role theories became diagnostic categories of pathology for children of alcoholics. Spouses, as well, became pathologized with labels including *enabler, coalcoholic,* and *codependent.* Labeling and sometimes blaming the family members for the alcoholics' problems is not in line with family systems theory. Systems theory is more interested in how the family patterns are maintained so a second-order change or shift in system dynamics can produce a reduction of symptoms and a healthy, functioning family.

Although the term *codependent* was originally used to describe spouses of alcoholics (particularly women), before the hysteria of the movement was over it spread to children of alcoholics, adult children of alcoholics, victims of abuse, and most of the population. Some definitions of codependency found in pop literature include:

- a disease
- an addiction
- a family problem
- anyone who lives with a neurotic personality
- anyone who lives with another person
- anyone who lives with, works with, or is around an alcoholic/addict

- immaturity
- toxic brain syndrome
- spouse of an alcoholic
- child of an alcoholic
- adult child of an alcoholic
- victim of abuse (Beattie, 1987; Cruse, 1989; Larsen, 1983; Mellody, 1989; Subby, 1984; Wegscheider-Cruse & Cruse, 1990; Whitfield, 1984).

Cermak (1986) even tried to have codependency added to the Diagnostic and Statistical Manual IV (DSM IV) as a personality disorder. John Bradshaw of Public Broadcast System's series on alcoholic families suggested that 96 percent of the population of the United States is codependent and all addictions are rooted in codependence (Bradshaw, 1988).

This proliferation of definitions and groups of persons defined as codependent made the word meaningless. Asher and Brissett (1988) interviewed 52 wives of men diagnosed with and treated for alcoholism. They found confusion and uncertainty among the women as to the definition of codependency. Most learned of the "syndrome" at family treatment programs. The researchers concluded that "becoming codependent is the result of a convolution of the illness metaphor and labeling process . . . this convolution is a twofold process involving, on the one hand, a deviantizing of the wife's behavior by other and self, and on the other, the medicalization of this alleged deviance" (p. 345).

The codependency movement was seen by many, including feminists, as a sexist attempt to pathologize women (Babcock & McKay, 1995). These critics believed that pop authors had taken women's socialized behaviors and created a pathological syndrome. They did not deny that women who lived with alcoholics suffered and often blamed themselves, but they did not agree that their caretaking behavior should constitute a disease diagnosis. Bepko and Krestan (1990a) provided a sociocultural view of this spouse relationship. They defined codependency as an adaptive response to stress or impairment in a family system in which one person is overresponsible for others and underresponsible for self in a social context that promotes this in women (Bepko & Krestan, 1990b). In other words, wives do what they have been trained to do as women when they are faced with the stressful situation of trying to be a "good wife" and a "good mother" and hold the family together, while hoping their alcoholic husbands will change. Their lack of self-responsibility is simply a self-sacrificing, problem-solving behavior that, for the moment, works.

Perhaps the harshest criticism of the codependency label came from those working in the field of spouse abuse. As the label was used as a simple explanation for complex relationship disorders, it was applied to women who were battered by their spouses, many of whom were alcoholic. Frank and Golden (1992) attacked this notion, saying, "Calling a woman who is living with a batterer a codependent is tantamount to victimizing her again. The prefix 'co' implies shared responsibility for the abuse, which directly opposes an important segment of the work with battered women—clarifying that women are not responsible for the violent behavior of their abusers" (p. 6).

To diagnose a woman who does not leave her abusive husband as codependent does not take into consideration the many complex variables that affect this decision. These include, but are not limited to, the legal response to physical abuse within her community, the number and ages of her children, economic factors, availability of shelters and community support programs, willingness of family and friends to help, and her employability (Frank & Houghton, 1987). This is further complicated by the statistic that more battered women are killed when they leave their abusive mates than when they stay (U.S. Department of Justice, 1983).

Other researchers tried to define codependency in spouses of alcoholics by constructing a measure. Spann and Fischer (1990) defined codependency as a "psychosocial condition that is manifested through a dysfunctional pattern of relating to others. This pattern is characterized by: extreme control focus outside of self, lack of open expression of feelings, and attempts to derive a sense of purpose through relationships" (p. 27).

The next step was to develop a scale to measure codependency in the individual trait-like characteristics (Fischer, Spann, & Crawford, 1991). The assumption was that codependency did exist and could be measured. Fischer, Wampler, Lyness, and Thomas (1992) tested the belief of Bradshaw that codependency was the underlying principle of all addictions. They reported:

> The results of this study challenge the widely accepted assertion that family dysfunction is closely linked to the development of codependent patterns in the offspring. Codependency was not predicted by number of addictions in the family of origin nor by the severity of the dysfunctions in the family of origin. Furthermore, the results also do not support the concept that codependency is the fundamental personal dysfunction underlying all other addictions and its corollary that someone who is codependent is at greater risk for developing other addictions. Neither alcoholism nor excessive risk taking were associated with high levels of codependency. (p. 30)

In fact, the development of a codependent pattern appeared to be related to reduced levels of risk-taking behaviors and buffered subjects from developing their own addictions.

## SUMMARY

Two conceptions of the alcoholic's spouse were presented: (1) the spouse as emotionally disturbed; and (2) the spouse in reaction to stress. The treatment implications for each were outlined. In the first instance, long-term therapy specifically focusing on the spouse's pathology was recommended. In the latter case, education about alcoholism and supportive counseling, along with Al-Anon, were advocated. In both situations, marital and family counseling were viewed as important during the recovery process, especially during the family's reunion period. A third perspective is the family dynamic belief that family-of-origin issues are at the base of most marital conflicts, and spouses of alcoholics should be encouraged to explore these root problems before current ones can be adequately addressed. It is clear that living with an alcoholic is very difficult and affects the spouse's self-esteem and sense of responsibility. It seems most useful to include the spouse in the treatment of the alcoholic, and if the alcoholic won't go to treatment to intervene with the spouse to shift the system.

---

## REFERENCES

Asher, R., & Brissett, D. (1988). Codependency: A view from women married to alcoholics. *International Journal of Addictions, 23*(4), 331–350.

Babcock, M., & McKay, C. (Eds.). (1995). *Challenging codependency: Feminist critiques.* Toronto: University of Toronto Press.

Bailey, M.B. (1964). The family agency's role in treating the wife of an alcoholic. *Social Casework, 44,* 273–279.

Beattie, M. (1987). *Co-dependent no more.* New York: Harper/Hazelden.

Bepko, C., & Krestan, J. (1990a). *Too good for her own good: Breaking free from the burden of female responsibility.* New York: Harper & Row.

Bepko, C., & Krestan, J. (1990b). Codependent or simply female. A workshop presented at the 48th Annual Conference of the American Association for Marriage and Family Therapy, Washington, D.C.

Billings, A.G., & Moos, R.H. (1983). Psychosocial processes of recovery among alcoholics and their families. *Addictive Behaviors, 8,* 205–218.

Bradshaw, J. (1988). *Bradshaw: On the family.* Deerfield Beach, FL: Health Communications.

Cermak, T. (1986). *Diagnosing and treating co-dependency.* Minneapolis; MN: Johnson Institute Books.

Corder, B.F., Hendricks. A., & Corder, R.F. (1964). An MMPI study of a group of wives of alcoholics. *Quarterly Journal of Studies on Alcohol, 25,* 551–554.

Cruse, J. (1989). *Painful affairs: Looking for love through addictions and codependency.* Deerfield Beach, FL: Health Communications.

Fischer, J.L., Spann, L. & Crawford, D. (1991). Measuring codependency. *Alcoholism Treatment Quarterly, 8,* 87–100.

Fischer, J.L., Wampler, R., Lyness, K., & Thomas, E.M. (1992). Offspring codependency: Blocking the impact of the family of origin. *Family Dynamics of Addiction Quarterly, 2*(1), 20–32.

Frank, P.B., & Golden, G.K. (1992). Blaming by naming: Battered women and the epidemic of codependency. *Social Work, 37*(1), 5–6.

Frank, P.B., & Houghton, B.D. (1987). *Confronting the batterer: A guide to creating the spouse abuse educational workshop*. New York: Volunteer Counseling Service.

Gomberg, E.S.L. (1986). Women and alcoholism: Psychosocial issues. In *Women and alcohol: Health related issues* (pp. 78–120). Washington, DC: U.S. Government Printing Office, National Institute on Alcohol Abuse and Alcoholism Research Monograph, 16. DHHS No (ADM) 86–1139.

Gomberg, E.S.L., Nelson, B.W., & Hatchett, B.F. (1991). Women, alcoholism and family therapy. *Family and Community Health, 13*(4), 61–71.

Haberman, P.W. (1964). Psychological test score changes for wives of alcoholics during periods of drinking and sobriety. *Journal of Clinical Psychology, 20*, 230–232.

Hansen, D.A., & Hill, R. (1964). Families under stress. In H.T. Christensen (Ed.), *Handbook of marriage and the family*. Chicago: Rand McNally.

Hill, R. (1949). *Families under stress: Adjustment to the crisis of war separation and reunion*. New York: Harper.

Jackson, J.K. (1954). The adjustment of the family to the crisis of alcoholism. *Quarterly Journal of Studies on Alcohol, 15*, 562–586.

James, J.E., & Goldman, M. (1971). Behavioral trends of wives of alcoholics. *Quarterly Journal of Studies on Alcohol, 32*, 373–381.

Kinsey, B.A. (1966). *The female alcoholic: A psychological study*. Springfield, IL: Charles C. Thomas.

Larsen, E. (1983). *Basics of co-dependency*. Brooklyn Park, MN: E.L. Enterprises.

MacDonald, D. (1956). Mental disorders in wives of alcoholics. *Quarterly Journal of Studies on Alcohol, 17*(2), 282–287.

Mellody, P. (1989). The roots of codependency. Audiotape produced by Listen to Learn Tape Library, Phoenix, AZ.

Moos, R.H., Finney, J.W., & Gamble, W. (1982). The process of recovery from alcoholism: II. Comparing spouses of alcoholic patients and matched community controls. *Journal of Studies on Alcohol, 43*, 888–909.

Moos, R.H., & Moos, B.S. (1981). *Family Environment Scale manual*. Palo Alto, CA: Counseling Psychology Press.

Moos, R.H., & Moos, B.S. (1984). The process of recovery from alcoholism: III. Comparing functioning in families of alcoholics and matched control families. *Journal of Studies on Alcohol, 45*, 111–118.

Morris, J.A,, Wise, R.P., Comensky, M.H., & Loney, T.E. (1992, October). *Bowenian predictors of spousal psychopathology in addicts*. Paper presented at the meeting of the American Association of Marriage and Family Therapy, Miami, FL.

Nace, E.P. (1982). Therapeutic approaches to the alcoholic marriage. *Psychiatric Clinics of North America, 5*, 543–564.

Paolina, T.J., McCrady, B., Diamond, S., and Longabough, R. (1976). Psychological disturbances in the spouses of alcoholics. *Journal of Studies on Alcohol, 37* (11), 1600–1608.

Pitman, N.E., & Taylor, R.G. (1992). MMPI profiles of partners of incestuous sexual offenders and partners of alcoholics. *Family Dynamics of Addiction Quarterly, 2*, 52–59.

Preli, R., Protinsky, H., & Cross, L. (1990). Alcoholism and family structure. *Family Therapy, 17*, 1–8.

Rae, J.B., & Forbes, A.R. (1966). Clinical and psychonectic characteristics of the wives of alcoholics. *British Journal of Psychiatry, 112*, 197–200.

Roberts, M.C.F., Floyd, F.J., O'Farrell, T.J., & Cutter, H.S.G. (1985). Marital interactions and the duration of alcoholic husbands' sobriety. *American Journal of Drug and Alcohol Abuse, 11*, 303–313.

Spann, L., & Fischer, J.L. (1990). Identifying co-dependency. *The Counselor, 8*, 27.

Subby, R. (1984). Inside the chemically dependent mariage: Denial and manipulation. In R. Subby & J. Friel (Eds.), *Co-dependency: An emerging issue*. Pompano Beach, FL: Health Communications.

U.S. Department of Justice (1983). *A survey of spousal violence against women in Kentucky*. Washington, DC: U.S. Government Printing Office.

Valentine, D. (1995). *Effects of family education and family therapy on spouses of alcoholics' coping behavior and perceptions of family environment*. Unpublished doctoral dissertation. United States International University, San Diego, CA.

van Wormer, K. (1989). Co-dependency: Implications for women and therapy. *Women and Therapy, 8*, 51–63.

Wegscheider-Cruse, S., & Cruse, J. (1990). *Understanding co-dependency*. Deerfield Beach, FL: Health Communications.

Whalen, T. (1953). Wives of alcoholics. *Quarterly Journal of Studies on Alcohol, 14(4)*, 632–641.

Whitfield, C. (1984). Co-alcoholism: Recognizing a treatable illness. *Family and Community Health, 7*, 16–25.

Wright, K.D., & Scott, J.B. (1978). The relationship of wives' treatment to the drinking status of alcoholics. *Journal of Studies on Alcohol, 39*, 1577–1581.

# CHAPTER 12

# Evaluation of Treatment

## EVALUATION OF FAMILY TREATMENT

Throughout this text we advocate a family systems approach for the amelioration of alcoholism. Many of the chapters specifically address a variety of family approaches in the hope that these techniques will be adopted and used by the reader. However, another pertinent issue surrounding family counseling has yet to be discussed—the evaluation of family therapy.

This chapter first reviews several approaches for evaluating family therapy that have been reported in the research literature. Following this, the results of these studies are discussed.

It is an understatement to say that attempts to evaluate family treatment have met with a multitude of problems, both from a conceptual and methodological point of view. As DeWitt (1978) pointed out, "In all, previous reviewers have all noted that the research evidence as to the efficacy of family therapy is disappointing in terms of both quantity and quality" (p. 550). The difficulties in measuring the success (or lack of it) for this treatment model are based in the following areas. First, there are no generally accepted criteria for successful completion. For example, many studies rely solely on the clinical impressions of the practitioners who provided the treatment. Others rely on the subjective evaluations of the client(s) following termination (usually in survey form), and still others use statistical data, such as length of employment, arrests, or recidivism following treatment, to verify success. Another problem in evaluation is the inability to use a control group—a similar population of families who do not receive treatment to compare with those who do. The problem here is that it is unethical to withhold treatment from distressed families for the sake of research. A final example of methodological problems is the difficulty in standardizing the type and quality of treatment offered. Indeed, even within most agencies there is a discrepancy between the styles and levels of expertise of treatment staff members. In general, the evaluation of family therapy presents many problems that, to date, have not been overcome.

Conceptually, the definition of family therapy remains nebulous. For example, many combinations of family members and therapists are possible under this heading. Family therapy may include the entire family with one therapist or two. In other situations it may include members of the family of origin, as outlined in chapter 3. Family therapy may involve the concurrent treatment of spouses and children, but in separate sessions. The term *family therapy* designates no consistent composition of therapist(s) and client(s).

Yet, given these (and other) obstacles, much attention and work have been focused on the evaluation of the family therapy process. Coleman and Stanton (1978) approached this problem by developing an instrument to measure the extent of family therapy involvement for different agencies, called the Progress Index for Family Therapy Programs (PIFTP), as shown in Exhibit 12–1. This instrument does not measure the effectiveness of family treatment per se but evaluates the agency's overall performance. The PIFTP consists of items deemed important by a professional task force. Each item is weighed on its relative importance and reflects what the agency considers cogent indicators of family therapy involvement.

Coleman and Stanton surveyed 500 agencies, including a preponderance of drug abuse centers. Many programs did, however, treat other problems (76 were community mental health centers). The results of this study were remarkable. The maximum score possible on the PIFTP was 58 (see Exhibit 12–1), but the overall mean for the total group was only 18.5. The mean for the community mental health centers was also 18.5. Coleman and Stanton additionally found that only 27 percent of the agencies had budgets for family therapy and only 4 percent conducted research to measure effectiveness. Another finding was that a mandatory requirement of family therapy for clients did not ensure as high a score on the PIFTP as was previously expected (42.5 percent of these programs scored less than 30 points). Finally, results showed that neither the characteristics (size) nor the client demography of the 40 most successful programs predicted a family therapy requirement.

The use of this instrument can help agencies determine their level of maturity in terms of family therapy and can allow a comparison with other programs. But again, the PIFTP does not provide direct evidence of treatment effectiveness.

A similar study was done, using some of the questions from the PIFTP, with 400 substance abuse treatment agencies that advertised a family program (Hoshino & Lawson, 1995). The following is a summary of some of the findings compared with the Coleman and Stanton survey.

**Exhibit 12–1** Progress Index for Family Therapy Programs

Family therapy in this index refers to therapy or counseling of family members in which a therapist or counselor helps a family solve its problems and achieve more positive and constructive ways of relating to one another. The family members who attend may vary from session to session, and it is very likely that all members do not meet together all the time.

| *Item* | *Response* | *Weighted Score* |
|---|---|---|
| 1. Is family therapy often or always introduced when the identified client enters treatment? | Yes___ No ___ | 1 |
| 2. Do families often or always remain in family therapy until primary goals are attained? | Yes___ No ___ | 1 |
| 3. Does family therapy take place in the home at least occasionally? | Yes___ No ___ | 1 |
| 4. Is family theapy mandatory for all clients? | Yes___ No ___ | 5* |
| 5. Is family therapy the primary or only form of treatment at your agency? | Yes___ No ___ | 5 |
| 6. Is the family therapist also the primary therapist for the identified client? | Yes___ No ___ | 1 |
| 7. Does the family therapist have primary responsibility for therapeutic decisions that will affect the identified client and the family? | Yes___ No ___ | 1 |
| 8. Does the family therapist have major influence on decisions regarding control of medication? | Yes___ No ___ | 1 |
| 9. Do family therapists have only a minimal role in establishing family therapy policies such as client selection, timing of treatment, etc.? | Yes___ No ___ | −1 |
| 10. Is there supervision of family therapy within your agency? | Yes___ No ___ | 3 |
| 11. Does training include group or individual supervision with live family sessions as a focus? | Yes___ No ___ | 5 |
| 12. Does training include group or individual supervision without live families? | Yes___ No ___ | 2 |
| 13. Does training include the use of audiotapes? | Yes___ No ___ | 2 |

*continues*

**Exhibit 12–1** continued

| | | | |
|---|---|---|---|
| 14. Does training include the use of videotapes? | Yes___ No ___ | | 5 |
| 15. Does training include the use of notes? | Yes___ No ___ | | 1 |
| 16. Does training include the use of seminars/lectures? | Yes___ No ___ | | 1 |
| 17. Does the agency have a budget allocation for family therapists' training? | Yes___ No ___ | | 3 |
| 18. Do family therapists attend professional family therapy conferences or workshops? | Yes___ No ___ | | 3 |
| 19. Does the agency provide funding for attending conferences or workshops? | Yes___ No ___ | | 1 |
| 20. Is at least 20% of the total time allotted for training devoted to family therapy training? | Yes___ No ___ | | 1 |
| 21. Is your agency doing any family therapy research? | Yes___ No ___ | | 3 |

22. Which of the following best describes the specific family therapy training of the average family therapist at your agency?

    a.   No training                              a ___          0

    b.   Conferences and/or workshops or course work in an academic program     b ___          2

    c.   Intensive inservice training or training with a family therapy institute     c ___          3

23. The average family therapist at your agency has the following amount of experience as a family therapist:    (Check one only)

    a.   1 year or less                    a ___          1

    b.   2–3 years             .         b ___          2

    c.   4–5 years                    c ___          3

    d.   6 or more years               d ___          4

*Originally received a score of 10 on this item.

*Source:* Reprinted with permission from "An index for measuring agency involvement in family therapy," by Sandra B. Coleman and M. Duncan Stanton in *Family Process*, vol. 17, p. 481, © 1978.

|  | *1978* | *1995* |
|---|---|---|
| Is family therapy offered? | 93% | 93.3% |
| Is family therapy mandatory? | 8% | 31.7% |
| Are live families used in supervision? | 33% | 35.8% |
| Is the agency conducting family therapy research? | 4% | 5% |
| Does the agency have funding for family therapy training? | 27% | 36% |

Although some advances have been made in the years between surveys, a shocking lack of research and funding still exists. Treatment agencies have still not made a solid commitment to treating families. Interestingly, although 93.3 percent of the agencies offered family therapy, 89.2 percent did not specifically employ a marriage and family therapist. The therapists who provided the family therapy had a wide range of education from a high amount, reflected by medical physicians (9.2 percent) and PhDs (4.2 percent) to a low amount, with 7.5 percent having only a high school education. The majority had a masters degree (59.2 percent).

More to the point of evaluating the actual effectiveness of family therapy, Tittler, Fiedler, and Klopper (1977) developed a system to determine change in families. To do this, they tailored four established measures to fit the characteristics of individual families. The instruments used are: (1) the family life questionnaire, (2) the outside activities checklist, (3) the felt figures task, and (4) a two-part, family interaction task.

The procedure used to tailor these measures for families consists of, first, determining areas of family imbalance and discordance, followed by the development of specific expectations as to how the family needs to change (based on the data obtained from the four instruments). Expectations are then formulated by the treatment staff and expressed in terms of the directions in which selected problems should change. These authors stress that expectations should be within the capabilities of the family. Change is evaluated on the measures by selecting 10 expectations for each family and assigning a score of +2 or –2 for each, depending on whether the change occurred in a positive or negative direction. This procedure can be employed both during and after treatment and can provide information about areas that need more attention. This method can also serve as an evaluation of family treatment after completion of therapy.

A similar approach was developed by Sigal, Barrs, and Doubilet (1976), who examined the interaction of the family and the emotional involvement of its members to see if these two variables could predict the outcome of family therapy. A questionnaire entitled "The Family Category Schema" was given to each of the 20 families in this study before and after treatment. Three judges then rated the various areas of family change based on these data to determine if improvement occurred. Families fell into three categories, according to the judges' rating: "great improvement," "moderate improvement," and "no change." Following this, the families' levels of interaction and emotional involvement (rated by the therapist) were compared with the three outcome categories. It was assumed that families who initially had higher levels of interaction and more emotional involvement would change more positively, but this result was not found. However, the approach demonstrates an improved way to use clinical evaluation to determine success—the employment of independent judges.

Minuchin, Montalvo, Gurney, Rosman, and Shermer (1967) also reported on the evaluation of family therapy. These researchers used the Family Interaction Apperception Test, a standardized instrument, in combination with the Wiltwyck Family Task (developed for their study) and a clinical evaluation of treatment. These measures were administered before and after treatment to determine if change occurred in the tested families. One drawback, however, is that both tests are projective in nature and require a considerable amount of interpretation. Nonetheless, this procedure represents the use of standardized instruments to evaluate therapy.

Another method for evaluating family therapy was reported by Martin (1967). His approach is unique because family communications are divided into blaming versus nonblaming statements. Martin compared families that received family counseling with a matched control group that did not. All the families were given pre- and post therapy evaluation sessions that were recorded and transcribed. Trained, independent judges made blind ratings from the transcripts and assigned all statements to blaming or nonblaming categories. The results of Martin's study indicated that families that received family treatment showed a greater proportionate decrease in blaming scores following treatment than did the control group. Although the results are not necessarily relevant to this section of the chapter, Martin's study illustrates the use of a defined aspect of communicational behavior, judged by independent raters, as a criterion of change in family functioning.

Similarly, Langsley, Flomenhaft, and Machotka (1969) reported a large-scale study that focused on the evolution of family treatment. A total of 300 families with one identified patient (IP) were tested; 150 were randomly given family therapy and 150 were referred for conventional hospital treatment. The two groups were then compared on several criteria before and after treatment and on a six-month follow-up. The criteria were rehospitalization rates following treatment; the Social Adjustment Inventory, which taps four areas of social and environmental functioning; the Personal Functioning Scale, which measures personal and emotional adjustment; and the number of days of lost functioning following treatment.

Although the differences found between the family treatment group and the control group were small in this study, the approach represents sound research methodology that could be applied in other settings. To review the study briefly, these researchers used a large population (300); pre-, post-, and follow-up assessment; random assignment of subjects into the experimental and control groups; and multiple outcome criteria that were measurable.

A retrospective design was used to evaluate family counseling in research conducted by Sigal, Barrs, and Doubilet (1976). This study involved the assessment of 93 families that requested help with a child at the Department of Psychiatry at the Jewish General Hospital in Montreal between the years 1962 and 1972. Families that participated in three or more family counseling sessions (63) were compared with those who participated in one or fewer sessions (following a diagnostic interview) and terminated contact against their therapists' advice. Because all families answered survey questionnaires four to five years following the termination of services, this study was retrospective in nature. The therapy provided was described by the authors as " psycho-dynamically oriented, interactional family therapy, typified by an emphasis on explanation or interpretation and reference to non-verbal expression in the family" (p. 228). Three criteria for effectiveness were used: (1) the status of presenting symptoms as reported by a parent at least one year after termination of contact with the treating facility, (2) the appearance of new symptoms, and (3) the parent's report of the degree of satisfaction with the family's current functioning. Information was also gathered concerning the informants' satisfaction with the contact, whether they thought their problems had been understood, and whether they had subsequently sought help elsewhere for the presenting problems.

Although the criteria for this evaluation model were subjective, the authors' rationale was that parents' reports of their children's behavior correlate well with reports obtained from outside observers (Glidewell, Domke, & Kantor, 1963). Furthermore, because consumers define the problems, it seems reasonable to ask them if they got what they needed (Mayer & Timms, 1970).

The results of this study, which are addressed in the next section, were not encouraging. However, as discussed earlier, the actual results of these research attempts are not germane at present. We are simply describing several methods of family therapy evaluation that may be used by the reader.

Finally, studies by Woodward, Santa-Barbara, Levin, and Epstein (1978) and Bond, Bloch, and Yalom (1979), respectively, are cited. These studies represent further attempts to refine outcome evaluations of family therapy.

The first study (Woodward, Santa-Barbara, Levin, & Epstein, 1978) used a scaling system for therapy goals. The goals for each family were individualized and constructed by the therapist. Each goal consisted of a five-point range, so that a level of attainment could be analyzed. It was stressed that once relevant goals were identified, they must be stated in the most concrete terms possible and also be behavioral and measurable. Next, the goal setter specified which expectations were least likely to occur and which were more or less desirable. The goals were assessed after a six-month follow-up period. Client deterioration or improvement was determined from the distribution of goal attainment scores. Any number of scaled goals could be constructed for each individual. Table 12–1 presents an example of goal attainment scaling (Kiresuk & Sherman, 1968).

**Table 12–1** Sample Goal Attainment Scaling

| Goal Weights / Outcome Value | Goals | | | | |
|---|---|---|---|---|---|
| | Fear of Sex Involvement 20 | Dependency on Mother 50 | Decision Making 20 | Social Functioning 30 | MMPI—78 10 |
| Most favorable treatment outcome thought likely (−2) | Avoidant Lives at home No dating No sex | No new decisions | Institutionalized made, still weighing same alternative (job, vocation) | Up at all over prison or hospital | previous score |
| Less than expected success with treatment (−1) | | Does nothing without mother's approval | Complains of being unable to make up mind | On probation Further arrests | Remains in double prime range |
| Expected level of treatment success (0) | Dating Petting | Chooses own friends, without checking with mother | Makes up mind on vocation, other major items | On probation No further arrests for peeping | Mid-60s T-score |
| More than expected success with treatment (1) | Some satisfactory intercourse | Returns to school | | No contact with police, states peeping no longer a problem | |
| Best anticipated treatment success (2) | Regular dating Regular satisfactory intercourse Marriage | Establishes own way of life Chooses when to consult mother | | | 40–60 T-score |

Notice that five goals for this client are outlined, each with a relative weight determined by the therapist. Also, the scale goes from –2 to +2, with 0 as the expected outcome. Goals can also be constructed for families as a unit objective, as opposed to goals for individual family members. The ability to objectively assess outcomes of treatment by using this method is obvious. Another advantage is that the model requires specificity and clarification of the client's issues, which is advantageous to the client, the therapist, and the family.

The second study is similar in that problems are targeted during the intake process and progress determined at a later time on these specific areas. However, Bond, Bloch, and Yalom approached the problem differently. Rather than developing goals, these researchers constructed a simple list of specific problems for each client prior to therapy. To evaluate success in these areas, agreement from three sources (patients, therapists, and independent judges) was examined relative to their appraisal of the effects of treatment after eight and 12 months. This method was helpful because it provided a check or comparison on the subjective perspectives on the effects of treatment. This is an uncomplicated way treatment personnel can obtain feedback on their counseling skills. The independent judges based their ratings on videotapes of the sessions. A team of three experienced clinicians viewed the pre-therapy tape and together constructed a list of the patient's main problems, prioritized on a nine-point scale of severity. They later viewed the patient again after eight months and rated each problem on a nine-point scale reflecting the degree of change, from 1 = "worst possible outcome" to 5 = "unchanged" to 9 = "best possible outcome." The procedure was then repeated with the 12-month tape. Patients and therapists completed the same procedure but based their ratings on their experience in treatment, not on videotapes. All three groups also rated the sessions globally at eight and 12 months (i.e., "improved," "no change," "did not improve").

## THE RESULTS OF FAMILY THERAPY EVALUATIONS

Reviews of empirical research on family therapy outcomes are not particularly encouraging (Sigal, Barrs, & Doubilet, 1976; Wells, Dilkes, & Trivelli, 1972). But as Lebow (1981) argued persuasively, the global question "Does family therapy work?" cannot possibly be answered in any one study, no matter how rigorous. Rather, he suggested, the knowledge base relating to the effects of family therapy must be constructed incrementally, using findings from limited studies that address such areas as specific treatment techniques, counselor characteristics, treatment goals, and outcome criteria.

An even more basic question is the feasibility of applying rigorous research methodology to this area of the human services field, given the multitude of subject, counselor, and outcome variables that must be somehow controlled. Wells, Dilkes, and Trivelli contended that although clinical practitioners paid only lip service to research endeavors in the past, all methods of therapeutic intervention can and must be submitted to experimental scrutiny. These authors did, however, concede that the clinical evaluations of professionals in the field do have a place. Lebow (1981) agreed:

> Family therapy is also an art. Thus, research is only one tool that can help in the development of family therapy. Scientific findings will never take the place of clinical wisdom. The isolation of the effectiveness of techniques alone will not suffice. What can be hoped is that family therapy outcome research will aid in the continuing development of the art, as art and science become an intermingled process. (pp. 185–186)

Paul (1967) concurred, believing that, as case studies accumulate, effective parameters for family therapy can be drawn even if not completely validated.

Indeed, the results of studies that rely on clinical evaluations to determine effectiveness indicate that family therapy does work. Wells, Dilkes, and Trivelli (1972) compared the results of family therapy studies (using clinical judgments) with similar global studies of individual psychotherapy. These results were tabulated along a four-point continuum, ranging from "improved," "some improvement," "no change," to "worse." The overall success rate (improved or some improvement) was 69 percent. The combined success rate for individual counseling was 66 percent.

What these two encouraging statistics indicate is that both individual and family therapy have been effective when evaluated subjectively. This is not hard and fast, valid data, but it may be as accurate (or more so) as studies using more stringent research methods due to the difficulty of applying methodological principles of evaluation to this treatment model at this time.

## Marital and Family Inventories

As the field of marriage and family therapy develops, more instruments are developed and refined to measure marital relationships and family dynamics. Some of the measures are observational in that family interaction is observed and then scored on several dimensions. The Beavers-Timberlawn Family Evaluation Scale is an example of this type of measure. The five dimensions on this scale are: (1) structure of the family, (2) mythology, (3) goal-directed negotiation, (4) autonomy, (5) family affect (Beavers, 1985).

In another category are the general marital satisfaction and adjustment scales. These scales are paper-and-pencil, self-report instruments for obtaining global assessments of marital satisfaction or family environment dimensions. Examples of marital adjustment scales include the Marital Adjustment Test developed by Locke and Wallace (1959). This is a 15-item paper-and-pencil inventory that takes two to 10 minutes to complete and is scored by the therapist. A newer scale is the Dyadic Adjustment Scale, developed by Spanier. This is an overall measure of a couple's adjustment but can also measure specific areas of the relationship. It is a 32-item paper-and-pencil test with four subscales: (1) dyadic consensus, (2) dyadic satisfaction, (3) dyadic cohesion, and (4) affectionate expression (Spanier, 1976; Spanier & Filsinger, 1983).

Two family scales discussed in Chapter 6 have been used to assess alcoholic families and to evaluate treatment outcome. The first, the Moos Family Environment Scale (FES) (Moos & Moos, 1981) is a 90-item, true-false, self-report questionnaire. It can be completed in 15 to 20 minutes. The reusable booklet comes with separate answer sheets that can be scored with a template; alternately, two-page answer sheets with carbons are available. The subject's marks are transferred directly to a self-scoring sheet. Scores are converted to standard scores that are plotted on a graph that compares the family with the Moos norms. Multiple family members' scores can be plotted on the same graph using different colors to assess consensus or differences in perceptions of family members. The ideal form of the FES can be used to identify how family members would like the family to be. This scale seems particularly useful in measuring problems of alcoholic families.

The second family scale that is widely used is the Family Adaptability and Cohesion Evaluation Scales III (FACES III) (Olson, Portner, & Lavee, 1985). FACES III is a 20-item paper-and-pencil scale. Each item has a possibility of five points. The scale is taken twice with different instructions: first, "Describe your family now," and later, "Ideally, how would you like your family to be?" The difference between the two scores measures the level of satisfaction. The scores can be charted in a family profile for interpretation. This instrument is currently being further refined and will be released as FACES IV.

In summary, the growth of interest in family therapy as an effective model for therapy is exciting. The process is still evolving and its exact uses are in need of further refinement. However, we think that family therapy is the model of choice for families with alcoholism or related problems, not only due to the traumatic effects problem drinking has on all family members but also because, we contend, the family, as a dynamic unit, should be perceived as the client.

## EVALUATION OF ALCOHOLISM TREATMENT

The idea of evaluating alcoholism treatment sounds at first to be a straight-forward proposition. Does it work? However, at the present time there is no clear-cut, comprehensive answer. As seen in the section on the evaluation of family therapy, both theoretical and methodological problems abound. First, definitions of program design are far from consistent. Residential or milieu therapy, for example, may constitute a variety of treatment models, lengths of stay, personnel qualifications, etc., making an across-the-board comparison of residential programs an apples-to-oranges situation. Also, population characteristics vary considerably; some programs primarily treat a chronic, skid-row clientele while others serve higher socioeconomic groups. Beyond this, consistent criteria for success have yet to be agreed on. Some evaluation studies consider total abstinence the sole criterion for success, while others take multiple factors (job stability, marital status, etc.) into account.

Nevertheless, many attempts have been made to evaluate alcoholism rehabilitation. The remainder of this chapter cites a few examples of evaluation techniques that may be adopted by the reader. Results of existing evaluations are also reported.

Godley (1982) developed a straightforward procedure for evaluating treatment outcomes for residential alcoholism programs. Godley advocated the accumulation of concrete, quantifiable data that minimally include reductions in drinking, reductions in the use of institutional facilities, and increases in productive lifestyling. He thought that these are typical goals of alcoholism facilities that lend themselves to quantifiable measurement, but he also stressed that other criteria can be easily added.

The first variable, drinking behavior, can be determined by dividing the number of days in which drinking occurs by the total number of days in the pretest and/or follow-up interval. This will yield a percentage that can be compared before and after treatment and can show trends in drinking (versus simple abstinence or nonabstinence).

$$\frac{\text{No. of days drinking occurred}}{\text{Total no. of days in pretest or follow-up interval}} = \text{percentage of days drinking}$$

The second variable, use of institutional facilities, can be determined in the same manner:

$$\frac{\text{No. of days in a hospital detox or other treatment facility}}{\text{Total no. of days in pretest or institutionalized follow-up interval}} = \text{percentage of days}$$

The third variable, employment, is measured like the other two but must account for legitimate days off. The formula for determining time employed is:

$$\frac{\text{No. of days worked}}{\text{No. of days in pretest or follow-up period}} = \text{percentage of time employed}$$

Similarly, alcohol-related arrests are a measure of alcoholism. In this particular case, however, it is recommended that a straightforward count of arrests be recorded rather than expressing it as a percentage like the other variables in terms of days. The rationale for this format change is that a client can be arrested and charged with an offense (e.g., D.W.I.) and not necessarily spend the night in jail.

## Data Collection Procedures

Godley thought that the best way to collect these data is by integrating it into the normal clinical routine. For example, pretest data can be collected on these measures at intake. This is not too awkward because at this point the counselor is interested in learning as much as possible about the new client. The pretest data are helpful as an extra assessment tool.

Similarly, follow-up data can be gathered as a routine function of the outpatient visit or the aftercare contact. Because of the possibility of relapse, it is always desirable to maintain contact with clients for a long period of time (perhaps 18 months). Contact points during this time frame afford the opportunity to collect data without creating a cumbersome new system. A sample format for data collection is shown in Exhibit 12–2.

Each client's data can be traced using this type of format. Also, each data sheet can be transferred to a summary sheet by converting ratios to percentages. An example of a summary sheet is shown in Exhibit 12–3.

Data can be summarized at pretreatment and subsequent three-month intervals by adding up each column for which data are available. This procedure also lends itself readily to computer systems.

A second evaluation technique is to examine objectives. This model helps program personnel define their mission in concrete terms and gives feedback on the extent to which goals are being met. To be written properly, objectives should have three elements: (1) conditions stating how the objective is to be measured (a

**Exhibit 12–2** Sample Data Sheet

| | | | Name or I.D. _____ | | |
|---|---|---|---|---|---|
| *FROM* | *TO* | *Number of days drank* | *Number of days employed full-time* | *Number of days institutionalized* | *Number of arrests* |
| | | | | | |
| | | | | | |
| | | | | | |
| | | | | | |

**Exhibit 12–3** Follow-Up Data Summary Sheet

| NAME OR I.D. | DRINKING MONTH | | | | | | EMPLOYMENT MONTH | | | | | | INSTITUTIONALIZATION MONTH | | | | | | ARRESTS MONTH | | | | | |
|---|---|---|---|---|---|---|---|---|---|---|---|---|---|---|---|---|---|---|---|---|---|---|---|---|
| | PRE | 3 | 6 | 9 | 12 | 18 | PRE | 3 | 6 | 9 | 12 | 18 | PRE | 3 | 6 | 9 | 12 | 18 | PRE | 3 | 6 | 9 | 12 | 18 |
| | | | | | | | | | | | | | | | | | | | | | | | | |
| | | | | | | | | | | | | | | | | | | | | | | | | |
| | | | | | | | | | | | | | | | | | | | | | | | | |
| | | | | | | | | | | | | | | | | | | | | | | | | |
| | | | | | | | | | | | | | | | | | | | | | | | | |
| | | | | | | | | | | | | | | | | | | | | | | | | |
| | | | | | | | | | | | | | | | | | | | | | | | | |
| | | | | | | | | | | | | | | | | | | | | | | | | |
| | | | | | | | | | | | | | | | | | | | | | | | | |
| | | | | | | | | | | | | | | | | | | | | | | | | |
| | | | | | | | | | | | | | | | | | | | | | | | | |
| | | | | | | | | | | | | | | | | | | | | | | | | |

survey form, interviews, etc.), (2) a behavioral verb stating the nature of the objective (e.g., reducing drinking, attending social activities, etc.), and (3) criteria, or levels of performance desired (reduction in relapse from six to zero times per year).

The following statement is an example of a behavioral objective for an alcoholic client. "Based on a monthly interview questionnaire, client X will reduce his or her relapse rate from two to zero times."

Two additional elements can make objectives even more meaningful. First, the objective should be time-limited, and second, objectives should be scaled so an approximation of the objective can be determined.

## EVALUATION RESULTS—INDIVIDUAL TREATMENT FOR ALCOHOLISM

The results of evaluation studies of alcoholism programs are equivocal, unfortunately, owing to the many issues already presented.

First, Alcoholics Anonymous (AA), the most pervasive of rehabilitation techniques, is examined. Based solely on face validity, AA seems to be helpful to many alcoholics. The millions of recovering persons who attend regularly bear witness to this. However, more rigorous examination of this model is difficult.

What, for example, are the relapse rates for those who attend? Also, what happens to individuals who attend a few meetings and then drop out? Due to the anonymous nature of AA, detailed, controlled follow-up studies are next to impossible. Another contaminating issue is that AA is also incorporated into treatment programs that offer individual, group, and family counseling. Therefore, it is not possible to determine which variable is responsible for success (or lack of it). In short, definitive outcome studies of AA are not available.

On the other hand, aversive conditioning models, especially chemical aversion, have reported success rates of 60 percent abstinence after one year (Wiens, 1976). Even though this sounds impressive, many criticisms are leveled at the claims. First, it is argued that those who choose or can afford this treatment are relatively intact, functioning members of society and would be successful in any program. Second, many of these models require six or seven booster treatments on an outpatient basis for one year following the initial treatment, which ensures the aversion to drinking for that first year. To be meaningful, drinking behavior must be studied with these clients after one year.

Other aversive models, particularly shock aversion, have unfortunately been shown by Nathan and Briddell (1977) to have short-lived and modest effects on clients.

An outpatient treatment model devised by Hunt and Azrin (1973) called the community-based reinforcement approach cited successes. According to the authors, patients (N = 8) who received standard hospital treatment plus community-based reinforcement drank less, remained employed longer, were hospitalized for a shorter period of time, and stayed longer with their families than did standard treatment patients (N = 8).

The effect of many of the other approaches (i.e., transactional analysis, psycho-analysis, etc.) is still questionable. Isolating a theory of treatment to compare it with others offers major obstacles. A definitive answer to the question of which model is the most effective cannot be provided.

## EVALUATION OF FAMILY THERAPY IN THE TREATMENT OF ALCOHOLISM

Even more limited than the acceptance of family therapy as a treatment for alcoholism is the treatment outcome research. Obviously treatment outcome data are needed to establish family therapy as a proven successful model. Some studies look at progress by measuring family problems before and after treatment and at follow-up. Other studies compare family therapy to individual and/or group treatment. This research is difficult, expensive, and time-consuming.

Edwards and Steinglass (1995) conducted a meta-analysis of 21 of these studies of family-involved therapy for alcoholism. They evaluated the studies for design adequacy, clinical significance, and effect size. They divided the studies into three phases of treatment: (1) initiation of treatment, (2) primary treatment/rehabilita-tion, and (3) aftercare.

In the first phase Edwards and Steinglass found that family therapy was effective in motivating alcoholics to enter treatment. The studies included three approaches: (1) the intervention model, (2) unilateral family therapy, and (3) community reinforcement training. The *intervention model* involves training friends of the alcoholic and family members in four to five two-hour sessions to stage a formal confrontation of the alcoholic. (This was the method used by the Long Beach Naval Station to get Betty Ford into treatment.) A single study was done to compare families who used this confrontation method with those who did not (Liepman, Silvia, & Nirenberg, 1989). The families who did interventions had more success in getting the alcoholic to enter alcohol detoxification or rehabilita-tion programs than those who did not (86 percent versus 17 percent). The confronted alcoholics were continually abstinent for 11 months compared with 2.8 for those who did not have an intervention.

*Unilateral family therapy* (UFT) is a more extensive model of treatment that includes an intervention option. The model includes:

- an initial assessment
- alcohol education
- unilateral relationship enhancement

- disenabling
- neutralizing old alcohol control behaviors
- preparation for alcoholic-directed interventions such as confrontation, request, and contracting
- support for maintenance of gains
- relapse prevention training
- help for the spouse in disengaging from his/her alcoholic partner and the drinking problem combined with help for dealing with emotional problems

Two studies tested the effect of UFT in getting the alcoholic to enter treatment and reduce drinking. Thomas, Santa, Bronson, and Oyserman (1987) found that if the spouse of an alcoholic participated in UFT the alcoholic was more likely to be rated "improved" than those whose spouse did not participate (61 percent versus 0 percent). UFT participation also decreased drinking by 53 percent and reduced spouses' life distress. In a larger study by some of the same researchers (Thomas, Yoshioka, Ager, & Adams, 1993) also found improved motivation to enter treatment, reduction in drinking, and improved UFT at follow-up (57 percent versus 31 percent).

The last study in the first phase is a study by Sisson and Azrin (1986) evaluating *community reinforcement training* (CRT). CRT for nondrinking spouses included how to reduce physical abuse, how to encourage sobriety by reinforcing the alcoholic for periods of sobriety and giving negative consequences for drinking, and how to encourage treatment. CRT, similar to UFT, is based on social learning principles. When CRT was compared with traditional treatment for spouses, CRT was more successful in getting alcoholics into treatment (86 percent versus 0 percent) and increased the amount of abstinence in the alcoholics, even though they were not in treatment, from 20 percent to 63 percent.

In the Phase II studies primary treatment or rehabilitation was examined. Family therapy treatment models fall into two categories: (1) family systems–orientated approaches, characterized by a focus on interaction patterns and the regulation of internal and external environments, and (2) behaviorally oriented approaches, all of which are based on social learning theory and include concepts such as reinforcement, reciprocity, and coercion (Edwards & Steinglass, 1995).

There were four studies in the family systems group. The first was a study of a psychoeducational couples group (CT) that was compared with treatment without spouse involvement (Corder, Corder, & Laidlaw, 1972). At a six-month follow-up the CT subjects were more abstinent than those without CT (58 percent versus 15 percent).

Cadogan (1973) tested a longer program that involved alcoholics and their spouses attending weekly multiple couples therapy for three to six months.

Compared with a waiting list group, no differences were found in marital satisfaction, but a higher abstinence rate was found (45 percent versus 10 percent).

McCrady, Paolino, Longabaugh, and Rosi (1979) compared individual therapy for alcoholics (I) with treatment that involved individual group therapy for the spouse and the alcoholic combined with couples group therapy (CI) and with joint admission therapy (JA), where both the alcoholic and spouse participated in the entire program. In a six-month follow-up both couples groups were more abstinent (61 percent for JA and 83 percent for CI) than the subjects in individual treatment (43 percent). Although there was improvement from pre- to post test on marital measures, there was no difference between groups. In a four-year follow-up of these subjects (McCrady, Moreau, & Paolino, 1982) there were no differences between the groups. Abstinence rates had dropped below the 50 percent baseline for clinical significance (33 percent for JA, 13 percent for CI, and 14 percent for I). The effectiveness of these treatments diminished with time.

The fourth study evaluated a treatment program for couples designed to affect the adaptive consequences of alcoholism and the role it played in the family's typical patterns of living (Zweben, Pearlman, and Li, 1988). This eight-session program (CT) was compared with a single session of advice counseling (AC) attended by the spouse and alcoholic. At the six-month follow-up, subjects in both groups had increased abstinence (36 percent to 52 percent for CT and 29 percent to 58 percent for AC). They also decreased their percentage of heavy drinking days. There were no differences between the two groups and there was also no difference at an 18-month follow-up. In general, family systems models seem to do better than individual treatment initially, but the results diminish in the long run.

Six groups of researchers have conducted studies of family-involved treatment models. The earliest was Hedberg and Campbell (1974), who tested four types of behavioral treatment. One treatment involved the entire nuclear family, which was allowed to pick either abstinence or controlled drinking as a goal—behavioral family therapy. The other three treatments were electric shock treatment, covert sensitization, and systematic desensitization. All four treatments consisted of 20 sessions conducted over six months, with 14 of the sessions occurring in the first eight weeks of treatment. Behavioral family counseling (80 percent) and systematic desensitization (60 percent) were more effective than the other two treatments in achieving abstinence (36 percent for covert sensitization, 0 percent for electric shock).

The community reinforcement approach (CRA) involves increasing social reinforcement to interfere with drinking, including marital counseling. A series of studies were done comparing CRA with a traditional program (Azrin, 1976; Azrin, Sisson, Meyers, & Godley, 1982; Hunt & Azrin, 1973; Sisson & Azrin, 1986). At six-month follow-up the first study showed a higher abstinence rate in the CRA group (86 percent versus 21 percent). The model was improved and the next study reported 96 percent abstinence compared with 45 percent in the traditional treatment group. Antabuse was added as a component to the behavioral treatment (BTA) and at six-month follow-up there was again an increase in abstinence rates (97 percent for BTA, 74 percent for Antabuse only, and 45 percent for traditional treatment).

The third group of investigators compared various behavioral couples treatments (McCrady, Noel, & Abrams, 1986). These models were minimal spouse involvement (MSI), alcohol-focused spouse involvement (AFSI), and alcohol behavioral marital treatment (ABMT). The pretreatment to six-month follow-up percentages of abstinent days were 26 percent to 88 percent for MSI, 36 percent to 75 percent for AFSI, and 25 percent to 80 percent for ABMT. At six-month follow-up, however, none of the groups had significant abstinence levels. This model was also tested with the addition of an occupational component by another group of investigators, who found significant improvements (Stout, McCrady, Longabaugh, Noel, & Beattie, 1987).

The fifth group of researchers compared behavioral marital therapy (BMT) with a more systemic marital, interactional couples therapy (ICT) and with a standard individual treatment (ST) (O'Farrell, Cutter, & Floyd, 1985). At post treatment all three groups increased abstinence (43 percent to 99 percent for BMT, 46 percent to 83 percent for ICT, and 21 percent to 91 percent for ST). Couples in the marital therapy groups showed improvements in their marriages and the couples in the standard treatment did not. Gains in abstinence and marital adjustment diminished at both follow-up surveys.

In the Phase III studies researchers investigated the value of involving families in the aftercare portion of treatment. One aftercare study looked at a group of inpatients discharged from a 28-day treatment program. The experimental group of these patients received a contract/calendar (CC) intervention that involved a contract between the spouses to reward attendance at aftercare and to display a calendar with the dates or meetings marked in red. This group did better at six months post treatment than those who did not get the intervention. They attended more sessions of aftercare. At 12 months the CC group members were significantly more abstinent (61 percent versus 21 percent) and had more functioning days when they consumed less than 2 ounces of alcohol (Ahles, Schlundt, Prue, & Rychtarik, 1983).

Two groups of couples were compared by O'Farrell, Choquette, Cutter, Brown, and McCourt (1993) to determine if adding a relapse prevention component that included an Antabuse contract to BMT would improve abstinence rates. The group members that received the relapse prevention at the end of the program were more abstinent than the group who received only BMT (94 percent versus 82 percent).

In summary, Edwards and Steinglass (1995) concluded that family therapy is effective for motivating alcoholics to enter treatment, but once the drinker enters treatment, the effect of family therapy is just slightly better than individual treatment. They believed that three factors mediate the effectiveness of family therapy: (1) gender, (2) investment in the relationship, and (3) perceived support from the spouse for abstinence. Also, modest benefits are demonstrated from spouse involvement in aftercare. The most recent studies address these issues by developing treatment models for women alcoholics and identifying factors to use to match appropriate treatments to alcoholics and their families.

## REFERENCES

Ahles, T.A., Schlundt, D.G., Prue, D.M., & Rychtarik, R.G. (1983). Impact of aftercare arrangements on the maintenance of treatment success in abusive drinkers. *Addictive Behaviors, 8*, 53–58.

Azrin, N.H. (1976). Improvements in the community reinforcement approach to alcoholism. *Behavior Research and Therapy, 14*, 339–348.

Azrin, N.H., Sisson, R.W., Meyers, R., & Godley, M. (1982). Alcoholism treatment by disulfiram and community reinforcement therapy. *Journal of Behavior Therapy and Experimental Psychiatry, 13*, 105–112.

Beavers, R. (1985). *Manual of Beavers-Timberlawn Family Evaluation Scale and Family Style Evaluation*. Dallas, TX: Southwest Family Institute.

Bond, G.S., Bloch, S., & Yalom, I.D. (1979). The evaluation of a "target problem" approach to outcome measurement. *Psychotherapy: Theory, Research and Practice,16*(1), 48–50.

Cadogan, D.A. (1973). Marital group therapy in the treatment of alcoholism. *Quarterly Journal of the Study of Alcohol, 34*, 1187–1194.

Coleman, S.B., & Stanton, M.D. (1978). An index for measuring agency involvement in family therapy. *Family Process, 17,* 479–483.

Corder, B.F., Corder, R.F., & Laidlaw, N.C. (1972). An intensive treatment program for alcoholics and their wives. *Quarterly Journal of the Study of Alcohol, 33,* 1144–1146.

DeWitt, K.N. (1978). The effectiveness of family therapy: A review of outcome research. *Archives of General Psychiatry, 35,* 549–561.

Edwards, M.E., & Steinglass, P. (1995). Family therapy treatment outcomes for alcoholism. *Journal of Marital and Family Therapy, 21*(4), 475–509.

Glidewell, I.C., Domke, M.R., & Kantor, M.B. (1963). Screening in schools for behavior disorders: Use of mother's report of symptoms. *American Journal of Psychiatry, 56,* 508–515.

Godley, M. (1982). Outcome measures for the evaluation of alcoholism treatment. Unpublished manuscript. (Available from Alcoholism Counseling Services, Marion, IL.)

Hedberg, A.G., & Campbell, L. (1974). A comparison of four behavioral treatments of alcoholism. *Journal of Behavioral Therapy and Experimental Psychiatry, 5,* 251–256.

Hoshino, J., & Lawson, A. (1995). *Family therapy programs in chemical dependency treatment.* Paper presented at the American Association of Marriage and Family Therapy Conference, Baltimore, MD.

Hunt, G.M., & Azrin, N.H. (1973). The community reinforcement approach to alcoholism. *Behavior Research and Therapy, 11,* 91–104.

Kiresuk, T., & Sherman, R. (1968). Goal attainment scaling. *Community Mental Health Journal, 4,* 443–456.

Langsley, D.G., Flomenhaft, K., & Machotka, P. (1969). Follow-up evaluation of family crisis therapy. *American Journal of Orthopsychiatry, 39,* 753–760.

Lebow, J. (1981). Issues in the assessment of outcome in family therapy. *Family Process, 20,* 167–188.

Liepman, M.R., Silvia, L.Y., & Nirenberg, T.D. (1989). The use of family behavior loop mapping for substance abuse. *Family Relations, 38,* 282–287.

Locke, H., & Wallace, K. (1959). Short marital adjustment and prediction tests. Their reliability and validity. *Marriage and Family Living, 2,* 251–255.

Martin, B. (1967). Family interaction associated with child disturbance: Assessment and modification. *Psychotherapy: Theory, Research and Practice, 4,* 30–35.

Mayer, J.E., & Timms, H. (1970). *The client speaks.* New York: Atherton.

McCrady, B.S., Moreau, J., & Paolino, T.J. (1982). Joint hospitalization and couples therapy for alcoholism: A four-year follow-up. *Journal of Studies on Alcohol, 43,* 1244–1250.

McCrady, B.S., Noel, N.E., & Abrams, D.B. (1986). Comparative effectiveness of three types of spouse involvement in outpatient behavioral alcoholism treatment. *Journal of Studies on Alcohol, 47,* 459–467.

McCrady, B.S., Paolino, T.F., Longabaugh, R., & Rosi, J. (1979). Effects of joint hospital admission and couples treatment for hospitalized alcoholics: A pilot study. *Addictive Behaviors, 4,* 155–165.

Minuchin, S., Montalvo, B., Gurney, B.G., Jr., Rosman, B.L., & Shermer, F. (1967). *Families of the slums.* New York: Basic Books.

Moos, R.H., & Moos, B.S. (1981). *Family Environment Scale manual.* Palo Alto, CA: Consulting Psychologist Press.

Nathan, P.E., & Briddell, D.W. (1977). Behavioral treatment and assessment of alcoholism. In B. Kissin & H. Begleiter (Eds.), *The biology of alcoholism.* New York: Plenum Press.

O'Farrell, T.J., Choquette, K.A., Cutter, H.S.G., Brown, E.D., & McCourt, W. (1993). Behavioral marital therapy with and without additional couples relapse prevention sessions for alcoholics and their wives. *Journal of Studies on Alcohol, 54,* 652–666.

O'Farrell, T.J., Cutter, H.S.G., & Floyd, F.J. (1985). Evaluating behavioral marital therapy for male alcoholics: Effects of marital adjustment and communication from before to after treatment. *Behavior Therapy, 16,* 147–167.

Olson, D.H., Portner, J., & Lavee, Y. (1985). FACES III: Family Adaptability and Cohesion Evaluations Scales. In D. Olson, H. McCubbin, H. Barnes, A. Larsen, M. Muxin, & M.

Wilson (Eds.), *Family inventories* (revised edition). St. Paul, MN: Family Social Science, University of Minnesota.

Paul, G.L. (1967). Strategy of outcome research in psychotherapy. *Journal of Consulting Psychology, 31*, 109–118.

Sigal, J.J., Barrs, C.B., & Doubilet, A.L. (1976). Problems in measuring the success of family therapy in a common clinical setting: Impasse and solutions. *Family Process, 19*, 225–233.

Sisson, R.W., & Azrin, N.H. (1986). Family-member involvement to initiate and promote treatment of problem drinkers. *Journal of Behavior Therapy and Experimental Psychiatry, 17*, 15–21.

Spanier, G.B. (1976). Measuring dyadic adjustment: New scales for assessing the quality of marriage and similar dyads. *Journal of Marriage and the Family, 38*, 15–28.

Spanier, G.B., & Filsinger, E. (1983). The Dyadic Adjustment Scale. In E. Filsinger (Ed.), *Marriage and family assessment*. Beverly Hills, CA: Sage.

Stout, R.L., McCrady, B.S., Longabaugh, R., Noel, N.E., & Beattie, M.C. (1987, June). *Marital therapy enhances the long-term effectiveness of alcohol treatment: Replication of an outcome crossover effect*. Paper presented at the Joint Meeting of the Research Society on Alcoholism and the Committee on Problems of Drug Dependence, Philadelphia, PA.

Thomas, E.J., Santa, C., Bronson, D., & Oyserman, D. (1987). Unilateral family therapy with spouses of alcoholics. *Journal of Social Service Research, 10*, 145–162.

Thomas E.J., Yoshioka, M., Ager, R.D., & Adams, K.B. (1993). *Experimental outcomes of spouse intervention to reach the uncooperative alcohol abuser: Preliminary report*. Manuscript submitted for publication.

Tittler, B., Fiedler, S., & Klopper E. (1977). A system for tailoring change measures to the individual family. *Family Process,16*(1), 119–121.

Wells, R.A., Dilkes, & Trivelli, N. (1972). The results of family therapy: A critical review of the literature. *Family Process, 1*, 189–207.

Wiens, A.N. (1976). Pharmacologic aversive counterconditioning to alcohol in a private hospital: One year follow-up. *Journal of Studies on Alcohol, 37*, 1320–1324.

Woodward, C., Santa-Barbara, J., Levin, S., & Epstein, N. (1978). Aspects of consumer satisfaction with brief family therapy. *Family Process, 17*, 399–407.

Zweben, A., Pearlman, S., & Li, S. (1988). A comparison of brief advice and conjoint therapy in the treatment of alcohol abuse: The results of the marital systems study. *British Journal of Addiction, 83*, 899–916.

# PART IV

## Prevention

In chapter 5 the relevance of etiology in terms of diagnosis, treatment, and prevention was briefly discussed. A major point was that the first step in prevention is understanding etiology. With etiology as a basis, it is possible to discuss prevention from a family perspective.

This is done in Part IV from two points of view. Chapter 13 discusses prevention from the perspective of the public health model. Chapter 14 examines the three levels of prevention—primary, secondary, and tertiary. As throughout the book, the family is the focus of these chapters.

# CHAPTER 13

# Public Health Model and Implications for Family Therapy

## VIEWING FAMILY TREATMENT AS PREVENTION

Family therapy can go beyond the remediation of current alcoholism and associated problems. The philosophy of viewing the family system as the client can stop the intergenerational cycle of alcoholism by also treating the alcoholics of the future—the children.

Because attitudes of self-worth and values surrounding alcohol use are formed at an early age, the involvement of young children in the overall treatment approach is essential. The development of positive self-worth and healthy values related to drinking and family relationships may indeed prevent children of alcoholics and their future families from experiencing the perils of alcoholism.

The goal is to free the offspring of alcoholics from the learned patterns that may lead them to abusive drinking in the future. This does not automatically occur for the child just because the parent enters treatment for alcoholism. The Booz-Allen and Hamilton report (1974) on needs of and resources for children of alcoholic parents found that the treatment and recovery of the alcoholic parent did not appear to reduce the problems experienced by the children. In the study group, 22 percent of the alcoholic parents had received treatment. Most of these had recovered or had significantly reduced their drinking. However, the type and frequency of problems among those children whose parents had recovered were not significantly different from those children whose parents continued to drink heavily.

The children from alcoholic families involved in a study by Cork (1969) did not find that family life became significantly better when drinking stopped. For the majority of alcoholics, the recovery process only begins with treatment and abstinence from alcohol. For some it is many years before they can be a fully functioning, effective parent. Without help, this may never happen.

Sometimes the alcoholism becomes an excuse for family problems. One client who brought her children in for therapy because they would not "behave" told her family therapist, "My children must learn to behave. I'm alcoholic, and my alcohol counselor told me I couldn't handle stress."

By the time many recovering alcoholics develop the ability to model healthy behavior, their children have already established negative patterns. In other cases children have already left the home due to divorce or other reasons. Therefore, they may have only experienced the alcoholic parent's prerecovery behavior.

Many of these children go on to become alcoholics themselves. It has been estimated that as many as 60 percent of alcoholics in treatment were raised in a home where there was at least one alcoholic parent. Many of those who do not become alcoholic themselves marry an alcoholic, and this pattern is known to repeat itself in second and even third generations. Even those children of alcoholics who do not become alcoholic or marry an alcoholic are reported to continue into adulthood with problems relating to intimacy, control, responsibility, identification and expression of feelings, and trust (Black, 1979).

Why are these children of alcoholics not helped prior to the development of serious problems in adulthood? There are several reasons. Research shows that alcoholism, in a great majority of cases, is not as much due to immediate stress as to earlier predisposition underlying some environmental stress (Moore & Ramseur, 1960). This environmental stress generally is identified as occurring within the family of origin. However, the major focus of treatment for the alcoholic remains on the individual rather than the family (Cork, 1969). Because of the disturbed nature of family relationships, alcoholism therapists find it easier to see the alcoholic without the family. The reasons reported by Booz-Allen and Hamilton (1974) for the lack of treatment of the children of alcoholics were:

- Alcoholism treatment programs do not present a substantial resource for children of alcoholics.
- Primary goals of these treatment programs do not include the family.
- When family therapy is included it is done to help individual alcoholics reach their goals.
- Family therapy is usually adjunct to individual therapy for the alcoholic.
- The child is rarely seen in individual treatment.

There appears to be a host of potential sources of help—nuclear and extended families; friends; community contacts, such as school personnel, clergy, physicians, child and family agencies; alcoholism treatment programs; and specialized resources for the children of alcoholics, such as Alateen—although many are not used by children of alcoholics. Often the children are too young or too embarrassed to ask for help. In some cases, the alcoholic might stop the child from seeking help through these groups.

Al-Anon, Alateen, and Alatot are the principal resources available for the children and family of the alcoholic. Most children who attended one of these groups think it was beneficial in helping them to adjust to living with an alcoholic. Unfortunately, only a small number of children ever attend.

Because these groups are associated with AA and alcoholism, many children feel stigmatized by attending them. They want to lose the stigma of parental alcoholism, not increase it. In addition, some children think that these groups are juvenile, overly religious, and unsophisticated. Some children do not have confidence in the ability of their peers to help them solve problems, and still others are not ready to accept the independent, laissez-faire attitude toward the alcoholic parent (Booz-Allen & Hamilton, 1974). Also, groups vary widely, depending on the individual makeup of the members. One woman who was in family therapy referred to her Al-Anon group as "Revenge Anonymous." This may have been a biased, subjective observation on her part. However, these groups, even though they all operate under basically the same guidelines, can be heavily influenced by their members. Just one member who has not worked through his or her anger toward an alcoholic can have a negative effect on the progress of the rest of the group.

Another problem with self-help groups is that they sometimes discourage members from seeking needed professional help, and sometimes they are seen as competition or as a substitute for family therapy. However, a family therapist with knowledge of the dynamics of alcoholism or an alcoholism counselor who does family therapy can use self-help groups to augment and enhance family therapy. Family therapy should be regarded as a complement rather than a threat to patients' involvement in AA, Al-Anon, Alateen, or Alatot. These groups, on the other hand, should not be thought of as a substitute for family therapy. The latter three groups are designed to help their members adjust to living with an alcoholic. They do this by helping the member to become independent of the alcoholic and by helping him or her to rely on the group rather than the alcoholic for support. One major difference between the two approaches is that the vehicle for change for the self-help group is group process and the focus in family therapy is on the family process.

Self-help groups and family therapy have several things in common. Both recognize that others in the family besides the alcoholic may suffer from the problems arising from alcoholism, and both make use of contact with significant others to facilitate change in drinking behavior. Furthermore, both operate on the assumption that family members can be a source of resistance to change by the alcoholic and can do things to trigger drinking by the alcoholic (NIAAA, 1978). The family therapist who uses both family therapy and self-help groups can have one reinforce gains made by the other.

The family therapist should be aware of two potential problems when both approaches are used. First, as family members begin to work on different problems in either the therapy or the self-help group, there is a resulting rise in anxiety. This may cause family members to avoid facing problems by escaping to the other group. Almost all worthwhile movement in family therapy toward a fully functioning family system that meets the needs of all members causes tension among family members. If family members are allowed to retreat to their own personal self-help group (e.g., Al-Anon, Alateen) and they do not work through the issue at hand, family therapy may suffer.

If the family therapist begins working with a family who is attending a self-help group and the therapist takes the focus off the alcoholic's drinking problems, the family may reject this approach and retreat to the self-help group, believing that the family therapist did not understand the problem. The family therapist should avoid shifting the focus and should assure the clients that alcoholism remains the primary concern of treatment.

The family therapist who establishes a clear purpose for therapy, creates a nonthreatening atmosphere, and conveys a genuine concern for everyone in the family will not be in conflict with self-help groups. While interpreting, clarifying, and rephrasing family interactions, the family therapist can keep the focus on the family system (and the dynamics of that system) without understating concern for the problem drinking, as well as keep the focus on the family unit and not the individual member (State of Florida, 1977).

By helping the family system to function to meet the needs of the family members, the therapist can help establish patterns in children that can be carried into the future to their own families, thus breaking the chain of alcoholism. Self-help groups, individual therapy, and other individual approaches to the treatment of alcoholism are justified in many cases because they are all that is available. However, they are not substitutes for family therapy and should not be thought of as appropriate substitutes. In the final analysis, a person can gain positive things from sources other than the family (e.g., self-help groups, religion, etc.) but these cannot replace a fully functioning family system that meets the needs of its members. If treatment professionals are to be successful in the treatment and prevention of future alcoholism (and other problems) among the children of alcoholics, they must focus their major efforts on the family. Treatment approaches that focus on the individual are very likely to be less effective than family therapy, and they do not have a built-in prevention focus. The hope for the future lies in family therapy and family systems that work effectively because this is the best type of prevention.

Prevention involves many things. The family system is the major aspect of prevention, but it is not the only one. Perhaps the best way to examine all the issues is through the public health model. The family should be viewed with regard to each of the factors presented.

## PUBLIC HEALTH MODEL

According to the public health model, alcoholism stems from an interaction between three factors—the host, the agent, and the environment (Nobel, 1981). The *host* is the individual and his or her knowledge about alcohol, the attitudes that influence drinking patterns, and drinking behavior itself. All these elements are influenced heavily by the family.

The *agent* is alcohol—its content, distribution, and availability. These areas are not directly influenced by the family but by cultural norms.

The *environment* includes the setting in which drinking occurs and the community mores that influence the drinker (Nobel, 1981). These factors are influenced by the family.

Intervention at any of or all these points is considered appropriate for preventing alcoholism. Each of the three factors is briefly examined, as are traditional prevention efforts. Following this, the role of the family in each area is discussed. It is important to note that the three factors may overlap or complement each other. However, the public health model is useful for understanding different prevention approaches.

### The Host

The majority of formal prevention programs deal with the host. One approach involves providing the host with information about the dangers of alcohol. The original idea was to change people's attitudes by approaching the issue morally and referring to alcohol as "demon rum," etc. The moralistic approach has long been used by parents and others in positions of authority to control all types of behavior.

It is true that in families in which there are extreme moral or religious sanctions against drinking, fewer children become drinkers. However, it is also true that children from such families who do choose to drink as adults have a disproportionately high rate of drinking problems, including alcoholism, when compared with children reared in families in which moderate drinking is the model (Fillmore, 1972). It is probable that both guilt and the lack of an appropriate drinking model play a part in the higher rates of drinking problems for this group.

Another common approach to prevention with the host involves providing grim statistics about the consequences of alcohol abuse. The problem with this method is that many individuals simply cannot identify with statistics and believe "it won't happen to me." For example, the link between cigarette smoking and health problems, such as lung cancer and heart disease, is widely known, but the smoker can easily rationalize that it only happens to others (a good thing for the tobacco companies). Perhaps one of the dynamics here directly involves the family. Children are warned so many times by parents about negative consequences that never happen that as they grow older they become desensitized to such warnings. Any behavioral psychologist can confirm what writers of children's stories have known for years—a person can only hear "wolf" so many times without seeing a wolf before the warning becomes meaningless. An additional problem involved in providing factual information to the host is lack of agreement among experts in the field. Many concepts of alcoholism have several sides and may become confusing to the public and professional alike.

A pertinent example is the disease concept of alcoholism. It is hard for average citizens to accept all the information given them concerning alcoholism when much of it conflicts with their own experiences. People hear that alcoholism is an illness and that alcohol is a drug. They may wonder, "Why don't we hear that heroin addiction is a disease? Isn't heroin a drug? Isn't nicotine a drug? Is smoking a disease? How about overeating? Doesn't that kill people as well?" A graphic example of this confusion was seen in an Ann Landers column. A woman wrote to Ann, saying:

> Dear Ann Landers: We are hearing a great deal about the "disease" called alcoholism these days. Do you have the guts to print this? If alcoholism is a disease, it's the only disease that is bottled and sold. It is the only disease that requires a license to keep it going. It is the only disease contracted by the will of man. It is the only disease that produces revenue for the government. It is the only disease that provokes crime. It is the only disease that is habit forming. It is also the only disease spread by advertising. And the only disease not caused by a germ or virus. Can it be that it is not a disease at all? (Signed) I'm from the Show-Me State.

Ann Landers wrote back:

> Dear Missouri: The experts whose opinions I respect say that alcoholism is a disease. But you raise some interesting questions. (As seen in the *Lincoln* (Nebraska) *Journal*. Reprinted with permission of Field Newspaper Syndicate.)

The experts that Ann Landers spoke of include no less than the American Medical Association, the American Psychiatric Association, the American Public Health Association, the American Hospital Association, the National Association of Social Workers, the World Health Organization, and the American College of Physicians.

Although it may seem like a digression, it is important to make the points that the disease concept has not been backed up by research, places the focus on the drinker, not the family system, and leaves little prospect for prevention.

When the motto "alcoholism is a disease" was first adopted by the National Council on Alcoholism (NCA), some remarkably complex concepts were involved. The persons concerned knew that alcoholics were sick individuals who needed help and were worth helping. In a rather special context, the American Medical Association (AMA) defined the word *disease* in such a manner that the individuals at NCA felt they could conscientiously make the statement that alcoholism is a disease. Their motivation was clear and commendable. They wanted to take the stigma away from alcoholism so that alcoholics would come forward and be helped. If alcoholism is a disease, then it is not a manifestation of weak will or poor character (Cain, 1964).

Prior to this time, medical treatment of the alcoholic was less than adequate. Some physicians provided a dose of moralizing along with the medical treatment, but others ignored the condition and refused to treat the inebriated alcoholic at all. When there was treatment, it often constituted cruel and unusual punishment rather than sound medical principles (for example, strapping the patient down during detoxification or withholding medication that would ease the process, or both). In defense of the medical community, its attitude only reflected the popular view of the time—that alcoholism is a moral weakness that calls for punishment.

Today many persons in the medical community defend the disease concept and condemn those that would see alcoholism as "only a symptom." In regard to the disease concept Gitlow (1976) wrote:

> But what of our reasons for retaining the title of "disease" for alcoholism? The ultimate reason for the designation of any individual as sick or diseased is for the singular purpose of separating him from the larger (normal) group in order to channel special resources to him. Whether the patient has a broken bone or is addicted, the "disease" label assists him in obtaining that special care which society reserves for its ill. (p. 6)

It seems Gitlow disputed his own point by his example. We separate many people from the larger group without giving them the disease label and that includes those with broken bones. They are classified as injured, not diseased. If alcoholism can't be cured but only arrested, are recovering alcoholics who don't drink diseased?

The final reason Gitlow gave for acceptance of the disease concept is that it "establishes alcoholism as firmly within the province of the medical profession" (p. 6). Would he make such a point if he were a psychologist or social worker rather than a medical doctor? The bulk of alcoholism treatment is done by paraprofessional alcoholism counselors, not physicians, who are often not trained in the treatment of alcoholism. We agree with Gitlow that the alcoholic is sick and in need of treatment. However, other than the medical complications of withdrawal, the medical doctor is usually poorly trained in treating the condition of alcoholism. In one survey of medical schools, drug and alcohol abuse accounted for less than 0.6 percent of the average curriculum. This translated into 25.7 average hours over the entire four years of medical school (Porkorney, Putnam, & Fryer, 1978). This is less than one day per year. Some medical schools offered no training at all in the areas of alcoholism or drug abuse.

Another major problem of the medical model or disease concept is that few strategies for prevention are suggested. Room (1978), a leading critic of the disease concept of alcoholism, pointed out:

> The logic of the disease concept requires that other preventive measures beyond casefinding be seen as utterly irrelevant to the behavior of the alcoholic, since the disease of alcoholism is defined by the individual's complete inability to control his drinking no matter what incentive or deterrents are brought to bear. (p. 48)

Given the medical model, the only logical prevention approach is to have everyone stop drinking. Few physicians would accept this approach to prevention either for themselves or their patients.

The disease concept also means the family approach is simply a matter of counseling the family members on how to adjust to living with the "disease" of the family member who is the identified patient. As was pointed out in the treatment chapters, we do not see this as family therapy. This approach treats the patient and educates the family but it does not treat the family.

Although the disease model has done a great deal to provide respectable medical treatment for the alcoholic, the full ramifications of the acceptance of the disease concept are not yet understood.

The disease concept has been questioned and possible negative results postulated. The limitations of the concept of alcoholism as a disease are summed up by Scott and reported by Cahalan (1970, p. 27).

> To assert that alcoholism itself is a disease runs the risk of obscuring the probable truth that it may be a symptom of a number of quite separate conditions; it also tends to direct the problem to medical practitioners who, with their tradition of requiring the patient to be the passive recipient of treatment, may perpetuate errors. Thus it is possible that some forms of alcoholism are not diseases of individuals but of society; some may drown themselves in alcohol as lemmings drown themselves in the sea, and both may be responding to social rather than personal cues. Epidemiological studies, for example, of the notable differences in hospital admissions for English and Scottish alcoholics, may be the appropriate corrective. Some forms of alcoholism should properly be grouped with other killing conditions such as obesity, smoking, posses-

sion of a high-powered motor bicycle. Looked at in this way it may be bad psychology to call these persons "sick" and to be squeamish about such terms as "immaturity," "lack of wisdom," and "self-indulgence" where they are manifestly justified. Such terms as "self-indulgent" or "unreliable" may be objective descriptions, to be sharply distinguished from moral judgments such as "shameful," "wicked," etc. Addicts need someone who will call a spade a spade in a realistic fashion without adopting a punitive, moralistic, or superior attitude. They know their weaknesses only too well and do not regard them as an illness, though they may secondarily bring illness. Certainly excesses of every sort may lead to illness or even to death, but we should guard against labeling everything which may shorten life as a disease, and the person who deliberately incurs risk as necessarily sick. (p. 221)

Cahalan (1970) concluded that the disease called alcoholism is not defined and that there is no specific treatment for it. Physicians can hardly be expected to apply a nonexistent treatment to an undefined disease in a population that denies the disease and rejects the treatment. Similarly, people working in prevention try to prevent an undefined disease in an unwilling population. Horman (1979) wrote:

I submit that the disease model is invalid and that the problem of alcoholism can be defined only as a highly complex political and behavioral problem. I believe further that alcoholism is in and of itself symptomatic of deep and significant societal and psychological problems. Unfortunately we have come to label alcoholism as a disease when it is merely a symptom of underlying diseases. Because we have decided to classify alcoholism as a disease, we have decided the appropriate treatment objective for this disease is abstinence. It is unfortunate that we have given this complicated problem an easy label and an easy cure. (p. 263)

Perhaps the most poignant case for deliverance from the disease model was presented by Cain (1964), who stated:

The fact is, however, uncontrolled drinking is an enormously complicated human phenomenon: almost as difficult of comprehension as human psychology itself. In their desperation to understand, control and prevent it, professionals and laymen alike have fostered upon anything that seems to work . . . . What we have in the final analysis is not one but two distinct concepts of "disease" when we say alcoholism is a "disease." These two concepts mingle most confusedly and slide back and forth most conveniently in our minds depending on what it is we want to believe at the moment.

Concept Number One: Alcoholism is a tangible, physical entity-in-itself which the alcoholic "has" just as people have cancer, heart disease, and tuberculosis.

Concept Number Two: Alcoholism is a collective noun which states that a number of people in a given society indulge in uncontrolled drinking. This is just like saying crime is a disease, or illiteracy or anti-Americanism.

It is difficult to imagine how anyone could dispute Concept Number Two. Not even the most ardent devotee of Bacchus and John Barleycorn would seriously assert that he favors uncontrolled drinking.

On the other hand, after many years of scientific exploration of the hypothesis, there is not one iota of acceptable evidence to support Concept Number One. There is, to the contrary, an overwhelming mass of experimental data to support the contention that uncontrolled drinking is fundamentally psychological in nature and in etiology—with, of course, a concomitant constellation of physiological, sociological and spiritual factors. (p. 38)

Cain also pointed out, as does our example from Ann Landers, that those who are not alcoholic find it hard to believe that alcoholism is a disease. "If so, they opine, secretly or publicly, alcoholics certainly seem to bring it on themselves" (Cain, 1964, p. 168).

From our perspective, one of the most disastrous effects of the disease concept is to take the focus off the family, both in terms of treatment and prevention. The disease concept of alcoholism provides a linear and singular cause approach that is contrary to the circular, multicausal approach accepted by family therapists. In the disease model, treatment and prevention start and end with the alcoholism itself. Although the family approach acknowledges that problems may begin with alcoholism, this is not a critical point because family therapists also believe that in many cases the alcoholism is the result of unresolved family problems. The point is, in most cases both family problems and alcoholism exist. In order to success-fully treat the alcoholic, the focus must be on the family system and not just on alcoholism.

It would be less confusing and more to the point to call the distressing and disabling disturbance of alcoholism a *condition* rather than a *disease*. Alcoholism is not a condition of moral weakness but a condition with multiple causes that can best be treated and prevented with the focus on the family. We realize that our society is very susceptible to rigid black-and-white, either-or thinking and that the primary resistance to rethinking the disease model comes from those who believe that the only alternative to this model is the moral weakness theory.

We believe that the majority of individuals in this country would gladly accept an alternative to both of these concepts. If we, as a nation, would spend the time and effort we spend convincing ourselves that alcoholism is a disease on training parents and pre-parents to provide a positive nurturing family environment for their children while meeting their own needs through the family, we would be providing the best prevention effort to date for the host, as defined by the public health model.

Three primary things can be done with the host: (1) provide education, (2) change attitudes, and (3) change behaviors. The traditional methods mentioned, as well as many others, have proven largely unsuccessful at accomplishing any of the above. School systems traditionally teach about the problems of alcohol, yet the school is the breeding ground for adolescent alcoholism. Similarly, the attempt to change attitudes about alcohol use through mass media campaigns is nullified by commercial advertisements sponsored by the alcohol industry. The picture is bleak but not hopeless.

The program most widely adopted across the United States is the D.A.R.E. (Drug Abuse Resistance Education) program. The D.A.R.E. program established a curriculum that is delivered in one-hour sessions by a uniformed police officer for 17 consecutive weeks and targeted toward fifth and sixth graders. Other curricula are aimed at junior and senior high school students (Koch, 1994). In a meta-analysis of the D.A.R.E. project across eight studies the reviewers concluded that the effect size means were substantially smaller than those of programs emphasizing social and general competencies and using interactive teaching strategies (Ennett, Tobler, Ringwalt, & Flewelling, 1994). In another evaluation of a psychoeducational risk reduction program, Gross and McCaul (1992) found little evidence to support the effectiveness of the intervention for reducing substance-abuse risk factors.

Although it was believed to be one of the major reasons adolescents use drugs, peer influence seems to have been overrated. Bauman and Ennett (1994) concluded that the strong and consistent correlation in drug use by friends is partially due to factors other than peer influence. They believed two additional explanations are: (1) the role of drug use in friendship formation (selection)—in other words, adolescents select friends that use drugs, and (2) attributing one's own behavior to the behavior of friends (projection)—that is, when adolescents report drug use by their friends they are more likely to report use like their own rather than what their friends are really using. Bauman and Ennett also believed that other variables, such as family characteristics and personality attributes, are often underrated in the literature because they are compared with correlations between friends that are artificially high.

The answer to successfully working with the host seems to be found in the family, in which most attitudes and values about alcohol are learned. Even more importantly, the attitudes individuals have about themselves, about their own worth, and their ability to deal with their environment come from their family. These are critical issues. They separate those who abuse alcohol from those who do not. They separate those who are mentally healthy from those who are not, and they separate those who become successful parents from those who do not. In a study of parenting styles and substance use during childhood and adolescence, Coombs and Landsverk (1988) found that prosocial behaviors were enhanced when behavioral expectations were clearly specified and reinforced with praise, encouragement, and other incentive rewards. Compared with users, nonusers felt closer to both parents and considered it important to get along well with them and to be like them when they grew up. Nonusers' parents more typically provided praise and encouragement, developed feelings of interpersonal trust, and helped with personal problems. These parents were also more likely to be perceived as stricter and to have rules about homework, television, curfew, and drugs and alcohol. Young persons who felt loved and trusted by parents wanted to emulate them, not bring them embarrassment by inappropriate behavior. In a study by Sher and McCrady (1984) a family history of alcoholism was related to a history of aggressive, acting-out behavior in school by male adolescents.

Another area that has some promise in prevention is locus of control. Locus of control, internal versus external, was shown to be predictive of a positive treatment outcome (Koski-Jannes, 1994). Those with internal locus of control are more successful in not drinking after treatment. Perhaps if parents helped children be more internally controlled they could resist external pressures to use alcohol and drugs.

The prevention of alcoholism or, for that matter, the prevention of any of the situations in which human beings seek to destroy themselves, begins with the family. As early as the first six months of life, babies make decisions about their world. Is it a world that meets their needs or one that does not? Is it a world over which infants have some control?

A baby reared in a home where its basic needs are met in a reasonable manner has a very different view of the world than a child who was neglected. The feelings of despair and hopelessness that are generated in a neglected child are the seeds of future alcoholism. Not every child who is neglected becomes an alcoholic, and not every alcoholic was neglected as a child. However, somewhere between childhood and alcoholism there were needs that went unmet, such as approval from others and learning to feel self-worth. A mentally healthy person is unlikely to drink alcohol when it becomes a physical threat and hurts those he or she cares about. Inappropriate drinking behavior fills some basic need for the individual, or it sends a message to others that there are needs that are not being met appropriately. Most of these unmet needs would not have become severe problems had they originally been met in the family.

There are many ways the family can prevent alcoholism in the host. The role of the family is discussed in terms of individual prevention at the primary, secondary, and tertiary levels in the next chapter. Presently, it suffices to say that prevention with the host is best begun in early childhood through a family atmosphere that allows for the development of a positive self-concept, coping and social skills, and decision-making skills that allow children to relate to the environment in a positive way. The family should provide an atmosphere in which feelings of self-worth can develop while a healthy respect for others is maintained. Parenting skills are not the subject of this book, but they are crucial to the early prevention of alcoholism. For more information in this area consult works by Rudolph Dreikurs, A.S. Neil, William Glasser, Thomas Gordon, Haim Ginott, and others who specialize in the area of raising children.

Outside the family, schools play the biggest role in the development of self-image. Schools have come a long way toward meeting the affective needs of students, but they still have room for improvement. For example, schools could spend more time helping students to learn communication skills rather than just teaching English. Students could be taught to deal with problems appropriately rather than deny they exist. Most importantly, schools could teach students (who are future parents) appropriate parenting skills. Many bad habits are passed on from generation to generation. Child abuse, incest, and alcoholism all run in families. Proper parenting skills can be learned, and the public schools would be an excellent place to begin. In addition, free day care centers in high schools for children of working mothers would provide an excellent training site for students as well as a much-needed service.

The prevention approaches that have been used in dealing with the host include:

- teaching the problems of alcohol use and abuse
- providing information
- efforts to change behavior or attitudes
- the development of interpersonal skills among nonabusers
- providing alternatives to abuse
- suggesting resources to help deal with related problems

All these are done quite naturally in the fully functioning family, and alcohol problems occur when they are not. Individuals are frequently motivated to engage in alcohol abuse by a perceived need to augment or to replace the constructive, pleasurable, and meaningful benefits that are naturally derived from healthy human development and an effective living environment, as these benefits relate to self-esteem, stress management, value integration, effective communication, recreation, decision making, and relating to other individuals.

Effective prevention efforts with the host or individual become attempts to promote healthy development around the areas just cited (McCord, 1981).

Many of those working in the field of alcoholism think prevention efforts should be confined to the host. This idea comes from a narrow conceptualization of the problems in general and inadequate definitions of problems in particular. This singular focus on changing individual behavior leads to an almost total neglect of the larger environment (including the family). As was pointed out earlier, all these issues are interrelated, and the relationship is not a simple linear one but one of mutual causality. One aspect fuels and supports the other and in turn is affected in a similar fashion. The family supports the alcoholism, and the alcoholic behavior supports the dysfunctional family system. If this is not the case, the family breaks up, as often happens when the wife is alcoholic. In this case, the behavior of the husband is strongly related to the environment, which makes alcoholism much less acceptable for women than for men.

The neglect of the role the environment plays in alcoholism was summed up by Wallack (1981), who wrote:

> The way we think about the nature of alcohol in society has not reflected a broad reaching effort to increase and enhance understanding but has indicated a need to reduce a complex problem to presumably manageable proportions. Disease concepts have been a convenient and popular way to organize thinking in this area. Such concepts have served to legitimize alcohol problems as a worthy recipient for treatment and minimize the moral onus associated with alcoholism. At the same time, however, the disease concept also serves to simplify the problem by locating the source as an individual deficiency seemingly independent of other influence. (p. 4)

Morgan (1981) suggested that the disease model provides an out for society in dealing with serious social problems by creating a need to treat the individual and thereby legitimizes the problem as based in the individual rather than in the larger system of social relations (the family, the school system, the church, the community).

## The Environment

It is unfortunate that prevention efforts have focused on the individual (host). Clearly, prevention programs are more likely to be successful if they result from the combined efforts of affecting the host and the environment, including families, schools, and communities. Very few programs that work exclusively with the host have demonstrated clear success or, for that matter, adequate evaluation designs. In addition, the relationship between alcohol information and its use is unclear. We next examine the problem of alcohol abuse from the perspective of the environment, with regard to both etiology and prevention. No group provides a better example for this than adolescents. They have problems with their environment that those 10 years ago did not have. Problems within the environment not only manifest themselves in alcohol and drug abuse but also in violent crimes, teenage pregnancy, etc., to the point that a significant number of young persons who reach legal age are unable to function within reasonable limits.

Glenn (1981) identified several reasons for the increase in these problems. First, it takes longer to achieve functional adulthood in the United States than it does in comparable nations, by about eight years, according to some estimations. This is due in large part to assumptions we make about our children. These are reflected in childrearing practices as well as in how we educate our children and see their roles. As Glenn stated:

> We do not need our kids. We definitely don't need them at 16. There are no jobs for them. There is nothing for them to do in this society. Those countries that need their young people have them solidly involved in important tasks by the time they are 16 years old. (p. 10)

Although contemporary teens mature physiologically faster and appear to be developing higher IQs than did adolescents 20 to 30 years ago, they have more mental and physical problems. Unfortunately, today's society is equipped to absorb them much later as functioning adults.

As an additional problem, Glenn cited poor moral and ethical decision making due to a modern focus on situational ethics or feelings rather than on true moral-ethical values. He believed this puts adolescents in the position of being expected to do things they do not perceive or understand. He claimed this is due in part to "adultism," which occurs when adults forget the childhood experience.

Slow development also appears to be related to a loss of role-taking opportunities. These involve carrying out tasks that are important to the welfare of the family or some other group. This situation resulted from many changes in our environment, such as changes in the nuclear family (including a vast decrease in the time the parents spend interacting with their children), reliance on television rather than role taking, and the lack of an extended family and close neighbors (Glenn, 1981). Similarly, the peer group does not perform the task of role taking for the adolescent. A successful peer group operates at a high level of judgment, but most adolescent peer groups operate on the level of situational ethics (which hardly gives the adolescent a chance to learn and practice higher-level judgments). Peer groups operate on the assumption that "Whatever we both want to do is probably okay," not on "Is it fair for us to do this?"

The point is that when we (the family, society, etc.) make a child feel unappreciated, unable to make a contribution, impotent, or unimportant, then problems develop. Prevention strategies that deal with the environment not only prevent alcoholism but rectify a vast array of other social problems.

Glenn postulated four principles for parents, a basic set of tools that individuals need to help children develop the ability to make decisions. First, he recommended that parents think small and concentrate on routine things that accumulate over time. For example, parents should let children make decisions that affect them very early (e.g., Do you want milk or orange juice to drink? How do you want your eggs?). Besides giving children an opportunity to practice making decisions, parents will find children respond much better when given a choice, even when both alternatives are unattractive. Second, parents should become learners. In times of change, learners do very well, whereas the learned find themselves beautifully equipped to deal with a world that no longer exists. Many parents fit into the learned category. Third, parents should recognize common ground. There are commonalties to all problems, and skills developed to deal with one situation often apply to another. It is helpful to generalize problem-solving techniques to new problems. (One of us learned a great deal about how to parent children from raising a Saint Bernard.) Fourth, it is important to learn to habilitate. Rehabilitation assumes the person was excellent before he or she developed the problem. If habilitation was used more generously, perhaps the problem would never develop.

More traditional prevention attempts with respect to the environment include arranging settings where alcohol is consumed to minimize abuse (lighting, seating arrangements, music, food). The research of Schoefer (1981), an anthropologist, yielded definite high/low-risk factors related to drinking problems in the areas of:

- lighting
- space design
- parking areas and their lighting
- male/female ratios
- music style via live/jukebox
- drinking styles
- age factors and social groups
- detox/emergency/taxi/referrals
- age regulations and ID checking systems
- hours
- crowd control
- beverage control
- art and decor
- bartender training/style
- food service
- alcohol breath devices
- serving regulations
- alcohol/driving education in place

These and other factors can and do affect the manner in which individuals drink in bars.

There are vast differences between the atmosphere of drinking establishments in the United States and European countries. Take lighting, for example. It would be difficult to find a pub in England that is as dark as most bars in the United States. Food is another area in which the two cultures differ. There is a considerable gulf between a package of stale potato chips, served American style, and a portion of steak and kidney pie or the sausage roll served in most English pubs. In fact, in Madrid, Spain, each tasca, or bar, is known by the special hors d'oeuvre it serves. Individuals go there more to eat than drink. The primary beverages served in most of Europe are beer and wine; a martini is vermouth on the rocks, no gin. Perhaps most importantly, drunkenness and losing control of behavior when drinking are looked down on in Europe.

Part of drinking behavior in American society stems from a Puritan background. Drinking is often seen as a clandestine experience—something one should do only in the dark in order to keep from being discovered. The first drinking experiences of many adolescents occur before the legal age and involve an attempt to keep from being caught. Very few persons teach their children how to drink, even when they come of age. Drinking is a behavior that is assumed children do not need to know about and adults should already know about. Here, again, Europeans take a different approach. For example, in Germany, at high school functions, even those held at churches, beer is sold to teenagers. Drunkenness or inappropriate behavior is seldom a problem.

People should learn drinking values from their families. If these values are unrealistic or are not taught in the family, they will be learned elsewhere, such as in the adolescent peer group under illegal conditions. If this is the case, these values will probably lead to some type of problem drinking.

This approach to the environment has been called the sociocultural approach, and the major idea behind it is that eradication of drinking problems requires changes in the social norms around drinking. Certain patterns of drinking are associated with low levels of problem drinking. Approaches to drinking not associated with problems include:

- reducing emotionalism about drinking and ambivalence about drinking norms
- making a clear distinction between drinking per se and drunkenness
- drinking in situations of restraint—that is, where drunkenness is out of the question
- drinking when drinking itself is not the focus of the group's activities
- drinking with food, both to integrate drinking with other activities and to reduce alcohol levels (Wilkinson, 1970)

Sociocultural approaches have led to the expectation that safe or responsible drinking should be the goal of alcohol policy. Although this cannot always be the case in this society because of religious beliefs, for those who choose this goal the five rules listed above are a good place to start to provide an appropriate model for children. Wilkinson (1970) also suggested the following regarding youthful drinking:

- The minimum age for drinking should be 18 and not 21, and those younger than 18 should be allowed to buy drinks with their parents.
- Drinking at home should be subject to no legal age limit.
- Mild alcoholic beverages should be served at teenage dances and parties without being the prime means of entertainment.
- There must be more alcohol education for responsible drinking.
- Colleges must provide supervised drinking places for students.
- Alcohol-related offenses for young persons should be decriminalized.

Some readers may assume these changes suggested by Wilkinson would promote rather than prevent alcoholism. There are two sides to every issue, and perhaps many sides to this one. From our perspective, having lived in countries where these ideas have been in practice for years, it is apparent that these approaches lead to a healthy integration of alcohol into society, resulting in fewer drinking problems among youths and adults. The cultural attitudes of societies that have low rates of alcoholism include:

- The children are exposed to alcohol early in life, within a strong family or religious context.
- Parents present a consistent example of moderate drinking.
- The beverage is viewed mainly as an accompaniment to food and is usually taken with meals.
- The beverages commonly used are wine and beer.
- Drinking is not viewed as proof of adulthood or virility.
- Abstinence is socially acceptable.
- Excessive drinking or drunkenness is not condoned.
- Alcohol use is not the prime focus for an activity.
- Most importantly, there is wide agreement among members of the group on these ground rules (U.S. Department of Health, Education and Welfare, 1976).

**The Agent**

Many of the suggestions above are prevention measures that deal with both the environment and the agent. The agent (alcohol) is most often controlled by laws.

Historically, our biggest effort toward controlling the agent was Prohibition. This approach not only proved to be unsuccessful as a means of controlling alcohol intake but also deeply affected society because criminal elements began to organize and prosper as a result of it, much as the gangs of today have organized because of and profited from the prohibition or war on drugs. When Prohibition was repealed in 1933, the criminal element that exploited it simply moved into illegal drugs, gambling, and prostitution. In retrospect, Prohibition did a great deal more harm than good.

Other approaches to prevention via the agent include strict pricing policies (the more expensive alcohol is, the less individuals will drink), limiting on-premises drinking, lowering alcohol content of beverages (light beer), limiting the number of retail and wholesale outlets, and enacting and enforcing strict zoning regulations. One approach that has apparently helped reduce the number of smokers involves the warning label on the tobacco products. This may deter at least some misuse, particularly among expectant mothers.

An effective prevention effort on the part of the family (concerning the agent) is to encourage the use of beverages with a low alcohol content (beer or wine versus straight drinks like martinis or Manhattans). It is also very important to provide alternatives for those who choose not to drink. Individuals should be respected not for their choice to abstain from alcohol but because each individual's opinions and values deserve respect. If children are taught to be suspicious of those who do not drink, it is unlikely that they will be abstinent as adults even if they believe abstinence is desirable.

Although prevention efforts most often involve only the host, these efforts are often not effective or have poorly identified outcome criteria. It is clear that effective substance abuse prevention efforts consider the ecological context in which the population functions and also address specific populations (Conyne, 1994).

In this chapter the role of the disease model with respect to prevention was examined in the light of its problems, including distracting the focus from the family. The host, the environmental factors and alcohol itself were examined in terms of prevention. Next, the high- and low-risk factors discussed in the etiology chapters are examined in terms of primary, secondary, and tertiary prevention.

---

**REFERENCES**

Bauman, K., & Ennett, S. (1994). Peer influence on adolescent drug use. *American Psychologist, 9*(49), 820–822.

Black, C. (1979). Children of alcoholics. *Alcohol and Research World,* 23–27.

Booz-Allen & Hamilton, Inc. (1974). *An assessment of the needs of and resources for children of alcoholics.* Prepared for the National Institute on Alcohol Abuse and Alcoholism. Springfield, VA: National Technical Information Service.

Cahalan, D. (1970). *Problem drinkers: A national survey.* San Francisco: Jossey-Bass.

Cain, A. (1964). *The cured alcoholic.* New York: John Day.

Conyne, R.D. (1994). Reviewing the primary prevention of substance abuse: Elements in successful approaches. In J. Lewis (Ed.), *Addictions: Concepts and strategies for treatment.* Gaithersburg, MD: Aspen Publishers.

Coombs, R., & Landsverk, J. (1988). Parenting styles and substance use during childhood and adolescence. *Journal of Marriage and Family Therapy, 50,* 473–482.

Cork, M. (1969). *The forgotten children.* Toronto: Addiction Research Foundation.

Ennett, S., Tobler, N., Ringwalt, C., & Flewelling, R. (1994). How effective is drug abuse resistance education? A meta-analysis of project D.A.R.E. outcome evaluations. *American Journal of Public Health, 84*(9), 1394–1400.

Fillmore, K.M. (1972). Abstinence, drinking and problem drinking among adolescents as related to apparent parenting drinking practices. Unpublished manuscript. University of Massachusetts, Boston.

Gitlow, S.E. (1976). Alcoholism: A disease. In A. Bourne & R. Fox (Eds.), *Alcoholism progress in research and treatment.* New York: Academic Press.

Glenn, S. (1981, February). *On prevention.* Presentation to seminar sponsored by the Nebraska Prevention Center, Omaha, NE.

Gross, F., & McCaul, M.E. (1992). An evaluation of a psychoeducational and substance abuse risk reduction intervention for children of substance abusers. *Journal of Community Psychology,* OSPA Special Issue.

Horman, R.E. (1979). The impact of sociopolitical systems on teenage alcohol abuse. In H. Blane & M.E. Chafetz (Eds.), *Youth, Alcohol and Social Policy.* New York: Plenum Press.

Koch. K.A. (1994). The D.A.R.E. (drug abuse resistance education) program. In Lewis, J. (Ed.), *Addictions: Concepts and strategies for treatment.* Gaithersburg, MD: Aspen Publishers.

Koski-Jannes, A. (1994). Drinking-related locus of control as a predictor of drinking after treatment. *Addictive Behaviors, 19*(5), 491–495.

McCord, W.J. (1981, April). *Developing prevention opportunities: A single state agency perspective.* Paper presented to conference on developing prevention programs, University of Nebraska, Lincoln.

Moore, R.A., & Ramseur, F. (1960). A study of the background of 100 hospitalized veterans with alcoholism. *Quarterly Journal of Studies on Alcohol, 21,* 51–67.

Morgan, P. (1981, February). *Alcohol, disinhibition, and domination: A conceptual analysis.* Paper presented to conference on alcohol and disinhibition, University of California, Berkeley.

NIAAA Information and Feature Service. (1978). *Family therapy seen complementary to Alcoholics Anonymous, Al-Anon.* National Clearinghouse for Alcohol Information, IFS No. 49, July 11.

Nobel, E.P. (1981). *Action on prevention of alcoholism at the national level. Preventing alcoholism.* Washington DC: Smithers Foundation.

Porkorney, A., Putnam, P., & Fryer, J. (1978). Drug abuse and alcoholism teaching in U.S. medical and osteopathic schools. *Journal of Medical Education, 53*, 816–824.

Room, R. (1978). *Governing images of alcohol and drug problems: The structure sources and sequels of conceptualizations of intractable problems.* Doctoral dissertation, University of California, Berkeley.

Schoefer, J. (1981). Presentation: Prevention of alcoholism, University of Nebraska, Lincoln, and Nebraska Division of Alcoholism.

Sher, D.J., & McCrady, B. (1984). The MacAndrew alcoholism scale: Severity of alcohol abuse and parental alcoholism. *Addictive Behaviors, 9*, 99–102.

State of Florida. (1977). *The family secret: Tips on counseling.* Public document.

U.S. Department of Health, Education and Welfare. (1976). *Drinking etiquette: For those who drink and those who don't.* (DHEW Publication No. ADM 76–305, Washington, DC: Author.

Wallack, L.M. (1981, April). *The problems of preventing problems.* Paper presented to conference on developing prevention programs, Nebraska Division of Alcoholism and Drug Abuse, Lincoln, NE.

Wilkinson, R. (1970). *The prevention of drinking problems: Alcohol control and cultural influences.* New York: Oxford University Press.

# CHAPTER 14

# Primary, Secondary, and Tertiary Prevention and Implications for the Family

Caplan (1974) first conceptualized the model of primary, secondary, and tertiary prevention. Primary prevention is the identification of those who are high risk and intervention to reduce that risk. There is some confusion in the field regarding the difference between treatment, intervention, and prevention. The greatest confusion seems to center on the distinction between primary and secondary prevention (Swisher, 1980). This chapter indicates how tertiary or secondary prevention for a parent may be primary prevention for the children of that parent. This chapter also demonstrates how very important the family role is in the primary, secondary, and tertiary prevention of alcoholism.

## PRIMARY PREVENTION

*Primary prevention*, as the term is used in the field of alcoholism, applies to preventing new cases. Ideally, it occurs before use or abuse of alcohol and involves such factors as government alcohol policy, public education and changes in customs, and values or mores that promote more satisfactory drinking or stops drinking from occurring in those who are under age. It also involves offering alternatives to drinking alcohol as well as opportunities for personal and social growth. The focus is often on those identified as high risk (e.g., children of alcoholics, adolescents). As mentioned earlier, confusion exists about primary and secondary prevention. In fact, there seems to be little agreement even about the goals of primary prevention. Personal opinions, values, and judgments all help make up an individual's idea of the goals of primary prevention. Most individuals agree a proper goal is to reduce alcohol abuse. But what is alcohol abuse? A medical doctor may define it as using alcohol to the extent that it causes physical problems. The law enforcement officer may define alcohol abuse as drinking and driving or drinking under age. The social scientist may define alcohol abuse as that level of drinking that is harmful to the individual or to society.

The latter of these definitions is chosen here. Primary prevention should prevent alcohol use that is harmful to the individual and/or society. To be more specific, primary as well as secondary prevention should prevent adverse consequences such as those proposed by Rockefeller (1975). These include:

- illness and death
- acute behavioral effects (e.g., paranoia)
- chronic behavioral impairment (e.g., apathy)
- intellectual impairment
- injury or death associated with conditions of use (e.g., nutrition)
- developmental difficulties (e.g., adolescent crises)
- barriers to social acceptance
- adverse consequences to society

This type of prevention effort is best done with complete cooperation between the family and all community resources, including schools, churches, and local and national governments. Such an effort may seem all but impossible. However, the family plays a more important role than all these other resources put together. Furthermore, the family is a social system that can be controlled and changed as necessary by its members. The school system, the community, and the church may not be as flexible or as responsive to individual needs. The best place to begin primary prevention is in the family. Starting with the assumption that alcoholism is a complex condition, what is the role of the family in primary prevention?

As seen in the etiology section, the family plays an important role in the development of risk factors for alcoholism in each of the three areas of risk—physiological, sociological, and psychological. The child of an alcoholic parent may have a risk profile that is high in all areas (Figure 14–1).

Primary prevention involves early identification of high-risk individuals and attempts to move the high-risk factors to low risk.

**Physiological Risk and Primary Prevention**

In the physiological area of risk, it is almost impossible to make a change in risk level without providing the child with a new genetic background. However, the physiological area is very useful in the identification of individuals at risk. Factors such as heightened natural tolerance and autonomic hypersensitivity can mean heightened physiological risk. Once psysiologically high-risk children are identified, prevention efforts can focus on the two areas that can be changed—the sociological and psychological areas. The goal becomes to make these two risk areas as low as possible. The individual in Figure 14–1 would look like the one in Figure 14–2 after a successful prevention effort.

Before we discuss how to lower risk factors in the psychological and sociological areas via the family, let us mention one possible area of primary prevention in the physiological risk area. Several of our clients have given histories of drinking problems that occur only on specific and identifiable occasions. Something about these situations triggered abusive drinking in these clients. For one college student, it was finals week. For one woman, it was the Christmas holidays. For another man, it involved visiting his family of origin.

These clients were all successfully placed on Antabuse several weeks before the precipitating event and were then taken off the drug shortly thereafter. Antabuse is a drug that makes any use of alcohol impossible without many adverse physical symptoms (vomiting, cramps). It temporarily makes a person at very low risk physically for alcohol use or abuse and can be used as a preventive method quite effectively under the right circumstances. Best results occur when the individual wants to take the drug and assumes responsibility for self-adminis-

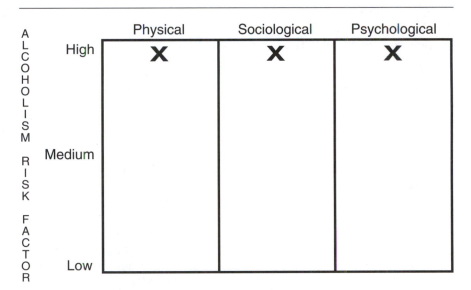

**Figure 14–1** Alcoholism Risk Factors

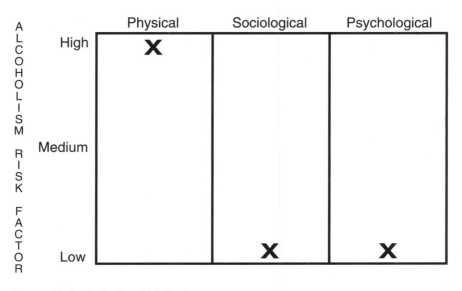

**Figure 14–2** Alcoholism Risk Factors

tration. It is not implied here that it is not worth looking into the reasons these individuals drink to excess on these occasions or that therapy would not be worthwhile. However, if Antabuse works to keep them from having alcohol-related problems, why not use it on these occasions?

### Psychological Risk and Primary Prevention

Perhaps the risk area that is the most amenable to primary prevention is the psychological area. Primary prevention can be done with those identified as high risk, such as children of alcoholics, or it may be done with children prior to the development of a risk factor. This includes working with a child from early development to produce an adult that is low risk. Either way, the family is the key to this type of prevention. Although many sociological variables are involved in prevention, only a few are in the psychological area. In their most basic form, these factors involve producing individuals who feel good about themselves and who can function positively in the environment. In other words, they begin and continue to have successful life experiences.

In chapter 4, seven inadequacies of psychologically high-risk individuals were listed: (1) low identification with viable role models, (2) low identification with and responsibility for family processes, (3) high faith in miracle solutions to problems, (4) poor intrapersonal skills, (5) poor interpersonal skills, (6) poor systemic skills, and (7) poor judgmental skills. The key to prevention here is to strengthen or develop intrapersonal and interpersonal skills, develop systemic skills (function in a system) and problem-solving abilities, and strengthen identification with the family and viable role models.

Research indicates that children who are at low risk for alcoholism come from families in which the parents provide a clear distinction between drinking and drunkenness, integrate drinking with other activities, and empower their children with effective problem-solving and social communication skills (Schoefer, 1981). Families that provide their members with a sense of self-efficacy through love, support, and discipline tend to produce significantly fewer drug-dependent children (Blum, 1972). However, discipline from authoritative parents who are firm but consistent is more likely to produce self-controlled, friendly, and self-reliant children than discipline from parents who are authoritarian, harsh, and domineering or parents who are permissive, nondemanding, and noncontrolling (Walters, 1994). Walters (1994) listed three family environmental factors linked to high-risk children:

1. parental deviance such as physical withdrawal, sexual promiscuity, or alcohol abuse
2. lack of affection caused by family breakdown due to events such as death or divorce
3. weak parental supervision

Alcoholics are often characterized as having low self-esteem, an inability to cope, an inability to relate to others, poor decision-making abilities, unhealthy dependencies, and a low tolerance for tension. All these somehow relate to the statements above. Primary prevention should involve providing a person with a positive self-image and skills to maintain successful life experiences. More specifically, children raised to have high self-esteem, good coping skills, good ability to relate to others, good decision-making abilities, independence, and a high tolerance for tension do not become alcoholics.

In terms of primary prevention, it is a matter of matching up what individuals think they are with what they think they should be. For families this means not placing unrealistic personal expectations on children. Parents should be satisfied if their children are happy with what they are doing. Also, parents should see that children get adequate vocational guidance and should provide children with many chances to try different things while they are growing up. These approaches can help children make difficult career choices later in life. If parents or other members of the family are unhappy with the way things are going, they should make plans to change things and work on their plans. If nothing seems to help, they should see a therapist or someone else who can help. Parents should take responsibility for their lives and teach their children to do the same.

## Sociological Risk and Primary Prevention

Primary prevention in the sociological area means dropping a person's risk level in that area from high risk to low risk. As stated in chapter 4, the reasons a person would be at high risk in this area include:

1. having parents who have strong moral or religious views against drinking
2. having a parent or parents who are alcoholic
3. coming from an ethnic background that is at high risk for alcohol abuse
4. belonging to a social group or having social values that allow for alcohol abuse
5. being in a position in society that is inconsistent with the individual's self-image

If any of or all these conditions exist, the family is the place to begin to neutralize them. If parents have strong moral or religious views against drinking alcohol, it is important that they discuss these views with their children. Parents should provide them with their rationale for making the choice. One of their parents may have been alcoholic, or the choice may be based on a religious belief. They could also point out that it is a personal choice each individual must make. Parents must discuss the pros and cons as they see them and should listen to what their children think without disparaging their opinions. They could provide their children with rules for appropriate drinking and point out persons who drink without problems as role models. They could discuss possible problems associated with choosing to drink. However, they must try to keep an open mind and not make their children feel wicked, guilty, or sinful if they choose to drink because those attitudes lead to problems.

If a parent is alcoholic, he or she should get treatment, preferably in a family-oriented program. Parents should discuss their problem openly with their children and inform them of the risks they might incur as a result of parental alcoholism. They should try to make sure their parenting skills are the best they can be, and they are well advised to take a course in parenting. In addition, parents should look for high-risk factors in their children and take corrective action. For example, if they think their children might be suffering from low self-esteem, activities could be provided to help reverse this problem. Children should be given many opportunities to experience success. Above all, parents should communicate with their children.

If parents are themselves children of alcoholics, they should try not to accept responsibility for their parents' problems but instead help as much as they think they need to. If these parents are still drinking it is important to confront the parents with their feelings. Condemnation or punishment is not advised. Personal feelings should be presented in this form: "When you drink, I feel . . ." or "Your behavior when you drink makes me feel . . ." They should not say, "You're an SOB when you drink" (even if it's true). It is also helpful to provide alcoholic parents with some alternatives. For example, they may be asked if they would prefer inpatient or outpatient treatment. A person can be 70 years old and still be affected by an alcoholic parent. However, even if the parents are dead, rehabilitation can include reconstructive therapy to deal with past issues. Parents leave their mark, which can be positive, negative, or both. It is difficult for individuals to develop to their full potential if there are unsolved problems with alcoholic parents.

With regard to high-risk ethnic backgrounds, primary prevention also begins in the family. The first problem becomes recognizing the high-risk group and then examining some of the reasons the risk factors are high. Irish Catholics are an example. Survey data rank Catholics nationally and locally the highest among religious groups for prevalence of alcohol-related problems. As Father Martin put it in his film *Chalk Talk,* "Any time you find four Catholics you'll find a fifth." Among American ethnic groups, the Irish rank the highest or near the highest in terms of heavy intake and loss of control (Cahalan, 1970; Cahalan & Room, 1974).

Although there has been much speculation as to why Irish Catholics have such high rates of drinking problems, the most frequently repeated reasons include studies that portray marriage among the Irish as an uneasy practical alliance providing little affection or intimacy. Sex and procreation were reported as duties rather than joys or expressive activities. Irish women, in their roles as mothers and wives, have traditionally been controlling matriarchs on whom sons and husbands were dependent (Messenger, 1969). Stivers (1978) postulated that heavy drinking became a significant characteristic of the cultural as well as masculine identity of the Irish male. Greeley (1972) presented a discussion of sexual relations and affective characteristics of Irish-Americans. He said that "the Irish are generally not very good at demonstrating tenderness or affection for those whom they love" (p. 114). He also described the domination of the Irish-American mother who rules her family by her strong will or by subtly manipulating the sympathies and guilts of her husband and children. Ablon and Cunningham (1981) presented case studies that substantiate these claims and provide an even clearer picture of the special problems related to problem drinking in this population.

After the identification of problems, primary prevention focuses on corrective measures in these areas. For example, Irish males can be taught how to express affection or how to communicate with their spouses. Each problem can be addressed with family involvement when appropriate, and by doing this, the cycle can soon be broken. Alcoholism can stop passing from family to family through the generations. The key here is to identify specific problems and address them. For example, if Native Americans drink heavily because they do not identify with the primary culture, they can be helped to relate or to have an acceptable culture of their own. If adolescents abuse alcohol because they feel alienated and powerless, they must be provided with something to do. Perhaps a year or two of public service for all 18-year-olds would not be a bad idea.

Sociological high-risk question number four presented in Chapter 4 is "Do you consider your friends to be heavy drinkers?" This indicates a logical prevention approach: Change friends. If a person's friends drink to excess, chances are he or she will also. Parents should provide their children with good role models. Very few heavy drinkers are good role models when it comes to modeling drinking. Single persons who want to cut down on drinking should find new friends who drink less or do not drink, or they could go to places where heavy drinking is not acceptable. As pointed out earlier, one of the reasons AA works is that it changes the social group of the individual. More than 50 million individuals in the United States do not drink. If individuals think they or members of their families have drinking problems because of their associates, they could find new friends who drink less.

With respect to the sociological primary prevention and the family, the reader should reexamine the 14 variables listed in chapter 4 that affect an individual's decision to drink, the six social psychological variables that determine the level of drinking maintained, and the eight characteristics of drinking groups that have low incidences of alcoholism.

These approaches to primary prevention seem straightforward enough. However, problems arise in their implementation.

The family is the logical place to teach good skills, and parents are the ones to do the job. However, many parents are poorly prepared to raise their children in a healthy manner, particularly if they have not developed constructive skills themselves. This is generally the case if their own parents never developed these constructive skills. In multigenerational alcoholism, poor parenting skills are passed along from generation to generation. There is no room for blame here. Often the parents who cause the most harm are the ones making the most sincere effort to be good parents.

The problem with the implementation of programs to prevent parents from being poor parents is that they are most often voluntary. The parents who need the training the most are the ones least likely to attend this training. Parents doing the best parenting job are often the ones who go to parent training programs.

The research concerning the effectiveness of parent training programs as a prevention technique is limited because too many problems with definitions and design render the results of most research unusable. However, this approach can be accepted at face value and research done later to substantiate productivity. For example, the acceptance of AA as the primary model for treatment programs is based almost entirely on face validity. If it is accepted that the family is the most effective agent in primary prevention, what can be done about parents who reject the training?

There are two places to begin alcoholism prevention via parent training. Alcoholism treatment programs must be solidly based in a family therapy model that has as its primary goal the development of a family system in which each member meets his or her needs. The parents learn to parent and the children in turn learn how to lead meaningful, successful lives. They feel good about themselves and others, and they learn to find something to do that they believe is worthwhile. However, this can prevent only children of parents who are in family treatment from becoming alcoholic.

The other place where this country can begin a prevention effort that will not only prevent alcoholism and drug abuse but also many of society's ills is the public schools. The schools should teach parenting skills, but the hard part here is designing and implementing a program to teach effective parenting to students. However, someone figured out how to teach English, math, and history in public schools, and it is very likely someone could figure out how to teach parenting. Many good programs have already been developed to teach adults how to parent, and with some minor adaptation, these could be used in the school system. A good school program would take into consideration the different values among students and would also recognize that adolescents, even juniors and seniors in high school, find it hard to imagine themselves as parents. Even if they are able to do this, often their preconceived ideas about how life will be when they are parents are overly optimistic, imagining only the fun aspects of parenting. The dirty diapers and 3:00 A.M. feedings are often forgotten until reality overtakes imagination.

It would not be too much to ask to have students spend one hour per day in their final three years of school to learn a skill that would make not only their lives but the lives of their children more meaningful and more satisfying, with fewer major problems (including alcoholism).

The first year of the program could be spent teaching communication skills (not English). The students could learn to identify and express their feelings. They could learn listening and reflecting skills and learn how to express both negative and positive emotions in an appropriate manner. In the second year, they could learn developmental psychology in a meaningful context. They could begin to learn parenting skills such as setting limits, how to handle misbehavior, discipline, building a child's self-esteem, answering difficult questions (e.g., Why is the sky blue? What is it like to be dead? Is God married? Why does Grandpa drink so much?), and many more. They could also learn to meet the psychological needs of a child. This would be like receiving an owner's manual with a child, something many parents wish for at one time or another. The final year of the program could be a hands-on placement experience. The public schools could offer day care free of cost or at a reasonable rate for single parents, working mothers, or anyone who needs it. High school students could be responsible for taking care of the children in day care; this would include changing diapers, etc. Such a program might also have the pleasant side effect of reducing teenage pregnancy. The program should be required for both males and females.

The result of a program such as this would be to give future parents the skills to develop families that function as families should, meeting the needs of each member and helping each other to develop and grow physically, emotionally, and intellectually.

Blum (1972) and his associates did an in-depth study of the role of the family in the origin and prevention of drug use. The findings are equally applicable to alcoholism. They found that no excellent family (as rated by clinicians as superior or good) was in the high-risk category. However, all troubled and pathological families were in the high-risk classification. Children from the excellent families stated that they derived self-confidence from their feelings of worth. In summary, Blum stated:

> In excellent families, the inner joy and strength is visibly expressed in harmony and in happy adjustment. In the troubled or pathological families, pain and chaos may take a variety of forms, all of which visibly reflect disharmony, disconnect and a search for elusive meanings and gratifications. Risk taking drug use by youngsters is to be seen in this light. (p. 21)

According to Silberman (1971), author of *Crisis in the Classroom*, the proper kind of education helps students to "develop the knowledge and skills they need to make sense out of their experience—their experiences with themselves, with others, with the world—not just during adolescence, but for the rest of their lives" (p. 74).

The parenting classes mentioned above would provide just this type of education. It is ironic that the most sensible and productive form of alcoholism prevention need not mention the word *alcohol*, but that appears to be the case. The most outstanding factor is that it would cost little more than is spent on education at the present time. With small shifts in priorities, the program could be underway. It is time for such a program for the sake of future families and for the primary prevention of alcoholism.

Conyne (1994) suggested that the elements of a successful primary prevention program include these features:

- Think systemically and ecologically.
- Intervene before the fact.
- Aim the programs at populations, not individuals.
- Work collaboratively.
- Empower.

- Use an interconnected set of methods, not one approach.
- Embed programs within naturally occurring situations.
- Include risk and protective factors relevant to target.
- Expand to include minority and low-income targets.
- Make programs culturally sensitive and valid.

## SECONDARY AND TERTIARY PREVENTION

Secondary prevention is the early identification of prodromal drinking as described by Jellinek (1960), or the provision of treatment or rehabilitation for these individuals so that they do not develop more serious long-term problems. So secondary prevention is done with individuals who are beginning to have alcohol problems. Tertiary prevention involves the treatment of serious long-term cases (leading to recovery) so they will not contaminate others by social influence, modeling, or setting bad examples (Smart, 1978). The definition of tertiary prevention is clear-cut. Alcoholics or alcohol abusers seek treatment and hence become "cases" or patients. They are self-defined. In some instances, tertiary prevention also includes institutionalization and/or detoxification. In any case, it is clear when tertiary prevention is taking place.

Another reason to provide individuals with parenting skills is that functional families can be productive in the secondary and tertiary prevention of alcoholism. As stated earlier, secondary prevention involves the early diagnosis of the alcoholic or problem drinker and treatment and rehabilitation. Tertiary prevention is treatment of serious cases. A functional family, by definition, is one that can identify problem areas and seek assistance for those problems. A nonfunctional family ignores or hides the problem. As pointed out in chapter 4, treatment of the alcoholic does not always imply primary prevention for his or her children. However, treatment of the alcoholic can be viewed as secondary prevention for that alcoholic, just as treatment of the chronic alcoholic can be seen as tertiary prevention. In both cases, a strong family system is helpful. One of the reasons for the low success rate among chronic alcoholic treatment programs is that often all family ties with the alcoholic have been broken.

In many cases, reestablishment of ties with either the family of origin or the nuclear family aids in the treatment of the chronic alcoholic. If this is not possible, reconstructive family therapy using surrogate family members can enhance treatment. Unresolved issues with parents, even if the parents are no longer alive, can be addressed. Past hurts, frustrations, and feelings of guilt can be discussed. If these feelings are not resolved, there is very little likelihood of successful treatment. The individual is tied to the family just as human beings are tied to their environment. The 55-year-old chronic alcoholic may still carry perceptions of his or her family of origin that developed at the age of five, and five-year-olds do not always have accurate perceptions. A small child may hear his or her parents fighting and think it is his or her fault. If the parents later divorce, the child may feel responsible for the divorce, a heavy burden to carry for life.

Just as a strong family system carries on after the loss of a member, it similarly continues to function and support its members during the loss of one member to alcoholism. When that individual reaches treatment, this family can be a great support and make the likelihood of successful treatment more realistic.

When the family is involved at all levels, prevention is more likely to be successful. The goal of primary prevention is to lower risks in the sociological and psychological areas and/or to raise children who are not high risks to begin with. The family plays a major role in such prevention and is also important in secondary and tertiary prevention. In fact, it may be said that the family is the key to the prevention of alcoholism.

## SUMMARY

Alcoholism is a widespread problem that has been frustratingly resistant to treatment efforts. In many respects, the development and maintenance of alcoholism are still mysteries, and effective treatment and prevention are yet to be discovered. However, this is not meant to disparage the gains made by dedicated practitioners and researchers in the field. This book should add to the knowledge base and serve as a helpful guide for the reader.

This book places alcoholism and its treatment in a family perspective. It is our strong belief that this conceptualization is critical to an effective understanding of the problem. In addition, prevention of alcoholism is shown from a family perspective.

It was our goal to provide, first of all, an overview of current thinking on the causes and nature of alcoholism, coupled with treatment approaches based on these theories. Although this information may be familiar to some readers, it was necessary to set the stage with background information on which the major themes of the book are built.

Following this, alcoholism etiology was described in terms of the family of origin and the nuclear family. Many reasons for the generation-to-generation transmission of alcoholism were explored. Much space was also given to treatment strategies for alcoholic families. Both the theory behind these techniques and specific applications were examined.

Finally, prevention efforts within a family perspective were delineated. Our goal was to provide an informative and useful document in the field of alcoholism treatment.

# REFERENCES

Ablon, J., & Cunningham, W. (1981). Implications of cultural patterning for the delivery of alcoholism service. *Journal of Studies on Alcohol, 9,* 185–205.

Blum, R., & Associates. (1972). *Horatio Alger's children: The role of the family in the origin and prevention of drug risk.* San Francisco: Jossey-Bass.

Cahalan, D. (1970). *Problem drinkers: A national survey.* San Francisco: Jossey-Bass.

Cahalan, D., & Room, R. (1974). *Problem drinking among American men.* New Brunswick, NJ: Rutgers Center of Alcohol Studies, Monograph No. 7.

Caplan, G. (1974). *Support systems and community mental health.* New York: Behavioral Publications.

Conyne, R.D. (1994). Reviewing the primary prevention of substance abuse: Elements in successful approaches. In J. Lewis (Ed.), *Addictions: Concepts and strategies for treatment.* Gaithersburg, MD: Aspen Publishers.

Greeley, A. (1972). *That most distressful nation: The taming of the American Irish.* Chicago: Quadrangle Books.

Jellinek, E.M. (1960). *The disease concept of alcoholism.* New Brunswick, NJ: College and University Press.

Messenger, J.C. (1969). *Inis beog: Isle of island.* New York: Holt, Rinehart & Winston.

Rockefeller, N. (1975). *White paper on drug abuse.* Washington, DC: Government Printing Office.

Schoefer, J. (1981). *Prevention of alcoholism.* Presentation made at the University of Nebraska. Sponsored by the University of Nebraska and the Nebraska Division of Alcoholism.

Silberman, C. (1971). *Crisis in the classroom.* New York: Vintage Books.

Smart, R.G. (1978). Priorities in minimizing alcohol problems among young people. In H. Blane & M. Chafetz (Eds.), *Youth alcohol and social policy.* New York: Plenum Press.

Stivers, R. (1978). Irish ethnicity and alcohol use. *Medical Anthropology, 2,* 121–135.

Swisher, J.D. (1980, April). Background paper for conference on developing prevention programs in treatment agencies and settings. Prevention Issues. Nebraska Division of Alcoholism, Lincoln, NE.

Walters, G.D. (1994). *Escaping the journey to nowhere: The psychology of alcohol and other drug abuse.* Washington, DC: Taylor & Francis.

# INDEX